Recovery of the Measure

Interpretation and Nature

ROBERT CUMMINGS NEVILLE

State University of New York Press

Cover by Beth Neville
"On the Theme of Air"

Published by
State University of New York Press, Albany

Printed in the United States of America

For information, address State University of New York Press, State University Plaza, Albany, N.Y., 12246

Library of Congress Cataloging-in-Publication Data

Neville, Robert C.
Recovery of the measure.

(Axiology of thinking ; v. 2)
Bibliography: p.
Includes index.
1. Philosophy of nature. 2. Hermeneutics.
3. Metaphysics. 4. Philosophy, American—20th century. I. Title. II. Series: Axiology of thinking series ; v. 2)
BD581.N48 1989 133 89-11444
ISBN 0-7914-0098-0
ISBN 0-7914-0099-9 (pbk.)

10 9 8 7 6 5 4 3 2 1

Dedicated to my mother
Rose Naomi Cummings Neville

Contents

Foreword

The specific idea for this book was conceived about ten years ago in discussion with Alexander von Schoenborn. I had explained the overall scheme of my project, an Axiology of Thinking, which called for a theory of interpretation as its third part. He responded that it would be worthwhile to develop a hermeneutical theory arising out of the American traditions of pragmatism and process philosophy, in contrast to the dominant approaches to hermeneutics taken by Continental and analytic philosophers. This very contrast has become a subtheme of the book, although I borrow heavily for my own purposes from writers such as Gadamer, Ricoeur, Derrida, Wittgenstein, and Searle.

In reappropriating the American tradition, which here is made to address directly issues that it had only obliquely touched, I have discovered again the brilliance of the interpretive work in American philosophy of my original teacher and now friend, John E. Smith. Further, I have followed his lead in attempting to extend that tradition in a self-conscious way.

The American tradition informs the two major foci of this book: the philosophy of nature and the theory of interpretation arising from it. The metaphysical theory of being and identity developed here as part of the philosophy of nature had its start in *God the Creator* (1968) and has been extended and reformulated in brief ways throughout my other books. Paul Weiss has been the person who most consistently through the years has pushed me to improve and extend that metaphysics. That is what I have attempted in chapters 5 through 12; those chapters can be read as an independent treatise on metaphysics. I thank the members of the Spring 1988 advanced seminar in metaphysics in the Boston University Philosophy Department for their interpretations, comments, and criticisms of a late draft of those chapters. The theory of value and the notion of discursive individuals—a notion developed to circumvent difficulties in Whitehead—

were first broached in *The Cosmology of Freedom* (1974). Process philosophers have been the most important to me in coming to understand value and individuality, and I am particularly indebted to George Allan, Robert S. Brumbaugh, John B. Cobb, Jr., Lewis S. Ford, and Charles Hartshorne.

In several previous writings, especially *The Cosmology of Freedom* and *Reconstruction of Thinking* (1981), I was heavily dependent on Whitehead for language even where I rejected his ideas. Now, most of the Whiteheadian language is gone, and his ideas have been internalized and combined with notions from other sources. My root disagreement with Whitehead, which underlies my critique of his theology (in *Creativity and God*, 1980) and of his theory of individuals (in *The Cosmology of Freedom*), has to do with time. For Whitehead in the end, the past and future are real only insofar as they function in some present time, whereas I think that they are also real according to their own modalities. Consequently, eternity is not a mirror of the present but a much more complex dynamism relative to the interactions of past, present, and future. Further, by acknowledging past and future as common fields, in their respective senses, a much stronger theory of space can be developed than was fostered by Whitehead's theory. On these issues I have learned most from Robert S. Brumbaugh, Peter B. Manchester, Anderson Weekes, Paul Weiss, and David Weissman.

The philosophy of nature in this book is developed for the sake of the theory of interpretation. Just as the metaphysics derives mainly from Peirce, so does the theory of interpretation. John Dewey has been the most creative and useful elaborator of Peirce's insights, in contrast to Charles Morris, for instance, or Willard Van Orman Quine, because he refused to assimilate the theory of signs to language. Rather, signs are features of behavior, and are to be understood in the broadest cultural and metaphysical context. I have followed Dewey in this naturalizing, anti-epistemologizing, approach to interpretation. ("Naturalized epistemology" is just epistemology that treats science as the authority on nature.)

My own practical experience in scholarly hermeneutics has been mainly in religious studies, interpreting world religions, especially Christianity, Confucianism, Taoism, and Buddhism; *The Tao and the Daimon* (1982) was a product of these studies. Tu Wei-ming has been my mentor in Confucian studies, Sophia Delza in Taoism, and Sung-bae Park and Lewis Lancaster in Buddhism. I have learned enormously about all of these topics from discussions with Steve Odin. Among the most influential friends for the more theoretical aspects of interpretation are Thomas J. J. Altizer, Langdon Gilkey, Ray L. Hart, Patrick Heelan, Alan Olson, Christopher Parr, John E. Smith, and Mark C. Taylor.

I have long taught Western philosophy and Christian theology, the classic sources for hermeneutic theory. But contrary to the customary contextless approaches to those traditions, I have come to interpret both within the perspective of philosophy of culture, the context within which we naturally study Asian philosophies and religions. I have learned about philosophy of culture from Filmer Northrop, Lawrence E. Cahoone, Joseph Grange and, most especially, David L. Hall. Fifteen years ago Hall and I had ferocious arguments about where we disagreed, and couldn't find any serious disagreement other than about terminology. Now, we quietly agree that there are vast differences between us although we've come to adopt and abuse each other's language; there is a deeper philosophical intimacy and friendship in hard-won disagreements than in distrusted agreements.

One of the chief characteristics of the theory of interpretation developed here is that it gives a central role to valuation and normative description. Mere "statement of fact" is a great abstraction, and itself betrays the values involved in selecting the descriptive vocabulary. This normative emphasis, which makes the book a true part of the Axiology of Thinking, reflects a focus on moral theory that was developed in *The Puritan Smile* (1987). Normative valuation functions much more broadly in interpretation than in merely moral uses. This book aims to elaborate some of that breadth.

I owe a general debt to Jay Schulkin who has been my critic and conversation partner through the last fifteen years. He has been particularly helpful in the discussions of philosophy of nature, and has been a friendly voice of encouragement and critical analysis throughout. Finally, I want to acknowledge my publisher, William Eastman, who has overseen this project from its inception. Not many philosophers writing on interpretation, from a metaphysical standpoint, with an eye to religion, have a publisher who is himself a philosopher, with a deep knowledge of world religions, whose very job is the material as well as formal reality of interpretation. I have been fortunate to enjoy his friendship and support.

The reader will think that, with all these brilliant influential friends, this book should be better than it is. Alas, one of the points in which Whitehead was exactly right is that we must reject most of what is valuable in the many influences that condition us, just in order to make their central contributions mutually compatible. The importance of the topic, rather than the disjunctive value of one's separate resources, must justify the cutting and filing. In this case, the importance of the topic is so much greater than my speculative imagination for addressing it, that I hope the reader has an adequate sense of irony about the fact that the professional philosopher is a modern replacement for the medieval court jester.

Introduction

None of the intellectual projects feeding our current preoccupation with interpretation sustains a developed philosophy of nature. The hermeneutics of Heidegger, Gadamer, and Ricoeur are late expressions of transcendental philosophy, a philosophy that gives the understanding of nature over to the sciences. The European semiotical, structuralist, deconstructionist, and postmodern approaches to interpretation award culture such priority as to ignore nature almost entirely. Surely they offer no way of conceiving culture as part of nature. The Marxist approaches, for all the naturalistic materialism of their early expressions, have focused on the dialectic of culture to the neglect of nature; this is especially true of critical theory. The Anglo-American approaches to interpretation in speech act theory, ordinary language, philosophical linguistics, and cognitive science are all on the wrong side of the "linguistic turn," committed to analysis of interpretation itself, and of nature only as represented or embodied in expressions.

As a result, these European and Anglo-American approaches lose the world, whatever their own insights.[1] They lose their grip on a sense of reality by which we would hope that our interpretations could be measured. They fail to register the commonsense fact that interpretations are carried out within larger contexts, contexts that may be grasped only with interpretation but that are real in their own right, with characters to which interpretations ought to be true. This is not to suggest that interpretations should always be about nature, nor that concern with culture is inappropriate, nor that interpretation itself is not wholly cultural. It is not even to suggest that the distinction between nature and culture is a viable one. The point is rather that a philosophy of interpretation without a philosophy of nature is inadequate because it loses the real as a context and measure for interpretation.

An obvious reason for the lack is that philosophy of nature itself is not part of any Western philosophical mainstream at the moment. Particularly, the European approaches to interpretation by and large accept Kant's critique of metaphysics, a critique that delegitimates philosophy of nature. The connection between philosophy of nature and metaphysics is intimate, as the sequel will demonstrate. The Anglo-American approaches, where they do not accept Kant's critique of metaphysics, do accept Hume's. Hume very properly called for metaphysics to be based in experience, but developed such an impoverished conception of experience as to make metaphysics impossible. Worse, Hume's conception of experience had a multiplier effect on the degeneration of philosophy of nature after Kant. If, as Kant argued, philosophy must limit itself to the conditions for the possibility of knowing, and is not a first-order kind of knowing itself, then philosophy of nature becomes philosophy of science, a kind of epistemology. In 20th century logical positivism, philosophy of science was wed to Humean empiricism and thus lost contact with the real practices of science. A recovery of philosophy of nature therefore must reconstruct a philosophic conception of experience as well as a viable metaphysics.

The American philosophic tradition flourishing in pragmatism is a distinct alternative to the European and Anglo-American traditions with regard to these issues. Consider first the problem of experience. Jonathan Edwards, the great 18th century American philosopher, adopted John Locke's language of "ideas" to express his theory of experience; but, like Whitehead in our own century, what he learned from Locke on the basis of his own philosophic genius was what most others missed. Two points stand out. First, for Edwards (1959) the confirmation of a putative experiential claim is not the forceful existence of an idea given from without (the devil, he thought, could counterfeit the existence of ideas), but its aesthetic power (if the devil produces good ideas, he does God's work). The theme of aesthetics as the controlling discipline for morals and logic held true in American philosophy down through Peirce, Dewey, and Whitehead.[2] Second, as indicated in the parentheses in the earlier sentence, Edwards was a proto-pragmatist. The aesthetic goodness of an idea includes its consequences, as the test of a reborn Christian is not in profession or personal feeling but in changed behavior; Dewey could not have made the point more forcefully. For Edwards, experience is thus not presentational immediacy or the contents of consciousness, but rather the various processes of experiencing, of engagement, of becoming experienced.

Though not formal philosophers, Benjamin Franklin and Thomas Jefferson continued and expanded this experiential philosophy. With them, experience is not as closely allied with metaphors of visual observation as it is with engineering, with trying things out. Emerson and Thoreau rightly objected to the manipulative elements in the engineering approach, but continued to value practical experience in their emphasis on participation. By great good fortune, Emerson thoroughly misunderstood Kant and construed his critique of metaphysics as a call for even bigger metaphysical ideas. The resulting Emersonian conception of the Oversoul has nothing to do with either the transcendental ego of Kant or the Absolute of Hegel. It is rather a magnificent conception of the communicating unity of all individuals with diverse unique natures. That conception required only the subtlest modifications by Peirce and Royce (1908, 1968:Pt. II) to become the pragmatists' conception of the interpretive community, a community rooted in the wildness and apparent infinite density of the American landscape.

Charles Peirce, if not an academic, was a technical philosopher in the modern sense. He understood the challenge of Kant's critique of metaphysics and answered it directly. Kant's critique is based on two premises. One is that metaphysics must claim dogmatic certainty, and the other is that science indeed has dogmatic certainty.

As to the first, that metaphysics must claim dogmatic certainty, it is a sufficient rebuttal to construct hypothetical, non-certain, theories of metaphysical notions such as identity, being, value, causation, multiplicity in unity, and so forth, and then to represent these theories as hypotheses. Even the theory of what an hypothesis is, and what would test it, is an hypothesis. Peirce himself constructed a hypothetical metaphysics, as have other pragmatists and process philosophers since. Further, it is far more fruitful to read Hegel, Leibniz and Spinoza, indeed Aquinas and Scotus, and Plato and Aristotle, as presenting metaphysical hypotheses, often presenting several to see how they relate, than it is to read them as dogmaticians presenting what cannot be denied without a contradiction.[3]

As a result of Peirce's work, there are now two conflicting uses of the language of metaphysics. One is the continuation of Kant's own understanding of metaphysics, perpetuated almost perversely by Heidegger in his concept of the "metaphysics of presence" and surely perversely by Derrida who knows of Peirce's work. The other is the conception of metaphysics as hypothetical that has been carried on by American philosophers. The deconstructionists' rejection and mockery of metaphysics might well be telling against metaphysics of the sort Kant had in mind, though there are few who have practised it after him. But it is surely disingenuous when directed at the American metaphysical tradition. That deconstructionism deconstructs the history of philosophy before getting the American side of it is a pity, for with that historical perspective it might be saved from the vain project of delegitimating contemporary American metaphysics with perversely misdirected polemic.

Kant's second premise, that natural science indeed has dogmatic certainty in the synthetic apriori truths of mathematics and physics, has long been abandoned by practising mathematicians and scientists. That both scientific and mathematical theories relate to the world as hypotheses, each in its own ways, implies that they are interpretations. How are we to understand them as interpretations? Philosophy of science attempts to provide the answers. Peirce argued that to understand the nature of hypothesis, it is necessary to understand nature (by hypotheses). Thus philosophy of science itself, for him, requires the philosophy of nature or philosophical cosmology. This is the thesis picked up, defended, and developed by subsequent pragmatists and process philosophers. In this regard, pragmatism and process philosophy are conjoined in a single effort (Rosenthal, 1986, ch. 5).

The purpose of the present book is to provide a theory of interpretation that derives from the American pragmatic-process tradition, with its emphasis on philosophy of nature. Though closely related by both issues and dialectic with the European and Anglo-American approaches to interpretation, my project is distinct in its orientation to cosmology. Generally put, interpretation is to be understood as a part of nature, as culture is part of nature. The categories required to understand interpretation thus will be specifications of categories used to understand nature.

The trajectory for this theory of interpretation derives neither from a critique of European and Anglo-American hermeneutics nor from an attempt to develop the American tradition. Rather, it is part of a larger project I call an Axiology of Thinking, the chief thesis of which is that all thinking expresses valuation. A previous volume, *Reconstruction of Thinking* (1981), explained the overall project (in its Part I) and developed a detailed theory of imagination (in Part II). The theory of interpretation in the present book is Part III. Subsequent works are intended to present theories of theorizing, Part IV, and of responsibility, Part V. Imagination, interpretation, theory, and pursuit of responsibility roughly correspond to the four levels of Plato's divided line. Part II emphasizes the senses in which imagination is a fundamental synthesis by which any conditions for thinking, particularly physical conditions, are transformed into the stuff of experience. Images are forms of synthesis. Imagination involves the creation of a self that engages reality, where otherwise there would be just one more thing reacting to other things in brute causal fashion. The imaginative valuation in such a self has to do with engaging well.

Imagination *per se* does not distinguish between the world imaged and the imaging of it. Thus, interpretation differs from imagination by supposing a dyad between the object of interpretation and the interpretation itself and by supposing, further, a triad in which the activity of interpreting encompasses both the object and the images or signs of it. Thus interpretations can be true or false, whereas imagination is merely more or less harmonious, well-formed, or beautiful. Philosophy of nature is not an issue for imagination *per se*, though it is for interpretation aiming at truth.

The reference to axiology is predictive of the fact that value will be a central notion in this book, not only for understanding interpretation, but also for philosophical cosmology or philosophy of nature. The centrality of value immediately implies a distinction between the philosophical cosmology advocated here and mainstream philosophy of science, and also between philosophical cosmology and scientific cosmology. As to the former distinction, the positivism in the dominant strains of philosophy of science has banished value from cognitive status. As to the latter, scientific cosmology has continued the sharp separation of scientific fact, which alone is allowed cognitive status, from value. This separation was articulated during the European Renaissance in the invention of mathematical physics, and is maintained today in practice despite the rejection now of almost all the other conceptions of early modern science. The axiological theory in all its dimensions—imagination, interpretation, theorizing, and responsibility—rejects the fact-value separation and provides an alternate metaphysical and cosmological conception in which facts *per se* and values *per se* are but selective conceptual abstractions.

The outline of the present book has four divisions, each introduced in some detail by preliminary remarks. Division I is introductory. Its first chapter explores the relation between truth and interpretation, and poses that relation as problematic. The second chapter reviews and criticizes various philosophic strategies for responding to that problem; it also discusses how philosophy made the relation problematic. Chapter 3 presents the hypothesis about truth and interpretation that will be defended in the rest of the book; the presentation is succinct and filled with promissory notes. Chapter 4 shows how interpretation is imbedded in nature by offering an analysis of four loci of participation required by interpretation: in human biology, in culture, in semiotics, and in purpose.

Division II is the systematic development of an axiological metaphysics that might serve as the commonsense presupposition for an adequate understanding of interpretation and truth. Its chapters deal with identity, being, value, and harmony respectively. Division III then elaborates a philosophy of nature or cosmology within which interpretation can be interpreted. The topics in respective chapters are time, temporal things, space and motion, and causation. Interpretation is a special kind of participation in the natural world by natural beings.

Division IV is an analytical presentation of the theory of interpretation made possible by the preceding discussion. Its chapter on network meaning deals with topics in semiotics. The chapter on content meaning shows how thinking is part of natural participation. The chapter on intentionality continues the theme of natural participation, and the concluding chapter on interpretation attempts to show how this theory does what other theories of interpretation do, but better.

DIVISION ONE
The World as Measure

Preliminary Remarks

Whitehead observed (1933, 313) that "it is more important for a proposition to be interesting than that it be true." The context for that remark was a discussion of the many functions other than assertion that propositions play in those who entertain them. Propositions beautify, intensify, simplify, enrich, and creatively modify experience, or do the opposite; they can do all those things, and more, irrespective of whether they are true or false. Propositions that are merely true are often dull, merely repeat (in some complicated sense) what they are about, and when considered for their truth alone trivialize the experience in which they function. This is what Whitehead warned about: propositions must be interesting.

Nevertheless, it is also often important that propositions be true, and that we be able to distinguish when they are and when not. For, it is by means of propositions functioning with a truth value that we "take the world as . . . " Not only when we describe, or think about something, but also when we are doing, enjoying, following a purpose, or engaging in any kind of performatory activity, we "take" the world and its proximate contents as being certain ways. To play on the familiar distinction, propositions are "being used" even when they are not "mentioning." Experience interprets the world by means of propositions even when it is not intending things about the world in those interpretations. Experience is wholly conditioned by interpretive suppositions, as I shall argue finally in chapters 15 and 16, and it constantly revises those suppositions, both intentionally and not.

Therefore, we have a fundamental interest in truth, and in understanding what truth is, in addition to acknowledging all the other functions of propositions and interpretive activity. In previous ages, people have had some common sense about the nature of truth. They thought it had to do with being faithful to the realities about them. In some basic way, truth was assumed to be the carrying over into experience of the nature of the things that experience might represent. This supposes that, whatever else experience is in intention, purpose, action, or enjoyment, it is also "representative" in diverse manners.

Beyond commonsense, philosophers have offered more exact reflective accounts of truth. Perhaps the simplest is that truth is the correspondence of a proposition with its object, where correspondence is something like a mirroring, or a one to one mapping, or an isomorphism in which, as Aristotle suggested, the form of the thing becomes the form of the mind thinking it. The standard criticism of this philosophic position is that there is nowhere to stand outside the object and its experiential representation to compare them. The more subtle recent criticism is the recognition that truth cannot be a two-term correspondence but must be a three-term interpretation; thus, the representation must be taken by some interpreter, a "third thing," to represent the object in some selective respect.

The recoil position from the collapse of simple correspondence is to say that truth is the coherence of all the propositions about a topic inclusive of all perspectives. Falsehood, by contrast, is present when there is reason to say something inconsistent with something else there is reason to say. The standard criticism of the coherence philosophy is that it loses the blunt dyadic sense of referring to the world, and ends in the tacit supposition that we know not only *with* ideas, but also *only about* ideas. The more subtle recent criticism, stemming from deconstructionist philosophy, is that coherence itself is impossible because the terms of assertion are internally related to the interpretive process, and thus keep changing, becoming "differant," to use Derrida's neologism, as the interpretation moves on (see Culler: 1982, ch. 2). Coherence would presuppose a constant transcendental ego keeping everything in mind at once while the process proceeds toward wholeness of vision.

Pragmatism is the third common philosophic theory for rendering the commonsense suppositions about truth as faithfulness. In its epistemological usage, a usage denied by the classical pragmatists themselves, "pragmatism" means that a proposition is true when acting on the supposition that it is true aids in fulfilling our purposes. This of course is a clumsy confusion of criteria for telling when a proposition is true, which successful prediction might be, with a definition of truth itself. Peirce recognized this confusion, warned William James against it, and made a further criticism: truth cannot be defined in terms of what serves our purposes because which purposes are worth having is among the most important things about which to have true knowledge. Logic (the study of truth) is the species of ethics that applies to thinking, said Peirce, and ethics is subservient to aesthetics, the study of what is good and worthwhile in itself, and why.[1]

There is no great disaster when philosophers fail to give an exact and persuasive account of something the culture knows vaguely in its bones. But it is indeed a disaster when the culture itself lacks the knowledge even in its commonsense, and this is what has happened with our understanding of truth. Perhaps the loss of the aesthetic sense of what is good in itself, of what is worth commanding our purposes and morality, has caused our culture's assumptions about truth to fall into confusion. Nietzsche indeed might be right about why this happened in the West. For whatever reasons, contemporary intellectual culture, East and West, is thoroughly confused about truth and has retreated to justifying rhetoric and sophistry in place of assertions about the truth. Concomitant with this, lacking an apprehension of experience as truly grasping the world, our culture has lost the sense of world. Truly, it has lost the sense of reality.

The title, *Recovery of the Measure*, indicates an attempt to recover reality as a measure of our interpretations so that we may recognize what their truth might consist in. The first chapter of this part explores the relation between truth, interpretation, and reality as a cultural problematic. It focuses particularly on the deep mythic level of imagination on which fundamental images for defining and grasping reality lie. The point of the chapter is to sharpen the contrast between the dyadic relation of asserted proposition to object and the triadic relations involved in interpretation. Does the fact that thought is interpretive mean that truth is impossible, and that reality is a "world well lost?"

Chapter 2 examines philosophers' strategies for dealing with the problem of truth and the cultural problematic. In particular, Descartes' view of mechanism is reviewed and criticized. That view derives from the more basic principle, almost unquestioned in our day, that to understand something one must break it down into its simplest or completely understandable components, and then reassemble it from those components in patterns that are comprehended because we make them. The Cartesian idea of components, or simples, is the root of many evils, and an alternate idea will have to be developed. Next, contemporary functionalism will be examined as a naturalistic epistemology aiming to solve the problem of truth. The limitation hamstringing that approach, I will argue, is that it accepts a Cartesian interpretation of functions as self-contained components. A contextualist theory of functionalism, such as Dewey's, is required instead, though this would be incompatible with functionalism of Fodor's sort. Hermeneutics as deriving from Heidegger, Gadamer, and Ricoeur will then be examined, and found wanting precisely at the point where the difference between triadic meaning and dyadic truth should be found. The subtleties of the hermeneutic position, however, must be incorporated into any viable theory of interpretation. The final strategy to be examined is pragmatism's, the starting point for the theory to be developed in this book. Of special importance is its theory of signs, as distinguished from the European semiotic tradition of de Saussure. For the latter, the interesting problem is understanding signs as codes. For Pragmatism, the interesting issue is how relatively vague and uncoded signs can become more specific or highly codified; pragmatism is interested in the genetic, more than the morphological, analysis of signs. Pragmatism's weakness is its dependence on the notion of the future to define truth as a present relation between sign and object.

After the review of the field of strategies, chapter 3 presents a preliminary statement of the theory of truth to be defended throughout this book. The thesis is that truth is the carryover of value from the object into the interpretation of it, as qualified by the biological, cultural, semiotic, and purposive elements of the interpreter. First, the chapter sketches the rudiments of interpretation, and then, the rudiments of the theory of value. The theory of interpretation will be comprehensively restated in chapter 16, and the theory of value will receive detailed treatment in chapters 7 and 8. Chapter 3 next examines the meaning of "carryover" and lays out the problems for a theory of nature that accounts for causation as the mediator of value between "external things" and "experience." The theory of nature will be developed throughout chapters 9 through 12.

Finally, in chapter 4, the causal transformers of human biology, culture, semiotics, and purposive behavior will be discussed for the bearing they have on carryover. These will be elaborated in more detail in chapters 13 through 16. Together they amount to a theory of participation, indicating how the process of interpretation, by individuals or by social groups, participates in structures that qualify but still carry over the realities about which interpretation can reveal the truth.

1

The Problem of Truth

European modernity bequeathed to us a nice distinction between mind and body that has become a wicked myth. The distinction was succinctly drawn by Descartes but echoed in nearly every one of his seventeenth century philosophic contemporaries and in their successors down to our time. The echo has not always been in the form of agreement. But the distinction has set the agenda for philosophy, for those accepting the distinction, for those attempting to overcome it, and for those developing one side while rejecting or subordinating the other.

The mythic embodiment of that distinction is a cultural imagination framing our politics, economics, ethics, social life, religion, art, athletics, and nearly every other civilized domain. For this reason, the distinction is vastly more important beyond the profession of philosophy than within; the profession, indeed, has domesticated it to a conceptual puzzle. The cultural mythic image of the distinction filters our civilization through a prism dividing the bodily aspects of things as objective from the mental aspects as subjective. The result is what some recent commentators (Lasch, 1979; Cahoone, 1988; Bordo, 1987) analyze as a pervasive cultural narcissism, a sick oscillation in personal and institutional attitude between a grandiose sense of self, viewing the world as made of objects to be worked upon, and a pseudo-scientific sense of reality as objective and valueless, with a reduction of the sense of self to an inertia-machine. There is a deep, pathetic irony in the fact that the deconstructionist center of post-modernism, the movement taking itself to have transcended the myth of the bifurcation of body and mind, asserts that the real is textuality (see Derrida: 1976, 1979; Harari: 1979a, pp. 37–44; Taylor: 1984, pp. 3–18). Compared to stars, seas, and mountains, to food, safety, and sociality, a text is effete body; compared to sensitivity, creativity, will, and passion, text-interpreting is effete mind. Deconstructive post-modernism reduces mind and body to the metaphors and tools of the academy, depriving the academy of its robust natural cultural context in the process.

The loss of philosophy of nature from the European tradition is a central thread in the development of the modern and post-modern mythos. From the Milesians through the early modern philosophers, including Descartes, Hobbes, Locke, Spinoza, and Leibniz, philosophy's interpretation of nature set the context and provided the springboard for most other philosophic interests. Descartes' distinction of mind from body, however, had the effect of handing nature over to science. Philosophy of nature was replaced by philosophy of science, an epistemological inquiry into the kind of knowledge science involves. Kant's critique of metaphysics was far more influential as a critique of philosophy of nature than as an attack on metaphysics, and after him the main philosophic movements left nature to science. Kant's heritage is transcendental, that is, limited to examining the conditions under which science and other claims to non-philosophic knowledge are possible.

There are three important exceptions to the abandonment of philosophy of nature in the West. The first (see Lucas, 1979, 1983) is Hegel and his idealist colleagues, especially Schelling. They did indeed produce philosophies of nature, but were limited by having forced nature into the vocabulary of mind: they saw nature as objective *spirit*. The idealists understood with perfect clarity the need for comprehensiveness in philosophy of nature. Perhaps their positive expressions of comprehensiveness in the terms of system and totality are unacceptable today, but the negative point is valid: no phenomenon, no question, no perspective can be left out of consideration.[1] One quick implication of a norm of comprehensiveness is that philosophy of nature is intricately involved with metaphysics and every other philosophic topic.

The second exception is Charles Peirce and the pragmatists, especially James and Dewey. Peirce easily circumvented Kant's critique of metaphysics by showing that metaphysics can be hypothetical, as mentioned earlier. This allowed him to elaborate a complex philosophy of nature, and to show how mind in all its Cartesian glory is a manifestation of nature. The limitation to Peirce's project is that his language for describing nature, ironically like Hegel's, is mentalistic. That is, the themes of his theory of signs are those employed to describe the evolution of mind; he called matter "effete mind" (1936, par. 25). By and large, Peirce's semiotics need not be given a mentalistic interpretation when read in its own context; but in the context of European semiotics, from de Saussure (1959) to Derrida, interpretation seems to be a mental phenomenon.

The third exception is Alfred North Whitehead (1925, 1933, 1978) and the process philosophers (see Lucas, 1983). While it may be arguable that Whitehead's language is mentalistic, his problematic of nature arises from the issues of twentieth century science and religion, and his philosophy is a critical response to the culture of modernity. The chief limitations in Whitehead are found in the ideas themselves, not the project. One way of undertaking a renewed philosophy of nature is by means of an internal critique of Whitehead, although that is not my purpose here.

Instead, my purpose is to elaborate a theory of interpretation complementing, but in crucial respects competitive with, those stemming from Continental hermeneutics and critical theory, and with those stemming from language analysis, linguistics, and cognitive science. Philosophy of nature is, in its rhetorical function, merely instrumental to the purpose. But because it has been so neglected, the strategy must be to present it in its own right. The controlling interest of this study is whether a theory of interpretation can acknowledge that reality is the measure of interpretive truth. Truth is the elusive but most important concept at issue.

Our culture finds truth deeply problematic, which is puzzling in light of our abundant intellectual life. The natural and social sciences have increased knowledge in the last hundred years far beyond any expectations a century ago. The arts and letters not only have enjoyed an extraordinary century of imaginative genius but have become self-conscious and accessible to criticism as never before in the West. The century's great disillusionments, about Progress, Modernization, Peace, Economic Fairness, National Character, Science, Technology, Psyche, and the Transparency of Consciousness, have been hard lessons well learned. Even if somewhat humbling, those lessons themselves are important truths. Yet our culture finds truth more problematic than ever.

The conglomerate nature of our culture is part of the problem. A single, well-entrenched tradition might have sufficiently deep assumptions that when some claim to truth emerges from its settled methodologies, its truth status is unquestioned. Our culture is not one tradition, however, but many. By no means unified or consistent, it is a mix of interactions among manifold traditions brought about by a world-wide economic system, a global political-military confrontation, a universal scientific base for technology, and by the vast outpouring of scholarship and popular writing within many traditions about the others. So the great disillusionments are embodied from many points of view, from that of the scientifically and technologically advanced but also that of the backward, from that of the guilty oppressors but also that of the bitter oppressed, from that of the literate but also that of the illiterate subcultures, from that of the elite in each society as well as that of the masses, from that of the Buddhists as well as the Freudians. Some cultures are disillusioned because they cannot modernize fast enough; others because modernization is destroying their old traditions; yet others because even the advance into post-modernized society hasn't brought the satisfactions sought. All these perspectives on disillusionment, mixed in the interactions of our real society, feed the poignancy of the problem of truth.

The problem is that truth too might be an illusion. Fundamentalists in the world's religions fear this when they try to protect their bit of the culture from criticism by the rest. Relativists fear it when they say truth is nothing more than having your own perspective. The masses, East and West, North and South, fear it when they abandon hope, pathetically giving in to the iron laws of natural and human oppression. The Western elites fear it when they despair, stylishly to be sure, by falling into the therapeutic mentality.

Not everyone believes truth might be an illusion. Many people fight for improved conditions, for self-betterment, for the welfare of others, for social peace and justice, for more accurate sciences, and for more sophisticated and profound arts and letters. This book is written out of a sense of identification with these people, not with the disillusioned. Nevertheless, when asked to explain and justify a serious commitment to truth, in the face of widespread disillusionment, we are hard pressed to know what to say. This book is an attempt at an answer.

The fear that truth might be an illusion is less about the status of our truth-claims than it is about reality. Our claims cannot be true when they seem to be if reality does not measure them. In fact, if reality is not the measure of our truth claims, then those claims can no more be false than true, only unmeasured, hence mere assertions. The goal, therefore, of an attempt to understand truth and its normative force in light of our century's disillusionments is to recover a sense of reality as the measure of truth. Hence the title of this book.

To recover a sense of reality as the measure entails attaining to a contemporary vision of nature in which intelligent beings can exist with capacities to represent things truly or falsely. A richer sense of nature is required by this than is assumed by sciences that treat nature as an object. A richer sense of intentionality as part of nature is also required than is assumed by philosophic traditions that treat intentionality as a matter of subjectivity. A richer sense of nature ought not to have to reject what science has discovered, and therefore it must be able to subsume a modern sense of objectivity; nor ought it reject what subjectivist philosophies have made plain, and therefore it must sustain a sense of subjectivity. Philosophy's response to the problem of truth thus involves developing an expanded sense of nature and intentionality. In this it is closer to metaphysics and philosophical cosmology than to philosophy of science, logic, or epistemology. My project here is to construct a "naturalistic" philosophy that makes apparent how reality is the measure of truth.

The key to a naturalistic philosophy that remains sensitive to the vast domain of subjectivity is a thematic exposition of the concept of value. A vision of nature in which each thing is an achievement of value, and each change is a transformation of value, may be rich enough to provide a context for an appropriate theory of truth.

Before examining the philosophic structure of the problem of truth and developing an appropriate theory, however, it is necessary to deepen the background analysis of truth as a cultural problem. An obvious way to begin that consideration is by asking where the metaphysical foundations of modern science locate the problem. The answer is, in the attempt to distinguish interpretations, which can be true or false, from imagination, which is the original synthesizing activity of experience.

I. IMAGINATION AND INTERPRETATION

A major achievement of our culture has been the recognition that the function of human imagination is so basic, and its powers so great, that in certain contexts it seems autonomous, or capable of autonomy, or worth being made autonomous. As to function, imagination is the capacity to synthesize the conditions of life so that they have the form of experience. Imagination turns external forces, sensations, environments, and bodily processes into "being in a world" where objects and ourselves appear against a background of other objects, where things have meaning, where "form" organizes processes and activities.[2]

Imagination is both inventiveness and a primary function that gives experience as such its shape. In its primary shaping role, it is presupposed by any specific judgments or activities taking place within experience. Also its syntheses, considered in this primary sense, need not be bound by any judgment or critical work that would guarantee that the "world" produced is true of reality. Realities, including our own nature, affect us causally, and imaginative synthesis is itself a kind of causality. But the synthesis of imagination need not necessarily produce a form of experience that is "true" of reality in the sense that it represents or is faithful to it in any sense. Therefore imagination in its primary sense is "autonomous" relative to the control of critical judgment.[3]

Imagination is inventive, as well as primarily shaping, in two related senses. In the first, imagination invents the various forms in which the world is experienced; these are necessary if we are to have an experiential world at all, and it is in this sense that imagination's inventiveness serves its primary shaping function. In the second sense, imagination is inventive of all specific cultural forms. By means of inventive imagination, we speak, build civilized societies, create technologies, the arts, crafts, and attain self-consciousness of culture. Cultures differ, of course, in their forms. To the extent cultural relativism is a serious truth, the distribution between the first and second senses of imaginative inventiveness is blurred: even the most basic forms of "world" are specific cultural forms and might be unique to given cultures, or colored by their special twists. Arising in the near autonomy of imagination to transform and thereby transcend nature, culture is both a glory and a terror.

The glory of the imaginative base of human culture is that it allows for the creation of values far more subtle and complex than that achieved by nature without imagination, values having to do with might-have-beens and could-have-been-otherwises. This achievement is a new complexity within the achivements of nature of such; culture is not intrinsically inimical to nature. The terror of culture appears with the recognition that the basic imaginative syntheses could have taken different forms (as they did in other cultures) and that maybe the entire cultural world is an illusion of imagination, a fantasy, a dream. The terror is that imagination may be so autonomous as to disconnect us from the reality we suppose to be experienced as our ground, context, and goal.

This terror is rather new with European modernity. Even in Descartes' philosophy, rigorous as it was about the separation of body and mind, imagination is the mental function that supposedly is directly moved by physical reality, the mediator of the outer world to the inner. When imagination becomes autonomous, as it has in late modernity, it loses the capacity to mediate. A naturalistic philosophy must restore that mediating function, and without the liabilities of Descartes' dichotomy.

Interpretation is to be distinguished from imagination as the cognitive activity of determining what is true, or enjoying, acting, and responding in ways shaped by assertions intended as true. In this broadest sense, interpretation involves both drawing out meaning and asserting that the meaning holds. The terms involved in interpretation may be imaginative products, and the very structure of imaginative forms may be the subject matter under consideration, as in much philosophy. But the structure of interpretation differs from that of imagination. The forms of imagination are subject to aesthetic norms of formal integrity, indeed of beauty in a basic sense (see

Neville: 1981, ch. 4). The norms for interpretation are the logical ones having to do with truth. Interpretation distances its signs from reality and asserts, perhaps with explicit or implicit reasons, that the signs are true of reality, that they interpret validly. Interpretation therefore sets itself up to be measured by reality. This is so even when the reality is other signs.

The model, common in Western modernity, of reality "out there" to be mirrored "in the mind" is no longer to be taken seriously. There simply is no way to compare the two, and this has been known since Hume, Kant, and Hegel, despite its appeal to our naively realistic scientific attitudes. The move from imagination to interpretation, if it can be made, thus involves introducing a dual modality within imagination. On the one hand, imagination is the synthetic human activity that constitutes the forms of experience such that we have a world. On the other hand, imagination is the medium by which we engage the world. Only interpretation can treat a part of imagination as a means of engagement, however. Imagination by itself might be appropriate for engagement, but the engagement does not take place without interpretation. Interpretation takes imaginative products as images and treats them as signs of the real; to do this it takes other imaginative products to be interpretants, asserting that the first signs do indeed interpret the real. The real is what the first signs are taken to stand for. Because imagination is a causal process and works with the products of the causal processes relating to people, imagination is a plausible connection between the reality of oneself and everything else.

Interpretation in an innocent sense is simply taking the world to be as we image it. Recognition of error leads to the loss of innocence. But the degeneration of interpretation occurs when we forget that the appropriateness of the sign is measured by the real it is alleged to interpret, and suppose instead that it is measured by the further sign asserting the interpretation. Of course, the temptation to degeneration is ineluctable because there is no obvious place to stand to compare the sign-images with the reality they are asserted to interpret. We revert instead to looking to further interpretation as the measure. This would not be so tempting were we to rest easy with a philosophic understanding of nature showing how signs do indeed mediate reality into experience. But nature is lost from our philosophy. Part of the terror of imagination's autonomy is that our culture construes it in disconnection from nature, and hence without any mediating function.

In the modern period, imagination has been identified with the individual ego, despite the fact it is a social phenomenon such that individuals are token-bearers of images. When the ego is construed as a subject, over against reality as object, imagination seems to be the individual's projection of personally created forms on a screen that remains subjective. Our culture thus rests in an ambiguous situation. On the one hand, truth depends on interpretation, which in turn depends on imagination, which in turn depends on imagination functioning as a genuine mediator of other things to ourselves. In a naturalistic theory, imagination is precisely this. On the other hand, the modern scientific culture has said that imagination is subjective. If so, then mediation becomes mysterious and all interpretive reference to the real things in the world is reduced to a reference to our imaginative representations. What do the imaginative representations represent? The real world? How could we know? Our creative imagination's projections? The terror of imagination arises when culture slides the latter way.

II. MYTH

The focus of the terror is on the mythic level of culture, because myth is the imaginative structure distinguishing what counts as the world from what counts as a representation of it. Myth is now widely regarded (Berger, 1969; Eliade, 1961; Smith, 1961) as a fundamental imaginative structure by which people organize experience so as to represent themselves as having some ground, context and goal. It is closely associated with cosmological forms imaging space, place, time, causation, life/non-life distinctions, human reality and destiny, and various other basic elements that can be objectified and conceptualized in philosophy. Mythological thinking has been modernized into a world view sensitive to science, but at the imaginative level such a world view plays roles similar to the ancient myths and their related cosmologies.

Myths are not merely imaginative structures, however, but also *assumed* or *asserted* structures. To believe in a myth, or to live with it as an assumption, is to take its structure as fundamental to the mode of the imaged world over against every creative imaginative product that might be questioned. The mythic structure is the way reality is imagined to be when any sign is interpreted as representing reality. The assertion of some fundamental mythic structure is the primordial component of interpretation. Without it one cannot distinguish within experience between one's fancy and reality. Myths identify the reality of the world that can measure our interpretive responses.

As the myths of the ancient and medieval worlds fell before modern science, a new secular mythology was born according to which the world is a wholly positive, factual reality. By controlled experiments, its nature could be discovered and knowledge could be accumulated in progressive fashion. This new mythic cosmology was coupled with a new myth of ground, context, and goal of human life. Reversing the golden age elements of many older mythologies, the secular myth postulated a definite historical development of the human race from animal-like primitivism to indefinitely improvable civilization. As for context, the secular myth postulated a universe of infinite inertial forces, with the human place seeming to be an accidental collocation of inertial forces, a place with no center, no limits save those determined by natural vectors. As to goal, the modern myth expressed an unstable ambivalence: on the one hand a progressive perfectability of human life and virtue, and on the other an accidental dissolution as our blindly running atoms disintegrate the human forms. Late modern consciousness thus tends to oscillate between bourgeois glorification of human achievements, marking the milestones of progress, and deep nihilism coupled with scientific resignation.

The romantic movement was religious rejection of the mythic structure of secular modernity. Sometimes romanticism seemed to hark back to prescientific, "gothic" mythic worlds. But its heart was in the creation of a new mythology of imagination itself. Let modern science define the natural world—the truer and better world lies in the creative genius of the human imagination. Romanticism was not just a twist on the myth of secular progress. It distanced the monuments of genius from the history of inertial progress. Or, more subtly in thinkers such as Hegel, romanticism turned history itself into a monument of genius; the inertial history of secular science and its progressive mastery of the world were relegated to an abstract place within the true history of spirit. That romanticism often identified the imaginative genius with God did not diminish its glorification of the human contribution.

The legacies of the dialectical relation between romanticism and bourgeois progressivism are many and sometimes paradoxical. There is the apotheosis of art and high culture, imagination's most exquisite products. Whatever one says about the decline of the West, the last century and a half have witnessed a blaze of cultural glory. On the other hand, romanticism revealed the seamy underside of imagination, its capacity to deceive and build a duplicitous culture. Marx, Nietzsche, and Freud would have been impossible without both the romantic aggrandizement of imagination which transcends nature and the progressivist mythic faith in positive facts to be uncovered. With these critics of deception, both the myth of secular progress and the myth of creative imagination have been deprived of their power to assert a real imaged world.

So we in the West find ourselves mythless now, and consequently impotent to believe our "world" is a real world. Our developing technology looked like progress in the short run, but nuclear war would reduce life to infinite, non-living inertial forces—no progress there. Increased knowledge has not meant improved civilization; instead we have invented "mass death," as Edith Wyschogrod calls it (1985). High culture suddenly seems real only for a small elite, while the truth for most people is hunger. Cultural leaders have lost their way, turning first from the attempt to make something of cultural value to making something to be applauded by their professional guild, and then to despair.

Meanwhile popular movements seek to regain a mythos, and thereby a world. The extraordinary world-wide resurgence of fundamentalist religion within the complex tissues of technological life is a case in point. The vain impotence of fundamentalism is that its mythic world is a different world from the creative technological and cross-cultural imagery with which we have to live. Therefore it cannot assert a reality for the living interpretations we need to test. Fundamentalism survives, indeed flourishes, by its capacity to isolate and protect from criticism a certain coherent image of the world that defines a way of life. But because that image is out of coordination with the terms of effective, historical life, it cannot function mythically to ground a world image that can be presumed real relative to those assertions the world should measure. The fundamentalist myth becomes then merely a psychological prop, attractive and psychologically effective for some, but not a cultural mythos.

The borrowing by Westerners of non-Western religion is another popular attempt to regain a myth, and thereby a world. Surely nothing can be said against cultural enrichment by such borrowing, and the mutual interactions of the world's traditional cultures are an important and valuable part of the contemporary scene. But non-Western religions can hardly provide a myth for contemporary life, whatever else they provide. The mythic structures of non-Western cultures were developed for conditions of those cultures, not the Western. And because modern technology has transformed nearly all the world's cultures, those traditional mythologies are in as much trouble in their homelands as the Western myths are at home. Although the story of the impact of modernization is different in non-Western lands, the outcome regarding the traditional mythologies is much the same as in the West. Most of what is said about the loss of a measuring world in the West can be said also about non-Western "developing" societies. If the traditional mythologies, East or West, can be rehabilitated to aid in the recovery of a measure, as they most likely can, the rehabilitation will involve radical surgery.

Not many of the developments mentioned so far have gone unnoticed by critics contemporary with their occurance. Indeed, the phrase "recovery of the measure" can be misinterpreted as a conservative slogan recalling us to "standards." The problem is deeper than the conservative appeal recognizes, however. The loss of the measure is the loss of the world, not the loss of the right interpretation of the world. Ours is an apocalyptic time from which there is no turning back, as Altizer (1985) so brilliantly has shown.

The loss of viable mythology cannot easily be repaired with a new and better myth because we have lost mythic thinking as such.

The logical problem is fairly simple. If the assertion of myth is the establishment of an imaged real world to measure assertions, what is the justification of the assertion of myth? This is not the relatively superficial question of justifying changes in a myth—the history of civilization details many shifts in mythology in which enough remains stable to justify the changes. It is rather the question about the very meaning of justification or reason-giving for mythic assertion if interpretation, justification, and reason-giving presuppose the prior mythic move distinguishing imagination in the mode of an imaged world from the imaginative creations that can be criticized. If the imaged world is an imaginative creation, how can it be true or real? If the imaged world is thought to be true, then it must be a sign of something. But of what could it be a sign that does not already partake of the very forms of imagination under judgment? If the imaged world is thought to be real, and thereby the measure of any image by which we might signify or interpret it, does this cast into unreality the elements of nature that have not entered into imaginative synthesis? If so, then imagination is the only reality, a terror of autonomy.

Let us not mistake where the terror lies. In a practical sense the imaginative structure of modern life is vast, has been developed in pragmatic concert with events throughout history, is common to anyone socialized into our perceptual and linguistic communities, and is common enough to diverse cultures because of biological similarities and historical interactions that it is impossible to describe more than superficial differences among the great literate cultures (Davidson, 1974). Much of our difficulty with mythlessness is that we have too many basic imaginative structures, inconsistent or even incommensurable with one another, and not coordinated by a dominant mythos; this is a usual phenomenon in times of cultural change, a cause for confusion and perhaps anxiety, but not terror.

The terror lies rather in the status of the world as a product of imagination, a creation of our own, something which requires a measure before it itself can measure our interpretations. Anything we look at directly seems to be a matter of interpretation. Our peripheral vision, however, seems to undermine the reality to which we interpretively refer our truths. And the truths become fantasies, to which we can agree to cling as our defining conventions, but which we can't really believe. Perhaps we ourselves are not really real. Heidegger asked the "question of Being" in an academic way: how can we know the being of Being rather than the being of things? He knew also that there is an existential side to the question: what is the being of the world such that it, and we ourselves in it, are real?

III. THE IMPERIAL TRIUMPH OF INTERPRETATION

Heidegger (1962), followed by Gadamer (1975, 1976), Ricoeur (1974), and others, popularized the notion of the hermeneutic circle. In its popular version, the notion is that thought has no intuitive, unmediated access to its subject but always engages in interpretation, bringing the thinker's predispositions to the subject in order to gain a handle, correcting those predispositions by the knowledge gained of the subject, and thus constantly moving back and forth between subject matter and self, bringing them into closer corrected coordination. Interpretation moves circularly from a view of the interpretive context to the thing interpreted, back to the context. The circle is not vicious since predispositions can be corrected in the process. On the other hand, there never is access to a reality without interpretive baggage. How can we then speak of the independence of the subject matter, its reality?

Heidegger was anticipated a half century earlier by Charles Peirce who was concerned less with interpreting texts (the preoccupation of the current hermeneutical movement) than with interpreting objects scientifically. Peirce (1934, pars. 213–217) argued that there is no first intuition, and that every interpretation takes its subject matter itself to be a sign. There is nothing knowable that is not a sign. Peirce had thoroughly abandoned the Cartesian separation of physical objects from mental or semiotic phenomena, and therefore he construed signs and the process of interpretation in terms of natural causation. Or, more interestingly, he explained the action of laws of nature on physical objects as special cases of interpretive process.

Peirce and Heidegger agreed that all interpretation is triadic, that is, a three-term relation. For Heidegger, an interpretation is defined essentially in terms of its movement between the object interpreted and the suppositions and particular understanding of the interpreter. To use Peirce's language, interpretation takes a sign to stand for an object in some respect; the interpretation here is another sign functioning as the interpretant. For an object to be specified as the object of the sign by the interpretant, the object is itself treated as a sign, as having its reality in the interpretation relation. Therefore, the relation between object and sign is always mediated by the interpretant, and when that mediation is in question, the interpretant itself is mediated to the object and sign by further interpretation. All cognition then is hypothetical, subject to further mediation.

Peirce is mainly right on this point, and the arguments will be developed below. More important, our culture has accepted the basic point, for it is the analogue within interpretation of the dilemma of imagination. No real world by which we can measure our interpretive assertions stands outside the circle of interpretation. Peirce's pragmatism has its greatest force in showing how to keep most interpretation stable as the measure of the interpretation in question, all the while looking to criticize any and all elements of the interpretive world.

By what grounds can an interpretation be criticized, however, if all criticism is only further mediation? Peirce had a dynamic view of interpretation in which signs constitute habits and expectations. An interpretation is criticized when reality frustrates the habit or expectation, saying No! Peirce called this Secondness, the overagainstness of reality. He pointed out correctly that reality, in contrast to interpretation, involves a dyadic or two-term relation. In some sense or other, reality "is what it is and is not some other thing," as Aristotle would put it.

It is important to identify in what the dyadic nature of reality consists, because a thing which is determinately different from another thing is in a triadic relation: *x* is different from *y* in some respect *m*.[4] Without the respect in which things are different, they are not determinately different. Over and above the triadic determinateness of a difference between two things, however, is the sheer fact of difference, the reality of the two things over against each other. Or even if there were only one thing, different from no other thing, it would be itself over against what would otherwise be nothingness. (Actually there could not be only one thing, because for a thing to have an identity it would have to be minimally determinate, which is to say minimally different from some other thing in some respect; see chapter 6, sections 3 and 4.) Reality is ineluctably dyadic in the sense that a real identity is itself *and not some other thing*. A real identity is also triadic in being determinately different from certain other things. A real identity can shape through shifts in the triadic relation. But it ceases to be real only when all dyadic relations fail to hold and it has no essential being of its own.

To be sure, reality includes processes in which real things are on the way to being other things, and it is the changes, not the beginning or end points, that are the reality of processes. Still, as real, the processes are just these processes and not some other processes, a dyadic difference. Reality might also include universals and generalizing phenomena—Peirce thought these are real; but again, the reality is these universals as contrasted with those, or with particulars; these generals and these vague realities, not those or none. So reality, however else it might be defined, involves the dyadic character of being this identity rather than that identity or no identity, regardless of how shifting, vague, or elusive the allegedly real identity is.

If reality has this kind of dyadic self-definition, then truth must also involve a dyadic character. As Aristotle said, a true assertion says of a thing what it is and denies of it what it is not. In the *Metaphysics*, Book IV, chapter 7, at 1011b 26, Aristotle wrote, "To say of what is that it is not, or of what is not that it is, is false, while to say of what is that it is, and of what is not that it is not, is true; so that he who says of anything that it is, or that it is not, will say either what is true or what is false" (Ross translation). Truth is very complicated in this regard because there are many respects in which assertions can interpret a thing. To say that a sugar cube is white is not to deny that it is also sweet. But interpreting a thing in a definite respect requires a definite, that is, a dyadically yes-no, attribution of each candidate character. Again, if the reality is a process, it goes from this to that character, which is its dyadic identity in contrast to another order of characters. If the reality is vague, such as tomorrow's dinner, it allows of certain contradictory predicates; for example, fish and chicken but not both when the dinner is actualized; its vague identity is still dyadically related to excluded alternatives—no mammoth steak. Therefore, despite the fact that a true assertion is in the triadic relation of being a sign interpreting its object (the reality) to an interpretant, the assertion is true precisely because of its dyadic relation to the object whereby it says of the object what it is and not what it is not.

Within interpretation, however, the dyadic truth relation is always mediated, and this creates the problem of truth. Perhaps a clever enough wit could prove that any assertion is true of anything to which it can refer by finding some context, some respect, in which it is true. Hitler was not a villain—he was the great leader who rescued Germany from the degradations of the Weimar economy. Two plus two is not four when applied to drops of water mixed in a puddle. The Michaelson-Morley experiments did not disprove the ether theory, because that theory can be reformulated to have the properties they observed. The difficulty here is that there are so many respects in which a thing can be interpreted that for any assertion there might be some respect, however far fetched, in which it can be true. Because the reality is connected to the assertoric sign by the respect in which the sign interprets it, the dyadic character of the reality is never allowed to measure the sign. For any putative measure, some respect can be found in which the assertion can be true. This is indeed far fetched, and impractical in the short run. In the long run, however, interpretation does not allow an alleged reality simply to be, and thereby to measure what is asserted of it. Interpretation makes the reality wholly maleable within the triadic processes, assigning respects in which signs interpret. The problem is not that assertions have no truth, but that all assertions can be true in some respect or other.

Thus the imperialism of interpretation domesticates reality and allows it to show itself only in the respects interpretation assigns. Immanuel Kant saw this point with brilliant clarity and expressed it in the remarks about his Copernican Revolution: whereas before Kant we were in the leading strings of nature, now we question her and she answers. But nature disappears.

The mediating character of interpretation would be benign were there a clear way to have reality apart from interpretation. For then we could say that a given reality does indeed allow of interpretation in these and those respects, and in these and those respects certain assertions are dyadically true. But in fact, we have realities only insofar as they are encountered within the triadic interpretive process. Put another way, they are not encountered except as imaged, and it is difficult to maintain the measuring status of reality if it is but the imaginative mode of imaged world in tenuous contrast to the imaginative mode of creative invention.

The outcome of the imperial triumph of interpretation is that reality cannot measure our claims to truth. The only measure seems to consist in what survives future interpretation. Neither the pragmatists nor Heidegger intended this at all. The pragmatists said that all judgments are fallible and any might be corrected in the future. But the correction would come because the future would supply a proper dyadic encounter with the reality, an occasion where reality in its dyadic secondness says No to error. Heidegger, particularly in his later work (1949, 1968, 1971), emphasized the activity of the object in making itself present to us, rather than the interpreting activity of the knowing subject. With due respect, however, to Heidegger and the pragmatists (and the later Wittgenstein), Richard Rorty (1979) has spoken the priestly word for the triumph of interpretation: reality can be dismissed as the stuff mind was falsely thought to mirror, and culture's quest for truth is simply an ongoing conversation, hopefully edifying.

Of course culture's quest for truth is a conversation, or many conversations. But is not their worth measured by the reality of their topic? And in a deeper sense, does not reality measure the appropriateness of the topics? These are not quite rhetorical questions, since Rorty might be right about the implications of truth-seeking as interpretation. If he is, however, the consequences are sad indeed. The cultural conversation, measured by nothing but its own future assessments, is only the language game of elite Western culture, with no worth except that found in its own enjoyment. Yet since the conversation has at least the form of a reference to reality, it is self-deceptive at its core, and the revelation of that self-deception will destroy it, sooner rather than later.

The questions are very nearly rhetorical, however, for the reason that they express the suppositions of the cultural conversation. The conversation is indeed about the real world, and it may therefore be an intrinsic part of that conversation to step back and re-examine the question of the impact of the triumph of interpretation on the measuring status of reality.

IV. FACT AND VALUE

Since Aristotle, a common assumption about knowledge is that it consists in obtaining in the mind the form of the object known. There have, of course, been many divergent accounts of the nature of form, of how form is resident in objects, and how it arrives and remains resident in mind. There have also been subtle accounts of the transformation of form as it is transposed from object to knower. In the modern period, beginning with Descartes' superb formulation, the difference between corporeal objects and mind was thought to be so great as to be a difference in kind of substance. Because, as Descartes said, the mind is more easily known than body, the nature of form as it lies in mind has been taken to be the clue to the way form lies in objects. Despite the divergences, the vague general assumption about the bilocation of form prepared the way for the plausibility of Wittgenstein's early thesis that the world consists of facts and that a fact is what is formally represented by a propositional function. The implications of this for interpretation are that an interpretive sign is a proposition, its object is what a proposition represents, namely a fact, and the interpretant relating the sign and object is just a proposition (or an act of proposition-asserting) to that effect. On this view it is clear why the real world appears only as a set of facts defined by their being represented, all a matter of imaginative form as ordered respectively into the fact-mode and the representing-mode by interpretive activity.

The assumption that knowledge or interpretation is a reiteration of form is not innocent. How can there be knowledge of the intrinsic values of things? The ancient Greeks did not doubt that things have values, both in themselves and for other things (Gadamer, 1986). Plato directed his entire philosophy to demonstrating how valuational knowledge has cognitive status. Like Aristotle, he suggested that knowledge consists in paralleling the object's form in the knowing faculty. But Plato's account of form was that it is a way of having things together so that they possess value, so that they express what he called "normative measures" in the *Statesman*; for Plato, the form of forms was the Form of the *Good*. Aristotle's account of form differed radically from Plato's. For Aristotle, form is structure. His account of value, which he intended to be as objective as Plato's, centered on the "final cause" of substances, the cause which brings the substance to completion. The "end" of things, according to Aristotle, is not some kind of aesthetic richness, as Plato thought, but rather a rounding out, a structural completion that actualizes as much of a thing's potential as possible.[5] The state of structural completion can be represented as a fact, with the consequence that the value dimension can be forgotten.

The European Renaissance pushed this Aristotelian view to an extreme. The invention of mathematical physics in principle allowed qualities or classes to be represented by quantities or mathematical ratios. Platonists, including many mathematicians of the Renaissance and later, might have seen value or beauty in mathematical ratios. But they finally abandoned the view that their beautiful mathematical representations represented the real values in objects. By the time of Descartes and Newton, physicists took mathematical representations to depict how parts of matter move relative to one another, and they took nature to be parts of matter so depictable. Strange geniuses such as Leibniz held out for a thoroughly valuational view of nature; but that view failed to discredit their overall theories in the new mythos that Whitehead described as dead matter for nature, duplicating or mirroring form for mind (see Whitehead: 1925, chs. 1–4).

The result of the victory of mathematical physics in determining the new mythos of secular modernity was that valuational thinking was deprived of cognitive status. Despite brilliant attempts to recreate normative political philosophy and ethics in the modern period, the best strategies have been limited to postulating some fact as the ground for norms, strategies that fall before arguments such as G.E. Moore's complaint about the naturalistic fallacy.[6] Social contract theorists, for instance, begin with a fact such as human aggressiveness (Hobbes, 1950) or appetite (Locke, 1947), facts modelled on analogy with physical inertia. Then they deduce political norms as rational ways of coping with the facts. Some ethicists (for example, Hume: 1888, Pts. II–III) postulated faculties of moral sensation or taste, but without a way of justifying the deliverances of the faculties except as what is in fact sensed. Others, for instance Kant (1956), appealed to structural or logical criteria such as self-consistency in order to determine norms, but there theories result in characters such as consistancy or autonomy for the willing subject without many positive moral duties or values. None of these approaches can withstand criticism of the sort expressed in the naturalistic fallacy: any fact alleged to ground normative judgments must justify itself as not a fact but a norm.

The twentieth century has seen a general turn from normative justification to an admission that normative judgments are either expressions of emotive responses (non-normative) or else consist in rationalizations of behavior in the face of universal personal selfishness (Rawls, 1971). The mythic base of secular modernity, exquisitely elaborated in its philosophical metaphysics and epistemology, turns the distinction between fact and value into a separation, and banishes the side of value. The undeniable appearance of value in human affairs must thus be reconstructed by secular modernity as a kind of non-normative fact if it is to fit into modernity at all. Real value usually is simply dismissed. In its place we talk of "values," and of "value-analysis," all of which refers to human preferences rather than to what is worth valuing; these preferences are to be respected because they are expressions of autonomy, of individual or group will, not because they are valid appreciations of real value in things.

Cultural experience follows philosophy; even more, it is shaped by the various forces that concurrently shape philosophy. Despite this, our cultural experience has not become wholly dead to the worths of things, to the normative call of duty, to the gratuitously delightful and the egregiously wicked. The usual attempt to reconstruct all value experience as a matter of support for or frustration of facts of personal pleasure might be carried out in theory but not in practice without calling the authenticity of practice into question. Of course, part of the loss of reality is that authentic practice is often called into question. But there is a self-referential absurdity to questioning authentic practice, since that questioning itself would have to be an authentic practice.

Culture's way of questioning authentic practice, or even its mythos, is through the trickster's devices—through parody, satire, and reversing the statuses of the socially elite and vulgar.[7] But the subversive methods of humor and deceit are never enough themselves to assert and sustain a mythos and metaphysics, not even the secular ones of modernity. The subversive methods are parasitic on criticizing some mythos and metaphysics that has independent authority. Modernity's culture is too enfeebled and confused now to bear the weight of much satiric criticism of itself. The result is that our now disordered experience of things as having value calls for a new mythos and metaphysics. This returns the discussion to the work of philosophy regarding the problem of truth.

Philosophy cannot perform the prophet's role of establishing a new mythos. But it can articulate an alternate metaphysical vision that gives expression to some of the forces and possibilities that can coalesce into a mythic foundation for culture. To do this, philosophy can embrace other philosophical traditions as well as elite Western culture, allowing its own form to change as the encounter dictates. Not to expand its experiential base is to commit philosophy to a metaphysical scale too small for the mythic structures of a global society. Philosophy is once again called to a task of speculative metaphysical daring, as it has been called in every period of fundamental cultural reorganization. Given the ambiguous success of previous attempts, as noted concerning Descartes, speculative philosophers should bring a sense of irony and humor along with their daring.

2

Philosophical Strategies

Philosophers in our century have not been blind to the problems raised in the previous chapter and have developed original and commanding strategies to deal with some of them. The focus of the present chapter is to examine certain of these strategies as they bear upon the attempt to conceive of the mental activity of interpretation as part of nature. Subsequent chapters will attempt a positive presentation of an appropriate naturalistic position. With such a naturalistic theory of mind in hand, it later should be possible to articulate a theory of truth in which reality is the measure of assertions.

If a naturalistic theory of mind is to be developed, the conception of nature is crucial. Descartes' was the most influential theory of nature in modernity, and it was mechanistic. Conversely, mechanism was made plausible because it is presupposed by Descartes' conception of understanding. Although mechanism has come in for severe criticism in several of the recent developments in physical science, the conception of understanding presupposing it has not been criticized equally. Further, Cartesian understanding has itself been something of a model, or leading metaphor, for contemporary conceptions of mind based on computer analogies. Functionalism is the philosophy in which a Cartesian conception of mind is revived with great power in the present day. The first two sections here deal with Descartes' views and with functionalism respectively. Both are criticized in terms of a principle of context-dependence.

The recent philosophy most sensitive to the subtleties of context-dependence is hermeneutics, the topic of the third section. According to hermeneutic philosophy, meaning is wholly context-dependent, and is to be interpreted through the hermeneutical circle. The limit of this approach is the difficulty it finds in distinguishing meaning from truth, and its vulnerability to the charge that at least some basic meanings are ideological distortions, that is, deceptively false. One source of this limit is that hermeneutics fails to interpret interpretation in a naturalistic way.

Pragmatism is naturalistic at precisely the right point and agrees in the main with the hermeneutic theory of interpretation, as the final section shall explain. Pragmatism also thematizes the importance of value and purpose in all interpretation and has been unaffected by the ideals of value-free science that so early influenced hermeneutics. The great limit of pragmatism, however, is in its particular suppositions about nature that overemphasize the mode of temporality of the present. Future and past are reduced to their roles for present or projected interpretation, a disastrous result for a philosophy that conceives that future consequences largely determine meaning. The discussion of these strategies sets up the strategy to be followed in chapter 3.

I. CARTESIAN MECHANISM vs. CONTEXT DEPENDENCE

It is commonplace among philosophical historians to lay significant blame on Descartes for providing basic dualistic conceptions that led Western philosophy astray.[1] The dichotomy between mind and nature for which Descartes is usually criticized is not his most important mistake, however. Rather, Descartes has been more disastrously influential in two other intimately related ideas. One is that proper analysis is to break things into their simplest component parts and then to reconstruct them in simple steps. Understanding is what results from this dissection and reconstruction. Although stated in many forms throughout his writings, and illustrated by his own practice, Descartes' most famous statement of this idea is in the second and third rules of the *Discourse on Method*:

> The second [rule] was to divide each of the difficulties which I encountered into as many parts as possible, and as might be required for an easier solution.
>
> The third was to think in an orderly fashion, beginning with the things which were simplest and easiest to understand, and gradually and by degrees reaching toward more complex knowledge, even treating as though ordered materials which were not necessarily so.[2]

For reasons to be made apparent shortly, this idea will be called the Cartesian Fallacy Part I. Descartes' second disastrously influential idea, to be called the Cartesian Fallacy Part II of course, is that the simple parts are foundational or certain, and that the build-up of knowledge from analysis of the parts is properly scientific. Descartes stated this idea in the first and fourth of the four rules in the *Discourse*:

> The first rule was never to accept anything as true unless I recognized it to be evidently such: that is, carefully to avoid precipitation and prejudgment, and to include nothing in my conclusion unless it presented itself so clearly and distinctly to my mind that there was no occasion to doubt it. . . . The last was always to make enumerations so complete, and reviews so general, that I would be certain that nothing was omitted. (1956, 12)

Foundationalism, as this position is called, has come in for round criticisms recently that will not be rehearsed here.

The Cartesian Fallacy in combined Parts consists in thinking that a thing is a whole of summed parts, where both the parts and the summing can be understood perspicuously. This is a fallacy because a thing really has parts only as a function of itself existing within a larger context. In this sense, a thing is always more than the sum of its parts, or, rather, a thing is a sum of its parts that exist themselves only as a function of more than the thing. Both mind itself and acts of mind (which might be true or false) are to be understood only in terms of larger contexts.

The twentieth century positions that have exemplified the Cartesian Fallacy—logical positivism, analysis, atomism, language analysis, Husserlian phenomenology, cognitive science, artificial intelligence, even hermeneutics—can all be characterized as facets of philosophical modernism. Modernism generally was the cultural movement that sought to embody intelligibility, meaning, and value in the artifact or subject matter itself, to the exclusion of continuities with context. In art, poetry, and literature, the modernist project led to abstractionism, for which the abstracted element has self-contained significance and worth. In philosophy, modernism manifested itself in what Dewey called the "quest for certainty" and the search for some simple part—a pure essence, a logical form, a *de facto* linguistic convention—that could be thoroughly understood and then combined with other parts to make a mosaic world. These are ramifications of Parts II and I respectively of the Cartesian fallacy. By its emphasis on context, hermeneutics would seem not to be Cartesian or modernist, and in many respects it is not. But the very idea of investigating meaning as such, without inquiring into truth, is the essence of modernism, and in this respect hermeneutics is modernist to a pitch that would warm T. S. Eliot's heart.

The pragmatic movement is essentially non-modernist by virtue of its adoption at the very beginning of what Kant called, in condemnation, "the method of hypothesis" (1956, B797–810). Pragmatism rejected both any appeal to simples or elementary starting points and any claims to certainty. Like hermeneutics, it emphasizes interpretation, context, and the growth of signs. Better yet, pragmatism is wedded to a naturalistic cosmology and therefore points in the direction our project aims to go. Best of all, pragmatism is based on an objective approach to valuation, a topic skewed in hermeneutics by its emphasis on meaning. Pragmatists knew that, in interpreting, a sign gives the worth of its object, and is itself worthy because of that.

The first part of the Cartesian Fallacy is a commitment to the metaphors of a mechanistic cosmology; the second part is a commitment to certainty based on mechanism. A machine is an assemblage of parts, each of which can be made by itself. Assembling the machine, the mechanic knows what relations are imposed on the pre-given parts. Therefore, there is nothing in the assemblage opaque to knowledge because there is nothing the knowing mechanic has not put there. Since each part is itself a machine, down to particles so elementary there is nothing more to know about them than their external relations with one another, the entire machine is thoroughly knowable. To conceive the whole world in mechanistic terms is to conceive it as thoroughly knowable.

The humanist and romantic attacks on mechanism make it easy to miss the extraordinary genius in the conception. The mechanistic thinking to which Descartes gave classic expression was a decisive invention and an historical turning point. The ancient Greeks and their heritage had discerned that nature has basic patterns, and identified many of them. But they couldn't conceive that nature might be such that it could be thoroughly known, only that, increasingly, its more basic patterns might be discerned. "What does the earth rest on?" "A turtle." "And the turtle?" "On an elephant." "And the elephant?" "It's elephants all the way down." When Plato in the *Timaeas* told the likely story of the demi-urgos' construction of the world, he could not conceive of a mechanical construction. Rather, the demi-urgos had to implant forms in a receptical or matrix that is infinitely obscure and subversive to form. For Plato, not the constructed world but only the forms could be known in the strict sense.

The Western monotheistic religions transformed the notion of creation from mixing antecedent realities to making things from scratch. Since the divinely created world is wholly positive—God made it all, and without God's creativity there is Nothing—it is thoroughly knowable in principle from the standpoint of divinity. But with what finite conception can the world be wholly knowable? With the conception of the world as a mechanism. Modern physics provides a conception of world adequate to traditional theism's creation theory.

Modern and even post-modern science is mechanistic in its presuppositions. What is it to "model" something but to construct a replica of the original out of "parts" that are unproblematic, to see if the model works like the original, and then to conclude that the rational part of the original is relations duplicated in the model? C. R. Gallistel, in his book *The Organization of Action: A New Synthesis*, a classic contemporary example of Cartesian science, describes his project the following way:

> In this book I assume that we are allowed no recourse to physically unrealizable principles and processes in order to explain what underlies the organization of action, no matter how intelligent that action appears. I reject, in other words, the distinction between "intelligent" actions and machine actions. I assume that the intelligence of animal action is simple a consequence of the intricacy and subtlety of construction in the machine that generates that action, namely, the central nervous system of the animal. Since an orderly temporal sequence of muscular contractions underlies any animal action, a scientific analysis of the organization of this action is concerned with specifying the types of physically realizable processes that underlie the generation of orderly temporal sequences of commands to the muscles of the body. Thus, one constraint imposed on the discussion at the outset is that we consider only processes that can be specified in sufficient detail so that an embodiment or physical realization of the process (i.e., a working model) can be built. . . . The dominating idea in this book and the one that governs its organization is the idea that behavior is produced by a hierarchically structured mechanism. At the bottom of this hierarchy are elementary units of behavior. The elementary units of behavior are like the elements of chemistry: All behavior is a compound of elementary units of behavior, just as all chemicals are compounds of the 96 chemicals elements. A chemical element is irreducible in the sense that it cannot be analyzed into anything else that qualifies as a chemical substance. An elementary unit of behavior is irreducible in the sense that anything less than that cannot explain a naturally occurring movement. In order to explain a naturally occurring movement you need: (1) one or more muscles, whose contraction is the mechanical cause of the movements; (2) an element that delivers a contraction initiating signal to the muscles; and (3), an element in which neural signals arise, either spontaneously or in response to a naturally occuring stimulus. (1980, pp. 4 and 10)

I quote Gallistel at length because he not only explains clearly what modeling is supposed to do but also because he illustrates the Cartesian idea of simples or elements and sketches a scheme in which the simples are reconstructed into large wholes that act in a unified way, that is, as dominated by the top of the hierarchy.

Scientists use the word "model" in several senses. Sometimes, and perhaps in the strictest sense, a mathematical model is meant, from which predictions can be deduced and checked out. Other times a physical model is meant, as when a hormone is artifically constructed from chemicals or when behavior is constructed from elementary behavioral units. In a looser sense, a conceptual model is meant, wherein categories are systematized and it is claimed that understanding the relations among the categories is equivalent to understanding the relations among the constituent elements in the subject matter.

To be sure, the idea of modeling does not necessarily presuppose a mechanistic conception of the subject matter. One can suppose that the elements in the model correspond to *important* elements in the subject matter, and mirror their relations, without supposing that the subject matter elements are mechanically insolable constituents. On this non-mechanistic view of modeling, the model brings out only certain aspects of the subject matter alleged to be important, not the elementary constituents. Other models would bring out other aspects, and all the models imaginable would still leave more to be known. On the non-mechanistic view, modeling is a form of interpreting, and by virtue of the triadic character of interpretation, suppose that the world is not thoroughly knowable. Nevertheless, the dominant scientific ethos is mechanistic.

Even the common interpretation of a controlled experiment presupposes the mechanistic philosophy in that it conceives holding certain of the parts steady while observing the effects of varying other parts, assuming all the while that the parts remain just what they are and are not affected by alterations in their relations. The nature of controlled experiments does not have to be interpreted mechanistically. The experiment can be interpreted as hypothetical relative to the experimental context, and the variables can be interpreted as aspects of the subject revealed in that context. But the dominant scientific interpretation is mechanistic and ignores the relativity of the results to the presuppositions of the experimental context.

The obvious advantage of the mechanistic philosophy is that it shows how nature can be thoroughly intelligible, and indicates what to do to understand it. As a philosophy, it provides a justifying rationale for modern science. But is it a good philosophy? Perhaps nature is not understandable in that wholesale sense. The recalcitrance of the problem of mind to a mechanistic analysis without destructive reductionism suggests that the mechanistic philosophy has severe limits.

How can we tell whether Descartes' apparently innocent assumptions—that there are parts to analyze things into and that the reconstruction employs only relations that are external to the parts—are valid? It does not help to say that science demonstrates that there are parts and that wholes can be understood as assemblages, because science presupposes that from the beginning; Cartesian science has no way of registering any counter evidence. One could employ a transcendental strategy and note, first, that modern science has indeed discovered an extraordinary amount and, second, that the world must be such that it is possible to understand everything. Mechanism represents how the world might make such science possible.

But there may be other philosophies that explain how science knows what it knows. Another philosophy could say that the world in some respects is like a machine and in other respects is not; science in its mechanistic form is applicable to the former respects. Or another philosophy could say that for certain purposes the world can be treated as if it were a mechanism, yielding the results science achieves, but that this is a selective abstraction from a richer, non-mechanistic world about which science is only a filtered approach. Any philosophy that would have to deny that science has achieved what it has achieved would be in an impossible position. But a philosophy could well accept the worldview of science in a limited way and give a larger interpretation of its results than could be possible on mechanist assumptions alone. One of the strongest arguments that could be given for a non-Cartesian philosophy would be a demonstration that it makes better sense of the activities and findings of science. A non-Cartesian philosophy cannot be anti-scientific.

Having called Descartes' views on dividing the subject matter into simples and reconstructing them into wholes a fallacy, it is necessary to show what is wrong with them. My claim, of course, is that reality is not made of simples and their aggregates; the basic difficulty with Descartes is his bad metaphysics. A non-Cartesian metaphysics (non-Cartesian on the point about knowledge coming from analysis into simples and reconstruction) asserts in some specific way or another that the definiteness of actual things is "context-dependent."

An actual thing's nature, according to this principle of context-dependence, is somewhat internally related to its context. To take the thing out of the context, placing it in a new context of analysis, is thus to change it. Since much of the richness of a thing comes from its context-dependence, to wrench it out of context into an artificial analytical context may be to impoverish it. Moreover, a thing's context consists of all the other things around, situated in their environing relations. Change something else in the environment and the context itself is changed.

Pushed to its strictest interpretation, the principle of context-dependence says that there is no actual definiteness apart from location in contexts. Thus there are no simples. Remove all contexts whatsoever and there is nothing left. Therefore, a Cartesian analysis into simples in the strict sense would lead to discarding the last onion ring, leaving only the essence. In a less than strict sense, a Cartesian analysis into relative simples, simples we do not bother to analyze further, results in distortion and impoverishment. In practice, such a Cartesian analysis leads merely from the rich context of actuality to the artificial context of the analytical constructs at hand. If one's analytical constructs are materialistic, analysis is materialistic reductionism; if one's constructs articulate facts but not values, analysis is factual reductionism; if one's constructs are ideal essences, analysis is phenomenological reductionism. The principle of the context-dependence requires that it be literally impossible to analyze into simples; what happens instead when the effort is made is the substitution of the context of analysis for that of reality.[3]

There is empirical support for the principle of context-dependence over the Cartesian analysis into simples and reconstruction. Empirical physics has utterly abandoned Descartes. Field theories of relativity and the undecidability principle of quantum mechanics are straightforward illustrations of context-dependence. Particle theory as well has abandoned the attempt to find atoms in the void. Historiography has reaffirmed the principle of context-dependence, of which it had rarely lost sight, and the current emphasis on social history, demography, biological factors such as disease, climate, etc., has brought the discipline to new degrees of excellence. The social sciences waver between their modernist desire to interpret their subject matters in clean systems of analytical constructs and the post-modernist recognition that the constructs are highly distortive outside the context of inquiry. After brief and scattered flirtations with Cartesian structuralism, the humanities in general remain firmly committed to the principle of context-dependence, except for the Cartesian philosophers of logical, phenomenological, and linguistic analysis (linguistic analysis frequently doubles back to make an anti-Cartesian point about context-dependence). The direction among the more advanced disciplines appears to be away from Cartesian suppositions. Those that are Cartesian are the ones still seeking to establish themselves, the new sciences that might be temporarily justified in acting *as if* the Cartesian metaphysics were true because, if it were, their task would be much easier. Biochemistry, for instance neuroscience of Gallistel's sort, psychobiology, and cognitive science have remained with Descartes under the guise of interpreting simples as elementary functions, to be understood in terms of biological systems. These last-named sciences are the ones apparently most promising for a naturalistic understanding of mind, particularly when they are cast into philosophical language by functionalism. That they remain Cartesian is particularly troubling.

Such quasi-empirical tests for metaphysics in the short run are inconclusive (in the long run they are the only kind that count). The short run needs an argument directly against the Cartesian theory. The argument is this: there are phenomena, especially those having to do with mind, that simply do not make sense apart from context-dependence. This will be demonstrated in the discussion of Cartesian functionalism in the next section.

II. FUNCTIONALISM

John Dewey was the outstanding proponent of the principle of context-dependence in our century. Beginning in his early Hegelian studies of internal relations and continuing through the writings of his long career, he argued that the affairs of human life are to be understood only in terms of their larger contexts. Most particularly, he railed against the epistemological tradition of modern philosophy for dealing with elements of knowledge in abstraction from the real knowing processes, knowing processes set within even larger processes of life. It is ironic that this virulent anti-Cartesian would be the father of functionalism. His contribution to the *Cyclopedia of Education* contains one of the earliest definitions of function and functionalism:

> FUNCTION. – Any process, sufficiently complex to involve an arrangement or coordination of minor processes, which fulfills a specific end in such a way as to conserve itself, is called a function. This may be illustrated by digestion. There are a number of chemico-physical processes sustained by various structures that cooperate together in such a way as to restore the wasting tissues of the body, the specific end; at the same time the processes react so as to maintain the conditions of their own maintenance. The sum total of functions, in their reciprocal adjustment to one another, constitute life, which, accordingly, is defined in the same way as a function. Life (or functions, activities) includes within itself the distinction of ENVIRONMENT AND ORGANISM (q.v.) . . . . In educational theory the fundamental character of the category of function is exemplified not merely in the increasing use of biological concepts, like ADAPTATION (q.v.), but in the attempt to introduce into the school modes of active occupation which involve control of materials and tools in a process of realizing results which are felt to possess immediate or intrinsic value (Reprinted in Dewey: 1978, pp. 466–467).

Dewey's statement can be read in two ways. What he himself meant, as is clear from the rest of his philosophy, is that a function is internally related to the environment in which it makes sense and is appropriate. When he wrote that a function "includes within itself the distinction of environment and organism," he meant to deny that the function is a property of the organism alone. Indeed, he held to the radical thesis that an animal or person is not an individual organism but the signficant functioning of that organism in its environment. An alternate reading, however, would say that because the function includes the end within itself, it is a relatively self-contained unit, a simple. On this reading, a life is an aggregate of self-contained functions reciprocally relating to one another in essential independence of the environment, or at least unaffected by the environment that tolerates them. The latter is a Cartesian reading.

The functionalism current in cognitive science is of the Cartesian sort. It came from the early pragmatic conception largely through the work of Quine, who, unlike Dewey, adopted and extended the epistemological tradition of Descartes and Locke. Quine called his project "naturalized epistemology." But he would be upset with the treatment of functions as relative simples; like Dewey, he believed in the principle of context-dependence.

In the work of cognitive scientists such as Jerry Fodor, functionalism is the philosophy that identifies mental acts with certain functions.[4] Regardless of what performs the function—a meat brain or a silicon computer—mental activity is the performing of mental functions. A function, as Dewey said, is the organization of activity to accomplish some end. Mental functions can be defined in terms of ends, for instance, calculations of specific sorts, discrimination of sensations, manipulations and articulations of objects, satisfactions of needs, hungers, lusts, and so on. A function can itself be an assemblage of other functions, or a recursive function, or part of larger functions. Cartesian functionalism is mechanistic in that it analytically decomposes mind into mental functions and studies their relationships. The structure of mind is a hierarchy of mental functions building on one another. A theorist such as Gallistel accounts for the unified and flexibly adaptive behavior of mind through the particular structure of the hierarchy: the dominating higher function gives vague orders to lower functions that have flexibility in carrying them out. In all cases, functions are systems that nest within systems and comprise systems, and Cartesian analysis that experimentally isolates them is the way to understand them. That is, they are conceived to be understood that way.

The great advantage to contemporary Cartesian functionalism is its versatility. It organizes a wide array of scientific investigations into kinds of mental functions, from reinterpreted behaviorist studies, through psychoanalytical investigations of interacting drives, to neuro-physiological experiments with psychobiological systems. The mind can be conceived as a set of innate or learned structures that perform mental functions when activated; intelligence can be interpreted as the integration of mental functions, especially the access they have to one another, building up complicated functions. The relations between the mental entity and the environment can be construed in terms of how the motivational functions and the discriminative functions can be exercised on the environment, and how the environment exercises a stimulating effect, triggering response functions in the organism.[5] The unity of mind can be accounted for as the integration of functions, according to patterns of mutual access and hierarchy, patterns in which higher order functions are built on lower order ones, and control them.[6]

The great disadvantage to functionalism as a philosophy of mind is that it runs aground the context problem. The context problem can be formulated in many ways, one of which is this: a function makes sense only insofar as it plays a role in some larger context, and the mentality of recognizing the function's fit in the context is not another function. For instance, the function of organizing behavior to get food makes sense only when hunger pangs and their potential alleviation are put in the complicated context of (1) an environment that might contain food, (2) the costs and dangers of seeking it, (3) the distractions from other activities, (4) the importance or urgency of this function compared with others, and (5) the role of this animal's eating in its own life and the life of its group.

No one would deny that functions are significant in larger contexts. A Cartsian mechanist, however, would give something like the following account. Beginning with some low-level functions necessary for bare biological life, combinations of those functions with fortuitous circumstances give rise to higher-level functions that allow a new and adaptive role to be played in the environment. The successful playing of the new role then is its own justification, and new combinations of functions can be discovered, up and up, until the function of discovering new and helpful functions is discovered, at which point we have not only intelligent behavior, but conscious reflection and inquiry. Indeed, this evolutionary account of the causal genesis of mental functions sounds plausible in a vague way.

The inadequacy in the account is its failure to explain how the fortuitous new behavior or happening ever is taken to be a new and adaptive function. The previous functions by definition do not take it to be so, because it is new. Perhaps one would try to redouble the evolutionary explanation and say that the new behavior is repeated, kept, prized, and routinized (so as to be a ready function) simply because the organisms that do that reproduce better. This would preserve the purely mechanical form of explanation, accounting for the repeated presence of the function on genetic terms. *Why* do the organisms with the new function reproduce better? Because the function makes the organisms more adaptive to the environment, and other evolutionary *etceteras*. This preserves the mechanical form of explanation at the price of eliminating the slightest plausiblity of calling any such function "mental."

Functions are mental functions to the extent they model intentionality; that is, seem purposive and intend an intentional field. This was one of

Dewey's main points. The organism is hungry and organizes behavior with the purpose of addressing that feeling; Dewey's model makes sense of the functions as mental, and goes on to explain how the organization of behavior reflects the identification of the function in the larger context. But if the mechanical evolutionary explanation is maintained, to the effect that organisms that get food when hungry reproduce themselves, and those that don't die off without passing on their genes, and that the causal reason some organisms function to eat is simply the algorithmic nudging of involuntary behavior like digestion, then there is no mentality involved. This is like a standard objection to determinism, that if determinism is true, the determinist is determined to say it is, which is no reason at all for believing determinism is true. Contemporary Cartesian functions don't make mental sense simply as the organization of activities in pursuit of ends; to that must be added the pursuit of those ends as itself meaningful as purposive in the larger context; Dewey's conception of function included the larger context in the conception of the end.

To summarize the problem of context, although the development of new functions can be explained, at least in part, on evolutionary grounds, the only justification for calling those functions "mental" is that they are performed with a grasp of their role in a life context. Without that grasp, they are not intentional, but only involuntary movements like digestion. Most functionalists suppose that the grasp takes place, but without realizing that it involves some kind of mentality other than a function.

The argument here has not been to deny that there are mental functions. It has been rather to imply that mental functions, such as calculations, discriminations, and so forth are mental because they are at the service of intentional behavior that fixes them relative to a context in which they are appropriate. Functions are the instruments of thinking; they can be discriminated only by holding them in the larger context of thinking life. A naturalistic theory of interpretation will have to explicate this instrumental role for functions, a difficult topic for philosophical biology. Cognitive science can identify functions as interpretive abstractions from that larger context. But it would be a mistake to believe that thinking is made up from an assemblage of functions. Although Dewey believed that life in the larger context is prior to specific discriminations within it, even his anti-epistemological functionalism lends itself to interpretation as a Cartesian construction from simples.

The practical significance of contemporary Cartesian functionalism is enormous. It interacts with and reinforces the computer model of mind. A computer can be programmed to perform functions, and the program can be made complicated so as to integrate the functions. Once the programmer introduces the structure of an end into the function, or invents a computer function of organizing other activities so as to accomplish ends, the computer can perform functions. But the functions are not intentional, and hence not mental; they do not intend themselves as appropriate against a background context; they operate rather according to the algorithms of the program.

Because the analogy of computers to minds doubles back to make minds analogous to computers, the functionalist interpretation of artificial intelligence is insidious. That the intentionality of mind is ignored in favor of identifying the functions mind performs is only part of the problem. The more important part is that mental life is wrenched from its real, rich, suggestive, allusive, adumbrative, and imaginative context to the context of the analytical constructs of functionalist cognitive science. Although it might help better to understand the mental functions instrumental to life, it is a terrible impoverishment to think of mental life as an assemblage of functions.

The most devastating arena of functionalist reductionism is education. In his own time, Dewey rebelled against the teaching of isolated skills. He criticized Maria Montessori, for instance, for preprogramming the skills children should learn.[7] His own method to provide stimulating but problematic environments in which children would invent the skills necessary to formulate and accomplish their goals. Education for Dewey was to be the development of habits of identifying worthwhile ends and constructing functions that achieve them, all presupposing life processes in an indefinitely large context.

Contemporary Cartesian functionalism, however, has taken the opposite track. Educators are encouraged to break learning down into discrete functional packages that can be taught in a programmed sequence. Verbal and mathematical symbol manipulation, interpretive skills, skills of historical and scientific analysis, have been identified and the teaching of them has been codified. From grade school onward skills are taught through the week and tested on Friday. If functionalism were true, then education could indeed be the accretion of skills building upon one another, each teachable in sequence and testable. The result of "skills" education, education in specific Cartesian functions, however, is miseducation. Given a set task within their repertoire, students can perform well. But as so many educators have said, they can't think. They can't approach a situation unless it is preformed to match their ready functions. They lack imagination in new areas and have no taste beyond knowing the worth of something for its use in some function. Worst of all, they believe thinking is performing a task, solving problems, accomplishing some end by the exercise of some skill. A review of any of the great examples of thinking—in Homer, Confucius, Lao-tze, Plato, Hippocrates, the Bhagavad Gita, the Bible, in the Gothic and Mogul architects, in Descartes, Newton, Shakespeare, Beethoven —will show that problem solving is only an instrumental part, often a small part, of the richness of mental life. Mental life is interpretive, appreciative, and directive, not much an exercise of task-oriented functions. To understand this better, we turn to hermeneutics.

III. HERMENEUTICS

The intellectual project *par excellence* that affirms context-dependence is hermeneutics. Hermeneutics arose as early as Spinoza as the project to interpret scripture with a recognition of an historic and cultural distance between the text and the interpreters. On an elementary level, hermeneutics sought to interpret the meaning of a particular passage in light of the whole text, and on a more sophisticated level, it sought to interpret the whole text in light of the larger culture. The overall project developed subtle distinctions between interpretation as explanation and interpretation as understanding. These distinctions were refined by the deep logical, sociological, and anthropological labors of the nineteenth century, and the project has come to fruition in the brilliant work of Gadamer and Ricoeur (see Bleicher, 1980).

The hermeneutical circle defines context dependence. That is, the very meaning of an expression depends on a nest of larger and larger cultural contexts. These include not only the contexts contemporary with the composition of the text, but also the historical continuities and discontinuities relating the interpreter and the interpreting culture of the text. Like Dewey insisting that his conception of life as a function of functions includes both organism and environment, hermeneutics takes interpretation to be *of a text* only as *in a cultural context*. There are no meaningful texts apart from cultural contexts. By the same token, the context is the cultural environment made up of other texts and socially meaningful or signlike things. No more than Dewey would allow that we have access to ends apart from the processes of experience, hermeneutics allows no independent access to the culture. Rather, we discover the lineaments of culture by interpreting texts, and we discover the meaning of the texts in terms of what we understand about culture, including especially the culture connecting text and interpreter. Interpretation thus circles round and round, from text to text, from text to context, from object of interpretation to the interpreting subject.

Because texts lie in an indefinitely varied and nested set of contexts, they have indefinitely diverse and rich meanings. The meaning of a text, being relative to context, is different for each context in which it can be interpreted. This is not to say there is no truth or falsity to the identification of meaning—a text means some definite things in a given context and not some other things. It is to say that all meaning is relative to some context or other and that for any text there is an indefinite number of contexts. Most important, because the interpreter's own situation is part of the relative context, and because the act of interpreting, of gaining understanding, may alter the interpreter's situation, the contexts for hermeneutics grow. A finished interpretation is hard to conceive. The text is not a Cartesian simple. Rather, there is no meaningful text *simpliciter*, only text-and-contexts. The definite actuality of meaningful texts is always context dependent.

Hermeneutics as the scholarly interpretation of arcane texts is pregnant with implications for a general philosophy, and this is the root metaphor for the hermeneutic approach to interpretation. All items of the world that can be experienced have social meaning, and can be treated as texts. But this supposes larger social contexts. In their re-assertion of the hermeneutic standpoint over the Cartesian functionalism in structuralism, the deconstructionists have generalized the notion of text to mean any significant, interpretable item. To take our world as meaningful, or to take anything in it as meaningful, is thus to be interpreting the item as a text; socially significant reality is "textuality." Now this may be the overuse of a good metaphor. The general point is well taken, however: the meaningfulness of anything requires that it be interpreted in terms of a context, and where there is cultural distance between the subject matter and interpreter, the context should control their connection.

The question of meaning in hermeneutics, however, is not equivalent to the question of truth. Of course, in the use of ancient texts for religious, philosophical, historical, or scientific purposes, we first must know what they mean in order to set up the project of judging whether they are right. But hermeneutics has pushed its philosophical cosmology farther. It has softened its sense that texts are signs of reality, to be judged true or false, and has allowed that the texts are the reality. The apparent justification for this is that, if the reality about which the text is a sign is itself significant, then it too is a text: if we have access to it, it should be interpreted itself; if we lack access, we interpret it through the texts about it.

In any case, the significant reality of a text is its meaning. Grasping the meaning is possessing the reality, and it is hard to identify as dyadic the relation between one meaningful text and another which purports to be about it: the relations are all triadic, it seems. Consequently, in his brilliant *The Symbolism of Evil*, Paul Ricoeur (1969) analyzes the ancient texts to show that a deep layer of the meaning of evil is uncleanliness, a stain. After showing the profundity of this meaning, it almost makes no sense to ask whether this is really what evil is. The very meaning he elucidates so forms our capacity to raise the question of the nature of evil that we can't distance the cultural meaning from any reality of evil except in sophomoric ways. Yet would we say in the end, as hermeneutics must, that the reality of evil is the interpretation the ancients and others down to ourselves give of evil? According to the principle of context-dependence, evil is not a meaningful reality except in larger interpretive contexts. But is its reality any more than the interpretation given?

The answer has to be No because we know that at least some of our interpretations are ideological distortions of reality. The important contribution of the Frankfurt School of criticism has been to show how entire strains of cultural meaning disguise as much as reveal. The merciful spirit, said Nietzsche in *The Genealogy of Morals* (1956), has been represented as good and god-like, but in fact is a glorification of weakness by the weak to make them appear strong. Whether or not Nietzsche is ultimately right, the fact his thesis can be argued proves that the reality of the merciful spirit, its real value in this case, is not identical with the standard interpretation of it. Ideology is usually linked to the interests of a group to make reality appear to favor those interests, disguising the unfavorable reality by creating a world of ideological interpretation.

One needn't limit examples to the false consciousness of ideology. Without any necessary intent to deceive, a metaphysics translated into common sense throws an interpretive screen over experience such that things can be interpreted falsely. Platonism, for instance, says value consists in a kind of aesthetic intensity, whereas Aristotelianism says it consists in formal completeness and fulfillment of development. Both philosophies have infiltrated elements of common sense and, depending on which interpretation is triggered in a given context, will make value appear one way or another; or rather, the values of the same things will be different depending on the interpretation employed.

Therefore, hermeneutics cannot be generalized to a metaphysics itself. One still must ask the question of truth. Is a given interpretation right, not just about what a thing means, but about what the thing is? The reality of the thing includes its meanings. Yet the meaningful reality of the thing should be the measure by which any given interpretation, or even strain of interpretations, is judged with regard to truth.

Hermeneutics must be made critical in a special sense that transcends the hermeneutical project. That project is already critical in the sense that it has extraordinary subtlety in correcting its interpretations so as to be ever more nearly right about what its subject matter means. The additional sense of criticism must ask whether the interpretation is right about what the subject is. This is a devious problem to grasp, for hermeneutics itself tends to the idealism that says the subject matter is its meanings. We have to drive a wedge between what the subject matter is, including its meanings, and the interpretation of what that meaning is. For, what the thing truly means *in* a given interpretation might be an ideological or other distortion of what it truly is and *ought to be* for that interpretation.

The clue to making hermeneutics sensitive to the question of truth lies in the triadic character of the sign relation. (1) Any sign interprets its object *in some respect*. That respect is a function of the culture's assessment that the object is worth interpreting in that respect. Is this true? To answer this question we need to know not only in what respects the culture interprets the world but whether these are the most worthwhile respects. The question of "what respects" is hermeneutical; the question of their worth is the special critical question. (2) Any interpretation uses a network of signs, or perhaps several partially overlapping networks. Hermeneutics can show how the structure of the network affects the interpretation. The special critical question is whether the network is the best for the interpretive purpose. Semiotics thus has two dimensions, a hermeneutic one (or phenomenological as Peirce would say), and a critical one; speech act analysis also should have those two dimensions. (3) Of course interpretation is also always for a purpose. Identifying the purpose and showing how it guides interpretation is hermeneutical; judging whether it is the appropriate purpose for the context is the critical task. The respect of interpretation, the system of interpretive signs, and the guiding purposes of interests are all selective principles for interpretation. The hermeneutical question is what selections are made. The question of truth is whether the selections carry over what is important in the object, or distort in some way. Is it possible to ask the question of truth without falling into the idealism of saying that what is important to be carried over from the object to the interpretation is simply what the interpretation carries over? Of course it is. Phrased that way, the idealism of identifying the reality of a meaningful thing with the meaning interpreted is not even plausible.

IV. PRAGMATISM

The philosophers who understood the difference between meaning and truth best were the pragmatists. (They also were the ones who, having distinguished them, most often confused them.) Even in the first crude formulations of the early Peirce and William James, pragmatism defined differential meaning in terms of the conceived difference a concept would predict for future experience, and truth was defined as the meanings that are confirmed by predicting real and observable differences. In the later Peirce and in Dewey, the pragmatic position became far more sophisticated.

Whereas the hermeneutic tradition arose out of a concern to interpret texts, pragmatism's concern was to interpret nature scientifically. Pragmatism was a theory of scientific interpretation, not literary. Consequently, the temptation to resolve the truth versus meaning question by appeal to observation made much sense. Hermeneutic scholars would think it somewhat silly to "observe" evil to determine whether uncleanliness and stain are significant elements. The observation is theory laden, a point with which the pragmatists would have to agree. Perhaps the most fruitful meeting of pragmatism and hermeneutic philosophy is in the recent work of Patrick Heelan (1983), who uses hermeneutical language to make the pragmatic point that even scientific perception is a matter of signs and hence formed by the sign-system. Dewey was the philosopher who understood best the principle of context dependence.

A deeper difference between hermeneutics and pragmatism, however, lies in their root metaphors. Whereas the root of hermeneutics is interpretation of texts, the root for pragmatism is experimentation. The significance of this is that the idea of "conversation" can encompass the full flowering of hermeneutics, from root to branches. Conversation has been made a totalizing category for philosophy by Richard Rorty (1982), focusing the work of Heidegger, Gadamer, and Ricoeur; David Tracy (1987) presents an integrated theory of hermeneutical conversation and discusses its social context and consequences. For pragmatism, on the other hand, the significance of the root metaphor of experiment is that interpretation is a kind of action, of which conversation is but an aspect. The full flowering of the pragmatic approach to interpretation is the claim that all action is interpretive by virtue of consisting in differential maneuvers in the environment, largely purposive, given intelligent formation by meanings. The pragmatists took signs not to be primarily communicators of meaning, but rather differential guides of action. To be actively living at all is to be interpreting, according to the pragmatic approach. Intellectual reflective interpretation, communication with others, conversation about things treated as texts, are all important in the pragmatic perspective, but built on the more fundamental meaning of interpretation as differential action. Philosophers of science such as Thomas Kuhn are often represented as pragmatists because they look first at science rather than literary texts; but the questions they ask about science are hermeneutic ones, treating science as a text to be discussed rather than an interpretive avenue itself.

Pragmatism introduced another crucial notion for interpretation that has yet to catch on in hermeneutics; namely, the power of signs to grow and generalize. Peirce expressed the point in picturesque language when he called it a power of evolutionary love (1935, pars. 287–317). That is, signs as mediators naturally tend to extend themselves to increase the field of their mediation. An idea generalizes itself beyond its initial context, and grows in richness as it does so. Growth begins with a vague, suggestive, metaphoric extension, and as the sign is actually lived with in the new mediating function, it becomes specific. The specificities are not delimitations of the initial vague sign, they are enrichments.

Thus for pragmatism's semiotics, the crucial question is how relatively specific sign-relations or codes arise out of less specific ones. Pragmatism here stands in contrast to the semiotics of Saussure and the structuralist tradition that treats signs only as coded. The pragmatic issue is how signs develop out of less coded situations, and semiotics is genetic as well as classificatory. Pragmatic semiotics essentially requires the history of the development of signs.

Unlike both the hermeneutic and structuralist traditions, however, pragmatism is thoroughly naturalistic. If the signs of human thought and communication grow, generalize, and extend themselves, then so do those of human institutions and of nature. Peirce went so far as to embrace a qualified Lamarckian theory of evolution because of this. It is unnecessary to go that far to appreciate his concern with how the significance of things develops through the interactions that interpret them.

Of special importance in the pragmatic theory of interpretation is the stress on purpose. As mentioned so often, the pragmatists recognized from the beginning that a sign interprets its object in some respect selected by the purpose guiding the interpretation.[8] A common European misunderstanding of pragmatism has been that its purposes are crass, materialistic, or egoistic ones, purposes held uncritically. There is reason enough for this misundertanding if one takes nineteenth century American industry as the exemplar of pragmatic philosophy. The pragmatists themselves, however, were clear that purposes are most in need of criticism precisely because of their ubiquity in interpretation (see Colapietro, 1988). The crucial question is whether the purposes guiding interpretation are the appropriate ones. Are our purposes worthy? Are they faithful both to the true values of human life and to the values of the environing things in and with which the purposes are carried out? Peirce argued that logic is a species of ethics, ethics a species of aesthetics applied to action, and aesthetics the study of what is intrinsically worthwhile. For Dewey, the guiding motivation for all interpretive having or doing is the securing of consummatory experience. So for the pragmatic tradition, an essential part of the truth of an interpretation is whether its guiding purpose allows for the relevant fulfillment or care of the values involved in the interpretive situation.[9] Pragmatism would not be surprised at to find that a line of interpretation is ideologically or metaphysically distorting, and it anticipated the Frankfurt School in accounting for this by reference to misguided purpose or interest.

All this is to the good of developing a naturalistic theory of interpretation sustaining a fast distinction between meaning and truth. The limit of pragmatism comes in its theory of time relative to interpretation. Peirce originally defined truth as the opinion ultimately fated to be believed by the community of investigators in the infinite long run. His supposition was that the community of inquirers would eliminate errors through criticism, so that in the infinite long run no error would be left. He subsequently gave up the optimism of this view of scientific integrity, admitting not only that the infinite long run would never come, but that the community might even work backward. Nevertheless, there is a future orientation to the definition of truth. If meaning is conceivable future consequences, the truth of that meaning must wait upon future demonstration. Hence the frequent pragmatic translation of truth into fruitfulness and warranted assertability. But what can the future be for pragmatism?

That question should be set in the context of pragmatism's orientation to the present. Interpreting is a present activity; interpreted objects are past, and the test of the interpretation is future. By focusing on the existential activity of interpreting, with its uncertain freedom and perhaps mischievous creativity, pragmatism has made a crucial contribution to the twentieth century understanding of the present. The future, for pragmatism, however, is nothing but the conditionals relative to present interpretation: that which *would* confirm or disconfirm an interpretation. Put generally, the future for pragmatism is what might carry on a present interpretive activity; it is open in part, but only conditional or hypothetical. If the future is only conditional, however, and is the locus of truth, then truth is only conditional—the truth is in the future and the future never comes. More to the point, it can't be said directly within the pragmatic framework that a present interpretation is now true or false, only that the future might make it so. Pragmatism surely is right that the future *among other things* has a conditional status relative to present interpretations. But without integrating those other things to give it a status of its own, the future collapses into a mere projection of the present.

The situation with regard to the past is even more unfortunate for pragmatism. The past supplies the objects for present interpretation, or the signs that lead us indirectly to intend past, present, or future objects. But the past has no reality of its own, since reality is the object of the opinion that is defined as essentially future. It is simple and obvious enough to say that Caesar's crossing the Rubicon is a past fact forever finished and about which we can be truly knowledgeable; it also makes sense to say that the criteria for testing our knowledge of that historical event includes further checking and criticism in the future. Peirce was clear that meanings are defined by the differences they make, and that they might be referred to past things; only the criteria for determining the truth of the meanings in that reference place the evidence in future experience. Nevertheless, pragmatism could give no account of the being of past things except as possible objects of interpretation. What about things that happened but fail, necessarily fail, to be interpreted? Further, even to function as possible objects of interpretation, past events have to have a status of their own not reducible to roles in interpretation. For, what is a potential object of interpretation if not caught up in some actual interpretation? Like the future, the past is reduced to its role in present interpretation, according to what pragmatism can say. This is inadequate for a theory for which reality measures truth and includes past and future as well as present things.

The limit of pragmatism is not so much in its theory of interpretation, as in its reduction of metaphysics to what follows the structure of interpretation. Like existentialism and process philosophy, pragmatism is a philosophy of the present, and this is too biased to sustain a serious theory of temporal reality. Most twentieth century philosophy shares this temporalistic limit, particularly insofar as philosophy has taken the linguistic turn. If reality is defined through the referring and interpreting activities of language, or other interpretive systems, it seems inevitably to have its modes of temporality defined by the present activity of speaking or interpreting.

If all reality is present reality and present efflorescences of the past and future, then indeed it will be impossible to break the triadic bond of interpretation and insert a dyadic relation of truth or error. As all philosophies of interpretation have pointed out, interpretation takes time. Any interpretation gives itself a history and future while happening. To break interpretation away from the reality interpreted, we must be able to conceive the reality of the three temporal modes in some independence from the present orientation of the activity of interpretation. The limit of pragmatism is that it had an insufficiently speculative metaphysical imagination. A theory of reality that can measure truth needs a realistic theory of time in at least the three modes of temporality—present, future, and past. This point sets much of the agenda of Division III following.

These remarks about time indicate a theme underlying the entire discussion: the contest between historicism and metaphysics. Of course the problem is that there are historicisms and historicisms, and there is metaphysics and metaphysics. Historicism in one central sense is undeniable: any thinking or intelligent action is a function of its historical setting. It can relate to those things to which its setting gives it access, and much of its excellence consists in pushing the resources of its setting beyond their inherited limits.

This is not to suggest, however, that historically conditioned thought cannot be about basic structures or metaphysical categories transcending its own and any historical situation. In this sense, metaphysics as hypothetical inquiry into the generic traits of existence (Dewey's characterization of the enterprise) or as the framing of a system of categories for the interpretation of the broadest and deepest elements of experience (Whitehead's characterization) is a natural intellectual activity for historical settings with certain kinds of civilization. It is a silly limit on thought, stemming from a simple logical confusion, to require that historically contextualized philosophy must restrict its topics to the interpretation of historical realities.

Underlying the logical confusion—indeed the only thing that explains why it traps so many intelligent historicists—is a fundamental metaphysical mistake about time: the assumption that only present time is real. If only present time is real, then we have access only to things that register themselves in present time; in fact their traces in present time are the only reality they have. So, of course interpretation seems to be the creative response to things whose only reality is their functioning in the present creative response. All things are only texts.

Yet if past things are real as past, then present interpretation is bound by a norm to be faithful to them. Truth as faithfulness to the past requires a temporally thick connection between past and present. Moreover, if the future is real as a field of possibilities that express differing values for actualization, interpretation is normed in moral ways as well as by faithfulness. If time indeed has three real dimensions, then interpretation, while "taking place" as a form of present activity, nevertheless is a temporally thick process comprising past, present, and future elements essentially related as each provides norms for actualization. This is a deeply metaphysical understanding of interpretation and truth, albeit historically conditioned as an extension of the process-pragmatic tradition and reacting to the historicism come to flower in deconstructionism. The following chapter sketches this understanding.

3

Truth: An Axiological Hypothesis

The discussion so far has revealed a need for an hypothesis about truth that is responsive to the problems reviewed in the previous chapters, an hypothesis both grounded in a philosophy of nature and exhibitive of the values in things. The purpose of this chapter is to present such an hypothesis and begin its explanation and defense. But first some introductory comments about "hypothesis" are in order.

To consider an hypothesis about truth is a peculiar enterprise. It differs on the one hand from a straightforward definition that can assume the understanding and general acceptance of its terms. Definitions can be given only within the context of a theory, and it is clear from the previous discussion that there is now no generally accepted theory of interpretation, or of reality, or of logic, capable of providing such a philosophic context. To present an hypothesis about truth is to recognize that the hypothesis itself is required to contribute to the development of a more general theory of interpretation that in turn might provide a context for the hypothesis. The hypothesis is thus doubly tentative. It needs to be made plausible within the context of a larger theory, and it needs to help make the larger theory plausible.

On the other hand, the direct consideration of an hypothesis differs from a discursive critical or historical discussion of views about truth, of the sort occupying the previous chapters. It pulls the elements of an hypothesis together for an overall examination, supposing that the hypothesis has been framed out of reflection on critical and historical discussions and that it can subsequently sustain itself in such consideration. As an hypothesis, it has formal elements that can be specified as reasonably well-formed formulas in the overall theory of which it is a part, once that theory is formed. Further, if the hypothesis is well expressed, its terms have resonances with many larger theories than the one to be elaborated here, so that it can be seen as a specification of various plausible overall points of view.

The logical point to understand about an hypothesis is that, although its own pattern is clear, it is vague with respect to its specifications. Its terms are high abstractions, and for it to be applied to anything, or understood in detail, it must be made specific. The hypothesis must be woven into the larger world-picture that provides its context. The present chapter expresses the hypothesis and comments on what yet needs to be specified. The rest of this book is aimed to specify it, to defend all the other hypotheses needed to make it plausible, and to show it to have application as a response to the problem of understanding how the world measures our assertion.

That the hypothesis is called axiological reflects a peculiar need. In the concluding sections of both previous chapters, it was argued that the dominant modernist and postmodernist approaches analyze interpretation and truth with a superficial or derivative conception of value. Only pragmatism and process philosophy, non-modernist theories, recognize the extent to which value is basic to interpretation. Indeed, it will be argued that value rather than form is the important variable in truth, hence the axiological character of the hypothesis.[1]

The hypothesis is that truth is the properly qualified carryover of value from the object of interpretation into the interpreting experience. The hypothesis thus supposes a theory of interpretation, a theory of value, a theory of carryover as a kind of causation, and an epistemological review of all this to see that the approach to truth does what an approach to truth is supposed to do. These are the topics, respectively, of the four sections of this chapter.

I. INTERPRETATION

The word "interpretation" is used here like a large umbrella to cover the cognitive processes involved in all sorts of assertion. An assertion might itself be an intentional act, or it might be presupposed in some other intentional act, as the suppositions about the nature of the world or situation involved in commands, question, promises, and the like. Assertions, to the extent they are not vague, are true or false of their objects, and thus fundamentally involve the dyadic true-false relation.

At the historical center of the development of theories of interpretation, however, is the conviction that knowledge is triadic, and that it involves representations. Knowledge is not the immediate intuitive entertaining of an object itself or its form, but rather the correct representation of an object with a propositional idea.[2] In this sense, knowing is a move away from the object, a re-presentation. Nevertheless, knowing must assert a connection between representation and object if one is to identify the object as that which is represented. The connection, however it be made, is what transforms the material reality of the representation into interpretation.

Because there are several words that have commonly been used as substitutes for one another—sign, representation, concept, proposition, and assertion—it is appropriate to lay down some stipulative conventions for the following discussion. These distinctions are not of equal importance for this chapter, but each will find its place in following chapters. Some of them will be reviewed and supplemented in chapter 13, section I.

1. *Sign.* "Sign" is used throughout as defined by its mediating function between an object and interpretant, according to the theory of interpretation put forward by Peirce and others. One of the major theses of this book (and of Peirce's writings) is that all of nature exhibits the process of interpretation in this general sense and hence everything is a sign. "Sign" and its cognates, such as "signify" and "signification," have the generality of the interpretive process in nature as well as human experience, a process to be explained in Part III.

2. *Representation.* Some signs are involved only in experience and are distinguished from the other signs by virtue of their connection with intentionality. The subclass of signs involved with human intentionality will be called "representations," and used in this restricted sense with cognates such as "represent" and "representative." Representations are not only verbal, but include any kind of gesture, perceptive structure, artifact, natural object, or instrumentally organized action that signifies in an intentional way. Except in discussing cosmology, for which "sign" has a much wider extension than "representation," the language of signs and the language of representations can be used interchangeably according to euphonic considerations, as the present chapter illustrates. The critical juncture where the two languages make a difference is where a non-experiential object, something that has not been subjected to the syntheses of imagination, is the object of interpretation; in this case a sign in its non-experiential extension is represented by a sign that is a representation. Here epistemology is displayed as a subject of philosophy of nature or philosophical cosmology.

3. *Concept.* A "concept" is a rule for representing, and it can be embodied in any appropriate representation; most concepts are best understood through verbal descriptions and metaphoric presentations. Whether concepts are Platonic forms, Whiteheadian eternal objects, or constructed entities, is a deep philosophic problem (addressed later) that should not be

prejudiced by observing that concepts are rules (that usage comes from Kant). Most words or phrases are representations embodying concepts, and frequently it is not misleading to discuss words as if they were the concepts themselves. Concepts should never be confused with the actual thinking of things through representations.

4. *Proposition.* A "proposition" is a complex conjunction of a concept and a logical subject proposing that the logical subject can be represented according to the concept's rule. All representations have the form of propositions, or embody propositions. A representation, however, adds an intentional subject to the logical subject. A proposition by itself need not be thought, or even be the form of a thought. A representation is a proposition that has the form of thought. An actually thought representation is a proposition whose logical subject is given some intentional embodiment in the actual world of the thinkers. "Intentional embodiment in the actual world of the thinker" allows that the intentional subject might be in the future, or a non-existent thing, or a fiction, as well as an actual object.

5. *Assertion.* Interpretation as triadic is a process. It involves the actual representing of an object, and the process can be understood as either dynamic or fulfilled. The object is one thing, the representation in itself is a second thing, and the interpreting of the object with the representation is a third thing when the interpretation is fulfilled or finished. As the process happens dynamically, the object is taken into the experience of the interpreter as represented with the representation, and the "taking into experience" is a third thing, though not as such an object subsequent to the first object and the representation. Insofar as a representation takes an object into experience with a truth value, the representation is "asserted." "Assertion" and its various cognates mean that the representation with its logical and intentional subject is taken to have a real subject in the world of the interpreter. Only the "third thing," the fulfilled interpretant, the dynamic process of interpretation, can assert. The interpretant can incorporate a representation as a sign of an object with many performative functions in addition to asserting truth value, as Austin and Searle have pointed out; but truth-value is the topic of interest in the theory of interpretation. A given representation can play at once three roles in interpretation: It can be an object of another representation, a representation representing its own object, and an interpretant asserting that another representation represents an object. Representations thus can stack up, and it is in virtue of this that there is the familiar continuity of thought, problematic as that sometimes is for clarity.

Interpretation is irreducibly triadic: it involves an object, a sign representing an object, and a further sign interpreting how the first sign represents the object. Or, to use the similar language of Charles Peirce, an interpretation includes an object, a sign of the object, and an interpretant of the sign asserting the sign to hold of the object. Put yet another way, a thing cannot be an object of knowledge unless it is both represented by a sign and interpreted as being so represented by another sign. As these three statements reveal, the triadic character of interpretation is embodied in each element—object, sign, interpreting sign. Each is what it is only by virtue of mediating relations to the other two.

Often interwoven with interpretation, there are other forms of thinking that are not exactly triadic in this sense because they are not assertive. For instance, imagination employs structures or "images" to form and integrate experiential elements; but its structures function as schemata, as integrating rules, rather than as representations asserted to represent objects. For another instance, there is cognitive envisionment that includes theories asserted to be true but that function as means for cognitively possessing the world, for organizing the world so as to have access to the various experiential and cognitive domains within it by means of formal theoretical structures. In addition, there is a kind of dialectical direction and redirection of thinking by which thought criticizes itself with regard to whether it is imagining, interpreting, or theorizing in the most important ways; although involving assertions, this kind of dialectic is more appreciative, critical, and directive than assertive. Whereas imagination seeks the aesthetically successful image, theorizing the unity of cognitive experience, and dialectic the good, interpretation seeks assertoric truth.[3]

Twentieth century studies of language have made abundantly clear the varieties of thought and expression that are other than assertoric. Speech act theory catalogues many kinds of illocutionary and perlocutionary dimensions of language (Searle: 1969, ch. 2). For instance promising, commanding, inquiring, emoting, cursing, praising, celebrating, seducing, and scaring. None of these kinds of thoughtful intention has its primary form the asserting of a representation as true. Nevertheless, each of them has an imaginative structure that the activity presumes to be true in the action's context and thus is indirectly assertoric. A promise, for instance, presumes a true identity for the promisor and the promisee, and a meaningful applicability of the terms of the promise. The act of promising therefore includes a host of assertoric interpretive elements, presuming them to be true. To make the promise is indirectly but necessarily to assert the truth of the interpretive presumptions. A fierce yell intended to scare away a predator presumes that, given the truth that predators are sometimes scared by aggressive behavior such as yells, a yell truly is at least worth a try in the circumstances. The fact that yelling behavior is an instinctive response when one interprets the situation as truly ready for it—that is, that one is in the presence of a possibly scarable predator—still allows that the instinctive response involves asserting interpretations as true. In this book, "interpretation" will refer not only to direct declarative assertions, but also to the assertions involved in any kind of intentional activity.

Interpretively to move away from an object in the direction of one sign or line of signification is selective. One could have moved off in a different direction. To note that the table is brown, for instance, is selectively different from interpreting it as expensive or old. In this sense, all knowing involves abstraction or simplification.

In order to recover full concreteness, one may dream of assembling all of the interpretations into a coherent whole, as in a Cartesian reconstruction. The principles for such assemblage cannot naively present themselves in the thing interpreted, however. At the very least, the assemblage must respect the history and the set of contexts of the several specific interpretations. Therefore, the interpreter, not alone the object, supplies elements of the reconstructed summary interpretation. In fact, the very selectivity of interpretation reveals that the perspective of the interpreter is partially constitutive of the knowledge of the object. More than that, the obverse is also true: the various selective processes of interpretation are among the crucial ingredients in the construction of an interpretive perspective. An interpreter comes to be in part through interpreting. An interpretation is a new natural reality beyond the interpreted.

The question of truth for interpretation becomes whether the sign stands for the object in the respect specified by the interpretant-sign that connects them. The respect of the representation's representing is all important, for without it there is no connection between object and sign that could be true or false. The apparently dyadic true/false distinction, determined by the norm of truth, is thus made internal to the triadic relations in the interpretive situation. Representation cannot be understood apart from an understanding of the principle of selection indicating the respect of representation. Therefore, an interpretation cannot be understood simply in its own terms, for further terms are necessary to explicate the respect of interpretation. The idealists are right about at least one dimension of representative correspondence: a potential correspondence needs to be fulfilled through a process of mediation (see Vaught, 1987).

From this point of view, the power in the pragmatist's association of truth with warranted assertability in a self-correcting community of inquiry is obvious. Warranted assertability differs from direct correspondence precisely by its reference to interpretation's triadic character. To warrant an assertion is to explicate and justify both the respect in which the assertion is made as well as the assertion, relative to the context, purposes, history, and needs of the situation. More exactly, to say that truth is warranted assertability is to note that the assertion is embedded in a context of inquiry that is indefinitely self-critical and liable to become unstable when a change in assessment of the nature and merits of the respect of interpretation shifts the truth value of the interpreting sign. The pragmatists correctly noted that the truth of interpretations is relative to common culture, shared goals, and mutually critical communication. An interpretation supposes a vast culture forming the imagination in such a way that things stand out as objects to be interpreted, that things function as signs, and that respects are articulated in terms of which it is culturally important to make interpretations. Cultural imagination presents a world relatively preformed with objects, signs, and relevent respects of interpretation. This is reflected in interpretations that presuppose language, in perceptions that presuppose perceptual categories and habits, even in specific identifications of what counts as cultural or as humanly significant.

Within the field of cultural hermeneutics, the recognition of this relativity has been extraordinarily liberating. We now come closer to understanding other cultures and our own distant past on their own terms precisely because we recognize that their terms differ from ours. The recognition of cultural particularity, our own and others, is at once the fulfillment of modernity's inquiry into knowledge and the beginning of post-modern relativity. Respect for difference at the profound cultural level marks the end of one of the main rationales for Western imperialism, and in fact is a new form of piety (Neville: 1982, pp. 230–247). It is not much of an exaggeration to say that recognizing other cultures to be profoundly different and yet true in their own terms is a fundamental religious perception.

The gods of cultural relativity, like most gods, are not entirely benign, however, and certainly not tame. For, is not the recognition of thorough cultural relativity the abandonment of the sense of reality? Just as a dyadic quality of truth is subsumed within the triadic quality of interpretation, so assertions within a culture seem to be true or false only within the culture. Because the very meaning of representing an object with a sign in a certain respect is a function of the larger culture, one cannot speak of true or false interpretations except insofar as those interpretations are embedded in some culture or other. One cannot say that contrary assertions in two different cultures might differ with respect to one another in truth value: they are true or false only relative to their respective cultures, not with respect to one another. The reality of things, which must be at once independent of any interpretation and yet connectable with any other interpreter, regardless of cultural selectivity, evaporates inexorably.

Of course, the divergence of different cultures cannot be all that great if we know in fact that they diverge. The vast majority of experience must be common to human beings who know they have different cultures, and surely this is so: human biology, development in the womb, seasonal variation, temperature extremes—there is a host of universal or continuously overlapping elements. But each of these elements takes on special coloring from its cultural context. And the experience of cultural relativity is not in the first instance an agreement to disagree, but a horrifying suspicion that there is no commensuration between one's own culture and the other's. The shock of relativity comes when the seemingly common and familiar suddenly becomes eery and strange in the usage of the other.

Another and even more basic element of interpretation needs to be recognized. A sign (as well as its object and interpretant) has some "material reality," as Peirce called it, such as a sound, a word written on paper, a neurophysiological event. This is as true for mental representations as for non-experiential kinds of signs. From a strictly logical point of view, this may be trivial, since all that logic requires is the function of representing; any material that can do the job is satisfactory. But from a more critical philosophical point of view, the natural reality of an interpretation is to represent the object in a certain respect *according to the form of the medium or material reality* of the sign as interpreted by the interpretant. Written words, spoken words, neurophysiological events, all qualify the sense in which they represent by their very own form. Peirce was concerned in his semiotic theory to classify the material way by which signs relate to objects—indexically through causation, iconically through isomorphism, symbolically through convention. But the analysis needs to be pressed further if the naturalistic elements of causation in interpretation are to be understood. Therefore there is a biological dimension to interpretation, the dimension by which we animals use signs and are related to the material elements of the natural world. The biological element is interesting for interpretation only insofar as it can express the appropriate triadic relations. Nevertheless, the plain biological structures involved in interpretation need to be understood in describing interpretive activity.

A special word needs to be said here about the connotation of 'object.' The terms in the triadic interpretive relation—object, sign (or representation), and interpretant—seem to have an atomistic connotation because of the logical differences they have within that relation. It is disastrous, however, to infer from those discrete differences to an atomism in the things that can be objects. Objects needs not be Aristotelian substances, or Whiteheadian actual occasions. An object is, by definition, anything that can be interpreted. Doubtless the most common object is a vaguely defined situation; this is the limit of the truth in Bosanquet's claim that the object of every proposition is the world. Discriminable parts of a situation, such as partially independent physical entities can be objects; so can their properties, relations, and aspects from various perspectives, their interactions, developments, histories and futures. Any representation can be an object. The metaphysical structures of reality, its unity and diversity, identity, value as such—all these can be objects. Indeed, anything real, including reality, can be an object. The clue to the discrimination of objects, of course, lies in their representations. The truth of that discrimination, however, depends on how realities measure their representations.

To recover the measure it is necessary and unavoidable to accept the triadic character of interpretation, and the cultural relativity to which it leads. Having accepted that, it may be possible to discover a deeper and more public meaning of reality of which the diverse cultures are expressions. In order to reach that conception of nature, however, it is necessary to suspend the discussion of interpretation and return to more fundamental issues, the task of Divisions Two and Three. At the present stage of the argument it is possible to indicate the lineaments of the axiological conception and to gather these remarks on interpretation into an hypothesis about truth.

II. VALUE AND VALUATION

As John Dewey so well pointed out, there is an affective tone in all things experienced, even in those that rarely if ever come to the focus of attention. The simplest way to account for this is with the metaphysical assumption that everything has a value.

There is a deep, unwitting peril in the use of the language of "value," however. 'Value language' has been appropriated by those affected by recent social science, for which values are the preferences, tastes, commitments, and appreciations of people. In this Weberian usage, value is something people feel about things, irrespective of whether those valuations are merited by the worth of the things. The benefit for social science of treating value in this voluntaristic and subjectivistic way is that it preserves factuality. Objects can be considered valueless themselves, or irrelevant with respect to value. Moreover, that a person holds a certain value about something is itself a fact, and can be classified and counted. The benefit for our culture making value subjective is that it eliminates any real disputes about right and wrong, and allows 'conflict resolution' to be mere negotiation of powers and the satisfaction of interests in compromise.[4]

Nevertheless, making value subjective, reducing value to valuation, and then valuation to value commitments, is a thorough corruption of value language. If Dewey were right, it is the things of the world that are filled with goodness, and our experience is a partial discerning of that goodness. The question of valuation is whether what we represent of a thing's value is true. Yet in common American discussions, a mention of something's value is almost inevitably interpreted to mean what someone feels is the thing's value. To speak of axiology as the analysis of value seems obtusely to mean "value analysis," the discussion of the intricacies among the values we hold dear.

Should we not then simply abandon the language of value and find some alternative? Heidegger and his followers handed over value language to the Weberians and wrote instead of intensity and authenticity. But this resulted in the elimination of moral philosophy, or normative political philosophy, from that approach, and opened the door to the romantic nostalgia of 'deep roots' and bigotry. Plato and Aristotle were far more critical than Heidegger and used the language of goodness. Indeed, the axiological theory to be developed below has many affinities with their theories. Yet "goodness" connotes a one-dimensional attribute, differing only in degree in its embodiments, and inviting easy comparisons. There are obviously different kinds of value, value in different senses, value that is defined by functional relations as well as by intrinsic properties. Value is intimately related to structure, and is as multidimensional as structure itself. This variability is nicely conveyed by value language. Therefore, it is appropriate to attempt to recover and properly qualify the language of value, bearing in mind the need to signal the objectivity of value constantly.

On the axiological theory, a thing's value involves its being a harmony of the features essential to itself with those by virtue of which it is conditioned by and conditions other things. Distinguishing essential from conditional features is as old as Plato and Aristotle, and the way of making the distinction here derives from Paul Weiss; chapter 7 provides a technical exposition. The conditional features constitute the things' relations, and these obviously structure the values we perceive objects to have; the conditional features also are the ones by virtue of which things are related to us as valuers. The essential features are those by virtue of which things have a being or integrity of their own, and the stubborness of value, most particularly the stubbornness of disvalue, evil, and ugliness, assures us that essential features are involved in a thing's values. The metaphysical point is that value is to be hypothesized as resident in the harmonic structure of a thing, including each of the concrete components harmonized. The values of things may thus be conceived as real, independent of the interpretation of them (except where the kind of value explicitly consists in value for an interpreter).

Valuation, on this hypothesis, is when the value of something becomes a value or plays a value-laden role in something else. With respect to interpretation, valuation is giving the thing a value-laden role in the experience of the interpreter or in the form of the interpretation that might be employed by a community. The problematic work of interpretation is that the value of the interpreted thing must be harmonized with the values of the other things entering experience; in the course of the interpretive process, the original thing's value is likely to be compromised. Valuation quickly becomes evaluation when the integration is done on a comparative level.

Interpretation is selective valuation in at least four forms, according to the hypothesis. First, the object is a harmony present in interpretation with its own constitutive value (this is not to suggest that the object does not also have its integrity and value irrespective of the interpretation). Second, the interpreter, by virtue of its own harmonizing essential intentional interests, places a value on interpreting the thing in a selective respect. Third, there is the representation that interprets the object in that respect. Fourth, there is the interpretant that asserts that the representation interprets the object, or that takes the representation as a sign in the relevant respect.

Without the fourth form, valuing the representation relative to the object in the appropriate respect, there is no assertion. Without the third form there is no selection, no distancing, no representation, and hence no advance whatsoever on the object by itself as uninterpreted. Without the second form there is no valuable or warrantable direction of selective representation, no connection with a context of meaning. Without the first form, there is no reality to be interpreted.

Both the philosophical and cultural problems of identifying reality so as to measure truth arise with the denial or neglect of the first form, the presence of objective harmony as a constitutive value. The principle historical argument for denying or ignoring the real object is that it is never present in experience without being interpreted. And when it is interpreted, it is always in the selected versions presented by the sign, the interpretant, and the respect of interpretation. We never objectify an object except in an interpreted form, and this is because we objectify objects only by making them constituents of our own processes in which they must be harmonized selectively with other constituents. Yet there is no reason to truncate the interpretive process, as this argument does, by denying or ignoring the valuable object-to-be-interpreted with which it begins. The process of selection begins with that from which selection is made.[5]

The most striking implication of this axiological approach to value and valuation is that interpretation is primarily valuation and only secondarily the representation of facts. "Factual description" must be an abstract part of normative description, which is what interpretation is whenever it is descriptive.

And is this not the case? Interpretations are guided in their selective respects by the general cultural and personal interest of human activity and enjoyment. It stands to reason that the aspects most often selected for notice in consciousness are the factual structures serving those interests. Modern scientific thinking greatly complicates this. Quite apart from engineering and technological interests, even purely theoretical interests in science have to do with locating universal, measurable, and replicable features of things, and these seem to be properties of a factual sort, shorn of their manifest values. But this is only selectively to prize those constitutive values that are universal, measurable, and replicable, values that we call facts. In our ordinary experience, we take things to be harmonic structures embodying some appreciable worth, even when this worth is subordinated to a factual function in an instrumental relation.

The important point to stress in the theory of value and valuation is that the value constitutive of the nature of a real object can become a constituent in an interpreting being, although only in ways compatible with the interpreter's other constituents. In contrast to the main drift of the modern Western tradition, which asks how we can reconstruct or represent things within us and concludes that the activity of reconstruction or representation is almost wholly a matter of our own creation and projection, the theory of value and valuation suggests a different question. Why do the specific values that interpreters objectify in their thinking differ from the constitutive values with which thinking begins? The answers to that question have to do with showing how the constitutive values must be altered to become compatible with the other elements in interpretive experience, particularly with the different physical reality of the interpreter, with the inherited or learned cultural values concerning respects in which things are to be interpreted, with inherited semiotic systems for interpreting, and with both cultural and situational intentionalities or leading interpretants. This is to say, the resources of hermeneutics are to be marshalled to explain the particular selectivities of any interpretation. They can explain why constituent values of objects in one person or culture are interpreted one way and yet these same value-laden objects are interpreted otherwise elsewhere.

III. TRUTH AS THE CARRYOVER OF VALUE

The hypothesis concerning truth guiding this discussion is that truth is the properly qualified carryover of the value of a thing (or situation, or state of affairs, or fact, or any complex harmony that might become an object of interpretation) into interpreting experiences of that thing. The achieved value in the thing is always a measure of the interpretation, and the dyadic character of the truth relation is thus preserved. Moreover, the reality of the thing with its constituent achieved value is manifest in the context of divergent cultures or lines of interpretation, because the differences between them are differences in the proper qualification of the carryover, and both are measured by the same real achieved value.

The definition of truth in terms of carryover of value rather than correspondence of form is a serious innovation. It can be made plausible if the more usual senses of truth can be shown to follow from it as special cases. The place to begin is with a discussion of 'properly qualified carryover.'

Carryover itself means that the value achieved in the thing not only enters into the constitution of the interpreters but is objectified in their experience. The practical as well as theoretical meaning of "objectification" is that other interpreters or the original interpreters themselves can later experience the value of the thing by getting it out of the interpretation. That carryover results in objectification means that truth is a relation between the objectification as an intentional object and that to which the intentional object "corresponds," the thing with its achieved value. On the other hand, that the carryover is a causal process means that truth is a character or norm for natural processes, even if indirect and filtered through many interpretive representations or when it involves inferring to the future. Enormous philosophical advantages acrue to having the same process be both intentional and causal in specifiable senses.

The proper qualification of carryover acknowledges the fact that selection and alteration are involved in any process by which a thing becomes a component of another thing, modified to fit with the other components. An indefinite number of different kinds of modifications may be possible for a thing to undergo when entering as a condition into an interpreter. The kinds relevant to truth, however, are those marked by the selected valuations involved in interpretation.

The first and most obvious kind of qualification consists in the independent physical make-up of the interpreter or the interpreting activity. Even though the object is carried over into the interpretation, there is a difference between the achieved value of the object in its own proper place and that achieved value functioning as a condition within the interpretive activity. There is a move from sunset to appreciative contemplation of the sunset, from written text to mental understanding, from historical event to the historian's reconstruction. In each case, the object must find embodiment within the biological structure of the interpreter interpreting, and for this reason we can call the first kind of qualification biological. Whatever the object—sunset, text, past event—it must find a place within the physical nature of human beings, and suffers the selective qualifications of that kind of embodiment. The reference to "biology" is shorthand for all the kinds of physical structures shaping the interpreter's response; there is perhaps no sharp line to be drawn between the physical and cultural formations of the interpreter.

The second kind of proper qualification is that carryover is limited to the respects in which interpretations are made. These respects are conditioned in part by physical considerations. But by and large the interesting selections of respects in which to interpret things are made by culture, minutely modified by personal history and idiosyncracy. Compare, for instance, the different ways in which a Sung Dynasty landscape painter and a nineteenth century American landscape painter would select respects of the same mountains to interpret. The cultural selection of respects of interpretation is the ground level of style; the next levels are the subgroup's and individual's further specification and idiosyncratic variation on the cultural selection. Only after that does style become affected by intention and vocabulary or medium. This second kind of qualification of the carryover of value can be called cultural qualification, with the notation that culture itself is a highly problematic concept.

Representations themselves, with their networks of syntax, semantics, general and special usages, constitute a third kind of proper qualification of carryover. Even after determining the respects in which things can be interpreted and the cultural layout that justifies these respects, the representational signs themselves make a further selection. The signs make the assertions that can be true or false. As remarked earlier, they don't have to be merely descriptive in order to be true or false. For instance, a performative command that itself doesn't assert a state of affairs may contain assumptions about states of affairs that are true or false—what Searle calls their "propositional content." The assertions or assumptions are true, on this hypothesis, to the extent they carry over the achieved values of their subject matter into the interpretations as qualified by (1) the biological reality of the interpreter, (2) the selective elements in the limited respects of interpretation, (3) the representations actually used to represent or objectify the subject matter, and (4) the context and will-determined purposes guiding interpretation. The third kind of qualification of carryover can be called semiotic.

Selective intentions naturally constitute the fourth kind of proper qualification of carryover. In a given culture, the same values determining typical respects of interpretation might also determine typical purposes, intentions, goals, prized objects and activities, and so forth. A semiotic structure also affects intentions. But the values determining intentions and purposes are likely to be more variable, more relativized to context, to small groups, to individuals' personal histories and particular contexts than would be specifically determined by culture and semiotic systems. Both culture and semiotic systems are vague with respect to an internal range of intentional use, and both can be deliberately called into question by philosophers, the insane, and other cranks. This fourth, intentional, kind of selective qualification of carryover can be called "purposive," with the understanding that "purpose" covers many spectra, from explicit to implicit, from conscious to unconscious, from focused to penumbral, etc.

To sum up, the hypothesis concerning truth is that an interpretation is true in the ways that, and to the extent that, it carries over the values in its object(s) into itself as qualified by biological, cultural, semiotic, and purposive selections. For an interpretation itself to be known, in addition to being engaged in or lived through, it objectifies these carryovers for further interpretation. For a true interpretation to be known as true, the further interpretation of it must interpret it somewhat critically in the respects it purports to carry over the values, subject to the qualifications. To interpret interpretations with respect to their truth or falsity, of course, is a cultural disposition. It might in fact be universal to all cultures, although we can imagine cultures that do not interpret interpretations in respect of truth. Indeed, we may be in the midst of a culture that does so only in deformed ways, asking, for instance, only whether the values in an interpretation are good for the interpreter (not whether they are carried over from a further reality), or only whether the interpretation embodies the selective principles of a certain culture (not whether the interpretation in the instance carries over any real value using those principles).

IV. THE HYPOTHESIS AS A THEORY OF TRUTH

However interesting the hypothesis about the carryover of value, what justifies the claim that it is a theory of truth? Why is it not just about the continuity of value? There are many levels to addressing this question.

The first and most obvious is to compare this definition of truth with some of the classical ones. Consider, for instance, Aristotle's point that truth is saying of a thing what it is and not saying of it what it is not. This is similar to Tarski's assertion that the saying "snow is white" is true if and only if snow is white. The underlying philosophy these two points schematize is valid, but we should note two unanalyzed elements.

What account is to be given of the "isness" of what is (and the 'is-notness' of what it is not)? Both Aristotle and Tarski (and most philosophers in between) work back by analogy from the form of the saying, that is, the subject-predicate form of a declarative sentence, to the theory that a thing is something to which properties can be predicated, a substance or logical subject. Suppose by a contrary hypothesis, however, that a thing is an achievement of value, or a sum of processes of achievement of values. Indeed, Aristotle's theory of final causes and of actuality and potentiality requires him to say something like this. Then, on this hypothesis to say of a thing what it is, and not to say of it what it is not, is precisely to show what values it achieves and not to suggest it achieves some other values.

The issue here is about the nature of reality. If reality is the achievement of value, then truth must say what that value is; and if this is so, then saying what properties a thing has contributes to truth telling only insofar as the bearing of properties is tied to the achieved value. For precisely this reason, a theory of truth supposes a theory of reality; an axiological hypothesis about truth requires an axiological metaphysics of the sort elaborated later in Division Two.

Of course, a thing might be many things besides achieved value. In Aristotle, a thing is also its material, its form, and the result of an antecedent process of causation, all these things individuated and combined with the thing's achieved value. In Tarski, a thing is not achieved value at all but rather a logical subject for a propositional calculus. The axiological definition of truth depends on a viability of the metaphysical theory of reality according to which the achievement of value is the encompassing nature of a thing, from which its other characteristics, dimensions, and relations are derived by abstraction. For instance, there is great plausibility in Aristotle's view that in some sense or senses, knowledge is getting the forms of things into mind, in the view that truth is a relation between a propositional form and a state of affairs, a picturing of facts. To encompass this insight, the axiological hypothesis would have to show that the relevant form in an interpretive objectification of things carries over the relevant properly qualified achieved value in the things. This can be done through an analysis of form itself as the instrument for making value possible, an analysis showing that the same form can be both in things and in interpretations of them. It would also be necessary for the axiological hypothesis to show that the form in the thing is what it is by virtue of bearing the thing's value. This will be argued in detail in Division Two.

The second unanalyzed element in the traditional definition of truth as saying "what is" consists in the nature of saying. This remarks is not intended to demean Aristotle's accomplishment in the logical writings. We do indeed know a great deal about what "saying" is. Nevertheless, Aristotle and most of his successors have analyzed saying in terms of language and speech. This is too narrow a view. Even if language is paradigmatic for all forms of thought, which it surely is not, saying is more than what is said and the act of saying. Saying is first of all a cultural activity. If the saying therefore represents its object, it is a representation in a cultural medium, unlike a footprint or smoke from a fire. To understand this is to understand the special limits and selective principles of cultural representation, and of a particular culture's representations. Within culture, saying takes place in a linguistic medium, and any interpretation has an interpretive medium. Aristotle knew a great deal about media, but not as media. Saying something is representing it in the terms and structures of the medium itself, and the limits and selective principles of the language need to be understood. Saying is also formed by the particular context of speech, with special circumstances addressed by the various purposes lying behind the acts of expression. These contextual dimensions of saying too need to be understood in order to have an analysis of *saying* what's what. They are, as will have been noticed, the biological, cultural, semiotic, and purposive qualifications of interpretation.

Truth, then, according to the traditional formula, is translating the nature of reality into the biological, cultural, semiotic, and purposive terms of interpretation. If the nature of reality is an array of achieved values, or values in process of being achieved, or values normative for future achievements, then saying of what is that it is, and of what is not that it is not, is translating the achieved values in the subject matter into the interpretive "sayings" according to the special qualifications of biology, culture, semiotics, and purpose. How does this differ from the axiological hypothesis about truth?

The previous paragraph used a weasel word, "translating," to indicate the relation between reality and the interpretive representation of it. On many modern theories, the translation is a kind of mirroring relation between objects and their reflection in mental substance, or between facts and the linguistic statement of those facts, or between objects and intentions of those objects. Those ways of interpreting the translation, however, lose the reality pole. Either we are stuck with the subject pole blankly looking out at a mystery, or we occupy a third position to compare the object and subject to pronounce that the relation is of the sort to mirror. That third position is the interpretant's, and if the object is to be brought into the comparison, it must be made internal to the interpretant. In both cases, we lose access to the integrity of the real object, the first through ultimate subjectivism and the second through reducing speech to conversation.

The alternative to the mirroring metaphor for translating is a causal relation: the object causes its representation in interpretation, subject to the qualifications of human biology, culture, semiotical elements, and purpose. This is the naturalistic strategy for recovering reality as a measure of our representations. It makes sense then to translate "translating" from its Latin roots to English and say that truth is the carryover of value from the reality in which it is achieved to the interpretation of it as qualified by biology, culture, semiotics, and purpose.

The argument for the appropriateness of the axiological hypothesis as a theory of truth is thus that it is the proper fleshing out of Aristotle's traditional notion. The fleshing out depends on the plausibility of an axiological theory of reality, and on the fruitfulness of an analysis of interpretation as a natural causal product of reality, subject to the qualifications of culture, semiotics, and purpose. It depends also on a proper account of the kind of causation involved in the carryover of value, an account that can show also how interpretations are intentional and can refer to their objects in appropriate temporal dimensions.

It is clearer now what must be discussed in order to make good on the hypothesis concerning truth. We need a metaphysical theory of reality that deals with value, and a philosophical cosmology that deals with causation, motion, space, and time. We need an analysis of the elements of interpretation itself. And we need an analysis of the ways we participate in biological nature, in culture, in semiotic systems, and in intentional or purposive life so as to constitute the context and stuff of interpretation. Participation is the crucial variable in giving a naturalistic or causal account of the relation between reality and interpretation such that the former might measure the latter as true or false.

4

Participation: The Context of a Philosophy of Interpretation

In its critique of Cartesian functionalism, chapter 2 argued that all intentional or mental acts are meaningful only within contexts. More generally, the logical structure of interpretation is insufficiently understood unless it comprehends the locating of any given interpretation in its context. Interpretation is the form of a thing's participation in its context. Most important, interpretation is the form of human participation in the world. As Peirce and especially Dewey argued, participation is the human way of being in the world, and it is what includes us in the world so that reality can measure our assertions.

What is participation? That question is hard to answer precisely because of its pervasive generality. Dewey and the pragmatists thought of participation as intentional behavior in the environment. Dewey was sharp that such behavior needs to be guided by the realities of the environment, and that the values shaping purposes in the behavior be the real values of the relevant environing things, not merely imagined values. One of the dimensions of participation therefore is framed by the particular historical purposes with which people live in their environment.

Another dimension of participation is the system of representations, the semiotic structures, by virtue of which we represent the environment and our purposes. By participating in semiotic systems, we participate in the environment through the give and take requiring representative direction. More than the pragmatists knew (except perhaps Peirce), participation in the world is participation in semiotic systems.

Of course, a third dimension of participation is that shaped by culture generally. Culture frames our imagination so as to provide the elementary valuations that form what we take to be important. Participatory experience is a dialectical process in which the formal valuations implicit in imagination are tested against the values in things. Precisely because we participate in the environment valuationally, we also participate in a culture so as to form our fundamental orientation.

A fourth dimension of participation consists in the fact that our interpretive activities are all the actions of our physical bodies, of our biological selves in interaction with the physical structure of the environment. Most important, interpretation involves physical elements entering our selves from the environment, and other elements returning from self to world. The biological or physical character of participation is a crucial dimension.

These four dimensions are the respects in which a valuable harmony is qualified as it is carried over from its own locus into that of an interpreter. This chapter shall review these in reverse order, moving from biological participation through cultural and semiotic to purposive.

I. BIOLOGICAL PARTICIPATION

If truth is to be understood as the carryover of value (or anything else, such as form) from things to the interpretation of them, then physical nature, including human biology, must be given a causal account that expresses the carryover. This is precisely the historic fault in Descartes' official view: he could not conceive how the causal properties of extended matter could effect changes in the causal structure of unextended mind. Yet he understood where the problem lay and addressed it far better than most of his followers. He tried to show how the nervous system was like a set of rigid rods immediately communicating motion from one end to the next, affecting the pineal gland in which the mind also is affected; and he argued that the process works in reverse. His psychology was an interactionist one, with plainly physical things affecting plainly mental ones, and vice versa. This is surely the situation needing an account. As Scrouge noted, an undigested bit of beef can cause dreams of ghosts; a nasty idea can accelerate the heartbeat and pull the trigger.

If the Cartesian view of nature as objective matter and mind as subjective activity of thinking is the total of our resources, there is no hope to gain an understanding of causation adequate to account for the carryover of things from nature into experience. Much of modern philosophy has been limited by Descartes' imagination. Thinkers enamoured of physical science have often claimed that mind is only epiphenomenal; others impressed with either the structure or feel of human subjectivity have accounted for the physical world as a special kind of ideal system. Both of these approaches accept Descartes' fundamental definition of the issue. Its advantage, to repeat, is that there are some things that are plainly physical, and others that are plainly mental, and they obviously affect one another even if the causation in that affection cannot be conceived.

Although there were many anticipations, particularly among the American pragmatists, Whitehead's was the first theory of causation to put Descartes aside. Roughly expressed, Whitehead argued that to be an actual entity is to grasp antecedent actual entities into a new unity, modifying them so that they cohere with one another. He called the past actual entities "objective" physical things. The process of modifying and integrating them into a new thing he called "subjective mentality;" once a new thing has completed its subjective integration, it is an objective physical thing ready to be grasped by a successor. To be sure, only the subjective mentality of things complex enough to use representations would count for what we ordinarily mean by mentality; Whitehead recognized this. His strategy was to articulate rudimentary "mentality" as categoreally basic in distinction from "physicality" all the way down.

Thus he recognized the genius in Descartes' distinction, allowing for plainly physical and plainly mental things. Whitehead's own genius was to define subjective mentality and objective physicality in terms of their mutual causation; subjective mentality is the integration of objective physical things, resulting in a new physical thing that calls for a further subjective integration with its neighbors, and so on. This is exactly the template needed for a theory of causation representing carryover from nature to experience, and from experience back into nature.

The core of Whitehead's advance on Descartes was his denial of what he called "simple location." Descartes and the moderns supposed that a thing is located only in its place. Thus for one thing to affect another thing causally can only be for it to bump it out of its place. Minds can't be bumped, being non-extended and lacking place. Therefore, for a thing to affect a mind it has to be represented in the mind; but a Cartesian representation is not the thing represented but *another* thing, and all the problems of comparing the representation with its object are born. Whitehead pointed out that "simple location" is merely a metaphysical assumption about place, and a bad one at that.

The alternative, which will be called "multiple location" later, is equally a metaphysical assumption, one introduced in Whitehead's theory of a thing. A thing has its own proper place in which it constitutes itself; indeed, for Whitehead, a thing constitutes its place out of the extensional resources of the physical things it grasps as it constitutes its own very self. But then a thing also has other places in the subsequent things that grasp it. Those places involve modification of its proper place, and they must be made to fit together definitely and coherently with the places of the other things grasped by the subsequent things. It is simply in the nature of a thing, according to Whitehead's metaphysical hypothesis, that its "place" is properly subjective and functionally objective in others. The thing grasped is really and truly in the thing grasping: not a representation (though the grasping thing can also construct representations if it is complex enough) but the real physical thing. According to Whitehead, when "modern" philosophers talked of physical things as objectively "out there," the "out there" ironically was the thing itself functioning in the interpretive experience of the perceiver. The nature of proper place for a thing subjectively coming to be as an integration of previous things is more like the "dwelling" of subjective intentionality than like the relational objectivity of modern science's theoretical projections. Whitehead thus restored the medieval meaning of "objectivity" "for a mind."

Despite the fact that all causation, according to Whitehead, involves subjective appropriation of objectivity, resulting in more objectivity to be subjectively appropriated, his theory also displays the continuity of physicality alone and that of mentality alone. That is, one can view the world in terms of the connections of finished facts, as history, discounting the "creative" contributions of the individual moments of subjective integration; all that is objective. One can similarly view the continuities of a mind thinking through a long stretch by paying attention to semiotic connections and ignoring the roles of brain states. But to understand either with much exactness requires attention to the other.

There are some very serious flaws with Whitehead's metaphysics, particularly having to do with time and motion. Nevertheless, it is important to appropriate his great advance in the theory of causation and to develop it in ways adequate to exhibiting the specific kinds of carryover involved in true representation. Divisions II and III will attempt that.

In addition to the general hurdle of finding an adequate conception of causation, it is necessary to obtain a model of interpreters as biological organisms if we are to understand how things quite different from human kind get to be represented in us. At some fundamental level, something of our representations is biological.

Psychobiologists and some cognitive scientists present the following picture. A biological organism consists of interlocking physical systems, each of which has several parts that interact to produce a bit of behavior. The digestive system is an example; its microstructures are the elements of metabolism. The organs for locomotion are another example, with nerve impulses contracting muscles as its microstructures. A hormone system, such as those producing insulin or adrenalin, is yet another. These sytems interlock in the sense that each is stimulated to "behave" by input from others, and is maintained in its capacity to behave appropriately by the organic interaction of the others. Thus, a locomotive act of putting food in the mouth stimulates a digestive process, which in turns provides energy for finding food. Sight or smell of the food stimulates the adrenalin necessary to catch it.

The picture of interlocking physical systems described so far is mechanical in the sense condemned above. Psychobiologists also emphasize a hierarchical organization of the system. At relatively low levels of organization, early in the evolutionary chain, the behaving systems can be conceived as relatively discrete and rigid: they do only one thing, and at any one time they are either doing it or not doing it. These organisms approach the sheer external relations of a mechanism. At higher levels of organization, however, the systems have access to a vareity of other systems, and can modify their behavior according to variations in the rest of the organism. The behavior potential is not rigid but vague, and is actualized in nuanced ways by internalizing the behaviors of other systems. At very high levels of organization, the higher systems of behavior not only modify their own behavior by input from other systems but behave in such a way as to control some of those other systems. Thus, certain systems can dominate and direct the overall behavior of the complex organism, as the behaviors of the nervous system dominate the body while receiving subtle input from all the body's systems.

Clearly, there is a large truth to this model, and contemporary biology and psychology are mapping the systems with great ingenuity. Therefore, in our understanding of the causal processes of carryover, we must understand as well how the systems of the body, especially the nervous system, causally change the things carried over. How can an event be transformed into light patterns that are transformed into retinal excitations, into nerve impulses, into a chemical play in the occipital lobe, and so forth? To neglect these physical processes in favor of assuming that "standard" conditions (of perception in the vision example) always obtain is too naive. It assumes a one-to-one correspondence between the world and our representative experience of the world, and that is simple unacceptably unsubtle. A scene viewed when hungry will look different from its aspect when you are sated, and the difference has to do with the differential effects of metabolism on the "vision system." Further, neglect of these processes flies in the face of the twentieth century's rediscovery of the bodily aspects of experience, of "the lived body," of experiencing with the "withness" of the body. The modern idea that we see things "out there" with representations "in here" is simply false to the content of experience; we see things out there in a hungry or sated way, with energy or with exhaustion. The interlocking functions of bodily systems provide the context as well as the mechanisms by which things "out there" are given a new, albeit modified, place "in here."

The limit of the psychobiological model, however, is that it gives precisely no account of context in behavioral functioning. The rest of the organism and its physical surroundings are the context from an external point of view. Ruth Garrett Millikan has developed an extremely sophisticated philosophy of mind from this point of view, which she calls realism (1984). Yet as a candidate for a model of experiencing, a functioning system is merely on or off, running or idling. It runs when stimulated, and shuts down when its behavior has reached closure with the stimulating environment. The "inside" of the function has no contextual view of itself. It doesn't act for the sake of the appropriateness of the function, but because it is mechanically stimulated to do so. Therefore, whereas the biological systems model serves rather well to account for an organized process of objective things coming up to a subjective thing in process of integration, it cannot account at all for the contextualizing aspects of the subjective integration itself. What those systems are is not mind, although they are some of the physical systems out of which mind makes itself.

It is tempting at this point to say that the biological systems approach just goes to the limit of the biological, and beyond that lies the mental or, if one believes in artificial intelligence, nothing. Experience should not be conceived in biological terms. Yet that temptation to respect the limits of biology caves in to Cartesianism and provides no help whatsoever in understanding the interaction of the plainly physical with the plainly mental. It gives up on understanding the biological context through which truth is the carryover of things' value (or anything else) into experience.

Philosophy of nature ought rather to enlarge the notion of biology. Whitehead's philosophy again supplies the clue in its claim that every physical event comes to be through a mental process. Yet the drawbacks of his philosophy threaten to spoil the clue. He conceived of experience as happening full-blown in a momentary occasion, given content to be sure by the past yet existing fully at a moment. This simply is mistaken about the kinds of experiences that humans can identify. All human experience is imaginative and interpretive, and these involve changes taking a stretch of time. What is needed is an account of the temporally thick biological functions carrying semiotic structures: the generation of representations, codes, intentions, and the like. These cannot be functions in the sense of behaving systems. They must rather be biological functions in Dewey's contextualist sense quoted in chapter 2. It is incumbent on an account of the biological context of experience to provide a philosophical biology that appropriates the biologists' model but that also transforms it to display full-blown intentional functioning. Divisions II and III build to such a model in Division IV.

The process of carryover from things (including representations) into interpreting experience participates in the physical structures of the world, particularly in the biological organization of interpreters. Our interpretations take their meaning, their modifications of reality, in part from the biological functions in interpretation. If computers are genuine interpreters, their experience has a silicone quality about it. We human beings experience with a meat brain.

II. CULTURAL PARTICIPATION

We also participate in and with culture, and are in some respects ourselves cultural artifacts. Understanding cultural participation thus requires a philosophy of culture. In recent years, discouragement at the possibility of understanding reality to measure our assertions has led some thinkers to believe that philosophy of culture is the sole legitimate form of philosophy. There is a vaguely Kantian, or specifically Neo-Kantian, impulse behind the attempt to see philosophy of culture as the container for all other kinds of philosophy; culture can be assumed to be the transcendental condition for all knowledge (see, for instance, Capaldi, 1987). Although an exaggeration, the emphasis on philosophy of culture has not only contributed to the understanding of culture but has brought philosophy into fruitful connections with social sciences and the arts. Philosophy of culture has often conceived itself to be unrelated to philosophy of nature, perhaps even dismissive. The use of both to explore participation in biological and cultural realms requires that categories be developed relating one to another. The categories for a rudimentary philosophy of culture will be discussed in subsequent parts of this book (see also Neville: 1974, Pt. III).

The important element of culture to notice at this point is that it is selective according to human values. Culture qualifies the carryover of value into experience by limiting what can be carried over to what can be registered at a certain level in cultural terms. Human biology makes a similar qualification: interpretation is limited to those things that can be carried in a biological medium. Cultural qualification is qualitatively different from biological qualification because it employs imagination.

It is not entirely arbitrary to distinguish the biological from the cultural by the use of imagination exclusively in the latter. Imagination is the causal synthesis by which causal impingements on the organism are restructured into the forms of experience. Culture always employs imagery, biology never. Imagery is not necessarily assertive, though it is employed whenever assertions are made (Neville: 1981, Pt. II).

Recall the role of imagination sketched in the first chapter. Imagination provides the sense of world assumed as background in any interpretive or other intentional endeavor. It also provides the elementary terms that are employed in any focused thinking. At any given time, therefore, interpretation takes place within a rough context given by imagination. There is a dialectical relation between interpretation and imagination, of course. Interpretive activity can change imaginative structure (and so can many other events), and shifts in imaginative structure alter the possibilities for interpretation, or the meaningfulness of interpretive terms.

Imaginative structures themselves have many dimensions, each responsive to altering stimulations from different sources. It is tempting to sort the dimensions as layers, with basic vague categories of things, relations, importances, time, and causation laid down first, then mythic dimensions that organize these into worldviews, then perceptual, kinesthetic, and agential dimensions, etc. But there is hardly a temporal priority to this layering, as is evident from a quick review of the kinds of variables that change each dimension.

Perceptual, kinesthetic, and agential imagination is structured in some part by our physiology, which is basic, ancient, and slow to change. But it is modified by the kinds of things around us, such as rectilinear buildings instead of merely natural forms, by media of communication and transportation, and by the instruments through which we see, move, and act. Biologically, the character of this dimension of imagination shifts radically with the age of the organism, but now technology in the form of reading glasses, hearing aids, vitamins, and somewhat controlled educational experience smooths out these shifts; we moderns see, move, and act with different imaginative possibilities than were available to a society like ancient India's that reflected sharp divisions between life's stages. Perception, movement, and action are functions of our bodies and their technological extensions, especially culture; the ancient physiological part is like a deep structure, but vastly vague and impotent without the artifices subject to invention, quick history, and faddish popularity.

Mythic dimensions of imagination obviously are affected by those of perception, movement, and agency. But they seem mainly to be sensitive to alterations in religious practices of ritual and spiritual discipline, most often associated with decisive historical events such as the Exodus, or with great founders such as Lao-tze, Confucius, Jesus, Zarathustra, or Muhammed. Whether or not the founders were historical personages, or their true stories known, mythic imagination personalizes its roots, perhaps because mythic imagination is grasped and re-enacted in personal activities of ritual and discipline.

Basic imaginative categories are sensitive to shifts of many kinds, including those mentioned. But they are sensitive also to basic deliberate thinking, to metaphysics, criticism, and philosophy generally. We don't recognize the contingency of our common sense imaginative assumptions about things until thought somehow objectifies them and points out alternatives. A culture's metaphysical common sense is rarely as coherent as a single explicit metaphysical system ought to be. After all, it likely derives from diverse metaphysical systems, reinforced by diverse fields of religion and technology. This is no difficulty as long as the incoherent parts can be kept apart. But when history requires a culture to act coherently, or when large scale technological changes ramify throughout a whole culture—the industrial revolution from steam engines to electronics illustrates both—then the basic imaginative categories of common sense fall into disarray. The function of metaphysical philosophy is to examine this and offer corrections. Whether suggested metaphysical corrections will be effective in altering common sense depends on whether enough other influences on imagination provide support.

Metaphysics is the abstract and controlled analysis of basic categories or common sense assumptions about things by virtue of which we take responsibility for those assumptions, and do something about them. The arts provide less abstract, and less controlled, avenues of approach to basic categories, but they are rarely, and never essentially, bound by a responsibility to develop true common sense assumptions. If the topic of interpretation, related as it is to confusions about truth and reality, is problematic because of problematic basic common sense assumptions, then metaphysics is essential to a philosophy of interpretation. If the problem with basic assumptions poses difficulties for interpretation, likely it poses difficulties for all pivotal topics. Therefore, metaphysics with its cognate modes of thought in non-Western cultures is an important task in any time.

Culture itself, on this view, ranges from experience formed by extremely elementary imagery to the very sophisticated. Some elementary levels of culture perhaps are universal because the experiences in which they are exercised are universal, for instance, the feeling of being in the womb, of being hungry, cold, or afraid. These elementary levels are quickly integrated with more complicated levels of imagery so as rarely to be pure. There are also levels of culture, such as orientation to spatial properties, distance, light, colors, styles of movement, and so forth, that differ in kind from one cultural group to another but that are too elementary to be represented easily in semiotic concepts. Only behavioral differences between cultures call attention to these cultural images, as when it was discovered that the African native carvers who could produce sophisticated, elegant wooden statuary could not imagine building a rectilinear box to ship them in.

Anthropologists might balk at allowing the notion of culture to sink so far down into the bio-psychic dance, preferring to limit culture instead to what can be taught or transmitted. There might be good methodological reasons for this. Nevertheless, any imagery with which teaching might take place is itself cultural. Rewarding a baby's attempt at speech with a womb-like hug acknowledges the experiential pleasure of the womb imagery. Images are webbed together not only with one another on a level, but among levels. A hug from a lover or friend recovers something of the womb, but is a great deal more as well. An adequate philosophy of culture would have to be able to articulate the kinds of relations and interacting modifications among levels of imagery. Freud's theory is so enlightening precisely because it recognizes this task and seriously addresses it.

The function of imagery is to select and organize data into the forms of experience. That it is selective means that it values the data, taking some to be important and the rest to be trivial. Of course this is too simple a view. Imagery values certain data by connecting them with other data so that they comprise a larger whole, which in turn can be valued in experience. Images as cultural forms are pre-selective valuations. A culture thus provides a valuative screen determining what can be experientially important. Cultures are fluid and "screen" perhaps is too static a metaphor. Cultural images are "taking-up mechanisms." Prior to conscious or even unconscious desire and deliberation, one's culture determines much of what will be taken up into experience, in what connections, and with what costs.

That culture is valuative emphasizes the distinction between the value a thing has in itself, or in its proper locus, and the value it has in the overall makeup of another thing, an interpreter, into which it is carried over. The value the thing has in the interpreter is a function of the roles it plays in the interpreter's life. From a pragmatic standpoint, there are many elementary carryovers that evolution has guaranteed to be constant. The pleasure a food contains had better be continuous with its real food-value, at least in enough foods enough of the time. In other areas of experience, the value for the interpreter can quite properly be quite different from the value of the thing in its proper locus. The interpreted value of the printed word is often far greater, even incommensurate with, the intrinsic material value of the ink on paper; this is different from the relation between real food value and gustatory enjoyment. In general, when the object of an interpretation is itself a representation, the role it plays in the interpreter's experience is related far more to its representative function than to its material reality. But this is not always the case. When a violent blow is a sign to "keep out," the whole issue of whether to trespass might be far less important than the reaction to the physical trauma itself. There is no purely formal answer to the question in any given case of whether the value carried over from the thing into the valuation of the thing is the right value. The carryover is qualified by the content of the culture at hand. Thc culture determine the array of meaningful respects in which an object can be interpreted or valued.

Although much of experience might be imaginative play, much also is interpretive; that is, assertive or assumptive of assertions. Within interpretation, the function of culture is to provide a ready selection of respects in which objects can be interpreted. Specific languages and particular purposes make further selections among the cultural options. But culture provides the first cut. Arctic cultures can interpret snow with respect to many different kinds, whereas most temperate zone cultures interpret snow as having only the few kinds skiers distinguish. Therefore, among the most important things to understand about a given culture is the array of respects in which it makes it possible to interpret the world. This is a technical way of saying the cultures give us ways of valuing the world. But in the cosmological scheme to be developed here, valuing is not mere projection. In fact, it is not projection at all. It is modification or qualification of the value the objects have in their proper places. Indeed, the process of qualification, here and in the biological, semiotic, and purposive spheres, is what constitutes the difference between the set of things to be interpreted and the separate reality of the interpreter. Human beings grasp things insofar as they can be carried over into their biological make up and into their culture.

Because culture is involved in a causal interactive process among people and the things they interpret, it is constantly in subtle modification itself, sometimes in unsubtle crisis. When a civilization finds its cultural imagery in crisis, the feared result is not just that mistakes or immoral abuse of things will be made. The fear is that the world will be lost. For the world cannot be possessed in the first place without a culture to provide valuative forms of imagination. To be without a culture is to take nothing up into experience. Culture is an indispensable instrument of participation in the world. Its loss would not return civilized people to savagery. It would deprive them of the capacity to participate in the world at all, even to have a world.

III. SEMIOTIC PARTICIPATION

It might seem that participation in semiotic systems is merely a subclass of cultural participation, and in many respects it is. But it is the subclass that defines interpretation *per se*; interpretation is intentional behavior employing semiotic systems as its essential medium. Human interpretation employs representations, and semiotics is the study of representations or human signs.

As has been suggested several times, most current theories of semiotics overstress language as the paradigmatic system. The interesting philosophic question, at this primitive stage of semiotic study, is what the array of different systems might look like. How do language systems relate to gestural systems for indicating emotional attitude, social roles, etc.? How do artifactual representations such as street signs relate to vision and behavior as well as to words? These are all crucial questions when semiotics is studied not as specialized linguisitics but as a crucial medium of human participation in the world. In the philosophic context of semiotic participation, the heavy use of any paradigmatic system is largely counter-productive. We need not the unifying themes, of which we already have too many generalized from language, but an assay of the diversity of semiotic systems.

Participation, of course, is not merely playing a role as defined by such a system. More actively, participation is using the system for contextually larger purposes, a use which then plays back to affect the system. Thus a participationist study of semiotics will emphasize the causal connections of the systems and their individual representation with the rest of culture, nature, and purpose. As Peirce argued, all signs are in the process of growth (some imperceptibly slowly). Human representations and their semiotic connections evolve as the systems are causally affected and effective in the larger contexts of life and society. Because any representation whatsoever, and any systematic network in which it might be connected, is in jeopardy of change because of the larger causal context, it is safe to say that any representation is metaphorical. "Literal" representation is merely representation in a system that is relatively stable, and the stability is only relative. Most representations acquire new connotations with use, connotations that can affect their syntactic as well as their semantic properties. Rigidly codified representation is a limiting case of metaphor.

In a study of semiotics as a participational medium, the interesting questions go far beyond the code-character of systems to issues of the development of codification, and of the breakdown of codes. What are the kinds of causal interaction involved in bringing only vaguely related representations to a more strictly codified form? What are the conditions that lead to the degeneration of codes into different codes or into dissociated or empty representations?

The field of issues lying under these questions is constituted by the question of causality relative to natural things, to human actions, and to representations. Here is another angle from which the necessity of a non-Cartesian theory of causation is obvious. The French tradition of semiotics and of structuralism is faithfully Cartesian. It will be important in Division IV to base the semiotic discussion on cosmological consideration of the sort that will be explored in Divisions II and III. Division IV will indeed develop rudiments of a causally grounded theory of representations and representing. Precisely because of the need for an appropriate philosophy of nature, that discussion is best postponed until the cosmology of Divisions II and III can be developed.

IV. PURPOSIVE PARTICIPATION

Participation as purposive activity integrates the other dimensions of participation so as to individuate people and groups. As Josiah Royce claimed (1899), purposive action is the way to concrete individuality. A human being has many parts, many of which are only indirectly and loosely coordinated. Purposive action puts these into definite order, whether the purpose itself is vague or explicit, conscious or unconscious, focal or of a background character. Of course, the purposes especially related to interpretation, those aiming at truth, or deception, or advantage, are of interest regarding the ways by which we participate in them. But the topic at hand is how reality is engaged by purposive behavior generally, for any kind of purpose can establish qualifications for the carryover of value.

The integrative function of purpose is especially important for a naturalistic perspective that recognizes the quasi-independence of biological subsystems and of causal vectors that pass through individuals. The structures essential to humanity are not "naturally given" but achieved through social and individual processes, and in jeopardy of being dissolved. Attaining to the level of purposive behavior, many new dimensions of integration are possible.

Participation in the world is both a necessary condition for and a by-product of purposive behavior. Without the biological continuities, there could be no actual participative behavior. Without the engagement given by imagination, there would be no purposive participation. Without the semiotic representation, there would be no distancing of oneself from the world so that participation rather than immediate enjoyment would be possible. On the other hand, without purposive behavior, biological action would be merely reaction, cultural imagination would be mere definition of roles, and symbolic representation would be mere play of signs. Purposive behavior is required to make the other dimensions of participation human in the ways we ordinarily think of them.

A discussion of purposive behavior must wait for a developed theory of intentionality, to come in chapter 15. At this point, however, it is helpful to recall that the pragmatists, especially John Dewey, elaborated a comprehensive theory of participation, interpreted as purposive (Smith, 1978). Dewey, of course, distinguished between doing and having, between acting and enjoying or suffering. Purposive behavior is not the whole of life. But the participative dimensions of having and enjoying, those elements that are not sheer immediacy, come from the fact that having and enjoying are modifications (modes, in Spinoza's sense) of ongoing purposive processes.

Perhaps Dewey's greatest contribution was to show in phenomenological detail how our purposes intrinsically aim at being purposes worth having. That is, just as we should conform our interpretations to the nature of the things interpreted, so we should form our purposes to intend what ought to be intended, what is most worthwhile. Pragmatism recognized that a purely voluntaristic conception of purpose, a conception that identifies the worth of a goal by the fact it is the object of purpose, is a contradiction in terms. Goals are not fixed orientations. They cannot be thought of as functions programmed into a computer. They are frames of purposive activity that itself is constantly seeking improvement in clarity, relevance, and sensitivity. Therefore, a theory of purpose depends on a theory of natural value, and of the carryover of value into an interpreter. The content interpreted constitutes the raw material, as it were, for the interpreter's own proper value, and the question is how that raw material is modified as it moves from its own proper place to its place in the interpreter. A successful theory of purpose demands an axiological theory of causation.

Dewey clearly saw that causation, as it concerns human activity, cannot be of the Cartesian sort. More than anyone else of his time, he drew out the phenomenology of human causal interactions with nature and society. But he failed to thematize causality theoretically. In his anxiety to remain relevant to the affairs of human beings, he avoided the commitment to develop a theory of causal categories, and it is ironic that he criticized Whitehead for doing so. His criticism (1984a, pp. 375-381) of *Process and Reality* was that it is just too hard to understand. Whitehead's own theory of causation, though a good start, does not go far enough. To advance beyond Dewey's sense of participation, to be more nuanced than assuming all dimensions of participation into purposive behavior, it is necessary to develop a subtler technical theory of causation.

If any single conclusion stands out from the previous diagnostic, critical, and exploratory chapters, it is that interpretation is not the topic of a mere essay. An essay assumes that its context, resources, and methods are pretty much given and understood, and it works these into an answer to its topic question. With regard to interpretation, all these are called into question, suggesting both that interpretation is a pivotal topic of our time, and that our time is philosophically confused and inadequate.

The previous discussion has indicated many of the angles that need to be developed in order to make good its claims, and one purpose of this chapter has been to pull these together into a helpful explanation of the outline of the rest of the book. Another and deeper purpose is to objectify the topic of a philosphy of interpretation in order to understand something of the shape of our philosophic situation. Because interpretation is such a central topic, what philosophy needs to do in order to address it reveals much about what philosophy needs to do generally. This book pursues only one approach to the topic of interpretation. That approach itself asserts that an indefinite number of interpretations of any philosophical topic can be given, each with its own value. Therefore, the situation for philosophy is doubtless far more complicated than expressed here. At the very least it is not less complicated.

The proposal is that reality can be recovered as a measure of the truth of our interpretations, and of our lives guided by interpretation, through the cultural adoption of a conception of thinking founded on valuation. The form of cognition in mathematical physics and its analogues in other "value free" sciences is an abstraction leaving out both felt values and imaginatively and hypothetically conceived values. The universality and elegance of the ideas resulting from that abstraction may justify, in certain contexts, the selective elimination of the valuational elements of experience. But reflective understanding of those contexts, and of the justification, requires a kind of thinking different enough from the model of modernity as to be explicitly valuational. Interpretation is an axiological process, to be understood with an axiological philosophy.

The general axiological hypothesis about interpretation is the following. Accepting something like Peirce's triadic theory of interpretation, truth is to be undestood as the carryover of value from the object interpreted into the interpretive experience, as qualified (1) by the biological nature of the interpreters, (2) by the respects in which the interpretation is made, which bears the culture's weighting of the importance of data, (3) by the form of the representations used, especially the systematic or code nature of the representations, and (4) by the purposes and intentional values guiding the interpretation.

Truth is thus not primarily a carryover of form, as in the Aristotelian tradition, but of value. Form is the means by which value is embodied, and the embodying forms might be different for object and interpretation. The crucial philosophical questions have to do with understanding the qualifications of value involved in the carryover. What happens to the value of a physical object, a mountain range, for instance, when truly carried over into the representations of a linguistic description, a description meaningful in a culture that interprets mountains in certain respects but not others, a description contrived for some human purpose such as sharing the enjoyment of the mountains' beauty?

It is one thing to define truth as the properly qualified carryover of value from object to interpretation. It is quite another to establish procedures and criteria to determine whether the definition is fulfilled in a particular case. Roughly speaking, the axiological hypothesis is pragmatic. That is, we test for truth by seeing whether experience positively or negatively reinforces our estimations of the values of things. But unlike the general drift of American pragmatism, the axiological hypothesis cultivates methods of distancing our interpretations from their objects while engaging them, holding reality off as a measure of our claims for truth. We should ask less whether reality conforms to our expectations than whether our interpretations, with their natural forms, purposes, respects of selection, and signs, are faithful to reality. The criteriological focus is on the integrity of the realities and our interpretive faithfulness to them. A crucial component of the theory of interpretation is a theory of the modalities of time. Lacking a sophisticated theory of time, pragmatism found itself easily accounting for the interpretation of the future but in some pain with regard to the past and present. A theory of time is necessary to understand "carryover" of value.

Explicitly pursuing truth in the axiological sense in intellect, morals, and the enjoyment and practice of life, automatically forces a distinction between the real world and the imaginatively formed interpretation of it at hand. The question of truth is always one of carryover of value from the former to the latter. The former might not have imaginative form, but still would have value. That the reality does not itself have imaginative form does not mean that it cannot be imaged, and through the image interpreted. The question of truth is then whether the value is carried through into the imaginative interpretation. Of course, whether that is true in a particular case must be determined by inquiry which also has imaginative form. Each of those inquiring interpretations is subject to inquiry regarding its truth, and there is no hopping outside imaginative form to an unimaginative form embodied, say, in a mountain range. It is necessary therefore to sketch a cosmology showing how unimaginative things like mountain ranges embody values in their forms and how these values can be carried over into interpretive assertions. The cosmology itself is an hypothesis, one which, if plausible, shows how human truth-seeking can in fact be faithful to real things that do not all have the imaginative forms of experience.

It is no solution to the dissolution of the sense of reality associated with the triumph of interpretation, to suggest that we can have intentional, cognitive, or intuitive access to things outside of experience. The solution rather is to legitimate our deep feelings that realities do measure us by their values and our responses. We do not feel realities as scientific forms, but as embodied values presenting themselves and laying claim upon our responses. The forms we deal with in interpretation embody values, in better or worse ways. "Feeling" cannot be left as a merely intentional or epistemological notion, however. It must be a causal notion, for it must be in natural continuity with the causal processes connecting real things with each other, including interpreters who transform the causal products into the imaginative forms of experience. The separation of logic and thinking as intentional away from the other processes of nature has been a modern mistake exacerbating our inability to conceive the continuities from non-thinking nature with intelligent human life. The axiology of thinking thus requires an axiological philosophy of nature.

DIVISION TWO

Philosophic Foundations for a New Common Sense: An Axiological Metaphysics

Preliminary Remarks

Paradoxical as it is, often the most practical ideas are the most basic and abstract ones, ideas saying very little that is special to any particular situation. Of the ideas investigated in the four chapters of this Division—identity, being, value, and harmony—all contribute to a comprehensive notion of reality. Reality is more basic and abstract than any of the four, being their sum in a sense, and yet each of the five is ingredient in just about any other idea that can be used, or in any thing to which reference can be made, or in any functional part of behavior. The paradox disappears with the realization that, because the most basic and abstract ideas are embodied in all other ideas, the subtlest nuances of their abstract character ramify throughout everything else. Everything of which one conceives, even a thing one conceives to be non-real, is shaped in conception by one's conception of reality. Whether or not one's metaphysical conceptions are articulate and explicit, still they structure the common sense supposed and used in experience.

What a fundamental practical disaster it is, then, when a culture's basic, abstract philosophical ideas are confused or inappropriate to its life, all the more disastrous when the culture is in serious transition. Consequently, speculative, ponderous, self-reflexive, metaphysical philosophy has the ongoing social role of emergency relief. There's something humorous about this. Surely the disabilities of lame philosophy are not practical disasters in the sense of geologic catastrophies, plagues, or barbarians. Nevertheless, the basic philosophic ideas, functioning as common sense, determine how we take the catastrophies, plagues, and barbarians; they determine in fact how we identify events as disasters in the first place.

The study of the most basic and abstract ideas, the ideas that apply to everything, is metaphysics. As the term has been used in Western philosophy since ancient Greece, metaphysics is the development of the big ideas that are presupposed by all other ideas, by all practical fields of endeavor, by all efforts in arts and letters, and by all the sciences. Perhaps it should be said that metaphysics is about ideas. Rather, it is the development of ideas that allow us to apprehend and interpret the most basic and universal traits of reality, what Dewey called "the generic traits of existence." Metaphysics is the attempt to get the biggest of the big pictures. Without the attempt, irrespective of success, a culture fails to be alert to the questions of greatest application.

In the history of the West, the word "metaphysics" has been used somewhat loosely, often encompassing what is called here "philosophical cosmology" or "philosophy of nature." Space, time, causation, and motion have often been called metaphysical topics, and often value or goodness has been excluded from metaphysics. The distinction between metaphysics and philosophy of nature or cosmology is observed here both because Aristotle distinguished them and because in the particular philosophic view to be developed, the notions of space, time, causation, and motion are specifications of the ideas of identity, being, value, and harmony, not the other way around. Charles Hartshorne (1962) distinguishes metaphysics from cosmology by saying that the former is the study of the traits that would be true in any possible world, whereas the latter deals with what is general in this world. To distinguish any possible worlds from this one is very difficult, however. Alfred North Whitehead made no hard and fast distinction between metaphysics and cosmology, calling his great *Process and Reality* a cosmology, but usually referring to other philosophers' alternatives as metaphysics.

Only in the modern era of the West has metaphysics been identified by a method, usually a method aimed at having a certainty presupposed by other ideas and methods and itself presupposing nothing else. The methodological preoccupations of Descartes, discussed here in Chapter Two, perhaps account for this modern approach, although surely there is no identifiable method *common* to, say, Descartes, Spinoza, and Leibniz. Descartes' method was to break complex things into simples requiring no further analysis, and then to reconstruct the original. Spinoza's method was modeled on geometry, intending to be axiomatic and deductive. Leibniz was a brazen hawker of brilliant ideas, turning each set of ideas into well-formed formulas so that he could represent them as logically coercive, but fully aware of the fact that different conceptions give rise to different systems.

In the history of Western philosophy, there have been extraordinarily diverse approaches to metaphysics, where "metaphysics" means the disciplined development of the biggest of big pictures. Plato employed the dialectical play of alternate hypotheses, of myths and likely stories. Aristotle's method was to generalize observation and common sense, and then rationalize the findings into a coherent and perspicuous whole. Augustine's method was to borrow freely from Plato, Aristotle, and their successors to rationalize a vision of a cosmos whose heart came from his religious convictions. Thomas and Scotus interpreted their wildly diverse experiences, with philosophical implications, by means of a deeply embedded Platonic and Aristotelian intellectual world. Hegel's system aimed at the evolution of maximum comprehension with minimal presupposition at each stage. Whitehead's was a metaphysics of rationalized empirical generalization. Peirce's metaphysics was guided by a search for the most abstract and general, Dewey's by a search for the presuppositions required for improving practice.

Indian and Chinese philosophies have metaphysical scope as broad as the great Western systems. The ancient Six Orthodox Schools of India had tightly formulated universal doctrines; the systems of Sankara, Ramanuja, and Abhinava Gupta are comparable to Thomas, Spinoza, or Hegel. Mahayana Buddhism is the most metaphysical of all religious traditions, and Neo-Confucianism, like Neo-Taoism, has been concerned with giving disciplined expression to the most generic traits of existence. Methods in Asia have included most of those employed in the West, often with an emphasis on giving expression to transformed consciousness, to the suppositions of social practice, or to profound experiences of participation in nature and human community.

The lesson to be drawn from these remarks on method is that method is nothing special to metaphysics, and attacks on a particular metaphysical method are not much about metaphysics and probably don't generalize to other metaphysical positions. Metaphysics is the attempt to formulate what is most basic in the world, of which other things are specifications, or to formulate ideas that are presupposed by other claims to truth. It has nothing to do with being more certain than anything else, or with being the foundation for other disciplines, or with grounding other enterprises.

It is necessary to make these defensive remarks in order to forestall the cheap shots many philosophers take at metaphysics, calling it foundationalist, totalitarian, and every other bad name. Whereas there are all sorts of valid objections to particular metaphysical systems, there can be no valid *a priori* objection to the attempt to develop a disciplined approach to the big picture that withstands critical analysis and deserves to form common sense.

The four chapters in this Division deal with basic ideas and are self-explanatory. The ideas are, as mentioned, identity, being, value, and harmony.

5

Identity

I. THE PROBLEM OF IDENTITY

The general purpose of systematic metaphysical reflection is to investigate the nature of reality and to clarify it with speculative conceptions. Three main topics or philosophical problematics are important to this purpose, phrased as questions. (1) What is identity, or what is it to be a thing? (2) What is the connection among things such that they all can be said to be, or what is being? That question can also be phrased in terms of how things can be many and one at once, or how there can be unity in diversity and diversity in unity. (3) What are the most basic categories of reality? The goals for a theory of reality are to give answers to these and their subsidiary questions.

Plato began the Western speculative enterprise with the intuition or hunch that reality is best defined in terms of identity. A thing is real insofar as it is not nothing and also not something else. It is itself. What is "itselfness?" Determinate identity. Plato added to this happy insight a less happy rider; namely, that identity must be static and unchanging. He reasoned that a changing thing is on the way from one identity to another, and concluded that changing things are not completely real and that the only complete realities are "ideas" that give changing things their determinations. Yet, as Aristotle saw clearly, there is an identity to a changing thing. Change can be identified by its own identity. Therefore, we need a conception of identity abstract enough to encompass both unchanging and changing identities. If we had such a conception, it would be appropriate to approach the issue of reality through the analysis of identity.

At the very least, to be real a thing has to have identity, to be determinate in some respect although not necessarily in all respects. For the reasons just mentioned, an account of identity or determinateness must be completely abstract. That is, it must abstract from any difference that might distinguish two things or kinds of reality, since both would need identity to be different. Therefore, we cannot define identity by explaining particular kinds of reality, for instance material objects, objects over against subjects, objects defined in terms of subjects, or things such as forms that maintain identity regardless of time.

Because natural science has remarkably interesting things to say about the nature of material things, it is tempting to believe that the identity it describes is identity as such, or at least is paradigmatic for identity. The materialism of our age feeds this temptation. But the temptation jumps too quickly to a particular kind of identity: if the claim is that identity is only material, there must be some meaning of identity that applies to the kinds to which reality is denied, or that are claimed to be analogous to material objects.

It is also tempting but premature to define identity in terms of objects standing over against subjects, in accord with the objectivism of the age. We might say that the identity of a real thing is what it is in itself to which our knowledge should conform; subjective knowers themselves can be conceived as objects to other knowers on this view. The difficulty with this approach is that identity as objectivity makes explicit internal reference to some other identity for the subject. That subjects can be objectified does not help the definition of objectivity in terms of the intrinsic orientation of subjects.

Recognizing this difficulty, transcendental philosophy takes the bold move of defining objects not as over against but as constituted by the conditions under which they can be over against subjects. The power in this move is that it can describe the difference between real objects of ideas (those that conform to the transcendental conditions) and merely imagined objects of ideas (those that don't); this gives a straightforward meaning to real identity. The weakness is that there must be some kind of identity, and hence reality, to the conditions themselves, and to the activity noting the conditions and their application. Ironically, transcendental philosophy becomes self-referential too quickly and hence can't stand outside itself long enough to explain itself.

In the face of these difficulties with identity, some thinkers reduced identity to the contents of the subject. Early in the modern period, subjectivity, or skepticism about objective knowledge, established itself as a resort for disenchantment with the vaunted certainties of the new science. Some kinds of subjectivism, those associated with idealism, were by no means ostensibly skeptical. In fact, some of the confident certainties of the Absolute Idealists fed the reaction of skepticism. The fundamental idealist strategy, however, was one of retreat from claims to know nature apart from the knowing. Given the failure of Kant's transcendental philosophy to give a properly cognitive place either to the reality of the transcendental conditions or to the transcendental knower, the idealists took the synthesizing activity of the transcendental knower as an account of concrete ego, or egos, and affirmed that the world plus the conditions of intelligibility plus the knowledge of all that, can be accounted for in terms of the knowledge of all that. Or, if there remains uncertainty in the face of relativism, "all that" can be accounted for in terms of the will or disposition to think that.

Materialism, objectivism, transcendentalism, and subjectivism are not merely briliant philosophic strategies of modern Western philosophy. They each express fundamental implications of the metaphysical foundations of modern science, implications that are also and more seriously expressed in culture. Materialism can be expressed as a clean theory, as it is by J. J. C. Smart, for instance. But its cultural expression quickly comes down to practices based on the view that material goods are the only ones that count. Objectivism is not only a theory, but a dimension of culture that takes the world to be alien to human life—not a context in which we move, but something defined over against human subjectivity. Materialist or non-materialistic, objectivist culture is pathetic alienated culture, literally pathetic because we are only moved by it, not engaged. The psychological result of objectivism is a narcissistic culture that oscillates between irrational self-deprecation regarding the non-objective life of intentionality and the irrational self-aggrandisement of an ego whose engagements with the world are too thin to provide a sense of real limits (see Cahoone, 1987).

Transcendentalism, the view that identity is given through transcendental conditions, is the parent of misplaced relativism. It moves from the recognition that all knowledge is mediated by categories to the mistaken view that objects of knowledge are constituted by categories, and that categories are all collected into relativistic systems. The effect of such relativism on moral and religious life has been disastrous, depriving both of any claim to truth when the only justified inference is that no system is absolute or complete truth. The failures of misplaced relativism are answered by subjectivism: We are not what we think, and since we have no good reason to think one thing rather than another, we are what we will. This of course is deadly boring. But worse, it can't be lived. Although we may identify with the subjective aspects of life, they are interwoven with so many dimensions that limit the subjective that in fact we cheat. Cheating on subjectivity, however, leads to bad faith, and our subjectivist culture shivers at the bitterness of bad faith's guilt.

Perhaps some of the cultural as well as philosophic implications of modern science can be short-circuited if we take another start from Plato. Platonism, following Parmenidean leads, defines reality or being as the identity which does not change, which simply is itself, for instance the form of being "larger than". This is a clear strategy, and its adherents often have the courage to say that things which do change identity are unreal, or partially unreal, or unreal in a sense (see Brumbaugh, 1984). But of course the interesting problems of life are those intimately bound up with the concrete changing processes of experience, as illustrated by the topics of Plato's dialogues: courage, piety, justice, education, statesmanship, and the like. The Platonic purpose in referring to timeless forms or realities is to throw light on the nature of the temporal. To distinguish the temporal from the timeless is to assert a more general sense of identity than that expressed in the latter. This is so even if temporality is some sort of compromise between complete and self-sufficient reality on the one hand and the forces of disidentity on the other. We shall return to Plato's point below, only noting now that it is fruitless to define identity by any special differentia such as changelessness or self-reflexive immediacy.

The account of identity needed for a theory of reality adequate for our culture must be so abstract that it applies to any possible kinds of identity. Put another way, it must be wholly vague with respect to what kinds of identity there are. Subsequent inquiry, presupposing but not presupposed by the theory of identity, can establish the kinds of identity. With respect to reality, anything that has identity is real according to the kind of identity that it has. Identity, or the conditions that make something determinate, is the topic of the most abstract philosophic inquiry, and it applies to anything to which one can refer. Given traditional usage, it makes sense to call the philosophic study of this "metaphysics."[1]

The considerations raised in previous chapters suggest that a theory of identity needs to account for how a thing can have its own integrity while being in intrinsic connection with other things. That is, part of the identity of a thing consists in its being determinate with respect to other things. For the sake of a name, this can be called the "requirement of identity in difference." If this requirement is met, it will be possible to characterize reality in such a way as to acknowledge a plurality of really distinct things that nevertheless are connected with each other by means of whatever relations inquiry discovers. The alternatives are either a monism that gives the lie to our experience of differences, or an atomism of disconnected things that makes it seem as if all relations were imposed by our minds, which would be false imposition.

A more specific consideration arising from the previous discussion is that the nature of connections between real things must allow for the specific kind of connection characteristic of the relation between real things and real knowers of those things. We have seen the need to account for knowledge as itself a kind of natural structure, with both object and knower existing as parts of a larger nature. In this context, our account should show how objects can be connected with knowers in such a way as to be known. The theory should account for how objects maintain their integrity so as not to be swallowed up in the knowers nor be transformed into mere representations. At the same time, the account should not suppose essential elements that ought to be known but cannot be because they must remain external to the knowing connection. This requirement, which cannot be met in full until the end of our study of interpretation, can be called the "requirement of ontological knowledge," ontological because of knowing the whole being of things. Without ontological knowledge, there is the danger that knowledge will be only of our representations of things, of the contents of our own minds. And so reality would be lost.

II. IDENTITY IN METAPHYSICS AND COSMOLOGY

Plato suggested in several places that there are three basic categories: Sameness, Difference, and Being. As argued above, an account of identity would express sameness in its self-identity, and difference in its other-relatedness. Being or reality is that which has both self-identity and other-relatedness, sameness and difference. Since sameness and difference are different, how do we account for their connection, or "sameness?" A different version of the question has to do with the ground of the difference between two distinct but connected things. The connecting features of diverse things provide some continuity between them. But the self-identity each has over against the other is excluded from the connecting continuities. How are those self-identities together in some other sense so that they can provide the real differences between the things? This is the old problem of the "one and many." Because of its intimate involvement in an account of identity as such, the solution one presupposes to the problem of the one and many colors every response to other things or to oneself.

Diversity is as problematic as unity. On the one hand is the cultural temptation to solipsism, to the view that nothing but our ideas measures our ideas. On the other hand is the modern common sense view of atomism, that things are different in isolation, and are connected only by the human imposition of mental patterns. What is needed, as seen above, is an account of diversity that exhibits real differences as co-constitutive with real connections. The problem of unity is thus transformed. Unity is not something over against diversity, but a condition of its possibility.

How can unity be a condition for the possibility of diversity? It is tempting to think of a unity for a diversity as some determinate unifying thing. For instance, it might be a property common to all the diverse things; but how would that property be unified with the other properties? By some other property, *ad infinitum*? Or unity might be an encompassing form of which the diverse things are proper parts, a perfect wholeness. But then we must ask whether the unity adds something to the diverse things that they lack without it. If the answer is yes, then we need some other account of the unity of the diversity with the unity. If the answer is no, then it remains a mystery how the proper parts of the unity are unified. The unity of a diversity, it would seem, must be something that is not itself determinately over against the diversity, or even determinate itself among the diversity. To the extent that high-level structures are determinate, they cannot provide the appropriate ontological unity. To the extent they are indeterminate (one thinks of Plotinus' One or the Indian Brahman without Qualities), they haven't yet explained how diversity is possible.

For metaphysical purposes, it might be satisfactory simply to account for self-identity and other-relatedness, noting that these two elements are harmonized within any identity, and noting as well that the diverse self-identities of different things are together in some ontological sense. But for purposes of knowing the world as the measure of our selective responses, what Heidegger called the Ontological Question must be pressed. We need an account of the One for the Many, of the Being that all beings have. There are two reasons for this.

First and most important, without knowing the Being of beings, we cannot know the otherness of beings. Hence the normativeness of the others is lost and our responses have no measure. Put positively, since Being is the condition for diversity, to know things other than ourselves, we should understand Being. The great religions have seen that this is the tendency of their queries, and the problem of the Ontological Question is indeed a religious one.

Second, and most insistent, diversity or complexity is what most wants an account. Wherever diverse things are together, forming a complex situation, it is legitimate to ask how they got that way. Whitehead called this the "ontological principle." It is the dialectical principle driving science and every other kind of inquiry, and many sorts of answers are appropriate in different contexts. The question becomes philosophically pressing when it is applied to the peculiar complex of "the world" and "the world's explanation." Suppose the explanation is a set of first principles. What is the explanation of the complex connection of the first principles to what they explain? Indeed, how do we account for the complexity of first principles at all? Obviously a different account of this kind of complexity is called for from those used to account for complexities within the world. Some philosophers, including Whitehead, decline to consider the bottom-line complexities as calling for an account. They assume that if first principles are really first, then it makes no sense to ask for a further account. But the account is called for not by the primacy of the first principles but by their complexity and by their relation to what they explain. That they are *first* principles means only that what can explain them will not be more principles. The explanation must be of a different sort (Neville: 1980, ch. 3). The study of these matters is generally called ontology because it inquires into the explanation of the being of things, not of the nature of particular beings.

Charles Hartshorne (1962, ch. 12) defines metaphysics as the study of what would be true in any possible world—determinate identity as such.[2] In contrast to such completely abstract metaphysics, we can call more specific study of what is real in this world, "cosmology." Physical cosmology is basic natural science. Philosophical cosmology is a somewhat more universal study relating physical cosmology to kinds of reality science might not address, asking questions about how the kinds of reality can be systematized. Philosophical cosmology is important for a naturalistic theory of interpretation and will be developed in this book through subsequent discussions of value, time, causation, and more particular issues. Indeed, the payoff for this study will be a philosophical cosmology that shows interpretation to be a special and interesting part of nature.

For the purposes of a theory of reality supplying common sense for culture, however, we need a primary cosmology, an identification of the most basic kinds of things to look for as real. This is more specific than an abstractly metaphysical account of identity, or an ontological theory of being. Yet it is more abstract than a model of the processes of the cosmos. Stephen Pepper (1942) understood the drive for primary cosmology in the pursuit of "root metaphors." Whitehead (1978: Pt. I, ch. 2) appreciated the need for it in the defense of his Category of the Ultimate. The categories defining his Category of the Ultimate are diverse (Many, One, and Creativity), incapable of being wholly defined in terms of one another, and yet undefinable individually out of relation to one another. Any particular reality would have to exhibit the primary cosmology, and thence to be definable in terms of all the basic categories. Although Whitehead's own candidates for the Category of the Ultimate might not be ultimate enough for the job, we will need to take up the job in order to articulate a common sense for reality. The sections that follow will provide formal, theoretical and dialectical accounts of identity; chapter 6 will extend that account to the ground of diverse identities in being, and of a primary cosmology.

Let us develop the initial suggestion that to be real is to be determinate. By characterizing determinateness, it will become apparent what the suggestion means and why it has some plausibility. To be determinate is to have identity, and there are two aspects to this. On the one hand, an identity is determinate with respct to other things, conditioned by them or conditioning them. This aspect of identity corresponds to the requirement of identity in difference, and is the source of the connections among things. On the other hand, an identity must have its own essence, or essential features. This is its self-identity. The categories of conditional and essential features constitute these two aspects of identity.

III. DIFFERENCE: CONDITIONAL FEATURES

For an identity to be what it is, it has to be that in contrast to being something else; this rather than that. By virtue of this contrast, it is also in contrast to a counter-factual state of non-being. Because it is something rather than something else, it is something rather than nothing; and if it is to be something rather than nothing, it must be some determinate thing rather than something else.

The above seems to be a fairly simple point, almost obvious once expressed. Yet it separates all the remarks that follow from it from positivism. Most generally stated, positivism is the thesis that a thing is simply itself, what it "positively" is. A thing can be "posited" by itself; for instance, as either filling or not filling a moment of time, as Kant argued. Descartes' conception of elementary simples posited by God in free creation is the paradigm case of positivism. The Cartesian positivist principle, that whatever can be conceived apart can exist apart, is surprising not for its direct assertion, but for its supposition that anything can be conceived apart. The "simple point" of the above paragraph is that things' identities consist in part in what they are not, and hence to conceive them is to conceive them in various kinds of distinction from other things. An alternative to positivism has to introduce some kind of negativity or nothingness—a "not being this other thing." For Spinoza, as for Plotinus before him, "all determination is by negation." For Hegel, any determinate state of affairs is the result of negating and transcending some other states of affairs. Our theory has to give an account of the ontological function of negativity in order to account for the determinateness of relevant differences.

Where an identity is wholly irrelevant to something else, or is undecided about several potential relevancies, it is to that extent indeterminate. A determinate identity does not have to be determinate in all respects, although it must be determinate with respect to some things if it is in contrast to something else and nothing.

The phrase "in contrast to something else and nothing" contains an ambiguity behind which lurks the fundamental ontological theme of reality. To address this, we will look first at the contrast with "something else," and then at the contrast with "nothing."

For a thing to be in determinate contrast with some other determinate thing is for it to have features relative to that thing that make it different. (The notion of "having features" is used informally for now, and means whatever common sense supposes when we attribute features, characters, aspects, attributes, roles, or anything else to the subject matter of discourse; subsequently "having features" will be characterized formally in terms of "containing components within one's harmony.") Since these features are the ways things condition one another so as to be determinate with respect to each other, they can be called "conditional features."

Although being a cause of another thing is one example of conditioning whereby things are mutually determinate, "condition" is used in a broader sense than "cause." A thing is a condition for, or conditions another thing, if it enters into the conditioned thing's identity in any way whatsoever, through whatever mediations. Since the conditioned thing includes the condition as but part of its own identity, it must itself be different from the conditioning thing. An important kind of conditioning is displacement; that is, the conditioned thing is structured to fit around the condition, displaying as it were the form of the absence of the condition, as a pillow is conditioned by the head, or a car's path in traffic by the other cars. Another important kind of conditioning is logical or formal, as when one term defines in part another term. The metaphysical use of the notion of conditioning is so abstract here as to be vague with respect to the kinds of things there are that might condition one another. The notion is vague, for instance, with respect to whether pure forms are real on their own terms or only as intended by minds; it is vague still with respect to any account of how an antecedent causes a consequent. Certain of this vagueness will be turned to precision in later chapters where relevant to the study; other aspects will be left vague, which is perfectly acceptable for the metaphysical purpose at hand.

Abstractly put, a thing is conditioned by another thing, has conditional features from it, when there is a respect in which the condition bears upon the conditioned. Expressed in the language of interpretation, the condition in a conditioned thing stands as a sign for the conditioning thing in the conditioning respect. How the conditioned thing integrates the condition within itself is its interpretation of the conditioning thing. Or if that expression suggests too much "agency" for the generality required of the concept of conditioning, we can say that the role of the condition in the overall nature of the conditioned thing is that thing's interpretation of the conditioning thing. That a thing has conditional features means that it is an interpretation of what conditions it. Crucial to determinateness as such is the fact that a determinate thing is an interpretation of other determinate things with respect to which it is determinate.

That determinateness as such involves an interpretive relation among mutually determinate things establishes the cosmological universality of interpretive structure. By "cosmological" I mean simply the aspect of things in which their relations to one another are constituted by the ways in which they condition one another. This is a specification of the earlier definition of cosmology as the systematic features of this world (in contrast to the features necessary in any possible world for determinateness as such). The cosmological universality of interpretive structure is the crucial fulcrum for the argument that knowers whose interpretations have the experiential form of imagination can interpret natural things lacking imaginative form. It is the commonality of interpretive structure that provides the needed continuity. Interpretive structure is not actual human interpretation. This theory is not anthropomorphic, since human interpretation is the special kind that employs experiential forms of imagination; only people, so far as we know, have imaginative experience. There is no reason to believe that there is any experience in the eight ball's interpreting the cue ball by moving sharply to the side, to use Hume's example.

To sum up the argument of this section so far, a determinate thing contrasts with other determinate things when conditional features on both sides define the things in part in terms of one another in relevant respects. This is a cosmological contrast and is necessary for any determinateness at all. There can be no determinateness without a plurality of things related by conditional features.

It was mentioned above that the contrast a determinate thing has with another determinate thing makes it contrast also with nothingness, or the state of its own non-being. This is a different but related sense of "contrast," a sense close to the heart of the problem of reality. The determinate thing is something, not nothing, and to be real is precisely to be something. It is important not to hypostasize "nothing" as if it were a funny "other thing" in relation to which the determinate thing has cosmological contrast. Nothing does not condition determinate things. Most important, nothing is not real, it does not exist. But the reason it is not real is because in fact there are determinate things. Were there no determinate things (a situation we cannot conceive because the very structure of conceivability is a complex determinate thing, "the Dyad," as Plotinus called it), there would be nothing. This nothing would not have being or existence as if it were a something. It would be the situation merely of a lack of determinate somethings. Ontology, the study of Being as such, focuses on the difference, the ontological difference, between determinate beings, which are real, and nothing, which is not. The contrast between a thing's being something and nothingness is an ontological contrast. The Being of beings is what contrasts with nothingness.

How does this relate to the dyadic character of reality? It might be thought that the relation between a determinate thing and its counterfactual non-reality is a dyadic one. But as a relation, that would have to be determinate, and the relevant non-being would have to be a determinate conditioned term, which would be nonsense. Rather, the dyadic character of reality consists in a thing's being in contrast with other things, determinately what it is in contrast to those others.

The contrast with nothing is precisely the contingency of the dyad itself. Contingency is not another determinate thing, but what might best be called an ontological status. The meaning of contingency as an ontological status is a puzzle deep in the heart of ontology, to which we shall return in connection with the account of the self-identity of things.

IV. SELF-IDENTITY: ESSENTIAL FEATURES

It is inconceivable that a determinate thing could only be a set of conditional features. There are at least two basic reasons for this.

1. What could make the conditional features a set? Perhaps it could be argued that one of the conditional features itself is the organizing principle and force. But how does that feature relate to the other conditional features in the first place? Only by being located with the others in the determinate thing. Therefore a prior, or at least concomitant, organizing principle is required to relate the dominant conditional feature to the others. Now, it is possible that a conditional feature also functions as an organizing principle within the whole set, helping constitute the order of the assorted conditions. But if it does so, that feature has taken on the function of an essential feature. An essential feature values or determines (partially) the order of the conditional features so as to make them part of the identity of the conditioned thing. This reveals the functional character of the distinction

> between conditional and essential features: conditional features function to relate a thing to other things, essential features to order the conditional features into a self-identity.
>
> 2. If there were no essential character to the thing, its set of conditional features would reduce simply to the other things that condition it. That is, there would be no determinate thing, only the other things that would be potential conditions (and of course the other things need to be determined in contrast to things other than themselves, and hence by regress there could not even be the other things). If the other conditioning things by themselves antecedently fit together as a set, then they are interrelated quite apart from the determinate thing they are supposed to condition. For a conditioned determinate thing to be conceivable or real, it must have essential features in addition to conditional ones, an essence of its own.

The essential features do two (only apparently) different things. On the one hand, they provide an ontological locus or position for the conditional features, something for the other things to condition. Ontological position is an extraordinarily universal trait, of which spatio-temporal position or location is but one illustration. But spatio-temporal position is a good illustration: by virtue of its locus in an existential field, a determinate thing can be the recipient of antecedent causal forces and the initiator of conditioning effects extending to other spatio-temporal positions. On the other hand, the essential features order the conditional ones, integrating them into a definite character for the thing.

Order in this (as in most) contexts means valuing. The essential features select among the possible conditions some to be important in the conditioned thing and others to be relatively trivial. This selection consists in arranging the conditions according to forms or patterns. A pattern is a way of putting certain things together so that other things can be together as well, as I have argued in detail (Neville: 1981, Pt. II). Selective ordering is indeed the achievement of ontological position. By having an essential integration, determinate things have position. Like ontological position, ontological ordering is completely universal, far broader than the ordering that goes on in a spatio-temporal thing, which nevertheless provides a good illustration. A spatio-temporal thing has as its initial givens or potential conditions all the things that have occurred earlier. To become itself, the thing must integrate these conditions, eliminating some, giving dominance to others, and arranging the set in a determinate, probably hierarchical, pattern. This completed integration exhibits the place and date the determinate thing achieves relative to its antecedent conditions. The antecedents have determinate natures of their own that set limits to what the emerging spatio-temporal thing can do with them, including the spatio-temporal coordinates open to it. In a spatio-temporal thing, some essential features might be unique to a given moment, spontaneous as it were and therefore unpredictable within the limits determined by antecedents. Other essential features, that is, order-giving features, might be past conditions that function essentially; in these cases the features would be both conditional and essential relative to the moment. Similarly, essential features could derive from future conditions, functioning both essentially and conditionally. For an enduring individual such as a human being, with a personal character which grows and exists only through a thickness of time, but that is embodied and operative within each datable moment, it is necessary that the essential features include not only those of the local moment, but those conveying past character and future commitments. For things that are not spatio-temporal, such as patterns or logical forms, the essential features do not have temporal distinction, but rather are simply the factors that give valuational order and integrity to the conditional relations the things have to other things, for instance to related forms or to potential existential embodiments.

It is necessary that a determinate thing have both essential and conditional features, for the reasons that have been traced. Without essential features, the thing would not be distinct from the conditioning things, and nothing would provide the conditioned thing's own ordering of the conditional features. Without conditional features, the thing would have nothing for essential features to integrate and it would not be different from anything. In its most basic metaphysical character, a thing is a harmony of essential and conditional features, each necessary and neither more necessary than the other.

There is a temptation fostered by the Western tradition (but not the Chinese or Indian) to regard essential features as "the real thing," and the conditional features as mere accidents. Aristotle distinguished between necessary and non-necessary accidents, but still gave the palm of true identity to essence. The temptation, however, betrays a bias toward independent substances, toward isolatable things, eventually toward atomism. The account defended here requires an exact balance between defining them through their relations (conditional features) and defining them through their unique and ownmost features (the essential ones). Such an account is necessary in order to provide a further account of diversity within the world.

I remarked above that a determinate thing contrasts not only with other determinate things through its conditional features, but that it also contrasts in a peculiar way with its own non-being or nothingness. The essential features constitute the self-identity or self-referential being of a thing by virtue of which it stands over against nothingness. Because of this, the essential features can be construed as a kind of existential power, or expression of the power of being, in deference to the tradition that marks the fact that contingent being depends on a self-contained power asserting itself in the face of non-being. The essential features are expressions of the power of self-being. Nevertheless, precisely because their function is to order the conditional features, and because they themselves would be indeterminate without those conditional features to order, there is no priority to essential features. Only as harmonies of conditional and essential features do determine things contrast with one another and stand over against non-being.

Harmony. To say that determinate things are harmonies of essential and conditional features is to deny that their unity is some kind of determinate "third thing" over and above the features that integrate them. The "third thing" argument is typical of idealism, supposing that any two or more different things require yet another to give them position or relation relative to one another. The theoretical difficulty with the "third thing" argument is that the third thing itself must be determinate to do any relating that the essential and conditional features do not do by themselves; and if it is determinate, then all the apparatus of conditional and essential features is needed to establish a relation between the third thing and what it integrates, manifesting a vicious infinite regress. To be sure, some things are contained in others, and hierarchical patterns are common. But in these cases, the container is not put forward as the very identity of the contained things together. Rather, the things are harmonized among themselves, and the containment by a higher level reality is an additional contrast. To mark the fact that within harmonies things just fit together, they can be called *de facto* harmonies. (That they are *de facto* does not mean they lack value—as the next chapter shall argue, all harmonies have some value or other; perhaps their value is the best, the appropriate, or even *de jure* as well as *de facto.*)

The harmony of essential and conditional features can be described with Whitehead's term "contrast," which has already been used informally. A contrast is a togetherness wherein the components do not lose their identity but indeed manifest it in juxtaposition to one another. In a formal axiology it can be argued that the greater the diversity in a contrast, and the more complex the relations between the things contrasted, the greater the value (see Neville: 1981, ch. 3; and chapter 6 below).

The word "contrast" has already been used to indicate the metaphysical relation between two determinate things, and with the association of contrast with harmony it must now be admitted that the contrast or harmony of any two conditionally related things is itself a thing. Further within any given thing, the components harmonized, both essential and conditional, are themselves harmonies, and their own components are harmonies down and down. In most circumstances, the interesting question is what kind of harmony is involved: some harmonies are very tight, such as enduring substances, and others are bare, such as mere logical relation, or evanescent, such as purely accidental events. Most concrete, spatio-temporal affairs are complicated harmonies of many different kinds of harmonies. In the present circumstance of characterizing reality, however, it is necessary to stress that anything is real to the extent it has determinate identity, that determinate identity is both essentially itself and conditionally related to other identities, that all things determinate with respect to one another constitute further harmonies or things, and that with respect to reality, all things have ontological parity, are equally real.[3]

6

Being and Primary Cosmology

I. BEING AND THE ONTOLOGICAL GROUND OF REALITY

Suppose the claim that "reality is determinate identity" wears well, and that identity consists in a plurality of things contrasting with one another, each thing being a *de facto* harmony of essential and conditional features. Is this metaphysical pluralism self-explanatory? No, for there is a crucial connection not accounted for in the simple reference to harmony. Consider two things mutually related by conditional features; each has conditional features from the other, and thus is an interpretation of the other. Each contains the other, or some elements of the other, by virtue of the conditional features. But by definition, the essential features of the other remain outside; if the essential features too are contained, the other is just a proper part of the first thing, nothing independent enough to supply the needed contrast. The togetherness constituted by the conditional features can be called cosmological.

But how are the essential features of the two things together, since in principle they are outside the conditional relations? It might be suggested that the essential features of the two things don't need to be together at all, that the things are together only in conditional ways. This argument, however, overlooks the fact that the essential features of each are necesary for there to be any conditional features of either. There could be no conditioning relations without the whole harmonies of the different things, because the conditioning relations depend on the terms of the relation; and the terms are the determinate things as *de facto* harmonies of conditional and essential features. Therefore there must be a context in which the essential features of different things are together, a context that is ontologically more profound than the network of cosmological relations of the mutual conditions. Let us call this the "ontological context of mutual relevance." It is the most fundamental context in which things with their mutually uncommunicating essential features are together so as to be able to be harmonies of essential and conditional features in relation to one another. Without acknowledging the ontological context of mutual relevance we would have to abandon the metaphysical pluralism of harmonies in relation, collapsing ontological relations to mere conditioning and casting essential features into mystery. What is the analysis of the ontological context of mutual relevance?

First, the ontological context of mutual relevance is so universal as to be accessible by only the most abstract of notions. It is not, for instance, the whole of time, for earlier and later moments have essential parts still external to one another; nor can it be a *totum simul* of time, for that fails to acknowledge that a dated moment changes its character as it changes from future to present to past. The context cannot be the whole of space, for space stands in contrast to other dimensions with which it has relations. The specific nature of the ontological context of mutual relevance is determined by the things in it, of course, and so there must be a way by which the essential features of external temporal things are related, a way for spatial things, and so forth. But the context itself is utterly vague with respect to the kinds of things that might be in it. Its sole character is to relate external things with essential features to one another. In this, perhaps it is best characterized as eternity, the perspective beyond temporal, spatial, and summary totalizing perspectives. The great religions have recognized this great Unity beyond unities and have struggled to give it symbolic form. Yet since all symbols emerge from determinate contexts that presuppose the very point to be expressed, the symbols are too small (for a more elaborate discussion of the ontological context of mutual relevance, see Neville: 1968, Pt. I).

Second, the ontological context of mutual relevance cannot be a determinate "third term" for the reasons discussed above, and hence the word "context" might be misleading. "Context" suggests a condition that makes possible the togetherness of the things contained in context, and yet the context cannot be a determinate condition without requiring an infinite regress of extra contexts to relate the determinate condition to what is conditioned. The *function* of the ontological context of mutual relevance is to put together diverse determinate things, each with essential features external to the others.

What can be the functional reality of the ontological context of mutual relevance? I propose that it is the creation *ex nihilo* of all mutually determinate things. That is, determinate things are simply created to be together.

This is an hypothesis, an ontological hypothesis, that can be explained in the following abstract way. Apart from creating, there is no determinate creator, no God, although given the creation the very act of creating constitutes the creator of this world. That determinate things are created together *ex nihilo* explains the sense of contingency in the dyadic character of reality noted above. The being of things is their being created together. The creator is the ontological ground of determinate things, but only insofar as actually creating. The creative act has no determinate character except that of being the creating of the various determinate things. Since time is among the things created, creation is "eternal," although in a fairly vacuous sense of that word so far as manifest here. Ontological creation thus has a three-term character: the source of determinate beings, the activity or power of creating, and the things created that are simply the *termini* of the creative act. So much for a summary abstract account of ontological creation.

The major religions give some kind of mythic fix on the ontological ground of reality through notions of a creator God, the emptiness of the Compassionate Buddha, Brahman with and without qualities. Each of these mythic forms is sensitive to the paradoxical character of creation: it is real if it happens, unreal if it doesn't. Therefore, the world is ontologically wholly dependent on its ground; the ground therefore must be independent of the world; but the ground is not ground without really creating the world. This is paradoxical but not contradictory. It cannot be contained within symbols and metaphors taken from within the determinate world, however. So the ontological ground cannot literally be conceived as a Big Person God, or a Super Mind Buddha, or a Soul so Pure it has No Nature. Yet culture cannot articulate a recognition of this ground of Being without some symbols or other. Hence, as Tillich argued, the important symbols must be regarded as broken symbols. The loss of reality discussed in the first chapter involves a loss of meaningfulness to these symbols, a death of God. One manifestation of the death of God, in systematic terms, is loss of contact with the essential features of others. Other people and things then disappear except as conditions within our own nature—ontological solipsism. And then since we ourselves are harmonies of diverse things, with no togetherness of our own diverse essential features, we disappear as real ourselves.

Let us remember the course of our argument. In order to account for identity, we were led to distinguish conditional from essential features, with the result that we finished with a pluralistic metaphysics. Then, in order to account for the possibility of the togetherness of diverse things with essential features explicitly external to one another, we noted that this entails an ontological context of mutual relevance. What can this context be except the actual making or creating of the things together? Ontological creation, by virtue of the total dependency of the created product, thus has three foci: the product, the act of creating all the things that are together, and the utterly non-dependent source of the creative act. Paradoxically, but not all contradictorily, the source depends on creating to be source. Now all of this is very abstract, far more abstract than any of the ideas arising through developing religious traditions, ideas such as God, the Buddha-mind, Emptiness, Brahman, The One, The Tao, or whatever, although each of these can be understood as particular and specific ways of pointing to some aspect of ontological creation (as well as to many other things).

The cultural death of God, and more generally the shaking of all traditional religions, does not diminish the point about ontological creation. That point stands as a fundamental explanatory hypothesis regardless of the fate of the religious symbols. Indeed, the strength of that ontological hypothesis might be sufficient to breathe new life into the religious symbols, properly criticized in their cultural contexts. To be sure, the religious symbols have undergirded whole concrete forms of life, and an ontological hypothesis cannot do that. On the other hand, if the ontological hypothesis becomes a new common sense, then it too takes on mythic functions. Regardless of the religious fate of the philosophic hypothesis about ontological creation, a rejection of contemporary religion does not constitute an objection against it. The hypothesis cannot be dismissed becase "we do not talk about God anymore."

What does the theory of creation *ex nihilo* say about Being, about the Being of beings? Underlying the dyadic character of reality that consists in a thing's being this rather than that, is the ghostly dyad of its being something rather than nothing. Because the thing indeed is real, it is something, not nothing. And this is possible because of the creativity in the ontological ground of being. When a true representation therefore refers to its object, it not only represents what the object is and does not represent it as it is not, but also it asserts that its object is. This is a ghostly dyad because the contrast to the assertion is not an assertion that the thing is not. Rather, the reference in the assertion simply commends the being of the object, the fact that it is real as so and so. Given that the being of a thing is interlocked with the being of other things, we can say that the Being of beings is the fact of their mutual coexistence. Being is thus the standing over against nothingness of things simply as determinate, prescinding from whatever their determinate characters might be. Put another way, Being is the product of the ontologically creative act. The activity of creating can be called the Act of Being, and the source can be called the Ground of Being.

It has been the mistake of many thinkers to attempt to do without one or two of these notions: Being, Act of Being, or Ground of Being. If one attempts to answer the ontological question with the notion of Being alone, it is necessary to make the notion determinate as a third term unifying the diverse many; but this leads to an infinite regress of connectors, as we have seen. If one attempts to employ only the notion of the Act of Being, without the produced unity of the product, Being, or without the Ground of Being as source, the question arises as to whose act it is; the consequence is either to posit a determinate creator, with the infinite regress difficulties of the determinate third term, or to fractionate the creative activity into the individuals created, which is precisely what will not explain the togetherness of essential features of diverse things. If one attempts to work only with the notion of the Ground of Being, one fails to acknowledge that ontological creation actually accomplishes the togetherness in the ontological context of mutual relevance.

The common sense outcome of this philosophical ontology is that the world and oneself are regarded bifocally. Looked at through one lens, the world is a tissue of really distinct but really related things, a pluralistic realm of Being. Through the other lens, that same world is regarded not so much for what it is, but for the fact that it is. The "that it is-ness" of the world both conceptually and emotionally involves acknowledging and deferring to the ontological creative act and its source. The fact that sensitive people can look through both lenses is the spring of natural piety, the respect for the world as such.

II. PRIMARY COSMOLOGY

The treatment of identity in chapter 5 began the development of a metaphysical theory, a theory of suitable presuppositions about reality, about what makes something real. The section above switched to the ontological question of being. It asked not about what things must be in order to be real but about the fact that there are real things. These topics are only abstractly separable, and indeed the discussions of them are only beginning here.

Another closely related topic needs to be introduced at this point, however, in order to be developed with the others. There must be some basic categories making up the world as we know it, categories that comprise what can be called "primary cosmology." The Milesians, for instance, thought the world is made up of basic stuffs, water, air, the indefinite, and so forth; the Pythagoreans thought it was numbers. The Neo-Confucians thought the world is a mixture of principle (*li*) and material force (*ch'i*). Whitehead thought the basic categories include actual entities, prehensions, nexuses, subjective forms, eternal objects, propositions, multiplicities, and contrasts; Paul Weiss thinks they include actuality, ideality, existence, and God.

As determinate things, these categories exemplify the metaphysical elements of identity. That is, each is a harmony with essential and conditional features, and they relate to one another in the complex ways constituted by their conditional connections. From one point of view, the categories of a suitable primary cosmology can be seen as species of the genus constituted by the metaphysical categories since they illustrate those categories, and yet alternate primary cosmologies also would illustrate them. The genus-species schema is not without its difficulties, however. As Thomas Aquinas showed, Being is not a genus of which metaphysical categories are species. Charles Hartshorne believes that metaphysical categories, as descriptive of any possible world, are generic with respect to the categories specifically descriptive of this actual one. Yet if the argument of the previous section has some truth, that the being of determinate things is a function of their being created, and thus involved in an indissoluble bond with ontological creativity and an ontological ground, then there are no determinate things without an actual world, in some sense of actual. Hence there are no metaphysical conditions for possible worlds prior to the existence of some actual one. Hartshorne to the contrary notwithstanding, there can be no uncreated conditions for possible worlds because they would be determinate and hence would need to be created themselves. Metaphysical conditions for other possible worlds are only extrapolations from what reality must consist in for this world to be real. Therefore, the relation between the primary cosmological categories and the metaphysical ones is simply the connection between two kinds of account, one of identity, and the other of the basic categories of things required to account for the world. Metaphysics is transcendental in the medieval sense, whereas primary cosmology deals with basic categories of reality, the summed connections of which constitute the world.[2] These points will be drawn out in what follows.

In the great literate philosophic traditions there have been three enormously influential primary cosmologies, each determining much of a civilization. In India, the Samkhya school gave clear formulation to the categories of prakriti and purusha. The former is creative natural process and the latter is consciousness with a capacity for ego-identification. In China, the Neo-Confucians combined the traditional insights of Confucianism, Taoism, and Mahayana Buddhism in their enormously complicated categories of principle and material force. In ancient Greece, Aristotle developed his theory of four causes, two of which, form and matter, are very roughly analogous to purusha and principle for the former and to prakriti and material force for the latter; Aristotle's other two causes, as is well known, are the efficient cause and the final cause.

The chief difference between Aristotle's four causes and the two-cause cosmologies of India and China lies in the importance given to time. For Aristotle, as for the entire Western tradition in its biblical as well as Greek roots, time has been so important in its asymmetry that he thought categories marking the actuality of the past (efficient cause) and the possibilities of the future (final cause) are as fundamental as those making formed things, or actualized forms. This is not to say that the Indian and Chinese cosmologies failed to make change important. Indeed, far better than the Western tradition they emphasized the dynamic quality of prakriti and material force. The omnipresence of change in Indian thought is what drives the philosophical and spiritual dialectic from the particularities of this cosmos to underlying realities. For the Chinese, the mixture of material force and principle is what gives rise to the ever-flowing transformations of yin and yang. In change as such, however, the asymmetry of temporal ordering may not be important; the Indians and Chinese had ways, of course, for distinguishing past from future, but those ways did not have a primary status in basic cosmology. For Aristotle there is not only change but historical change, so that even the present status of a form-matter product is understood in terms of the antecedents that brought it to be and the future consequences contained in its present potentialities.

Aristotle's theory of four causes has been influential down to the present day as a classification system for ideas, most notably in the work of Richard McKeon and others of the Chicago School. Yet it has not been able to provide an interpretation of modern science, and the Renaissance thinkers often characterized their science as a rejection of final causation. Indeed, much thinking about modern science from Kant's time has abandoned use of the categories of form and matter, transferring the notion of form to the relation between a thing and its efficient cause. Modern science itself has been surpassed by scientific developments during the last century. The account of causation I will present in chapter 11 below is neither Aristotelian nor modern in the sense of Galileo, Descartes, or Newton.

Aristotle's primary cosmology has a flaw that was noticed before the rise of modern science. On the one hand, the causal process is supposed to flow from an efficient cause to a caused substance. On the other hand, change takes place only within a substance as it actualizes potentiality or substitutes properties on a substratum. Aristotle's theory makes it very difficult to conceive how one substance can causally affect another, and the very continuity of a stretch of time that he wanted to lift up in importance is put in jeopardy. The brilliance of his theory should not be underestimated. Not only did he propose the understanding of a substance in terms of four causes, but he provided separate accounts of substance from the standpoint of each of the causes. Thus, from the standpoint of form, a substance is to be understood in terms of the distinctions between genus and species, with essential and accidental conditions. From the standpoint of matter, substance is the inherence of properties in a substratum, and change is the alteration of properties to their contraries. From the standpoint of efficient causes, substance is the actualization of potential. And from the standpoint of final causes, substance is the coordination of form and matter so as to achieve some completion of structure. Yet in all this there is a lack of continuity from one thing to the next, because the actualization of potential jumps from the material substrate of the causing substance to that of the affected substance. Of course there are many Aristotelian ways to circumvent this consequence with other distinctions, but the flaw lies deep in the primary cosmology's account of the basic causes.

My own belief is that one of the first to perceive the difficulties with Aristotle's view was Plato, who offered his own alternative to the four causes in the *Philebus*. This historical claim perhaps sounds strange because we are accustomed to thinking of the influence being one way from Plato to Aristotle. But Plato, who was the world's greatest philosophy teacher (except perhaps for Socrates) because he produced the world's greatest philosophy student (except perhaps for himself), was surely smart enough to learn from his best student, Aristotle. The *Philebus* was written with the later dialogues around 354 BCE, and Aristotle had been at the Academy since around 367. As a seventeen-year-old freshman in 367, Aristotle is not likely to have produced the theory of the four causes. But seven years later, he surely would be an advanced graduate student with all the precocity that comes from forming one's own view over against the master. It makes sense to think that Plato moved from his simple opposition of the limited and unlimited in the *Phaedrus* to the more complex primary cosmology of the *Philebus* through discussions with Aristotle. And of course Aristotle continued refining his own theory to its later clear statement in the *Physics*, although it pervades his work as an organizing hypothesis and was surely an early inspiration. At any rate, whatever the order of discussion, Plato's late primary cosmology is advantaged over Aristotle's.

In his mature work, the *Philebus*, Plato developed a cosmology with four fundamental categories: limit, the unlimited, mixture, and cause of mixture. None of these was claimed to be real in itself or to exist independently of the others, and each needs the others to help define it. Limit means pattern or form, one of the chief themes of Plato's earlier work. The unlimited or indefinite is that which form is to measure; it has no feature except the capacity to take on pattern, and as if to counterbalance this it also has the feature of not being able to sustain the forms it takes on because of its intrinsic dynamism. The mixture is the individuated concrete world we live in, formed in many patterns but exhibiting an indefinite dynamism, an overflowingness, an infinitude of potentialities for other patterns that bespeaks the unlimited, a mixture thus of limit and the unlimited that individuates them. A mixture is not the mere combination of limit and the unlimited, but the actualization of possible combinations. A mixture has an existential dimension over and above the analytical components of limit and the unlimited. By "cause of mixture" Plato did not mean antecedent or efficient causes, which are themselves just other mixtures. He meant the reason why, or the justification of, mixtures in the first place, and his analysis of this was in terms of value. The cause of mixture is the goodness to be attained in it. The main intellectual plot of the *Philebus* is to describe the virtue most important to embody, namely goodness itself, and Plato's description involved a description of balance, appropriateness, measure, and the like.

Without meaning to enter into a critical interpretation of Plato's text, I want to use his notions as themes for a primary cosmology. In contrast to Aristotle's theory of the four causes of substance, Plato's four categories are not the cause of anything except their own intermingling. A mixture is to be understood as a long process with a past of determined actuality, a future of possibilities, and a present in which potentialities are actualized. The dynamism of the process comes from the unlimited; its possibilities and actualized forms from limit. Its value comes from getting the right forms in the right places, and the existence of the mixture itself is the process of actulization. Whereas for Aristotle, the problem of causation is to explain how one thing affects another thing, for Plato, the problem of causation is to describe the course of actualization in a temporally extended mixture, and to relate how mixtures of various sorts affect and interweave with one another; in particular, for Plato the topic of primary cosmology is to show what onging mixtures are conditions for mixtures of higher worth, and to provide a normative analysis of how to achieve and sustain the mixtures of highest goodness. This, I submit, is precisely the topic for a primary cosmology that serves to make sense of the process of interpretation. An additional advantage to Plato's view has to do with the acount of value. For Aristotle, value is acknowledged in the form of final causes, which are those states that would complete or perfect the substance at hand; his theory requires that the world be made up of individual substances, a requirement denied not only by modern science, but by our common experience that relates to situations far more often than individual enduring integral organisms. For Plato, by contrast, value is an aesthetic characteristic of the way form or limit relates to the unlimited or the components to be formed.

All mixtures, for Plato, exhibit some value and perhaps ought to exhibit more; but only those that are intentional or, like society, are intentional artifacts, have teleological drives. In a way, this reduces teleology to a sphere that is unexceptionable to the modern consciousness. In another way, however, Plato's claims for value are broader than Aristotle's, not just concerning one of four equally basic causes. Although but one of four categories in the *Philebus*, the cause of mixture is what brings the other three categories to bear upon one another; and we have no reason to think they have any reality apart from their commingling. For Plato, and for our own common curiosity, the kind of answer that addresses our ultimate question of why things are as they are is one that shows how and why those are good ways to be. The answer might also point to other ways it would be better or worse to be. These are precisely the questions of explanation that guide and shape the interior structure of the process of interpretation.

III. FORM, COMPONENTS, ACTUALITY, AND GOODNESS

The primary cosmology to be introduced here is not intended as a critical interpretation of Plato's primary cosmology, but rather as a contemporary elaboration of its themes and metaphors.

As harmonies of conditional and essential features, determinate things are mixtures. For an imagined minimally complex harmony with only two components (an essential and a conditional feature), the togetherness of the components exhibits a pattern. If the components are considered apart from their patterned togetherness, their relations to one another are indefinite or "unlimited." Whatever they might be in relation to other things, considered apart, the components are indeterminate with respect to one another, and they have no essential features harmonized with conditional features from each other. (If the components are not incidentally determinate with respect to things outside the harmony, they are wholly indeterminate and hence are nothing, unreal.)

A given harmony has an indefinite multiplicity of components organized with a finite form making certain components important and others trivial. Further, each component is filled with components, essential and conditional, and so on down and around. That there is an "actual infinite" in any finite thing would be a profound philosophic conundum were it not for the fact that at each level of harmony, the harmonizing pattern distinguishes the important from the trivial; and the trivial can be forgotten in analysis except as presupposed background for certain important components.

In a practical analysis of a thing as a determinate harmony, one can go down to its "matter" as it were by investigating its components. So long as one attends to the conditional features the components have from each other by virtue of being harmonized components of the thing, one views the components in their roles as components. Many kinds of harmonies, however, bring together as components things that have independent careers of their own. The analysis of components, then, can take the form of following out the careers of things extending beyond the original harmony, as a newspaper writer investigates background on diverse people who come together only in an incident. Going down into components of components, and so on, harmonic patterns of many kinds might be found, some allowing the components strong integrity of their own outside the harmony of which they are components, and other depending in organic ways for their very being on the integrating harmony.

If one's primary cosmology were classical atomism, or Aristotelianism, or modern pre-twentieth century physics, one would expect the analysis of components of components to tend toward some elementary particles, some basic set of kinds of "atoms." On the primary cosmology offered here, however, any possible component must itself be determinate, and hence divisible into at least a few essential and conditional features, which themselves are divisible, and so on indefinitely. There is nothing elementary in this cosmology. In the *Timaeas*, Plato suggested that the Demiurgos made the building blocks of the universe by giving algebraic and geometrical forms to the Receptacle or Unlimited. Nowadays physicists suggest that mathematical properties such as "charm" define the elementary forms of organization. The Platonic aspect of this is that what is elementary is not the littleness of the stuff but the ratio of the form. There is no sense, according to twentieth century physical cosmology or to our primary (Platonic) cosmology, in hunting for some natural bedrock; at best we can hope to find some stable and balancing forms of organization. This point is an independent route to the principle of context-dependence discussed in chapter 2.

A component-oriented analysis of things reveals the fragility of the complex forms of natural, social, and personal organization. The higher level forms depend on the stability of lower level forms. Since so many components have careers independent of many of the harmonious things into which they enter, the environment is constantly shifting, and stability then means adaptability. The image of the unlimited revealed in component-analysis is thus of a great stream of changes, filled with many eddies and currents, to which the mixtures we care about must constantly adapt. Plato himself was so shaken by this vision of the maelstrom of change that he feared deeply for the fragile civilization he prized. Both as a philosopher and institution builder (the first university president) he developed a conception of reason, not for contemplation, but for ruling, guiding, exercizing statecraft. Yet he remained pessimistic about the powers of reason, and finally in the *Laws* worried about how to entrench rational policy in as unchangeable a way as possible (which was not very much). Conservatives today respond to the same vision of the powers of the unlimited to undo the mixtures that give life meaning and value. Radicals look to change as providing opportunities, causal openings, for making improvements.

To speak of the dynamism of the unlimited, of the independent and heedless careers of things relative to the high-level harmonies through which they pass, is to suppose some account of change and of time. Chapters 9 and 10, on time and temporality, will elaborate this category of the unlimited as temporal passage and dynamism.

Form is never found outside a plurality of things formed, nor imagined without also imagining some kind of plurality for formation. Form is what Plato in the *Statesman* called "normative measure," a togetherness of things achieving some value. Specifically, as mentioned above, any finite form integrates an infinitely large mass of components by giving certain of them importance and trivializing the rest. Further, form establishes hierarchies. That is, by harmonizing certain things as components, form determines the forms of the components to be contained within itself on a lower level, and so on down to the forms of the components of components. The most general requirement of form we have noted so far is that it unite essential and conditional features. The essential features determine the values of the conditional features and order them; the conditional features are arrayed according to forms that exhibit some as important, others as trivial.

Just as the analysis of a determinate thing can go downward, as it were, to its components, it can also go upward to examine higher forms in which its form participates. There are many senses of higher form—higher genera, more inclusive systems, inclusive ratios. To the extent that formal analysis prescinds from the actual components of the determinate thing, it abandons that thing's reality. A formal analysis might proceed by acknowledging only the forms of the components of a form, mathematics being the paradigm example of this. A formal analysis that maintains contact with the actual components is at least incipient philosophy.

A form is a way of having a particular set of components together. There may well be other ways of having these components together, and those other ways would achieve different values from that achieved in the initial form. Therefore, a crucial aspect of the analysis of a thing's form is a kind of normative analysis of how that form compares with alternate forms that can be imagined. Insofar as the normative analysis uses the imagined forms of potential components rather than real determinate things, one can vary the set of possible components as well as the harmonizing forms, and play with an unfixed array of possible values; this is something like an aesthetic analysis. But insofar as the forms analyzed are related to real determinate components, there is a fixation of the array for alternate patterns to harmonize, and the analysis is more like an ethical one.[3]

Because determinate things are mixtures of unlimited components and limited forms, they are not "positive facts" as that phrase has developed through modernity, but rather "actual achievements of value." Therefore, it is fundamentally impossible for things to be described in the ways positivism, including phenomenology, has advocated. For, a true analysis or "description" would have to indicate how a value is achieved by harmonizing these components with those forms, and in addition, it would have to display how different forms would have given different achieved values. And insofar as what is being described is a process, it might be important to indicate how different forms could have made different components relevant to the process, an aesthetic power in temporal causation. To be true to determinate things, therefore, is not to describe in the sense of setting forth the "facts," but to give a critical assessment of what's happening. Within this primary cosmology, there simply are no bare facts, only mixtures of limit and the unlimited, and these mixtures are achieved values.

To develop the notion of form employed here, it is necessary to undertake a theory of value, showing how form itself is the expression of value. This is the topic of chapter 7.

Would it not be enough in our primary cosmology to end with mixtures of limit and the unlimited, or with determinate things harmonizing components with forms, with valuable form? The remaining question is how these work together, the true and most universal question of context. Granted the mixtures, why are there mixtures? Granted that mixtures are efficiently caused by other mixtures, what is the power or force in efficient causation? Granted that mixtures achieve value, why is there the achievement of value? These questions sound strained because we are unaccustomed to asking them, conditioned as we are by the positivist mentality that would say things are just there because they are there. But if positivism cannot even be true to determinate things, then its response to these questions cannot be binding. Further, these questions are the most fundamental Why questions, and they deserve an attempt at an answer. Therefore we need a theory of causation that integrates the efficient causality so important in science with the causal forces of value and existence as such. Because most theories of causation have neglected both value theory and temporality, our treatment of causality will be postponed to chapters 10 and 11.

Let us recall that the four categories of our primary cosmology are invoked to indicate how there can be determinate things. The primary cosmological categories carry promissory notes to explain specific determinate things, such as structured temporal processes. The categories are not defined in terms of each other—that would allow any one of them to be reduced to the other three—but rather in terms of how they conjointly make up determinate things as harmonies of essential and conditional features. The categories have no independent reality: they rather are four coordinated routes by which ontological causation takes place. In the previous section, we noted that ontological causation creates determinate things with conditional feature *vis a vis* one another, and with essential features over against one another so as to maintain real difference. Now we can suggest something of how that creation takes place. It is by the joint creation of the unlimited, the limits, the mixtures, and the cause of mixture. Or, it is the creation of the world of determinate things through the joint agencies of infinitely rich components, forms, harmonies of these, and a causal process integrating all.

Language about "creation of the world" has undeniable religious overtones. Indeed, the religious traditions have emphasized one or several of these categories as the agency of divine creation. The unlimited, the infinite density of components of any finite thing, is the appearance of the divine as Dionysos, the Mother, Siva/Shakti, Samsara, the Tao that Cannot Be Named, Power, Fecundity, Plenitude. The limit is the divine appearance as the One, Brahman, the Buddha-mind as Absolute, the Law. The mixture is divine creation as Act, as Existence, Concreteness, Yahweh, Person. The cause of mixture, The Divine Heaven, Earth, and Man, is the most complex appearance of divine creation exemplified in theologies formed by philosophies such as Hegel's, Wang Yang-ming's, and Ramanuja's; these theologies subtly or blatantly rename the old divinities within their integrated totalities. But the cause of mixture cannot totalize the other categories, only bind them together, perhaps imperfectly, and only for a while; the old divinities break out again. Their effects in the world of determinate things are not wholly subsumed in the Cause of Mixture.

Whether the primary cosmology introduced here has much plausibility depends on the fruitfulness of subsequent specifications of it in the discussion of value, temporality, and causality, and in its application to problems of truth, reality, and interpretation. The cosmology is introduced here as an initial response to the question, how can a thing be real? The answer suggested is, by being a determinate harmony of essential and conditional features in relation to other such determinate things, exhibiting an unlimited inner richness, value-giving organizational limits, mixing these together in actual definiteness, according to the causal processes of the universe. The four categories of primary cosmology are the routes through which ontological creation takes place.

IV. A SUMMARY THEORY OF REALITY

The purpose of this chapter and the previous one has been to develop a theory of reality that might direct a reorganization of our common sense about the most basic elements of thinking. A summary can indicate some of the directions for common sense.

1. To find reality, to develop a sense of what is real and not fantasy, look to identity. Even a fantasy is real in its identity as fantasy.

2. To grasp identity, look for mutual relations among things such that each is reflected in the others, in conditional features.

3. For identity, look also to the essential features or self-identity of determinate things. In reflecting on what things are, locate the conditional and essential elements by which they are in relation and in themselves.

4. Identities are harmonies of features that do not reduce to one another. No thing is just one thing, but a harmony of many.

5. Reality means that these identities are what they are rather than simply not being. Their very diversity testifies to their contingency and to a deeper unity than that provided by their conditional relations.

6. The being of things consists in their being created out of or over against nothingness. Therefore, an appreciation of things notes not only what they are but that they are. There is more to the real world than meets the eye, but it is not more real world.

7. Any thing can be understood in terms of an infinite richness of components,

8. and in terms of the forms of value it embodies or might embody,

9. and in terms of how it mixes these first two,

10. and through the comprehensive causal elements integrating form, the unlimited, and the many mixtures.

The last four points are the most enticing because they indicate particular things to examine in order to get a hold of reality. They are extraordinarily vague, however, and need to be made more determinate through discussions of value, temporality, and causation. Before those discussions we can contemplate how the theory of reality so far addresses the problems of interpretation raised earlier.

1. The focus on identity is crucial for an appropriate relation between the real and the true. If reality finds its fundamental mark in identity, then an interpretive assertion can be true or false if it correctly describes or assumes that identity. Further, truth is dyadically related to reality, and measured by it, if, as Aristotle prescribed, assertions assert the reality's identity and do not assert what is not its identity.

2. The nature of identity as such involves the determinate relations of an identified thing with other things; interpretation thus affirms an identity, in part, by tracing out those relations. The root metaphors of interpretation thus are not predications of properties but focusings of networks of relations. This suggests what I shall later argue is the case, that interpretation is always metaphorical in being relational.

3. Interpretation is not merely the tracing of relations, but the identification of things by their essential features that order or position their relations. A metaphorical reach to things by their relations must terminate in a move beyond the relations to the thing's essence. Of course, the essence is not separable from the conditions, and so identity is preceived as a harmony of essential and conditional features. Interpretation requires using signs so as to balance both sides.

Further, just as realities to be interpreted have essential and conditional features, so do interpretations. Just as the essential features of related things keep them from collapsing into one another or one being reduced to the other, so realities have their harmonic integrity that cannot be reduced to interpretation and that thus can measure it. And on its own side, the interpretation includes the intended realities as its conditional features, but its essential features consist in what it does with those realities. An analysis of the essential features of interpretation reveal the qualifications by which the worth of things is carried over into the interpretation of them.

4. No interpretation can ever be complete because it never succeeds in identifying all the components of a thing. Nor does it ever exhaust all the respects in which a thing can be interpreted, these being functions of its own essential features.

5. While not assuming a determinate transcendental signifier or principle of unity, interpretation does assume a context of mutual relevance for the things whose identities refer to one another. It thus embraces a kind of non-being, a this-and-not-that, within the unities it notes among objects when it makes assertions about them.

6. In noting that each thing it identifies is not only itself relative to other things but also not nothing, the assertive element of interpretation takes being as the first object of its intellect, as the medievals would say. Without a metacommentary on it, any assertion says of its object not only what it is but that it is, in whatever modality of reality it might truly or falsely have (for example, spatio-temporal existence, cultural fiction, mere imaginative object).

7. The infinite richness of things suggests not only that the interpretation of an object can never be complete, but also that there is an indefinite number of interpretive frames that can be employed. Each culture provides a finite "take" on things, even if that take itself is internally infinitely dense. But there can be any number of such takes, as relativists have argued. Knowledge of the vast relativity of cultures, coupled with the knowledge that one always lives within some culture, even a metaculture about culture, gives rise to an ironic dimension to all interpretation when it is self-aware.

8. That all forms or orders are ways of achieving value, as will be argued in more detail in the following chapter, means that interpretation always involves an element of appreciation. In knowing the forms of things, there is indeed a carryover of value from the object into the interpretation of it. Part of that value consists in the forms as such that are grasped. Given the relativity of alternate frames of forms, the aesthetic mode of appreciating the values marked by each frame is juxtaposed to the moral evaluation of frames from the standpoint of one's own. This is a deeper irony.[4]

9. But more important, the value of a thing consists in how its forms in fact organize its components at all levels. Actual value is form forming, or components functioning together as components. The actualized mixture constituting a concrete thing (usually a process) is the locus of real value.

10. The relational or conditional elements of things, together with their essential elements, require that interpretation approach things in terms of their interactions, interactions exhibiting both mutual conditioning and independence. Further, interactions are themselves kinds

of mixings, and the norms for patterning those mixings are themselves revealed in interpretation. Or rather, interpretation guides itself by seeking out the ways things are or are not harmonized, and how they might be harmonized other ways with other resulting values. Thus interpretation not only involves the values that are carried over into it from its objects, but also the values that guide its own process as justified by the measure of its objects in their real contexts.

7

Value

The point to which the previous chapter brought the argument is the need to develop a theory of value that has metaphysical universality. Specifically, it was claimed that to be determinate as such is to have value, and the present chapter will explicate that thesis. Further, it was argued that value is found in two ways among the basic categories of the primary cosmology. In one way, any form has the ideal value of integrating its potential components in the way it does. In another way, the existential mixtures of form and components have real values as functions of the degrees to which they get the right forms in the right places at the right times, building the complex hierarchies of ongoing mixtures that we prize enough to name and recognize with appreciative language.

Moreover, a detailed account of the nature of value is required by the theory of truth as the carryover of value, an integral part of the larger theory of interpretation. A sketch of a theory of truth was provided in chapter 3, enough perhaps to indicate the categories required for such a naturalistic or causation-oriented approach to truth as was taken there. It is now necessary to develop the theory of value directly and dialectically. The point is to show that anything that is a patterned togetherness of components has a value that can be carried over into the interpretation of the thing.

I. HISTORICAL REFLECTIONS ON "VALUE"

The claim that everything has value is not unique. Both Plato and Aristotle asserted it in their own ways, and Christian philosophers such as Augustine, concerned to show that everything God creates is good, thematized the convertibility of "being" and "value." By the medieval period in Europe, goodness was considered a transcendental.

Two conditions have made our own century so unfriendly to a theory of value with metaphysical universality that a special apology is needed in order to put one forward for philosophic consideration. First, the development of modern science has introduced a sharp distinction between facts and values, and excluded the latter from cognitive status. Second, as J. N. Findlay has recounted in the admirable history of the subject in his *Axiological Ethics*, the beginnings of metaphysically universal value-theory in this century were overwhelmed by the antitheoretical, especially antiaxiological, influences of Heidegger and Wittgenstein. It is therefore appropriate to introduce the discussion of value with some historical comments about how to approach the topic.

"Axiology," from the Greek *axios*, meaning "worth something," "worthy, deserving," or "fit for its place," was introduced into philosophy by Wilbur Urban, according to Findlay (1970, 1),

> in 1906 in his heavily excellent book *Valuation: Its Nature and Laws*; it was used to translate the *Werttheorie* which the Austrian economist von Neumann had introduced into economics, and which the Austrian philosophers Ehrenfels and Meinong, concerned at all costs to follow the lead of 'science', had tried to cultivate in the field of aesthetic, moral, scientific and other values. 'Axiology' meant the study of the ultimately worthwhile things (and of course of the ultimately counterworthwhile things) as well as the analysis of worthwhileness (or counterworthwhileness) in general.

This is exactly the right set of connotations for the study of the nature of value in which it is asserted that every determinate thing is valuable. There is an irony in the scientistic origins of axiology in German thought, for the impact of a successful axiology of the sort developed here would be to undermine the very fact-value distinction supporting scientism. Before launching into such a formidably theoretical topic as axiology, it is worthwhile to survey an array of alternate approaches to value.

The first set of approaches comprises those centering on human practice: ethics, aesthetics, and politics. Human activity in fields that appear to be governed by norms provides the most urgent quandaries about values. The step is small, and often practical, from wondering what one should do to wondering what makes something better to do than something else. Practice is often translated back to the Greek word *praxis* in current discussion, and the nature of value raised in that context. As Richard Bernstein has shown most persuasively, the motive for the back-translation is to pick up on a particular reading of Aristotle's distinction of *praxis* from *theoria*.[1] Within *praxis*, values emerge contextually, and action is concretely rather than abstractly normed. By the emphasis on *praxis*, the discussion resonates with interests from recent Marxism and from the pragmatism of John Dewey. In addition, it provides a ready ground for analytic philosophers who are moving from meta-ethics to practical issues and for continental thinkers attempting to develop an ethics out of existentialism and phenomenology. By means of the contextual origin of values conceived in *praxis* language, a cognitive status is recovered for the normative disciplines. But precisely because of the use of the Aristotelian distinction of practice from theory, values are not treated in a theoretical or axiological fashion. Paradoxically, John Dewey, the great hero of *praxis*, provided some of the century's most interesting axiological ideas in *The Quest for Certainty* (1984, ch. 10). and *Theory of Valuation* (1939).

There is nothing to be said against the discussion of *praxis* except for its willful anti-theoretical bias. Values are indeed contextual and we have properly learned in this century to distrust both the application of abstract "values" to concrete situations and the deliberation about concrete problems in terms of neatly defined "values." Both language philosophy and hermeneutics have made this point, relying in part on the development of the social or human sciences. Whitehead was most exact when he warned against "the fallacy of misplaced concreteness." He was also right, however, that the best protection against this fallacy is not an increased emphasis on concreteness, but increased attention to the abstractions. All intelligent behavior is selective, no matter how concrete, and the guiding elements of selection are abstractions that should be examined as such. Further, if our basic common sense is formed by abstractions that include those of metaphysical generality, and value-notions do not appear there, then our common sense will continue to enforce the objective-fact/subjective-value distinction despite *praxis*.

It is appropriate here to stress that the word "value" is used in the axiological metaphysics to signify worth in things, not an ideal prized by persons. Ideals will be called ideals, and ideas about values will be called value-notions or some such. The discussion here has no association with the common interest now in "values analysis" or the fostering or justification of arranging one's life according to "values." As "values" is commonly meant in those subjective and individualistic contexts, it supposes a drastic lack of objective grounding, precisely the opposite of the thesis defended here, that determinate things as such are valuable.

Ethics is the most obvious field of normative human practice, and it is the field in which value questions are most pointedly raised. Broadly understood, ethics is the philosophic study of the values or worths of things that need to be respected in human life, and of how to respect them. For practical purposes the range of values in ethics is universal and a reflective study of what makes those things valuable can give rise to characterizations of all the values that might possibly enter human experience. In this sense, ethics provides the range of values for axiology.

The specific focus of ethics, however, is on the transition from the worths of things and the general obligation to respect them because of their respectibility, to specific responsibilities to individuals and groups for doing the things in which proper respect consists. Ethics, in other words, concerns the movement from the values in things to those values being normative for specific potential actions. Most ethical discussions are about the rightness of actions and the goodness of their fruits rather than about the claims made by various elements of the situation for proper respect. As the word indicates, ethics is about behavior rather than about the values to be respected in behavior. Concerning values as the ultimate determiners of behavior, Charles Peirce (1923, pars. 196–200) pointed out that ethics is derivative from aesthetics, the study of what is valuable in itself (see Potter, 1967).

Aesthetics is an indispensable discipline for the study of value. Bounded on the one hand by the study of art and on the other by the study of cognitive or appreciative faculties for discerning aesthetic value, aesthetics indeed includes analysis of what makes things appreciable in themselves. There is a strong analogy between the appreciation of art and the appreciation of any other value for its own sake. Control over that analogy, however, is hard to gain. To what extent is artistic value isolatable within human experience, isolatable in ways that the values of persons or institutions, say, are not? To what extent is artistic value a surface value, a value that consists in what presents itself rather than building on and containing hidden features?

Twentieth century modernist art has emphasized the formal, and to this extent lends itself to our thesis that a thing is valuable by virtue of having form. But by the same token, modernist art focuses on the formal elements by abstraction from content and context. If value is universal in the way suggested in the previous discussion, then it must be associated with form that is not abstractable but is expressed in the connections between abstractable form and its content and context. Whereas modernist art has emphasized abstract form, and modernist ethics abstract rules or quantifiable units of goodness, both have been succeeded by a reverse emphasis on contextuality and the importance of concrete, comparatively uninterpreted symbols. (Marxist post-modernism is an exception; while it emphasizes contextuality, it also treats symbols as relative to its own ideological theory, however subtle this might be in the hands of critics such as John Berger or Donald Kuspit.)

The limit of aesthetics as an approach to a philosophy of value is in identifying the "in itself" in phrases such as "valuable in itself." If the thesis is correct that to be determinate is to be both self-identified by essential features and other-related by conditional ones, then value must have both sides as well. And just as a determinate identity contains components with components and more components, opening onto vast reaches of the world as the thing's own depths, so value is inclusive to the point of not being "in itself." Whereas ethical value is normative for action, and aesthetic value normative for appreciation, value itself can be expressed in relations that include both poles of the ethical and aesthetic relations—the norm and the normed.

In a profound sense, the most inclusive practical field in which we face values is the political. In its most general range, politics is the activity of caring for the environment within which life, including private life, takes place (see Neville: 1974, ch. 9). Among other things, politics has the responsibility to care for ethics and aesthetics. Philosophy began in ancient Greece and China as a special approach to politics, and surely the justification of abstract philosophy that has been given here is a plainly political one.

The limit of politics as an approach to value is its very mutifariousness. Everything practical must be taken into account. This means that, when politics moves to the theoretical level, it is abstracting from the most comprehensive human responses to the embodiments of value rather than from valuable things as such. A theoretical axiology might well be a necessary instrument of practical politics. Indeed one should expect this in a complex world where half the problems are to preserve civilization from the forces of chaos and the other half are to destroy and rebuild unjust social structures: a formal understanding of what makes things valuable or countervaluable, for better or worse, is a crucial compass reading. But this very necessity means that a properly theoretical approach to value is independent from the directions of politics.

Whereas theory is doubtless useful, it is not merely a component of normed behavior. Value cannot be understood theoretically by an analysis of how values norm behavior, although examples of values norming behavior need constantly be employed to check out axiological theory.

II. THE "OBJECTIVITY" OF VALUE

If one accepts the assumptions of much modern philosophy and culture, the above discussion of values in relation to human practice is deceptive and pointless. The modern assumption is that values are not "objective" and that therefore those practical fields involve values only insofar as they are projected onto the allegedly valuable objects by human emotions, interests, tastes, or imagination. According to this conclusion, there is no proper study of values, but instead the various scientific studies of emotions, interests, tastes, and fantasy.[2] If this modern assumption is correct, then not only is the axiological metaphysics fundamentally mistaken, but so is the theory of truth as the carryover of value and the theory of interpretation as measured by the achieved values of things. There are, however, three principal reasons to reject the modern assumption.

First, it is self-referentially mysterious. If there be no legitimate normative values, then why would anyone submit to the rigors of science? That some people just like science is no explanation because the norms are binding on the practice, whether one engages in it or not, because of the worth of the cognitive product. The difference between well-founded theory and irresponsible opinion is a normative difference, not a mere factual difference between two ways of having ideas. In point of fact, the scientific pursuit of knowledge has attained something of the sacral respect and obligatoriness that religion had during earlier times. The conclusion is that with regard to scientific practice, there are values both appreciated and accepted as binding that are not acknowledged by the assumption that only facts are real.

Second, the assumption that only facts are "objective" is part of the wider metaphysical foundation of modern science. That science was developed during the European Renaissance as a brilliant integration of quantitative and qualitative modes of thought. The paradigms of mathematical science excluded valuational thinking, however, in distinguishing facts from values, and enshrined that exclusion in the distinction between objectivity as knowledge of the knowable, and subjectivity as the activity of the human subject whose only norms lay in being objective. Those basic modern distinctions are now under round attack from many segments of contemporary culture and philosophy, and the present study is part of a larger examination of alternative ways of conceiving thinking, ways that include valuational thinking. Admittedly, the rejection of the modern assumption does entail the development of an alternate metaphysics and cosmology to undergird a non-modern common sense.[3]

Third, the modern assumption is flatly counter-empirical. Our experience is pervaded by values that we appreciate in many ways, by which we are attracted and repelled, normed and seduced. Some of these values come to explicit attention. William James and John Dewey were masters at the demonstration of this. Underneath the explicit, however, is the universal sea of implicit valuation. Everything we experience we grade in order to provide some role in our experience. We respond to everything selectively. The value we give something for ourselves is always some compromise between the value it presents and our need to accommodate it to the other values in our lives. Some people might argue that a thing is just a fact with no value of its own, and that we give it a place in our experience solely on the basis of our own interests. But how could it have any bearing on our interests, how could it contribute anything (or its exclusion make something else worthwhile possible), if it did not have a valuable character itself? Where would our own interests come from, our own emotions, tastes and imaginative fancies, if not from the combined values of our conditions? To deny that things are experienced as bearing value is to deny what confronts us at all levels of personal and social life. It is to deny that poetry is true.

The problem concerning the objectivity of values is more deep-seated than all this, however. Indeed there is a cognitive dissonance for Western thinkers between our actual practices of valuing and our official theories and assumptions. But many seem to prefer to live with that dissonance than to criticize the official theories. Underlying this preference is a nihilistic mourning of the loss of innocence regarding the cultural system of European civilization. On the one hand, the innocence was lost in the encounter with other great civilizations and the rise of cultural relativism. On the other hand, the twentieth century's wars, its oppressions, its military threat to the whole ecology, and the general shifting of demographic power to the East, indicate that the West is betrayed by its own values: their outcome is not what it was supposed to be. The West is not merely one cultural system among others but a deeply flawed one.

The proper outcome of nihilism is to take a new look at the nature of what, if anything, is worthwhile, unencumbered by uncontrolled allegiances to one's own cultural perspective. This is yet another reason to undertake an axiological metaphysics that reconciles our practical experience of valuing with viable theoretical perspectives. Further, there is all the more reason to undertake an inquiry into whether, behind the relativism, there is a reality that can measure our interpretations.

III. A THEORY OF VALUE

What does a theory of value look like? The presentation here will begin with the aesthetic standpoint and characterize the surface structure of value as harmony. That presentation will be deepened in chapter 8 by an analysis of what it means to be a "component" in a harmony, as promised earlier. The present section will give an overview of the theory that will be detailed in the following section and in all of chapter 8.

As a preliminary characterization of value, we can turn to the notion of harmony introduced in the discussion of identity in chapter 5.[4] A harmony integrates components that would not be compossible in the context without the harmony, or some other harmony. The first element of value a harmony has, therefore, is that of sustaining its components together. The second element is the cumulative sum of the values in each of the components, since each of them is also a harmony. The third element of value is the novel value produced by the particular pattern of harmony. With the exception of two limiting conditions, a harmony creates new levels of reality over and above those involved in its components. The new level of reality is an achievement of value in its own right. Of course, the value may be a disvalue in context: every stew is a new reality compared to its ingredients, but some stews taste very bad. The two limiting conditions are: when the harmony is a bare conjunction of items such that none is affected by juxtaposition to the others; and when the harmony's components are all alike, pure homogeneity.

From this preliminary characterization, we can discern two variables in a harmony, complexity and simplicity. Complexity consists in the array of different things to be harmonized. It can exist on several levels. Consider the ideal case of harmonizing three things. At the base level, there is a threefold complexity. At the level of their harmony, a fourth thing comes to be, creating a fourfold complexity, and these may be related in any number of ways with the possiblity of much greater complexity. Further, each of the base things is itself a harmony with components, and components of components. (So the idea of a base level is a fiction, a necessary fiction for the moment.)

A *de facto* harmony has a given complexity. We can imagine, however, that the complexity is varied. What would happen if new elements had to be integrated? What would happen if these or those elements were eliminated? As moral and artistic experience show, the value of the harmony changes with changes in the things to be harmonized.

Simplicity consists in the order of togetherness of the components. The lowest form of simplicity is mere conjunction. At any level of simplicity, the form is a contrast of items fitted together. The higher forms of simplicity build on the lower forms to reinforce and intensify, to particularize and individuate, the contrast; from a high contrast looking down, as it were, the lower levels function efficiently to find expression in the higher. The simplicity of a harmony has a form or order. We can imagine variations on the form of a given *de facto* harmony, and these variations achieve different values.

In point of fact, the value of a harmony is a function of its degrees of complexity and simplicity together. Any harmony always has some degree of both. We can imagine varying complexity while holding the form of simplicity constant, or vice versa. Increasing both complexity and simplicity is an absolute increase in value, an increase both in the things integrated and an increase in what is made of the integration. One can increase one and decrease the other, perhaps resulting in an overall enhancement, or diminishment, or in a break-even. Alternate ways of increasing or decreasing one or the other give rise to different values, not always comparable. The essential point is that value is having your cake and eating it too, to some degree. Great complexity with minimal simplicity yields maximal unimportance. Great simplicity with minimal complexity yields boring homogeneity.

Any feature contributing to complexity is a conditional feature of a harmony, and any contributing to simplicity is an essential feature. Some features play both roles, as when a particular integration results in a new thing to be integrated with the lower levels at yet higher levels. Without the essential features, the harmony would not exist, only the otherwise potential components. And sometimes the potential components could not exist on their own without the harmony to sustain them together; organ systems in the body are an example.

The common sense habits sustained by this axiology of the surface of value are these. Although we might take something as having a certain worth naively, we ascertain and appreciate that worth by making two kinds of related thought experiments. On the one hand, we imaginatively construct similar things that differ from the original and from each other by virtue of having somewhat different contents. Then either by past experience or by imaginative appraisal, we compare the values of our original and its alternatives. On the other hand, we perform similar thought experiments that vary the form of organization, and see how different values are achieved. And then, of course, by imaginative construction we imagine variations of both variables.

All of these evaluative responses to a thing involve complex interpretations that pick out the items constituting the complexity, isolating for attention the particular forms contributing simplicity. Indeed, we attend to things as meaningful identities because our intellectual habits latch on to their significant essential and conditional features. Even where the identifying interpretations are attentively intellectual and not just the exercize of intellectual habit, they might be mistaken. We easily misconstrue the value of something if we mistake what makes it up, and how it is put together. Our intellectual habits, particularly those enshrined in language, frequently overdetermine our suppositions about form, and underdetermine the suppositions about complexity. So pervasive as usually to be unnoticed, we continually correct our appreciation of things as we learn more about the nature of their complexity and simplicity. At any stage, however, the grasp of a thing is valuative in that it takes the thing as having whatever we then understand of its complexity and simplicity.

Experience is not merely analysis toward some further end. It is also the enjoyment of things as having perceived value. This explains both the occasion for the fact-value distinction, and its ultimate falsity. One may respond to a thing by interpreting its complexity or simplicity, attempting to find out what makes it up and how those things are put together. The tools for this response are oriented to facts: *that* such and so is here produces a certain effect. Science is both the cataloguing and the discernment of organizing principles for the components of harmonies. The isolation of the factuality of harmonies from their value is ultimately false, however, because each item isolated is itself a harmony whose coherence is appreciated as a value. Only if the explanatory parts and principles are identified exclusively in terms of their own potential for further analysis does one fail to stop at the explanatory things to appreciate them as harmonies themselves. In concrete experience, our attention is determined by bafflingly dense vectors of intentional forces, some of which are analytical and therefore attentive to fact alone. But most of the time in experience, our enjoyments, especially those functioning contextually and as goals of intention, are felt as value-laden harmonies whose interpretation is implicit. Experience is pervasively valuative.

There is a strain in our common sense that looks only to order or form for value. This strain owes a great deal to the phenomena and forces that have fueled the Platonic and Neo-Platonic traditions. If our axiological theory is correct, however, any value is equally the product of multiplicity, of the indefinite, the principle of plenitude. For, a valuable determinate thing is as much the components to be ordered as the order itself. So the emphasis on existence and fecundity is equally to be stressed, perhaps best expressed in the traditions of the Tao and the Goddess. The balance between limit and the indefinite as axiological contributors to determinate contributors to determinate being has found its most elaborate expression in the concerns for Heaven and Earth, principle (*Li*) and energetic matter or material force (*Chi*) in the tradition of Neo-Confucianism. For purposes of our own thinking, the balance in the axiology reminds us to avoid, in the quest for greater and more appropriate value, reductive searches either for greater order or for more luscious and particularistic diversity. Each must be balanced with the other, and a search for one should be accompanied with a concern for what that will do to the other.

IV. FORM AND VALUE

The discussion at this point needs to make good the claim that value derives from realizing a pattern or form in a thing. The claim is that a determinate thing, a harmony, has value because a multiplicity of components is integrated with a pattern. We have seen something of the connotations regarding value that center in the complexity and simplicity of a harmony. Now we must analyze how pattern arranges components so as to exhibit complexity and simplicity.

The nature of form or limit is a complex dialectical issue. One position, structural realism, characteristic of British Platonists (including Whitehead and sometimes Russell, though not Plato) and many mathematicians, is that form is determinate logical structure, and that things that are formed partipate in that structure. On this account each form is a pattern of definiteness, real by itself and ready to ingress (Whitehead's word) into actual process whenever there are things that could be formed according to it.

The difficulties with this structural realist theory of form were thoroughly explored and exposed by Plato in his *Parmenides*. They have to do with participation. As that dialogue indicates, every sense in which a thing can be said to have a form, where that means being related to it as a determinate structure, presupposes some more basic sense in which the concrete thing is already formed so as to be able to participate in the determinate form. In the language of the previous discussion, if the form is determinate itself, then the participatory relation is between two determinate things, with conditional and essential features, presupposing already the notion of being formed. Plato's own suggestion is that forms are norms more than structures, and attain structure insofar as there are things to which the norms apply.[5]

An alternative account of form, a nominalistic one, argues that forms are merely conceptual abstractions from concrete things, and are applied to more than one thing by the powers of the mind to represent many things with one. The most fundamental objection to this account is Peirce's, namely, that if the abstraction can be applied to more than one thing, this proves that the several things all contain that to which the abstraction refers, and the problem returns to that of participation. If a term can be applied generally, the several things to which it applies must conform to it.

The ancient dialectic between these two positions has given rise to three principles that a theory of form must satisfy. First, forms must be what they are regardless of whether anything participates in them; otherwise, they could not be evoked to explain differences or unities. As patterns, forms remain the same while concrete things exchange one pattern for another and severally exhibit diverse patterns. Second, forms must take on their structural character in relation to what they form rather than possessing it independently of what they form; otherwise, the relation of form to formed is that between two determinate things and the problem of participation is unsolvable. Third, forms must be able to be shared by several things; that is, be applied generally.

My hypothesis, following Plato, is that there is only one true form, the Form of the Good. In itself, this form is wholly indeterminate, hence not structured. Nor is it good in itself, because to be good a thing has to be a structured harmony. But it is not in itself. As Plato remarked in the *Republic*, in a passage that few can reconcile with the traditional interpretation of Platonism, the Form of the Good creates the visible and knowable world, and the perceptive and cognitive faculties of people, accommodated to one another.[6] Referring to my own account of the primary cosmology in the previous chapter, the ontological creativity of pattern-making is one crucial aspect of ontological creation. In the present section, this aspect shall be explained as the ontological creation of things as both formed and normed.

Let us say, with Plato in the *Statesman*, that a form is a normative measure, a good way for certain things to be together. A normative measure contrasts with a standard measure such as a yardstick which is laid beside what it is to measure for comparative analysis.[7] For Plato, a normative measure is discerned contextually by a statesman after thorough dialectical studies of all the kinds of things that require integration in society, and after long experience learning taste and timing. Plato described the discernment of normative measures to be an ability to judge how much of one thing to mix with how much of another to achieve justice. The determinateness of the normative measure thus comes not from some objective structure of its own but from the diversity of things to be harmonized, and their own diverse determinate natures derive from the fact that they in turn embody normative measures. To say simply this, however, is not yet helpful, because normative measures must somehow be objectifiable if indeed they are to measure something that needs measuring. We must be able to say something about the internal structure of forms as normative measures.

A clue to the internal structure of forms is that they suppose degrees of vagueness and specificity. (This is what Plato was getting at in the *States-*

man in the funny discussion usually interpreted as an inadequate account of genera and species.) Let us say that primary vagueness is the state of minimally discriminable contrast: a/not-a. This is determinate only in the sense that it measures elementary multiplicity as such. Secondary vagueness is where the "a" has some character—colored/not-colored; tertiary vagueness is where both terms have some character and therefore a relation—a/b, or tall/short. Lower order vagueness, that is, forms that are more specific, add determinateness to the terms and their relations. In all cases of increasing specificity, the specificity depends on elements in the multiplicity to be measured that require determinateness. Suppose we are considering a tall, red vase. To be applicable to an actual, or actualizing-in-the-potter's-hands, vase, the tallness must be specified relative to all possiblities of being taller or shorter; the red has to be specified as to all the possibilities of just this clay and just these glazes; and the vase has to have just one shape and no other. With respect to any order of vagueness whatsoever, that level of order is compatible with contradictory further determinations; to be colored, for instance, is compatible with red/not red, to be red with crimson/not crimson, etc. How these determinations are made depend on the precise components presented for harmonization; the vase can not be scarlet if the clay and glazes at hand yield only crimson.

The least level of vagueness, or complete specificity, is total individual determinateness for all the actual components that might be harmonized; the complexity of this depends on the complexity of the multiplicity presented for harmonization. There is a qualitative jump from any form containing any vagueness whatsoever to the individuality of an actualized pattern. The actualized pattern is an individual nature, an haecceity as Scotus would say, a "this." No other harmony could have that pattern because the pattern is wholly determinate with respect to the individuating elements of the harmony's unique position in the extensional field, the elements of its position. Another way of putting this is that the individual nature is ordered completely by the essential features of the actual harmony.

A "common nature" is a form of any degree of vagueness that can apply to more than one thing because it is vague with respect to the elements that individuate the things. "Three foot tall red vase" is a common nature because it is vague with respect to all the elements that would distinguish between vases of that description. In terms of our primary cosmology, mixture is a different principle from limit, or a different aspect of ontological creation, because it moves a common nature to a haecceity by mixing it with specific components.

That forms are structured in orders of vagueness by their relativity to the pluralities they are to measure, poses a special problem. It would seem that there are no forms except those actualized in the world, for it is the world that supplies the plurality. But if that were so, then forms could not norm the world; they would derive from it. In order to acknowledge the independence of form from the world's actual processes, we should say that its mode of being is subjunctive. That is, form is as it is, in vague orders, upon the condition that it be pluralized. *If there were this plurality, a, b, and c,* then forms x, y, and z would apply to them. Because of the subjunctivity of form, we can imaginatively create a multiplicity, as we do in mathematics or any use of the imagination whatsoever, that is still vague in itself but is specific enough to determine some yet vaguer forms. We thus can imagine a world of forms, even the most specific of which are still vague with reference to how they could become embodied exactly. Subjunctivity is a notion that cannot be given a complete analysis prior to an analysis of time. In temporal terms, a form is subjunctive as a future possibility for integration of components, and subjunctive in a different sense when actualized because it remains one of several forms that could have been actualized even when actualized.

The theory of form here provides a solution to the old nominalism-realism controversy. An individual thing exhibits a wholly individualized haecceistic form, and perhaps can be grasped as such. Nevertheless, included within that form are all the orders of vagueness that in fact are fully specified but subjunctively need not be: the tall, the colored. These constitute common natures, or universals, or Thirds as Peirce would call them, that are intrinsic to the thing and really in it. That a vase is three feet tall does not mean it ceases to be merely tall relative to a plate. It is by virtue of these common natures that things can be known and signified, for the common natures function as signs that could be applied to other things, and connected with other signs. Further, the common natures in a thing might be far more important than their haecceistic specifications. The vase is valued because it is tall, not because it is taller than 2' 11 15/16" and shorter than 1/8" higher; Mary gains more importance from being a person rather than an ape than from being her parent's second rather than third daughter. The fault of nominalism is believing that, because things have unique indiviudal natures that as such can only be indicated and named, they do not also have the vaguer and therefore more universal common natures that are the source of the power to be interpreted and may also be the more important sources of value.

This solution to the nominalism-realism controversy is extraordinarily important for a theory of interpretation. Because it acknowledges that all actualized things are haecceities it can say that there is an individuality or suchness to at least some objects of interpretation; a technical way of saying this is that interpretation can identify harmonies by their specific contrasts, their essentially ordered features, rather than by approximation alone. Because the theory of forms also acknowledges that vague forms remain in actualized things as common natures, it is possible to identify indiviudals by general signs, and to interpret their general characteristics.

What can be said about form in a concrete thing? It is a complex layering of more and less relative vague forms, the latter specifying the former. Because the concrete thing in a harmony, the pattern of layering (a phase to indicate the complicated form) is not merely an order of genera and species, with the (relative) species being responsive to the plurality to be harmonized. Rather, in a harmony the base components are formed into valuable intermediate components, upon intermediate components and on upward to a final complex contrast. The forming of the intermediate components is guided both by the starting point (contrast) of actualities that are potential components and by the ending point of an individual harmony. Therefore the pattern of layering has to exhibit simplicity, an order that, among the many possible orders, sustains as much as possible of the original components in attaining to an intensity and elegance of harmony in the new individual product.

Is there an internal pattern to the pattern that gives simplicity? Whitehead suggested rightly that what he called an "organic" order exhibits four traits: triviality, vagueness, narrowness, and width.

1. Simplicity in a pattern of layering has *triviality* in that it can contain a vast host of things without giving them noticeable importance. Without the capacity to contain components in a trivial way, the harmony would brutely have to exclude most things. Like the motes in the sky, like the gravitational pull of the grains of sand on beaches in the other hemisphere, most things enter any harmony as utterly trivial background. That they are present at all means that, in principle, given the right selective techniques, they might be brought to importance.

2. Simplicity has *vagueness* in that a harmony orients itself to and registers the trivial multitude with some vague common natures – the blue of the sky, the averaged gravitational attraction of the "ground." The sky on a particular morning to a particular person seems a very particular shade of blue – but that is to call attention to the aesthetics of the instrument by which the person contains the trivial motes. Just about any old blue, not brought to much attention, would serve to let the motes be effective in the person, or in any person that morning with a normal human visual apparatus. The vase in Boston might be held on its table by the gravity of specific grains of

sand on China's coast, but the gravitational pull effective on the vase might be equally effective if the China coast were all rocky with no sand. Triviality and vagueness are the tools by which simplicity accommodates vast complexity.

3. *Narrowness* is that trait by which simplicity builds its many layers to create and sharpen stark, intense contrasts of individual features in an individual harmony. The mass of components contained trivially and vaguely is a background for focus on distinctive individuating traits. The foreground focus comes from relating many things so as to reinforce some fews things that in turn stand in sharply defined contrast to one another. A person, for instance, filters a vast array of stimuli through a nervous system that reduces the influences to messages of certain restrictive types that can be separated off from the mechanical causal matrix and employed to refer, interpret, and guide. An amoeba, by comparison, does very well by triviality and vagueness but seems to have minimal narrowness of experiential focus. Experiential examples are easy to give, but the point applies to the dumbest physical object: narrowness has to do with the depth of layering achieved in making parts reinforce parts so as to achieve individual definiteness. A volume of gasses has little narrowness; sunlight passing through clouds and shining at an acute angle to the earth has great narrowness. So does a crystal.

4. *Width* is the trait of simplicity by virtue of which the layering of relative forms of vagueness provides an orientation toward other harmonies. In our previous terms, width is the element in the focal part of a harmony that highlights the conditional connection with other things. Whereas narrowness calls upon essential features to turn the harmony into something far more than its components, width is faithfulness to the connections constituted by the conditional features. Harmonies lacking width also lack reinforcement from their environment except at the trivial level.

Although essential features are more prominent in the traits of vagueness and narrowness, and conditional features in the traits of triviality and width, it is the essential features that determine the hierarchical ordering of the thing's overall pattern. That is, certain kinds of vague properties allow for a multitude to be contained trivially, and certain kinds of narrowness allow for width of connection.

A thing's pattern is the whole array of layers of vague forms exhibiting both simplicity and complexity. In this sense, the pattern is an individual contrast. But how do we abstract patterns from the thing to compare the thing with others, or to imagine alternate patterns? An answer to that question can be gleaned from reflecting on what an artist does in representing a scene. Say, the artist draws the scene with a charcoal. In this case, the artist picks out crucial contours, not every outline, but just those outlines that suggest what the picture might contain were it to be filled in. The outline is subjunctive, as it were, suggesting what the scene might be in detail without specifying the details. Similarly the pattern of a thing consists in common natures instantiated in its focal, that is, its narrow and wide, elements. Because the pattern picks up focal elements, it suggests a background that can have trivial and vague elements. Because the pattern is vague and has common natures rather than the haecceities of the focal elements, it is both representable in a variety of media (charcoal, paint, visual images, verbal description) and can be found in other things (the drawing, although derived from a scene in New York State, might just as well be of Missouri or Korea).

The patterns that we represent to ourselves are highly selective, subject to the language, culture, context, and purpose of interpretation. By virtue of the infinite depth of harmonies, there is an infinite number of ways to pick out their patterns. There are often a great many ways to accurately represent important patterns. In moral deliberation, we attempt to pattern things, and then vary the pattern, examining alternate complexities and simplicities, as discussed above. But too often we discover tragically that the patterns we identified were not the genuinely important ones, only the ones that most struck our aesthetic sense, or were representable in our linguistic terms. The variability of interpretive patterns does not mean, however, that an individual thing does not have its own real pattern or form. It has that form, and it relates through its width to a great many other things in interpretive ways. Human curiosity might never have real hope of getting all the patterns of things. But the important question is whether it can hit on the most valuable patterns, both those that are expressive of the thing's essence relative to conditional features, and those that express its potential effectiveness for entering into other harmonies, for functioning as a condition itself.

The discussion of value so far has focused especially on its surface structure, particularly upon its form. This is only half the story, for a valuable thing is a form ordering components. To pursue the other half of the story, it is necessary to consider harmony in its wholeness.

8

Harmony: A Theory of Components

The discussion up to this point has assumed a common sense understanding of what it means to be a component of a harmony. Yet our common sense is likely to be inadequate to the demands made by this complex theory. For, according to the axiological theory, a component is anything that conditions a harmony, and is itself conditioned *ad infinitum*. There are two elements in our common sense that must be altered in order to accept this notion of harmony.

First is the image, deriving from both atomism and substance philosophy, that the components of a thing are contained within its skin separating it from other things. On this view, to be a component of one thing is precisely to be in that thing rather than in others; identity consists in having one's own components over against other things with their components. The "skin container" image cannot recognize relations as definitive of identity, however. Nor can it show how things do condition one another since it must imagine a magical transfer of effect from one thing to another. Rather, if we are to acknowledge an interlocking world, as defined by the characterizations of identity with conditional and essential features, then we must be able to explain how genuinely other things can be found among the components of a determinate harmony.

Second, our common sense still is bound up in what Whitehead (1925, ch. 3), more than half a century ago, called "simple location." Simple location is the doctrine that a thing is located in its own proper place and not anywhere else; hence, if that thing conditions something else, or is known by another thing, only a representative or substitute can be in the other thing. Whitehead indicated how simple location is incompatible with twentieth century physics and with the possibility of knowledge. The discussion above will have indicated how it is incompatible with conditioning. Instead of simple location, we need a doctrine of "multiple effective location." Multiple effective location supplements a thing's own "proper location" with the locations in other things in which it itself, not a substitute, is effective. If the image of multiple effective location were to become ingrained in our common sense, it would free up and valorize our pervasive experience of things functioning in many minds, of systematic forms of causal conditioning, and of the multilayered organization of reality.

The hypothesis to be developed here is that there are four senses in which things are contained within harmonies or function as components or contents: as (1) claiming components, (2) patterned components, (3) achieved components, and (4) harmonized components. Each component is contained within the harmony in all four senses.

The four senses reflect the four categories of the primary cosmology. That is, as claiming, the components express the indefinite, the principle of plenitude and multiplicity, each insisting on its own value, daring the harmony, as it were, to include it with respect. The self-worth conveyed in presenting their own claims to the harmonizing situation is also the ground of potential disrespect to the harmony that can result in its eventual dissolution. In connection with temporality, to be explored in chapter 9, the claiming character of components provides the force for change in the present.

As patterned, expressing limit or order, each component presents itself as a unity of its own components, with a form that must be accommodated in the larger harmony. Insofar as there is a temporal ordering, the pattern itself is first a future ideal or way of having the component's components together, then an actualization of that way. Also, as patterned, the components exhibit forms or common natures that might be replicated in the form found for the larger harmony, or altered through combination to yield a new pattern.

As achieved, components express mixture. That is, every component is a definitive mixture of pattern and its own components, a mixture that presents a claim regarding its own value in the context of larger harmonies. The mixture is fixed, and respecting temporality is effected in the present, and it characterizes the past. Creating the mixture in present temporality is actualization, and simply being the mixture in the past is actuality.

As harmonized, expressing the cause of mixture, each component stands in the harmony as itself a harmony of harmonies and, as participating in larger harmonies, harmonized with the whole to the extent both participation and the whole are determinate.

These four senses in which things are components of harmony will be analyzed in detail here. Claiming and patterned components will be discussed together as a base for defining the extensionality of the existential field and relating this to intentionality of value. Achieved contents will introduce the topic of continuity and causation, and harmonized contents will provide an occasion for addressing the question of cosmic unity, or lack of unity. Finally, the chapter will sum up the discussion of contents by showing how an understanding of the contents of harmony in the four senses specified leads to knowledge of things as valuable.

I. CLAIMING AND PATTERNED COMPONENTS: EXTENSIONALITY

Components present themselves to a harmony as themselves having achieved specific value as harmonies of their own components, thus making a claim in their own right. If the containing harmony can sustain the whole value of the components, it will at least equal them in value. But of course the components must be made compatible with one another, and so are subject to modification within the containing harmony. The modifications may but need not be important.

The point is that as claiming components, they occupy two "positions": the value each component achieves as its own harmony of components, and the value each presents as a function in the containing harmony. When a thing becomes a component in another thing, being thus multiply located, an extensional field is created. The extensional field is constituted by the harmonizing container that gives the claiming component a place in itself, thereby introducing a diversity of locations for the component. The containing harmony has its own determinate being in part as an extensive field giving the components a place the components would not have otherwise. As harmonies in their own right, the components are themselves field extensions, and so the containing harmony must render these diverse extensions consistent with one another by means of an integral extension of its own; each of the components had done the same thing with its own components.

The most obvious illustration of the notion of extensional field is the existential field of space-time. Harmonies thus have their own time and place, and these are defined relative to the times and places of their components. The notion of extensional field must be broad enough, however, to encompass any kind of harmony. One can talk about logical space, for instance. Chapters 9 and 10 shall give the discussion much greater specificity about temporality, and chapters 11 and 12 shall do the same for space and causation; it will be clearer then what domains other than space-time, if any, need to be interpreted. With the caveat that the dimensionality of space-time is far more complex than common sense notions, common sense illustrations can suffice. (Perhaps the most complicated sense of field extension is required to understand the nature of dialectic and certain kinds of dramatic literature and poetry.)

The theory that the extensional field is constituted by a harmony that turns another thing into one of its components stands in contrast to the more common account that sees the field as a pre-existent medium in which things are located or happen. Paul Weiss, for instance, argues that there is an existential field whose nature is to divide perpetually, and also that there are enduring substances that reassert their identities across the dynamics of the division wherever possible (1958, chs. 1, 3). The difficulty with all such accounts that make the field a determinate thing rather than a function of harmonies is that some analyzed super-field must be invoked to account for the relation between the field and the contained substances. Weiss recognizes this and invokes other fundamental modes of being to effect the relation; but the problems of how one thing can be in another are only multiplied this way.[1] No sense can be made of the assertion that things are "in" an extensional field; to be "in" at all is simply and already to be extensional.

Whitehead was more nearly right in arguing in *Process and Reality* that the extensive continuum is constituted by the newly emergent entity as the form in which it integrates its components. The limit of Whitehead's view, however, is that it does not consistently maintain the reality of the component in itself, especially a past component. On his view, a past occasion is contained within a present occasion, albeit perhaps in modified form. He also argues in places, an argument carried out consistently by Hartshorne, that once an occasion is finished it needs to be prehended in some subsequent entity in order to be real; in fact, in order that some reality not be lost, there must be a perfect divine prehender who cannot modify anything. The result of this view is a commitment to what Heidegger and others have called the "metaphysics of presence": to be real is to be real relative to some present. It puts Whitehead's account of the extensional field in danger of subjective idealism; namely, the doctrine that extensional relations are matters of subjective projects.

To say that the extensional field is constituted by harmonies that make other things components of themselves is to build in both otherness and identity to the account. There is the otherness between the component as it is in itself, as the achievement of its own value, and the component as valued within the harmony. The component is in itself just what it is, regardless of its participation in larger harmonies (although of course many things could not exist as harmonies in their own right without also being taken up into other things). In temporal perspective, an earlier thing is real, with whatever reality it achieves, irrespective of whatever it might become as a component in some later thing. If there were not this exteriority involved in the very notion of an extensional field, it would be impossible to maintain the externality required for the dyadic nature of truth as the measurement of interpretations by the real. The objects of interpretation would be internalized and transformed into the mere representations of them. At the least, logical space must involve externality or difference between the component as its own achievement of value and the component as component, in order for truth to be the carryover of value from one to the other when the harmonizing container is an interpreter.

The identity involved in the field consists in the fact that it is the same achieved value, the same determinate thing, that is both in itself and a component of the containing harmony. This is a fundamental metaphysical or cosmological point. If the extensional field were an independent medium in which things are located, then a thing in one place could only be represented in another place by another thing, giving rise to all the conundra of representative knowledge and of the continuity of force. That the extensive field is constituted by the harmonies themselves means that a component in fact can have two or more positions. If modified by containing harmonies, it changes but still is the same thing.

This theory thus agrees with most substance theories in claiming that a determinate thing can be extended spatially and temporally, enduring change by virtue of multiple location. But it agrees with process philosophy in claiming that extensiveness is the product of a harmony containing a component that presents its own value, the extensive field being a cumulative product of the harmonies of components of components. Because of the latter claim, it must reject the doctrine often associated with substance philosophies or atomisms asserting an independence for the extensive medium. And because of the former claim it rejects the reduction of all temporality to the role of the past and future for the present, a reduction characteristic of process philosophy.

That a determinate thing presents itself with its value claim to be a component in a larger harmony constitutes an intensional as well as extensional field. The component is not merely a representation of what has achieved value in its own right, but the real achievement, though perhaps modified. Moreover, the components of the components themselves are real achievements of value, *ad infinitum*. Although the modifications for the sake of compatibility at each node of harmony might diminish the value of the components in themselves, there still is continuity through a line of infinite remoteness. "Remoteness" is perhaps the wrong word, for the most remote elements, down to the least measurable triviality, are still intensionally present. Further, their extensional properties, however trivially, still play some role in the extensional character of the containing harmony.

The density of value in a harmony is thus both extensional and intensional. Extensionally, a thing's components are other things (with their own components and so on down) with their own determinations of extensionality integrated by means of the containing harmony's contributions to the extensional field. The "place" of a harmony (including logical place) includes the places of its components as "placed." The "boundary" of a harmony is a function of the nature and degree of modification the containing harmony places on the component. If there is no modification, the component fits wholly inside the containing harmony as a proper part; the organ systems in an animal body are illustrations. If there is great modification, the boundary lies between the potential component unmodified and the component modified; there is a boundary thus between food and the animal that eats and digests it. The problem of boundaries is complicated by the fact that the nature of the modification often rests on context; modifications are important in some contexts and not in others, with the result that there are significant boundaries in some contexts and not in others.

The claiming aspect of components is associated with the indefinite, the principle of plenitude, because it defines the extensional field dynamically. That is, the various components each press their diverse claims to have their value recognized, and the containing harmony is perceived in this aspect as making itself yet a new thing that contains them, with a new extensional place. Within temporal things, this is the locus of change and novelty. The indefinite is one expression of Whitehead's category of creativity, the many becoming one, increasing the many by one. It is also akin in its extensionality to Plato's Receptacle, which, however, sometimes seems to be an independent medium.

Each component is itself a unity of components and that unity exhibits a pattern. Hence, another sense in which a component is in a harmony is as patterned. According to previous arguments, the pattern cannot be a "third term" that unites the components by containing them under its own aegis. Rather it is simply the way the components fit together as modified to be compatible. In the course of modification, components can be combined and recombined, and higher levels of combination can be third terms for levels two or more down. The components at the top level of a harmony simply fit together in a complex contrast, each being what it is, as modified, relative to the others.

As discussed earlier, the patterns in a harmony exhibit complexity, in answer to the diverse components, and simplicity, in answer to the need to integrate them. Simplicity will be discussed further in the following sections on value and form. Here we may note that patterns contain both extensional and intensional matrices. That is, as contrasts of components, they exhibit how these components, and components of components, relate to one another.

The special contribution of the aspect of patternedness among components of a harmony is its unique contribution to value. As a thought experiment, consider patterns apart from the components they are to unify. In themselves they are simply logical forms according to which things might be fitted together, if there were any of the right things. If indeed there are the right things, then the patterns are normative for fitting them together. Since the values integrated are in addition to the values achieved in disjunction, their integration is a plus value (even if a different integration would have been a much greater value, and even if it would be better not to have that integration all things considered). Further, the form of integration might have some degree of simplicity higher than mere conjunction, which adds to the value of the things separately. Of course there is always a trade-off between the loss in value that would come through modifying the components so as to make them compatible and the increase in value through simplicity.

Given the claim of components to have their achieved value respected in the larger harmony, the patterns of unity are more or less normative according to how they maintain that respect. In themselves, the patterns are purely subjunctive: they are ways certain things could be together, achieving the value of that togetherness, if there were any such things. If there are indeed such things as the components for a harmony, then the patterns are normative for those components potentially harmonized. Alternate patterns for a given set of components differ in value by means of differences in simplicity; patterns that differ in virtue of harmonizing different sets of components differ in value relative to complexity.

That in a set of components to which a harmonizing pattern relates primarily is the patterns of the components. The pattern thus would harmonize "these kinds" of things, but not "those kinds." This is the truth in the idealist position that interprets integration in terms of the connections of universals. The limit to the idealist position, however, comes in the subjunctivity of pattern. A pattern would integrate subordinate patterns of certain kinds, if there were any. The subordinate patterns in turn are integrations of sub-subordinate patterns, if there are any, and so on. Conceptually, of course, we may simply posit some definite complexity of universals; we do this directly as mathematicians, and in common sense we assume that the patterns we see in things are real patterns that can be integrated at higher levels. In fact, however, there are real components with extensionality and the dynamism of the indefinite, as well as with their own patterns. Indeed, it is only because there is extensionality all the way down that there can be patterns all the way down. With respect to pattern, a thing is a component of a harmony because its pattern fits into the thing's overall pattern; contrarywise, the overall pattern is possible only because the thing contributes itself to be integrated.

In one sense, the value in a harmony comes from the fact that its pattern is the way it makes its components compossible, in the ways discussed above. Pattern is thus the bestower of value, and the components of a harmony are valuable because they are actualizations of their own value-pattern. Plato had a profound insight in associating the Good with form.

A pattern as common nature can be reiterated from one thing to another, so long as all have components with the right patterns to fit into the reiterated patterns. According to Leibniz' principle of the identity of indiscernables, however, if two things have absolutely no differences in pattern, they cannot be two. We cannot say that the same wholly definite pattern can be in two places in the extensional field, since the difference in places is a diference in the pattern of the field. Therefore, because patterns obviously do have reiterations, we must distinguish again between patterns as partially vague, allowing many iterations without caring about trivial differences, and patterns with haecceity made wholly concrete and unreplicable. This leads to the discussion of achieved components.

II. ACHIEVED COMPONENTS: ACTUAL SPACE-TIME

A harmony is not only a collection of components to be harmonized plus a pattern to harmonize them, but also the actual mixture in which the individuality of the harmony consists. A pattern is a way of integrating types of sub-patterns, and is indifferent to the details. The details are settled by the sub-patterns with respect to their own sub-sub-patterns, and so on down. Patterns, in other words, need to be accomodated to wholly definite patterned individuals in order to be wholly definite themselves. On the other side, a collection of wholly definite individuals that are potential components of an integrating harmony may have a great many alternative possibilities. They are, disjunctively, vague with respect to how they can be harmonized definitely and need to be brought to some one definite pattern. Therefore, neither the principle of limit nor the principle of the indefinite is sufficient to provide an analysis of a harmony.

Harmony as mixture is actuality. Actuality involves the transformation of vague, replicable pattern into singular definite nature. Duns Scotus was the first to see the importance of this point, in his distinction between common natures and haecceities. Patterns are common natures, but harmonies are "thises." On the other side, actuality involves the choice among possible forms of harmony to give a definite and singular way things are. Whitehead was perhaps the clearest philosopher on this point, at least in a temporal mode, in his doctrine of creativity as rendering the many past entities, which are potentials for a new thing, into a unique new individual, thereby increasing the many by one.

At this point, it is necessary to anticipate to some degree the discussion of temporality to come. For, harmonies are not entirely actual; they are actual only as past, as having become wholly definite. Insofar as there is a process of becoming, of becoming actual, harmonies are yet partially vague with respect both to how their components will be integrated and to how they will completely specify their possibilities. And insofar as harmonies are regarded with respect to their future, they are very vague indeed, depending on the intermediate careers of a great many decisive factors. Many of the most important elements of certain kinds of harmony, such as the capacities to grow or to think, depend on crucial incompleteness of definiteness as being essential (essential and not conditional). Nevertheless, harmonies must be at least partially actual, therefore at least partially achieved mixtures, because their components are actual and their patterns cannot be wholly indefinite.

An actual thing presents itself as a potential component for a containing harmony. Included in its actuality is the value it achieved by contracting its pattern to its own components; this value is its haecceity, its thisness. In its turn, it contains its own actual components, and their components, and so on, with the result that there is an infinitely dense achievement of value presented in each component.

The "problem" for a harmony is to reconcile the actualities of its components together in a patterned mixture of its own. This may require cutting off, paring, substituting, or excluding potential components. It may also involve harmonizing them on many levels, excluding some of their reality on one level in order to bring it back enhanced on another. Insofar as the process of actualization is temporal, it is not possible for all actuality to be carried on in the present: its disjunct elements must be compromised, with some loss. Nevertheless, once there has been an actual achievement, that actualization stands with its own achieved nature in its proper place in the extensional field. Perhaps only some of its actual nature attains multiple location in subsequent present harmonizations.

Therefore the achieved contents of a harmony give it actuality and connection with the rest of the actual world. It bears within itself the value achieved by its contents. Is there any sense at all in which the achieved contents of a harmony are different from those actual things in themselves, or is each harmony the container of the entire realm of actuality up to its time? There is a difference, of course, in that a harmony may change many of its contents in order to integrate them with one another. So, the full reality of an actual thing is one thing, its modified reality is another. This difference cannot be understood, however, without reference to the extensional field. An actualized thing with multiple effective locations has its own full reality in its own proper place in the extensional field. Insofar as it enters into other harmonies as a condition, it is modified, and the modifications, along with those of the other components, go to make up the proper place of the containing harmony in the extensional field. If we were limited to a doctrine of simple location, we would have to say that the actual achieved mixture is exhausted in the reality it has in its proper place. But instead, by virtue of acknowledging that a mixture is an achievement of actuality, we can say that its proper place is the fullness achieved by its satisfaction of all the constraints of integrating its own components, and that its multiple effective places are still its own reality as effective in other places. Because of the compromising necessary to integrate that component with others, its full actuality might not be present in the containing harmony; but such of its actuality as is effectively present is the same actuality that portion possessed or possesses in its own proper place. There are not two actualities for the component, its fulness and a diminished representation; there is one actuality in whole or partial effectiveness.

The continuity of actuality in multiple effective locations aids in understanding the sense in which a harmony constitutes its own proper place in the extensional field. What does a harmony have to work with, as it were, except the potential conditions each in its own proper place and perhaps some as effective in modifications of one another? The very potentials for a unique proper place for the containing harmony thus are the proper places of its components as subject to modification. The intrinsic nature of the extensional field is not something apart from all determinate things, but is rather constituted by what each can do with the proper places of the others that are actual for it. The apparent continuities and regularities of space-time and of logical fields come because each of the actual mixtures must cope with others that have coped with others and so on back. Perturbations in space-time come from perturbing actual events, not from wrinkles in an independent extensional field. There are logical, emotional, and social perturbations as well, because any field-character derives from the ways in which each thing achieves its own actuality by putting together elements of its potential component actualities.

The achieved value in a component is what makes a claim for a place in other potentially containing harmonies. The elementary origin of obligation comes from the achievements out of which a new achievement can make itself. The secondary origin of obligation comes from the various values in the patterns by which integrations are possible. The primary obligations give determinate content to the secondary ones.

It should be remarked here that the essential features of a harmony are those involved in modifying and integrating the achieved potential components so as to make up the harmony. At least some of these essential features are concerned with creating the unique proper place of the new individual harmony, and these features are expressed in the final actual achievement. From the standpoint of the proper places of the component actualities, the elements contributing the unique proper place of the containing harmony are "spontaneous." That is, even though they may express a continuity of a matrix extending from the actual extensional field, they make up precisely what is not contained with the actualized components: the proper place of the containing harmony. As remarked earlier, a thing's own position *vis-à-vis* other things is at the heart of what is essential to it.

A final remark needs to be made about achieved components and actual things. Because actuality, mixture, always presupposes the success of actualization or mixing, it has the character of a past tense, a *factum*. And the past does not change except insofar as it is effective in subsequent changes. This is not to suggest, however, that actualities are static. The Chinese would go so far as to say that there are no static actualities, only actual movements. Indeed, most actualities are moving things or movements. To account for this a critical notion of temporality is called for. One must beware of a premature closure of that account, however, that would come by conceiving of actuality as a slide show of once-present presents that are now collectively past. The actual world consists mainly, it appears, of things whose very essence is to be temporally thick and in movement. The principle of mixture is equi-primordial with limit and the indefinite; there would be no multiplicity determining patterns, or patterns integrating disjunct plenitude, without the individualizing *esse* of mixture.

III. HARMONIZED COMPONENTS: COSMOS AND CHAOS

The fourth sense in which things are contained within a harmony is precisely as being harmonized there. Not only is a component part of the larger containing harmony, it is itself a harmony of harmonies of harmonies. Not only that, the harmony of which it is a component is itself a component of harmonies upon harmonies upon harmonies. In a profound sense, a thing's identity is its place, or movement through places, in the great cosmic harmony.

This might be dangerous thinking, however, if the degree of cosmic harmony is exaggerated. In no sense can we assume that the cosmos is a totality, for in every movement there are things lost and things gained. Hegel saw this point better than most, and it is ironic that he also believed that the cosmos constitutes a totality. He purchased his belief, however, by leaving aside those things, the irrational, which do not fit into his principle of totalization, reason. All actualities have their proper place and value, contrary to Hegel, even if they are not multiply effective so as to condition other important actualities. The overall continuity of the extensional field, which is usually what is meant as the basic condition of totality, depends on the actual conditioning of one thing by another. Where that conditioning does not take place, and one thing is indeterminate with respect to the other, the extensional connection is also indeterminate.

There are of course a great many kinds of harmony: organisms, assemblages, trajectories, events, groups, mental and emotional things, cultures and civilizations, elementary particles, supernovas, bare conjunctions and homogeneous masses. These interplay with one another, changing and affecting one another in myriad ways. Part Three will sort some of these out.

From the standpoint of a harmony in process of actualization, the possibilities sought in order to achieve integration of the components are those that position the harmony itself so as to achieve value. That is, the harmony's value is not only what it makes out of its components, but how its particular way of integrating its components gives it valuable places in the larger harmonies in which it exists or will exist. Most things play roles in many systems, and although they have an immediate value as integrations of what those systems bring to it as potential components, they also have contributing values to the systems as such. In physical systems, things might not have much latitude of variant integration. But in social systems, people at least have a great deal of latitude about how they integrate themselves day by day, contributing well or poorly to this or that larger harmony—family, society, civilization.

The essential task of spiritual perfection—finding the central Tao, the way that makes one's own positions centered in the larger harmonies, most valuable in harmonizing and being harmonized—displays a crucial part of the ontological character of determinate harmony. A thing's overall worth consists in how well it harmonizes and how well it contributes to its containing harmonies. This obligation to fit in does not compromise freedom since there are many valuable ways of harmonizing and being harmonized, and freedom is what poses our problem in the first place: rocks can not go wrong. With whatever kinds of interlocking harmonies the cosmos contains, a thing's value consists in large part in how it contributes to the values of those harmonies in which it is or could be effective.

The question of the unity of the harmony of harmonies is a profound one. To be sure, a unity of interpretation is imposed in three ways. First, reality is filtered through what is biologically representable in human interpretation. Then there are the unities imposed by culture, language, and singular human purposes. But suppose there are non-biological interpreters, with different cultures, languages, and purposes. Different unities would be imposed, or discovered. Yet is there a unity to things over and above those that necessarily are employed in order to interpret? Should interpretation necessarily deconstruct its functional unities in decribing the cosmos? Should interpretation deliberately insist that each thing it interprets has its own perspective on reality, with its own order? Is chaos the sum of all orders, as David Hall (1982) has argued?

All of these questions ultimately turn on empirical issues. Is a given harmony conditionally related to another given harmony in a certain respect or not? If so, then an interpretive perspective is possible that recognizes that. But whether the relation in that respect is compatible with relations in other respects may not be representable within the interpretive perspective. There is no *a priori* guarantee that some superarching persepctive will be able to reconcile and make commensurable the diverse interpretive truths brought out in diverse frames of reference. There is, however, the *a posteriori* commitment to search for such a reconciling perspective whenever two frameworks make incommensurable claims. Because of the infinity of intensive value, no finite perspective can be exhaustive, no matter how comprehensive. Therefore there always will be a contrast between the finitude of all interpretive perspectives and the infinite richness of the world. Any perspective then will be somewhat arbitrary, although it may well be able to be shown to be a very valuable perspective. There is no escaping the irony of the contrast between the infinity of the world, expressed aesthetically, and the finitude of finite interpretations, that inevitably have a moral dimension.

The discussions in these last three sections have explored four senses in which things are components of harmony. They have opened up a theory of extensionality, as well as a theory of the intensionality of value. These themes will be further explored in the chapters on temporality and causation.

IV. KNOWLEDGE OF VALUE

Properly speaking, a discussion of how value is known in things is out of place here. That discussion lacks the generality of this axiological chapter, and its topic is in fact the topic of the whole book, dependent on the theory of interpretation. Nevertheless, the common assumption that we cannot know values in things is a stumbling block to the serious consideration of the theory of value. Further, a plausible account here, even if preliminary in light of further complications to come, can reinforce the common feeling that of course we do know the values in things despite the fact that we are not supposed to.

The argument begins with another reminder of the just-mentioned fact that we do know things as valuable. We take our surrounding aesthetically as beautiful or ugly, intriguing or boring, important or trivial. We appreciate the people in our lives for their various characters, good and bad. And we also construe things for how they help, hinder, lure, guide, or disabuse our purposes. In all these instances our naive appreciation is for the value characteristics in the things. Only as a secondary move do we say that they give us pleasure or pain, move us toward or away from them, or are to be construed in terms of how they are valuable for us. The secondary move is of course important, essential to individual self-identity, to personal value, and to appropriating the objective characters of the valuable things. The secondary move is the way by which other valuable things condition us. But we must not be misled to think that the value consists only in our own value feelings projected onto things. That runs directly contrary to what we experience.

Equally impressive in our experience is that our grasp of the values achieved in things is fallible and corrigible. Experience teaches that our initial sense of things' worths are often misleading or plain mistaken, and as we discover what really is going on we correct our evaluations. The more we know about something and its context, the more subtle our appreciation. It is hard to conceive denying this aspect of experience.

Where does the impediment lie to acknowledging the value-laden character of our relatively naive experience? Historically, there are three impediments in the modern period: the distinction of primary from secondary and tertiary properties, the assumption of representative perception, and the triadic character of interpretation.

Accepting the assumptions of modern physics about the nature of the real natural world, John Locke and others distinguished between the primary qualities science deals with in things, and the secondary or tertiary qualities that the mind ascribes to them because of its own structure. Color appearances are obviously a function of the seer's visual apparatus, not of the light waves or particles, and so are screens by which real things appear to mind. Values are even more subjective assessments of secondary qualities, depending on will, taste, or perceptions of inner sense, according to one philosopher or another. Now therc is a firm truth in the belief that things are modified and transformed as they manifest themselves in the various media transporting them to our experience. It is probably safe to say that we transform all things into the forms of our nervous system and subsequently to the experiential forms that work with that data. The theory of extensionality suggested above, to be developed in chapter 11, makes transformation the expectation. But what is there to suggest that value is not among the original, primary qualities, subject to modification but nevertheless partly continuous from object to experience? Only an alternative cosmology that postulates that value cannot be among the primary qualities. The answer to that alternative cosmology is one such as that being developed here that shows that value is the implicit contribution of form. This axiological cosmology allows all of the scientific hypotheses to be possible in their positive assertions, but supplementing them with an account of the value from which they abstract. The axiological cosmology allows the *prima facie* sense of value in experience to be asserted realistically.

The assumption of representative perception is a more direct attack on the reality of values in things because it seeks to cut off the causal continuity between primary qualities and their registration in experience. Representative perception, or representative knowledge, is the belief that, things having simple location, their function in a perceiver or knower must be through a representative with a different substance from themselves. To be sure, we do make representations of things; all signs have a representative function. But is there no continuity between things and their representation? A dualist separation of physical from mental reality must deny the continuity, although Descartes tried hard to give a causal account of their interaction in the pineal gland. (His account failed because it suddenly assumed that mental elements were not representations but were physical-like motions.) Immanuel Kant denied the continuity by dropping real things with primary qualities and admitting only a distinction between the subjective order of our personal representations and an objective order of representations which he labeled the empirical world. Charles Peirce, on the other hand, argued that the character of natural causation in the world has the form of sign-interpretation; on the basis of this he could show that human experience is just a particularly interesting part of the natural process, preserving the continuity. William James argued that experience itself, interpreted according to his "radical empiricism," provides the continuity bewen things and the interpretation of them, with the difference between the things and their interpretation being due to their different contexts. Alfred North Whitehead provided a complex theory of self-constitution and connection of natural things which showed how every emerging thing has a moment of mentality and that complex emerging things such as the higher animals have experiential contact with their conditions and the field in which they project their own actions; he called this the vector quality of experience. The account developed in the previous and succeeding chapters continues this tradition of naturalistic interpretation of the relation between real objects and experience. If this tradition can be developed and defended, this by itself constitutes and adequate answer to those who say that all perception and knowledge is by representation alone, with the corollary that values are a function of the representations, not the real objects.

The most serious challenge to the *prima facie* validity of the experience of things as valuable comes from the claim that interpretation is always triadic. That is, anything we can know or say about something is always mediated by a sign of the thing, and a questioning of whether the sign is well-taken always involves further, usually more removed, signs. Value thus can be found in a summary judgment about something interpreted, but not in the object itself; or if it is in the object itself, it can't be known there through mediating interpretation.

The challenge posed by this construal of interpretation is to show that the object itself is not lost in mediation, that meditation does not mean total alienation and replacement of the object by signs. This can be shown in the logical character of interpretation itself. An interpretant takes a sign to stand for its object in a certain respesct. The "taking" of the interpretive relation is a fourth thing over and above the object, sign and interpretant. It is in fact an intuitive, unmediated harmony that includes the object as a proper part. The taking, of course, is fallible—perhaps most of our interpretations are mistakings. As with our value-experience, further experience corrects these intuitive harmonies. But the harmonies are indeed inclusive of the object with whatever value it has by virtue of embodying its form in its content. This conclusion follows naturally from the account of the senses in which a harmony contains its components. Interpretation is a particular kind of harmonizing of the components that go to make up the object, sign, and interpretant.

"Intuition" is not used here to denote an unmediated grasp of the object. Therefore it cannot be thought infallible or used as an epistemologically certain building block in a certain edifice of knowledge. But it is used in the sense of an immediate grasp of things together. Intuition is the grasp of a harmony as harmonious, and as containing the value achieved in the harmony. Intuition is thus intrinsically appreciative.

Were we not to admit an intuition of this sort, it would be impossible to see how we could grasp things as harmonious. What could that grasp be except a seeing of how the various components of a harmony interpret one another (through conditional features in essential positions) so as to produce the integrated whole? The immediate unity in the making of an interpretation is an example of the immediate unity of the components of a harmony together; the complex pattern of disposing conditional and essential features according to triviality, vagueness, narrowness, and width is a special kind of interpretive pattern. In correcting a valuation, we rarely stand back to examine the signs used in interpreting it. Rather we examine the interpretations of its parts, one to another, to see whether they are as we had assumed. We usually see through our experiential signs to the signs and sign relations in the object. Thus it is simply to be expected that the values experienced in things are really there or, if they are not, it is because their values are different from what they originally seemed.

To show that we do experience things as valuable is not by itself to demonstrate that everything with form is valuable, for there are many things we don't experience. But I have argued that what makes things valuable for experience is their harmonic structure, and that this is the object of our valuational intuitions. This harmonic structure is the same structure hypothesized for any determinate thing. Therefore if it makes objects of experience valuable, it makes any determinate thing valuable. Or at least the argument puts the burden of demonstration on those who want to make something special about objects of interpretive experience that gives value to them but to nothing else. The more universal hypothesis is by far the simpler.

The axiological theory I am proposing is a speculative, empirical hypothesis, highly mediated and intuitive only in the sense that one grasps its meaning. It supposes, however, that an empirical survey of valuations will reveal experience to be interpreted as intuition of the sort hypothesized. In both the experience of works of art and moral experience there are moments of "just seeing" that things hang together. There are other moments in which the previous valuation comes apart because the components believed harmonized turn out to be other than they seemed. The theory also supposes that in criticizing a value judgment, we vary complexity and simplicity, intuiting the imagined results. Further, the intuition of value involved appreciating the simplicity of a thing's pattern as having triviality, vagueness, narrowness and width, any of which can be objectified for analysis. Subsequent chapters will make this analysis far more nuanced and subtle. What has been said so far, however, indicates the plausibility of trusting that we experience the values of things and that, when we find ourselves mistaken, the mistake is that the value is different from what we thought, not that things do not have values.

The purpose of this chapter, following its predecessor, has been to begin weaving a complex contextual tapestry for a theory of value. The chapter has indicated something of the place of value-theory or axiology in contemporary thought, and it has presented a preliminary categoreal interpretation of what makes things valuable. This interpretation has grown out of the metaphysical language of the previous chapter and aims to remain in continuity with the philosophy of nature to be developed subsequently. Absolutely central to the thesis of this book is that value be given an account as a universal trait of nature or determinate being. Only if this is so can truth be understood as the carryover of value from object to interpretation, properly qualified.

DIVISION THREE

Philosophy of Nature: A Cosmology of Participation

Preliminary Remarks

The thesis that truth is, among other things, the carryover of value from objects into the experience interpreting them supposes that interpretive activity participates in all the things about which there might be true faithfulness. Yet modern epistemology has presupposed a philosophy of nature in which this is difficult to conceive. Expressed in various ways, the modern cosmology supposes that, regarding truth about the natural world, the objects have primary qualities whereas the experience of them is exclusively in terms of secondary or tertiary qualities. Or, the world is objective fact whereas experience is of and by a subjective stuff. Or, the world is a concrete existential thing whereas experience is of ideas or essences. These and many other common philosophic expressions represent the world as alien to the stuff of experience, with the result that most philosophies, and the common sense notions expressed in them, either construe the world to be real and experience "merely" subjective or even epiphenomenal, or construe experience or consciousness to be real and the world to be a construction of experience. What is needed is a cosmology that can be shown to contain the full richness of human interpretation as a special domain of nature, participating interpretively in all the other domains.

The first obstacle to such a rich cosmology is a failure adequately to conceive of time's three modes: past, present and future. Most modern cosmologies have assumed that the "time lines" characteristic of past time also apply without modification to present and future time. So, physicists can speak of cosmic time as being in principle reversible. The twentieth century has reacted against this by emphasizing the existential spontaneity that characterizes present temporality. Existentialism, process philosophy, and pragmatism share this focus on present change. Yet, I will argue, they fail to appreciate the intrinsic characters of past and future temporality, acknowledging them only insofar as they are implicated in present time. This is clearly inadequate for a theory of participatory interpretation, since an interpretation takes time and therefore involves past, present, and future together. Chapter 9 distinguishes and relates the three modes of temporality.

Chapter 10 then elaborates a theory of enduring things that observe the temporal modalities. The usual approach to this issue is to treat individuals and environments, or individuals alone. Yet, there are many things that endure, including individuals, non-individual functions within individuals, situations, historical events, causal processes, and the like. Especially important are interpretive processes in which many people are involved, such as a constitutional deliberation, a family quarrel, or the rise of a new style of music.

The great difficulty in accounting for enduring things is not temporality, once the three modes are adequately distinguished, but rather their spatiality. Space has been a neglected topic in recent philosophy, neglected in favor of concern for time. Why Heidegger, for instance, said that time is the horizon for human being, any more than space, is a mystery; yet most thinkers have taken his word for it. Perhaps the linguistic turn itself has led to the neglect of space as a topic; language seems to be temporal and not spatial, especially if the study of language assumes a Cartesian or Kantian cosmology.

The theory of space that will be defended is particularist and immanentist. That is, space is a characteristic of spatial things, and places are the result of all the things that have happened in their coordinates. Such a theory makes it difficult to conceive of motion, which seems easy enough to conceive when one assumes that things are bodies traveling through an empty void. Chapter 11 develops both a theory of space and then a theory of motion.

Chapter 12 then undertakes a summary discussion of causation, attempting to illustrate how various kinds of experientially observed causation illustrate the cosmological idea. It concludes with a theory of participation whereby both the continuities and discontinuities of things in interaction can be understood. This sets the stage for the particular kinds of interactive participation required for interpretation.

9

Modalities of Time

Interpretation is a temporal activity. As an action it takes place in the present. The objects interpreted, or signs of them, are finished facts given from the past. The purposes and other aspects of intentionality guiding interpretation are oriented in certain necessary respects toward the future. Present, past, and future are modes of time, strikingly different from one another. How are they related? Time and temporality have been greater problems for twentieth century thought than for that of any other period.[1]

It might seem that temporality is not intrinsic to truth if truth is some kind of mirroring or correspondence, an isomorphic topological relation. If God is omniscient and eternal, as was assumed in certain prior ages, then it is difficult to see how temporality could be important to having true knowledge. Hegel argued, however, in the very case of God, that truth involves moving from non-representative immediacy to an alienation that allows of representational marking of sameness and difference. Truth can not be an adventitious isomorphism, but one that causally arises out of a special process of alienation, or one that arises from a process of taking an adventitious isomorphism to be a sign of an object. Existentialists, process philosophers, and pragmatists construe temporality as a fundamental condition not only for human life but for the making and having of truth. How much more is this a condition for a philosophy that says truth is the carry-over of value from objects to their interpretation?

The purpose of this chapter is to develop a theory of time and its temporal modes, making good on some of the promissory notes of previous chapters and setting the stage for a temporal theory of interpretation. The first three sections will begin the analysis of time by characterizing the differences between present, past, and future respectively; this will require development of the categories of temporality and timeliness. The fourth section will discuss the being of time, relating the theory to the metaphysics developed earlier, and noting how very much more complicated time is than our common sense representations, such as the time line, would lead us to believe. Chapter 10 will ask what it means to be in time, and respond with a theory of endurance, change, and perishing throughout the temporal modes; it will also treat time-consciousness with special attention to how it relates to interpretation.

Despite the length and density of these two chapters on time, they will seem curiously partial. Time cannot be understood without reference to space: chapter 11 must then take up that topic, developing the notion of extensional field introduced earlier. Further, endurance through time cannot be understood apart from motion across space-time.

I. PRESENT

Process philosophy, existentialism, and pragmatism have demonstrated in their respective conceptual languages that the present is the mode of time in which change takes place.[2] The timeliness of the present, what time is in the present, is the decisive action that renders previously given actualities into a new actual situation, a new harmony. Perhaps the new situation is internally innovative, but perhaps it is only numerically distinct from the old situation, with merely the novelties in the extensional field that this entails. To say that the present is decisive is not to suppose that it contains deciding agents; it is not to adopt an anthropomorphism of the sort of which process philosophy is often (unjustly) accused. Rather, the present is decisive in the sense that the diverse potentialities given by the past are actualized in some one definite order out of the many possibilities of arrangement. The decisive present cuts off possibilities for realizing larger possibilities, and actualizes but one, as Wallace Stevens pointed out, a glorious transformation from possibilities lit by past actualities into new actuality.[3]

The present-timeliness of a present moment can be analyzed indirectly into before and after relations, before this or that aspect of decision versus after. The reason for this is that any unit of change can be analyzed into logical elements of "reduction of the vague to determinateness." As will be argued at length shortly and in later chapters, the structure of real future possibility is such that it is somewhat vague. That is, as a whole possibility it will be realized, but there are several ways in which it might be realized. Part of present activity is to decide in just which way to realize it. A possibility that is completely determined has haecceity and is thus already actualized. To be future, a possibility must involve at least a bit of vagueness so that its actualization is the reduction of that vagueness to determinateness. Because of the logical interconnection of future possibilities, the resolution of one possibility from vagueness to determinateness has ramifications regarding other possibilities. In some, there will be a concommitant reduction, as when deciding to sit or stand determines whether the chair will be under pressure. In other cases, the resolution of one vague possibility makes other possibilities more vague, as when a decision to leave home opens new opportunities for experience. The analysis of a complex moment of change is a logical investigation of the relations among the various reductions of vague possibilities to determinate actualities. Such an analysis can be performed by noting what in fact has been changed in a given moment.

But the timeliness of a present moment cannot be analyzed into earlier and later segments, for that would suppose not a single present action but an earlier action that would be a finished potential for a later action, or a later action that would be a possible sequel for an earlier. Objectively, present-timeliness consists in a series of stages; before and after decisions are made to reduce the relative indefiniteness of the before-decision stage to the relative definiteness of the after-decision stage. The stage achieving complete definiteness or individuality is not earlier or later than any other stage in that present; when it is reached that action is complete and it has past timeliness.

In itself, the timeliness of a present moment cannot be directly analyzed, only felt. Subjectively, present-timeliness consists in the decidings themselves. The immediate subjectivity of a present moment is simply the active decision to wreak this immediately contained given set of conditions into some individual outcome that determines possibilities. The present always involves a process of deciding, creating toward complete definiteness but not having it until the moment is past.[4]

"Timeliness" has been used to indicate what time is like for the present, and shortly will be used to characterize the timeliness of the past and future. Timeliness is to be distinguished from temporality. Temporality is the way by which something, including a mode of time, relates to time as such, or is constituted by time. Unlike its timeliness, the temporality of the present includes an earlier past and a future that shall come after. The reason the logical analysis of present timeliness discussed above was called indirect is precisely because it had to appeal to the future, and thus to the present's temporality. This temporality is internally constitutive of the present as present; otherwise there would be no essential relation of present to past and future. Past and future are essential to present temporality, not mere conditions. This is to say, time is not present existence alone, but present, past, and future as essentially connected. The discussion of enduring temporal things will elaborate this point of essential connectedness through time.

Present temporality includes causal conditions as past, with their own timely and temporal structures. Part of the essential temporality of the present is to have a history leading up to it, providing its situation and its multitude of contents to be resolved. Past actual achievements are potentialities present action has to work with, and may be combined and altered according to the structure of possibilities. "Potentiality," thus, is a word to be reserved for association with the past; it means the actual resources providing raw material, as it were, for present change. "Possibility" is a word that ought to be reserved for reference to what the future provides to a present moment of change. "Causation," of course, is to be understood as that mixture of possibility and potentiality effected by present action resulting in an individual actualization of vague possibilities. Although the timeliness of the present as such is decisive action, the temporality of the present includes an inherited past with which to act and a real future as an arena of action. Because of this we can be unaware of our momentary bondage to the present when, in explicit decision-making, for instance, we assume connection with an effective past and an urgent future, neglecting conscious awareness of present conditions entirely. As mentioned above, present temporality also includes the future as the source of possibility for combining the achievements of the past into an individual outcome.

The discussion of this section, as well as that of the next two, has an air of arbitrariness. Technical terms and distinctions are used to describe time as if they were merely read off the phenomenon. What are the arguments for the plausibility of these notions? There really cannot be arguments in any strict sense because the issues at stake are about the highest level assumptions that we can make. The only genuine argument in their defense, apart from local polemics with alternative schemes, is that to assume them is to be open to recognize and understand more in our experience than is possible with alternative assumptions. The underlying question is, what should we assume about time to recognize it most clearly and to deal with it at its natural joints? The underlying polemic here is that, in contrast to most twentieth century views recognizing only present time, the reality of past and future temporality is equally important.

II. PAST

The timeliness of the past is objective everlastingness. Once having happened, a change is an addition to what had happened before, fitting into its own past according to its character. To call the past "objective" is to indicate that it has a fixed character that can be an objective condition for subsequent present moments of change. It has that character by virtue of being a finished change, not by actually being involved in a subsequent change (although, according to the theory of multiple effective location, it may in fact be so involved). The asymmetry of time demands that the past have whatever character it has irrespective of what comes after; and it has that character everlastingly: nothing can change it. That a past moment is objective does not entail that a subsequent moment in fact is able to accept it as a condition; its causal influence might in fact stop with itself, and still it would be objective, ready to condition anything that could accept it.

In those periods of our history in which notions of a synoptic divine mind were unexceptionable, people had little difficulty recognizing the objective everlastingness of the past. They also recognized the difference between that objective everlastingness and the various roles that past things might play in subsequent events. As objectively everlasting, a past thing never changes from what it became at the proper date of its actualization. As involved in subsequent events, a past thing can change its nature, contours, and significance in extraordinary ways. Thus, for instance, at the time of its actual completion, the Parthenon was a glorious event for its architect and the citizens of Athens. That was its "proper" location in time and space. Over the centuries, the Parthenon has been subsequently located in a continuity of other events, growing old, changing from a religious edifice to an armory and finally to a cultural monument. The temporally thick Parthenon is located through all those events, with its several changes having proper dates yet being taken up in subsequent events in its career. Further, the originally completed Parthenon has been variously located in the memories, drawings, and reflections of those who have seen it and visited its precincts, undergoing many changes by virtue of being conjoined to representations of itself in human experience; we have forgotten the architect, however. There is neither a conceptual difficulty nor an experiential one in recognizing that the Parthenon's original glorious completion is fully real as objectively past while also located in multiple events of the temporally thick continuity of the building and of its enjoyment by admirers. Even common sense assumes that past things are real as past, that they are often real as an accumulation of continuous events, with various forms of unity, and that they are real in the experience of being represented.

In our own period, however, in which objective reality has come to mean "reality for a knower," many people have great difficulty with objective everlastingness, and believe that the past is real only in some present memory. Many process philosophers, for instance Charles Hartshorne and John Cobb, believe that there must be a God who is always present and who bears in mind all the things that happened in the past. This belief assumes that only present existence is real. On the contrary, the past is real precisely as past, as finished fact, and it is this whether or not anything else comes along, and whether or not the past makes a difference to anything else. The past, in becoming itself, makes a difference to itself, and that difference is everlasting even if uninfluential. The finished quality of the past is entailed by the very meaning of change as actualizing decisions among diverse possibilities for integrating potentials. Having finished becoming, a thing is simply actual, occupying its proper position in the extensional field and bearing the values achieved intensionally. To say that it then mysteriously becomes nothing unless remembered by or influential in a being in current present time is to introduce a needless complication. How could it "become nothing" if its time of change is past? How could anything at all happen to it in its now past dated proper location?

In contrast to its timeliness, the temporality of the past is to exhibit matrices of cohabitation among its own elements and in relation to the present and future. These matrices are structures of togetherness, such as temporal relations of precedence and consequence, spatial relations, and all kinds of causal relations in terms of which one thing conditions another. All disciplines of inquiry contribute their own representations of matrices that, to the extent they are truthful, pick out dimensions of coordinate structure; physics treats many more dimensions of space-time than the usual four of common sense. Since each past thing was once a present moment, each has a wholly determinate relation to what was in its own past. Apart from the fact that a past thing once was present, and determined its relations in its present timeliness, the borders of past things are trivial relative to the matrices constituting their togetherness. In reference to the past, therefore, it is often relatively unimportant which were the items or events that had individual present immediacy. What is important are the structures they variously constitute together. A present moment in its own temporality receives the past not as a set of individual past "presents," but as a structured environment, a complex group of lines of influence, a unified past set of growing identities. Further, the matrices of the structures of past temporality can be projected beyond what has in fact been actualized as past, projected into the future. Past temporality thus represents the temporality of the present and future as like its own—conforming to wholly determinate actualized structures. Science, which models its notion of "thing" on the past (as process philosophers and pragmatists since Bergson have noted), deal with reality insofar as it can be identified and manipulated according to its coordinate structures. Sometimes modern scientific thinking adopts the temporal structure of the past for the whole, thereby missing the decisiveness of the present and the vagueness of the future. Analogously, present temporality can represent the past and future as like itself, looking for individual decision points in the past, which is a tissue of actual achieved structures, and in the future, which is lacking precisely the decisions. It is pointless to speak of process philosophy's "actual occasions" in the temporal past. The point is to speak of the things constituted by the coordinating structures of space, time, and causal inheritance. The structured things may have been made by the actions of many actual entities in their present moments, but by how many and which ones does not matter. What matters is the kind of structure actualized, how tight it is, how the structured groups interact, and so forth. The most sophisticated analysis of kinds of structure relative to kinds of time is Robert S. Brumbaugh's brilliant *Unreality and Time* (1984).

Because the structured thingness of past temporality is what environs, calls up and funds all present moments, present actions should be thought of as actions of temporally thick things. Similarly, the temporal future is structured by the ongoing careers of temporally thick things, acting moment by moment. "Temporal thickness" is not the specious present (a characteristic of the temporality of the present) but rather is the character of things whose identity includes some past, present, and future, temporally related and comprehensively including the diverse timeliness of past, present, and future.

The temporal structure of the past may be more or less tightly unified. There might be one single time and space, as Kant thought, or there might be several branching off and dwindling to mutual irrelevance. However tight or loose, the structure of the past as such is determinate as far as it goes. The temporality of the past as it extends to the present and future might very well allow of partially vague matrices yet to be rendered completely determinate. That is, from the standpoint of the past, the matrices allow of contradictory determinations in the future. The temporality of the past relative to the present is to be structured potentialities for change, maybe with important vagueness for present decision-making; the temporality of the past for the future beyond the present is vaguer potentialities waiting upon the present. The effectiveness of the past upon the present is not only to convey vectors of causal forces through its extensional structures, but also to convey the massiveness of value through its achieved intensionality.

III. FUTURE

The timeliness of the future is the subjunctive normativeness of good ways of harmonizing things. It is, indeed, the structure of pattern or form as value. To identify form as value would seem strange in many circumstances because of the common assumptions that forms are facts (the early

Wittgenstein had a typical modern interpretation of the connection of form and fact) and that values are subjective projections onto facts. But the distinction between fact and value was one of modernity's most vicious mistakes. In *Reconstruction of Thinking*, Part II, I presented a detailed theory of form as intrinsically expressive of value. Earlier here, in chapter 7, an appropriate theory of value was developed in terms of complexity and simplicity, and expressed through the traits of vagueness, triviality, narrowness, and width. This was related in the succeeding chapter to a theory of formed things as harmonies. In the present circumstance, therefore, it is not strange but rather to be expected that form is identified in tight, technical ways with value. The point of the current argument is that form is the timeliness of the future, and enters into concrete things through present changes that actualize what had been future.

The future's timeliness is the non-date-referred condition that pattern *x* harmonizes *a, b,* and *c,* with *m* value, *y* harmonizes them with *n* value, *z* harmonizes *b, c,* and *d* with *o* value, and so forth. This is the realm of Platonic forms, the Limit, wholly subjunctive and not very timely in any usual sense at all. Normative patterns are wholly indeterminate without a multiplicity to harmonize, and by itself the future's multiplicity is strictly hypothetical. By itself, the future is not "in time" except negatively, by being not yet.

The temporality of the future, in contrast to its timeliness, is to be those patterns that can integrate the past as it is being changed in the present. Therefore, the temporal structure of the future is to be a constantly shifting set of patterns of possibilities for which the past provides and the present exercises potentialities. More specifically, the far future consists of very vague patterns for achieving value. The immediately next future consists of patterns only so vague as can be resolved by the present decisions. In between are patterns of intermediate vagueness that shift as things become determinate. That a pattern is vague, as discussed in the previous chapter, means that it can be actualized in more than one way (the morrow can see either a sea-battle or no sea-battle—Aristotle). The temporal structure (in contrast to its timeliness) is thus extraordinarily dynamic; the future is always changing, depending on what is happening.

The distinction between possibilities and potentialities is important to observe. A potentiality is an actual thing that, by virtue of multiple effective location, is ready to enter into a subsequent present as a condition. As a present thing is actualized, it harmonizes potential conditions together, and the patterns of harmony are possibilities given it from the future. A thing has far more potentialities than it can accept at full value, an infinite number in fact. Its possibilities for integration are far more limited, and have the structure of layers of vagueness, described earlier, arranging the potentialities so as to exhibit triviality, vagueness, narrowness, and width. Possibilities apart from actual potentialities that give them determinate multiplicity are either totally vague or merely subjunctive—they are what would integrate the multiplicity if there were a multiplicity. The timeliness of the future, real as subjunctively normative but non-existent, is pure logical form. The temporality of the future turns those logical forms into real possibilities.

The temporalities of present, past, and future are connected. The temporality of the present is to inherit the structured past and to determine the vague, normative future by its decisions. The temporality of the past is to provide structured, achieved actualities as potentials for subsequent events and to delimit hypothetical normative possibilities into real possibilities. The temporality of the future is to provide ways by which dated present decisions can combine the actual structured conditions of the past into new achievements of value; the shifting temporality of the future derives from the fact the different presents of decisions come each with its own date. The temporality of dating consists of the timeliness of the now, the timeliness of the past fixed timeline, and the timeliness of the logical relations of vagueness and specificity relative to the harmonizing pluralities. The timeliness of each mode is special to itself. Temporality involves the unity of time in all its modes, from the standpoint of each one.

It must seem paradoxical, perhaps even perverse, to have such controversial descriptions of time laid out as if they were obvious. The characterizations of the temporalities of present, past, and future that have been given so far involve something of a new use of language; but what is most paradoxical about them is that the three temporalities are not reduced to one. There is no single meaning to time or to "being in time," as Brumbaugh has argued so eloquently. For all its complication, Heidegger's approach to time was much too simple, modeling the whole of temporality on that of the present which, by itself, does not even acknowledge a real distinction between early and late; past and future are reduced to horizons for a temporality of the heroic now. By the end of the discussion to come, I hope that the paradoxical "descriptions" will seem to be simply accurate and insightful descriptions. But before this can happen, the paradoxical quality of time itself must be deepened.

IV. THE BEING OF TIME

What is the being of time? This is the ontological question directed toward time itself. In order to frame the question we may recall certain of the metaphysical distinctions introduced in Division Two.

As argued there, a thing in the most abstract sense of "thing" is a harmony of essential and conditional features. The essential features are those it has unique to itself; the conditional ones are those it has by virtue of which it is relative to or "conditioned" by other things. Since a thing's identity is always determinate with respect to something, it needs conditional features relating it to the something with respect to which it is determinate. Since a thing cannot merely sum up its relations but must be something that does the summing, it needs essential features. The features of a thing are themselves things in this abstract sense, and so have their own conditional and essential features. A thing is a harmony of essential and conditional features in the sense that they simply fit together; there is no "third term" required to relate them because that would be just another thing which would have to be related to them (implying an infinite regress of relations).

With regard to time, the timeliness of the modes—present, past, and future—display the respective essential features. In a present moment, what is essential is the actual deciding that creates a new determinate state of affairs out of past actualities functioning as potentials. Among the essential elements are the novelties of subjective form as they develop, and the creative energy, as it were, in the decision-making. "Subjective form," a Whiteheadian phrase, means the forms an emerging entity acquires in its emergence, over and above those found among its antecedent conditions; based on the theory of value, the subjective forms are the instruments of simplicity. Whereas the creative energy may have a field-character common to many present moments, it is essential to a given moment by virtue of being creative with its initial data, its decisions, and its individual outcome.

With regard to the past, what is essential is its objective, everlasting fixity. The past lacks the present's capacity to change and to participate actively in any existential field, although it exhibits the structured coordinations of its temporality. Among the essential elements in the past are its structures and the values achieved by having those structures.

What is essential to the future is the normativeness of its logically possible ways of harmonizing hypothetical multiplicities. Without reference to the other modes of time, this hardly has determinate status except as conventional articulations are imagined for it; hence the essential features of the future are often taken to be merely the realm of formal logic.

It is possible here to make the distinction between timeliness and temporality more precise. Temporality is the way by which each mode of time relates to the other modes of time. Timeliness is the collection of essential features for each temporal mode, to be contrasted with the conditional features by virtue of which each relates to the others.

According to the distinction between essential and conditional features, the modes of time could not be what they are without the conditional features as well. So the essential decisive dynamism of the present could not be itself without the conditions of the past to give it specificity, to supply initial data, and without the normative structures of the future to provide possible outcomes to be decided on. The essential features of past fixity could not be distinguished from mere logical possibility without the decisions of those moments when present, and couldn't even be logical possibilities without the future. The normativeness of the essence of the future would be wholly indeterminate without the fixed characters of the past to provide the multiplicity to be realized and the dynamism of the present to make the logical normativeness relevant to realization. So each mode of time contributes conditional features to the other modes, making them what we commonly know them to be in conjunction with their essential features.

Temporality is the harmony of the respective timely essential features and the conditions the modes of time give one another. The temporality of each mode is precisely its own essential features as harmonized with the other modes, and time as such is the harmony of all the modes of temporality as characterized above. That is, the present inherits the past and acts decisively now further to determine the future. The past provides actual content as causal ground to the present, and structures the future with its multifariousness. The future provides the ideal, normative and logical structure that will be exhibited in the past and that lure present decision-making.

Time is the sum of the temporalities of all things, in all their temporal modes. For each thing within the time, there is a shifting locus of its temporal embodiment *vis a vis* past, present, and future, depending on which moment is the relevant present "now." Since process philosophers, existentialists, and pragmatists are exactly right about the way by which the present "now" cuts between a determined past and a partially indeterminate future, the shifting locus of the now shifts not only the date, but the determinate reality of temporal beings. As Kant pointed out, time is concrete and single (though perhaps not as consistently unified by coordinating structures or geometries as he thought). The question of the being of time, therefore, is how the temporalities of all things can be real as a sum. "Sum" is a cheat word in this context, and needs an analysis.

The temporality of each mode of time (past, present, future) provides one form of togetherness for the three kinds of temporality. The past unifies the temporalities according to the chronological time line (and perhaps other more sophisticated coordinates). This does justice to the essential fixity of the past, and to the conditional traits of the present as fixing things to be past and to the conditional traits of the future as providing possibilities for future extensions of the coordinates. But the past's temporality does not touch the essential inner decisive dynamism of the present, nor the essential normativeness of future form itself. And therefore the temporality of the past cannot successfully provide the togetherness needed for the three temporalities, although it is easy to see how people enamoured of coordinate temporality would try to make it do so. Existentialists and process philosophers rightly protest the deadness of the past relative to the present; ethicists and artists rightly protest its "mere factuality" when severed from the normativeness of the essential future which any past once included.

The temporality of the present unifies the three temporalities as inherited past and future potentials for present action. This does justice to the essential dynamism of the present, to the conditional readiness of the past to influence the present, and to the conditional structures supplied by the future for possible actions. But it neglects the essential objective, everlasting fixity of the past, and also the past's achieved values, because it treats both only as potentials for modification in the present's creative actions. And it neglects the essential intrinsic normativeness of the future by transforming it into what merely satisfies the need to achieve determinateness, relative to past conditions, in the present moment. From the standpoint of present temporality, past and future function as horizons for identity in the now. The past merits a respect, however, and the future a sense of obligatoriness that are not registered within the temporality of the present alone. Philosophies emphasizing present temporality tend to collapse the fixity of given fact and the normativeness of external obligations—science and ethics—into an aesthetics of the moment. By neglecting the essential features of past and future, the temporality of the present cannot fully or adequately unify the three temporalities.

The temporality of the future unifies the three temporalities as the lure for increasing ideal definiteness, the final cause. This does justice to the future's essential normativeness, to the conditioning of the future by the past as providing multiplicities, and to the conditioning of the future by the present as constantly shifting the relative determinateness and indeterminateness of possibilities. But it fails to recognize the essential objective fixity of the past's temporality insofar as it treats the past merely as potentials for limiting logical possibility. And it fails to recognize the essential dynamism of present temporality which it treats as a principle, not the action, of selection. From the standpoint of futural temporality, past and present are merely specifications of otherwise vague ideal possibility.

That each of three modes of temporality is insufficient to unify the three into one temporality (or, concretely, time) illustrates an important characteristic of the problem of the one and the many. Stated abstractly, if there are two things, each with essential and conditional features, each can include the other with itself by means of the other's conditional features; but by definition it cannot include the other's essential features, without making the other just a proper part of itself. Therefore, a solution to the problem of the one and the many cannot be reached from the standpoint of any one of the many alone. We have seen how any attempt to define time from the standpoint of the temporality of any mode of time, present, past, or future, leaves out exactly what is essential in the other modes of time.

Therefore, that time which is the unity of the three kinds of temporality is somehow simply a fitting together of those three, a harmony of them. But how can this be characterized? Not by appeal to any of the senses of temporality within the harmony, by virtue of the above arguments. Must we then adopt the classic position of defining temporality in terms of "eternity"?

I believe we must indeed appeal to eternity to understand time. For, there is a togetherness of the modes of time that is not a function of any of the kinds of temporality. Put most paradoxically, there is a togetherness of a thing's youth, when its maturity is still undetermined, with its age when nearly everything is fixed. Temporal sequence is not the whole of the togetherness because the thing's determinate character is different at different stages in the sequence. Being horizoned by past and future is not the whole, because the center constantly shifts and the horizons gain and lose. The process of determining vague possibilities is not the whole because it neglects achievement and the action of decision. Therefore there must be some kind of non-temporal or eternal togetherness.

But what can eternity be? It cannot be the *totum simul* eternity opposite present temporality precisely because there is no "at once, or *simul*, registering that a thing that is indeterminate at one date becomes determinate later; *totum simul* eternity presupposes complete determinism in the temporal process, and cannot account for the passage of time making any difference. This eliminates many theological answers to the question of time. Nor can eternity be the opposite of past temporality, the eternity for which time is its moving image; for by citing eternal coordinates, this answer separates eternity from the actual movement required, and cannot account for movement; the eternity of coordinates is in fact as deterministic and static as that of the *totum simul*. Nor can the eternity be the Aristotelian completeness of the final cause that moves by attraction, not moving itself; for that eternity accounts neither for the existence of actual things to be moved nor for the moving, and hence is too vague to relate to time at all.

The eternity making sense of time, I suggest, is that of the ontological or divine creative act creating things that are in time, with successive present dates, etc., but that itself is not in time and hence not temporal. Only the created things are in time. As such, temporal created things succeed one another in timely fashion. Each present thing, as present, has a fixed past and a perhaps partially open future. Each past thing, or part of a thing that is past, has a character achieved in itself and also available to enter into and condition subsequent entities, and to restrict future potentialities. Each future thing is a normative pattern for harmonizing increasingly determinate possibilities that are in the way of being actualized. As time passes, a self-identical thing shifts temporal modes from future to present to past, changing its nature as it does. There is no ontological date at which a thing's participation in time is simply what it is; there is only the temporal date, when it is past, at which the thing can no longer participate in time in a changing way. Time simply does not exist wholly at a date. Ontological divine creation is temporal only because temporal things are created. To ask, for instance, whether the future is divinely determined presupposes a present to which that future is relative; and from the standpoint of that present, of course the future is indeterminate in part. But that present does not register the whole of time. The act of creation is temporal only in its products, not in its actions.

The unity of the act of creation consists in whatever is involved in the diverse essential features of what is created. With regard to time, this means that the divine creative act provides a context of mutual relevance in which the essential features of the present (decision-making, etc.), those of the past (objective fixity, etc.), and those of the future (normativeness, etc.) are together. Because the essential features are together, it is possible for the three modes of temporality to condition one another and therefore have the conditional features required for each to be itself. Each mode of temporality is a harmony of its essential and conditional features. The conditional ways by which the modes are together constitute our three temporal ways of unifying time. But the very existence of the conditional ways presupposes a more basic togetherness in which the diverse essential features are unified. Without the togetherness of the essential features, there could be no togetherness of the conditional features. The ontological divine creative act is eternal in the sense that its function as a context of mutual relevance is a precondition for all temporal relations, as displayed above.

Apart from creating things, there is no character to the ontological ground or divinity, since all "character" requires essential and conditional features, all of which must be created. The identification of the ontological ground comes from noting that there are indeed finite, temporal things that must be grounded. I call that ground "divine" because creation makes the affinity for each other of essential features that have no worldly contact save through conditional features; this is profound love or compassion, deeper than the conditional connections of things that can be brutal beyond belief. Lao Tze understood this point about the Tao deeper than movement that makes movement possible:

> The Tao that can be told of is not the eternal Tao;
> The name that can be named is not the eternal name.
> The Nameless is the origin of Heaven and Earth;
> The Named is the mother of all things.

Also:

> Heaven and Earth are not humane.
> They regard all things as straw dogs.
> The sage is not humane.
> He regards all people as straw dogs.[5]

Time is simply the created togetherness of the modes of temporality. But the modes are not determinately consistent within time. From any point within time, regardless of the mode, the essential features of the other modes are opaque. The modes are determinately consistent only within the eternity of the ontological divine creative act by which the things are made to be together each with its own shifting dates. To say anything simpler than this is to render impossible the recognition of some essential part of temporality, which is to be strongly untimely. Time is real enough. But it is not difficult to see why it appears unreal if one starts with a prejudice for some one mode of temporality over the others, or if one starts by taking definite reality to be the capacity to create ontologically. But the creator is unreal except as actually creating, and the individual modes of temporality are partial embodiments of what we know of the fullness of time.

Ontological creation commonly is construed as bringing something into existence, and this is an adequate construction for those things that exist. In a present moment, for instance, the dynamic decision-making brings a new entity into existence out of the resources of the past things; what is new is spontaneously created. The past resources in turn were themselves once new, with their novelty being an existential spontaneity at the date of their emergence, combined with their own antecedents, and so on back. The creation of actual existence takes place in present dated moments through the spontaneous harmonization of previous entities, which themselves were once created. The future does not exist, and hence is not created as an existent. It is real, however, since it has identity, even shifting identity. The creation of the future therefore has to be appropriate to future reality, to normativity. The general notion of creation required is that the ontological creative act makes a thing's essential features in harmony with its conditional features; since the latter entail other things to provide the conditioning, the same creative act must create those other things, with their essential and conditional features. This creation of all related, different things together, with their individual harmonies of essential and conditional features, is the ontological ground functioning as the context for mutual relevance. Only a theory acknowledging the mutual relevance of diverse things with uncommunicating essential features can do justice to the metaphysical pluralism our world displays, especially with respect to time.

The remarks about existence and the future in the previous paragraph reflect a construction of creation from the standpoint of the temporality of the present alone. It is more or less consonant with process philosophy which emphasizes that standpoint.[6] From the standpoint of the temporality of the past, creation means sustaining the objective fixed contingent actuality of things everlastingly; and it means connecting the coordinating structures of the past to future possibilities and present actions. This sense of creation has been associated in the West with the creative mind of God, from the speculations of Augustine through those of Newton. In the East it has been captured in large part by the idea of the Buddha-world. Deep as these metaphors for creativity in the temporality of the past might be, they display only part of ontological creativity. Creation in the mode of future temporality has not received the attention it deserves because of the prejudice that believes only existing things are created. Plato was getting at it in the *Philebus*, however, when he wrote about the cause of mixture that achieves value in combining the limited and the unlimited; he also knew to say, in the *Republic*, that the Form of the Good creates both the visible world and invisible world (the forms), as well as our capacities to know them. Creation of future temporality alone is just as limited a sense of ontological creativity as that of present and past temporality.

At the heart of the deep mystery of time is the fact that time's true and whole creation, the creation of all three modes of temporality mutually conditioning one another, can be apprehended only at the metaphysical level in which their essential and conditional features are acknowledged and distinguished. Time does not exist within time, nor is the creation of it temporal. Whether by metaphysical dialectic or mystic vision, one must attain to the juncture of eternity with time to appreciate time as such.

10

Temporal Things: Endurance, Perishing, and Change

I. ENDURANCE

The discussion of time's ontology leads to the problem of what exists within time. What are temporal things? What must a thing be to enjoy temporality? The first observation to make is that the initial formulation of the question is misformed, even if the common one. Nothing exists "in time," or "in space" for that matter. To be "in" at all is already extensional; that is, temporal or spatial and whatever else might be extensional. Only by virtue of being temporal can a thing be "within" the time of an hour or a year, or an incident "in" the life of a person. Being temporal is what gives the possibility of being in other things that are temporal, and containing components that are temporally within oneself. Similarly for space: being spatial is what makes possible being in a place, in a larger space, and having components spatially within oneself. Thus, in a strict sense, things are not in space and time, but are spatial and temporal; and by consequence, are in other spatial and temporal things, and contain such within themselves. Leaving the question of spatiality to the next chapter, let us now ask, What are temporal things? What must a thing be to enjoy temporality?

Aristotle addressed this problem with his theory of substance, and the difficulties process philosophers find with the substance theory center on its inadequacy with regard to change, an essential element of present temporality. In fact, the substance theory is largely, though not completely, wedded to the temporality of the past, emphasizing actuality and achieved structure. Attempting to explain change, the substance theory does not acknowledge the dynamism of the present, except as an afterthought, and instead emphasizes the power of realizing potentials as that power lies in already achieved act. The future is reduced to that which completes what is already in act, ignoring the integrity of its own norms. Or put more exactly, Aristotle's theory of final causes construes the future as what will complete the actualization of potential of each substance, minimizing the fact that the future is also the structure of compossibility, a common field given multiple articulateness by all actualities together.[1] Despite its limits, the substance theory does indeed hold up for attention the fixed integrity of actually achieved structure, and the coordinated continuity of this through time construed as a stretch of past impinging on the present and shaping the future.

Process philosophy focuses on the first lacuna of the substance theory; namely, the account of change. To be temporal for process philosophy is to be an actual occasion, inclusive of past actual occasions as inherited and anticipatory of future occasions as superjected. Change is not the realization of potentials by past realities, but is rather the treatment of past actualities as potentials for integration by the spontaneous creativity of the present. Genetically analyzed, an actual occasion is temporal in the sense of its own present emergence. Coordinately analyzed, it is temporal in spatial and temporal relations to other occasions, as determined by its actual nature and the nature of its neighbors.

Endurance through time is impossible for an actual occasion, on the process view; an occasion can only have the proper time of its own dated presence, and the borrowed time of the future present dates of the subsequent occasions that prehend it. The price paid by Whitehead for the ability to give an integral account of change is a temporal atomism of individuals. But surely at least some individuals endure through a thickness of time so that they have a youth and also an old age. Paul Weiss has made this criticism ever since his earliest book, *Reality*, in 1938; process philosophers have not answered his persistent questioning except to cite, not individuals, but societies: societies occupy a stretch of time but do not endure.

An enduring entity, according to the account of process philosophy, is at its tightest a society of actual occasions given common identity by virtue of the causal reiteration of something of the same pattern through the sequence of occasions. It is understandable that reiteration is a satisfactory account of endurance from the standpoint of present temporality, because it expresses the appearance of temporally thick things as data in a present moment: from the standpoint of organizing the present, past data are significant as having a common identity mainly if they have a common form. But reiteration does not give temporal thickness. No matter how intensely an actual occasion reiterates pattern, the past it has is the past of the world. It has no past of its own except in the general sense that it inherits the past world. From the temporal perspective of the past, however, most actualities do indeed have temporally thick careers. At any present moment they are extensions of beings that existed previously and seem to have at least a little future. The career of an actuality is not the career of a form through many reiterations, nor is it the career of an actual occasion through successive prehensions, to use the language of process philosophy. The career of an actuality takes shape through the accumulation of time, and it changes while maintaining its individual identity. Moreover, from the temporal perspective of the future, the endurance of an actuality is the successive achievements of value as each normative possibility is realized. The values might not be the best possible, and indeed can be evil, but they are still values. Because an actuality realizes successive values, and faces the future as the possibility to enhance or diminish value, an actuality even in the present is not normatively exhausted in aesthetic resolution. Rather, there is normative (for humans, ethical) obligation, objectively determined, that addresses the actuality as achieving, bearing, and living up to a normative identity through time (see Neville, 1987).

Since at least most actual things exist in time, with a past, present, and future, an account of endurance must be given that respects all three modes of temporality. A temporally thick thing can be called a "discursive actuality" because its identity consists in the movement from moment to moment, accumulating a past of achieved structure and taking possession of a future. Let me begin the account by saying that I accept the major contribution of process philosophy to the explanation of the temporality of the present, as far as it goes (Neville: 1974, Pt. II). My intent here is to supplement it with those aspects of being temporal that result from past and future actuality.

II. PERISHING

My account of the development of an enduring, temporally thick actuality stresses the cumulativeness of enduring character, and relativizes the importance of the present, and of conscious experience that is fixed in present time. In contrast to cumulativeness, does nothing perish? This is a crucial question for process philosophy because of its claim that only the present is real, and the past can be real only by being in the present. Two senses of perishing are paramount for an understanding of time: the perishing of subjectivity and the perishing of achieved value.

It almost goes without saying that the subjective immediacy of the present moment perishes with the achievement of finished actuality. When a moment has finished becoming and is ready to condition subsequent moments of creativity, it has lost its subjective immediacy. That immediacy consists in the intentional dynamism of working the plurality of conditions into a definite harmony: it is the aim at the elimination of vagueness, and its activity is decision-making. Subjective immediacy is the mixing that arranges patterns into an individual haecceity uniting the actual components. In the case of the higher creatures, subjective immediacy can have the sense of an experiential orientation to the world in the diverse modes of temporality. In lower creatures, there seems to be no reason to believe that they synthesize their conditions with the forms of experience, or have any "awareness" of the sort associated with consciousness. Both past and future have their own essential features, and therefore are "subjects" of their own characters; but neither has the subjectivity of the act of existing characteristic of the present. The past is thus "dead" and the future "unborn."

From an ontological or theological motive, some philosophers have argued that the subjective immediacy of a present moment is itself ready to be prehended by subsequent divine (if not finite) moments. Charles Hartshorne wrote (1980, pp. 93–94):

> I hold that the satisfaction contains its process of becoming ("the being cannot be abstracted from the becoming"), so that to prehend a past satisfaction is to prehend the becoming, the subjective immediacy itself, of the past actuality. The past presentness, the past becoming (which did not prehend itself, it simply was itself) is now prehended. And I see Neville's and others' arguments against this as verbal confusions. Nothing is lost, with the qualification that all non-divine prehending is more or less indistinct (Whitehead's "negative prehensions") so that, except for God, much of the past is dismissed as irrelevant and in this sense is indeed lost. But not for God, by whose adequate prehending actualities "live forevermore."

John Cobb continued the line of argument (1980, p. 100):

> For Whitehead, the way in which one moment of my experience flows into its successor is not denuded of immediacy by the fact that it has attained satisfaction. What is felt by the later occasion are the feelings of the earlier occasions. It is true that modifications are introduced into the later occasion and that in the temporal flow the immediacy of the earlier feelings fades. Whitehead's intuition is that in God this immediacy does not fade.

Hartshorne and Cobb both admit that the only elements in the present available as subsequent conditions are those that are objectified in the finished satisfaction. This may well include the elements (propositions) which function at intermediate stages in concrescence, and hence are still partially indeterminate. It may also include whatever elements of subjective form accrue to the process of deciding out the indeterminacies—the "how" of a process is contained in the "what" that is produced. In this sense, the objective satisfaction of a moment might include whatever the concrescing moment thinks "about" its own process (if anything—Hartshorne doubts self-awareness within conscrescence itself). But what is not objectified is the immediate process itself, including its own affect where the process is experiential. (Rather than construing natural process on the analogy of human experience, as process philosophers sometimes do, I would construe experience as a complicated natural process whose temporally present key elements come from the immediacy of the process of decision-making. Thus, rather than claiming, with Hartshorne, to be a pan-psychist for whom material nature is a special case, I would claim to be a pan-naturalist for whom cases run from mere matter with no psychic development to psychically subtle nature in which matter is no longer "mere." Models of nature from, say, physics, deal with the special cases for which they are designed.) What is lost from any moment, when it becomes past, is its own subjective immediacy of changing. This is the very heart of process philosophy's crucial distinction between the modes of time.

As to the theological interest, there is less reason to worry about the past as living on as a condition of some present reality (divine or other) than to account for the relation of divinity to the past precisely as past. The process conception that God is primarily an experiencer is not helpful here, for that conception turns the past into a mere condition for the present. The ontological conception of divine creation as the ground for the temporality of the past as such (as well as of the present and future) suggests a divine intimacy with creatures that is religiously more satisfying.

The second important sense of perishing is the loss of structure. As past achievements, of course, the valuable structures are eternally what they are. But the issue regarding this kind of perishing is whether they continue to be important conditions for multiple effective locations in the present and future. "The grass withers and the flower fades." Evil structures perish as well as good ones, and since evil so often consists in misplaced structures it might have even less adaptive advantage than the good. But all achieved value passes from enduring effect, and change is not always for the better. Process theology mitigates this sense of loss by saying that all achieved structured value continues always to be enjoyed subjectively by God. If we accept that such a God is real, then the divine experience is cumulatively rich without end. But the loss of achieved value is felt by the finite world irrespective of the divine experience, and for the world the past involves perishing. From the worldly standpoint, there is the constant problem to determine whether the loss is bad or good, and what to do about it. The perishing of achieved valuable structures raises practical questions about whether to recreate them, to mourn their loss, or to celebrate it. The poignancy of this dilemma comes in large measure from the contrast between the temporality of the present, impoverished by the perishing, and the temporality of the past in which the perished achievements have slipped to ineffectual fixities. To remark that "the word of the Lord remains forever" need not mean that God learns and never forgets; it can mean that the creative word is what it is outside of time such that it relates the components which severally compose time.

Let us return now to provide a direct account of discursive actualities, acknowledging the perishing of the subjective immediacy of present moments as they become past and alert to the fact that structures can fail to be continued.

III. DISCURSIVE ACTUALITY

The form of a proper account of a discursive, temporally thick actuality is to show how, in the being's present, past, and future, the other temporal modes are always present as essential features. That is, it is essential to a thing's past that it have a relative present and future. It is essential to its present that it have a past and a future. And it is essential to its future that it contain its past and relative present. Whereas a thing's past, present, and future are always conditioned by a vast assortment of things in other respective temporal modes, the thing's own past, present, and future are the elements essential to it. That this is "the form" of a proper account of a discursive, temporally thick actuality stems from the fact that it includes the essential and conditional features of all three modes of temporality in the being of one actuality, with the temporality of the present shifting from date to date relative to the other two. The mutual relevance of the three modes of temporality, each an independent harmony with its own essential features, reflects the fundamental ontological character of the one and many.

Consider a present moment in a discursive actuality. With respect to its present temporality, the past things enter as conditions to be harmonized together in the creative moment. But with respect to past temporality, at least some of those past things are the actuality's own past identity, and hence they are essential to the present. What does it mean to say they are essential this way? They are essential if they contribute to the way, to the subjective form, by which the present moment integrates its conditions. The essential timeliness of the present itself involves spontaneous essential features of the moment. The essential features from the past are in addition to these. An actuality's own past thus functions both as a set of conditions to be integrated in the present and as essential elements influencing the integration. The essential effectiveness of the past in the present constitutes primarily the discursive actuality's character, and secondarily the potentialities that give it normative commitments.

A discursive actuality has temporally thick character by virtue of achieving enduring structures. The process of achievement might consist in fortuitous circumstances or in hard, deliberate work (in the case of intelligent beings). The structure achieved is not exhausted at a moment but rather, in accord with the temporality of the past, extends over the coordinates of the spatio-temporal field in which the actuality exists. With regard to the present, the past's temporality provides a history of the development and exercise of the structure, and delivers to the present the intensional field of value actualized in the past. At each present moment, that structure must be re-enacted through an addition to the extensional (and intensional) field; the re-enactment is the actualization of the structural potential generated by the past achievement. Further, each re-enactment provides a potential for future embodiment, and part of the meaning of the present re-enactment is to provide that future potential. If we were not to admit the essential past temporality of historically achieved structures, we would never be able to distinguish an enduring actuality's own past states from all the other past states entering as conditions into a present moment.

The phrase "discursive actuality" covers many kinds of enduring things; in fact, any kind of enduring thing that has essential identity across time. This includes situations, transitions, institutions, organized singularly acting aggregates, and organic individuals such as the biological ones that were Aristotle's prime analogue for substances. These differ by virtue of how tight the essential features of a present moment bind its past and future to it, and this tightness is a function of the kind of structure that they have. For purposes of the present discussion, the test case is the extremely tightly organized individual, such as a person. This extreme can be called a "discursive individual" and will be the focus of the rest of this section; section III of chapter 12 will provide a summary account.

There are many structures in a given discursive individual because the individual has to relate to so many diferent factors in the environment. Further, the structures change and develop as the environment changes. Enduring individuals that themselves are mobile need structures for changing their own structures in accord with change of place and external relations. Indeed, the structures of a discursive individual build on one another, interacting in many ways. Perhaps the clearest kind of interaction is hierarchical development: given the achievement of lower structures, higher structures become possible, and when realized, make possible even higher structures. The higher structures sometimes can interact with lower ones, however, as when a high-level conscious decision endangers one's low level bodily existence. The variables in relation to which an individual's structures change, grow, and diminish include both environmental factors and factors internal to the individual such as other structures and spontaneous happenings.

Given the complexity of the enduring structures of, say, animal life, it is clear that the environment itself must exhibit many levels of stable structure. The stability of the environment includes other enduring individuals, of course. But it may also include merely reiterated structures whose continued embodiment depends on the failure of possible alternatives, as in an ecosystem. In between discursive individuals and merely reiterated functional patterns are many kinds of aggregates whose components might be discursive individuals but whose overall patterns are merely reiterated. The constant flux of even apparently stable enduring entities should be stressed, since the most tightly integrated discursive individual is a temporal harmony of many parts. Not all the parts are themselves discursive individuals, although most would be discursive actualities of one sort or another; the parts that are themselves discursive can have careers of their own. There is hence a poignant fragility to the stability on which civilized life depends, on which life itself depends.

The primary connection between present and past temporality in a discursive individual is the continued development of structural character, which is inherited and reenacted, perhaps with modifications, in each of the individual's present moments. By virtue of that reenactment, the historically developed character is essential to the present activity of actualization.

The secondary connection is that the past constitutes the individual as having normative commitments. Perhaps it sounds peculiar to say that enduring individuality itself involves something like moral obligation. Surely only human beings have moral obligations, not ducks or tigers. True enough. Nevertheless, if being formed is to have value, and if the continuity of an individual through time involves essential relations among its formed states, then the relations among the values of those states are definitive of individual continuity. Relations among values that are temporally ordered are normative commitments. This sounds peculiar because we are accustomed to assuming that moral obligations derive from our commitments or contracts: obligation, on social contract theory, arises because of the agreements into which one has entered. The moral theory espoused here, however, says that obligation arises out of one's character existing in a context; that is, out of normative commitments constituted by relations among formed things (see Neville, 1987). Agreements can only limit or channel obligation, relieving one of the necessity to do all possible good at once by virtue of parceling out some of the job to other roles. This kind of conception, peculiar to hear in the modern era, would have been intelligible and natural to Plato or Confucius. In order to provide an analysis of normative commitments, it is necessary to examine the bearing of future temporality.

With respect to a discursive individual's present temporality, the future consists of the slightly vague patterns that would give definite individuality to the conclusion of the present attempt to come to harmony. That definiteness includes the value that would be achieved by integrating the moment's components according to the pattern, which perhaps contains alternative patterns within it. The temporality of the future itself extends genuinely into the distant future, far beyond the immediate possibilities so nearly definite that present decisions would be able to individualize them. It consists, as discussed above, in a shifting set of layers of vague forms that are possibilities for actualization relative to the past conditions a present moment has to integrate. Therefore, in a present moment, a discursive individual faces a temporally diverse distant future. That future is partially structured because it can be realized only by means of the actual things relative to which its pure forms are possibilities; and these actual things have structures. The future is partially indeterminate, however, because the process of actualizing possibilities is the work of present moments that have their own originality. The act of "mixing" is more than the conditioning potentials and the ready-to-be-completely-determined possibilities. Where the present does not have serious options, the future is highly structured and can be predicted (in principle) in the serious ways. With the passage of time, the future's structure shifts radically as decisions close off options and open others. And as each layer of the future is actualized, decisive determination is given to its later moments.

The essential point of future temporality is the normativeness of the patterns for integration. Each pattern is such that when it integrates a set of components, the resulting harmony has the value of integrating them that way, with that particular complexity and simplicity and that narrowness, width, vagueness and triviality. Therefore, every present results in creating something with value, and every structure achieved and historically continuous through the past has a value. With the passage of time new value-structures are actualized and new potentialities become multiply effective.

The primary bearing of future temporality on the present is to provide a normative common field for activity. The future contains the normatively discriminated possibilities for action. Since the structure of the future includes the relations of all past and present things to one another to the degree that they are connectable, all contemporary things share a more or less common future. Sometimes that future is divided into separate possibilities for the different actors. But often structured possibilities are integrated for joint action. It is part of the being of a discursive individual to share both past and future with other beings. I accept the view of process philosophy and existentialism that in the present moment of coming to be, the essential timeliness of the moment is subjective, inward, and isolated from other contemporary moments. But the temporality of the present essentially includes conditional features as well as its essential timeliness. Because the individual does indeed have a past with past temporality, and a future with future temporality, the individual is not existentially isolated; at any present moment it is not only present but also the possessor of past and future. This is to assert what is so often forgotten in the modern period, that the present moment in an individual's life is only a small part of the person's reality, albeit perhaps decisive in great ways.

In a present moment, a discursive individual acts in such a way as to affect a wide variety of things in the future. The primary normative content of that action is the values actually achieved in the action (relative to what could have been achieved); these include value effects on everything in the future conditioned by the action. A secondary but in some cases more important normative content is the value achieved relative to the discursive identity of the individual itself. Only some elements in the future are the individual's own future self. But those elements have their identity in part as continuities, developments and modifications of the individual's structures achieved in the past and reenacted in each present. In part, a discursive individual's future states will have the value they earn by their actions when they themselves become present. But in other part, they have the value that accrues to them simply by being the future of an agent who acts normatively in the present. One's normative character tomorrow depends in part on the worth of what one does today; one may enjoy blame or credit tomorrow for today's deeds. Therefore, a discursive individual faces the normative future in general, and its own normative future in particular.

We are now in a position to discuss commitment. A discursive individual always acts with reference to its world, of which its own past and future are but small parts. Nevertheless, the character it has itself, embodied in its achieved structures, gives it special norms with which to act in the world. Those norms determine that it would be good to actualize things so as to take advantage of the values made possible by that character. Trees have a *prima facie* commitment to provide shade, and parents a *prima facie* commitment to provide nurture. This commitment involves not only living up to the past but also attending to the function of future character in the future. At the level of human structure, this means that we can be guilty or meritorious for the past, and obligated to be truthful and fulfill promises in the future. Being structured so as to have commitments does not require the higher order levels of consciousness or universal morality of human life, however. It simply means that one's present action is not governed by the norms of the moment's aesthetic harmony alone, but also by the norms of an enduring self-identity. Since an enduring self-identity is a changing identity, a thing's commitments also change. As a special subcase of commitment, the fact that a thing has developed certain structures might provide a commitment to develop others, as in a hierarchically organized organic being. Thus the internal development of an organism is normed by commitments that arise successfully from its own nature.

Process philosophy, along with existentialism and pragmatism, rightly has focused on the present as the arena of action. By complementing its account by reference to the temporality of the past and future, we can see how a temporally thick enduring individual is possible. In any given present moment, a discursive individual is also its achieved past and is faced with a partially structured future which likely contains its own future states. (Whitehead saw the importance of acting for the future in his doctrine of the superject; but he could give little acknowledgment to a reality for the future save as an anticipation in a present concrescence.) The togetherness of present, past, and future temporalities provides for a temporally changing structured actuality; that actuality embodies a definite value moment by moment and at every moment is normatively affected by commitments arising from its own achievements.

The account of discursive actualities has gone about as far as it can without an explicit consideration of space and of the commonality of the spatio-temporal field for diverse interacting beings. These are the topics of the next chapter. It is appropriate, however, to conclude the present chapter with some general reflections on the human experience of time, perhaps the dominant theme of the philosophy of our century.

IV. THE TEMPORAL STRUCTURE OF HUMAN BEING

Twentieth century accounts of human time have been decidedly anthropocentric. This may not seem surprising since the topic is *human* time. But it is one thing to say that the contours of human life are shaped within time and quite another to say that time is a construct of the ontological character of human life. Insofar as the twentieth century philosophies of process, pragmatism, and existentialism emphasize the temporality of the present and interpret present action on the model of abstracted human experience—as concrescence, Dasein, having and doing—the resulting time-sense is decidedly human. Existential and phenomenological approaches to time agree with the process focus on present temporality by their attention to consciousness (consciousness is an exclusively present temporal phenomenon); an interpretation of time in terms of horizons for awareness repeats the anthropocentrism. Even linguistic philosophy, when it pays attention to time at all, does so in terms of its embodiment in human language.

The most striking feature of the account of time in three temporal modes is that it makes time the measure of human embodiment rather than the other way around. The temporality of the past presents a nature measuring human life, a nature to be respected for itself, irrespective of human interests except insofar as contained there. The temporality of the future presents a realm of norms obliging human life by their intrinsic worth, irrespective of human interests except as those interests lie among the future possibilities. The temporalities of past, present, and future together present an objective, dynamic, value-laden time in which human beings find roles appropriate to their personal and social natures. The eternity of the togetherness of the modes of time is the ultimate measure of human truthfulness about the topic.

An account of human time relative to past temporality must emphasize the obligation to truth, both to representing things truly and to being true. Truthfulness is not the temporal mode of relation only to the past, but also to present and future insofar as these exhibit the coordinate objectivity of the temporality of the past. We are to be true to present and future insofar as they have objective characters that will or may become achieved. Both in representation and in life, past temporality implies a kind of piety toward the objectively real, toward nature. Past temporality means that there are things to which we must conform if we are to realize human time. This stands in contrast to the diminished position that says that there are only things we are to use, things whose reality is exhausted in their being conditions for our own present existence. Whether in past, present, or future, the temporality of the past gives things a dignity to which human time implies respect. How paradoxical it is that the cry, "to the things themselves!" was uttered by philosophers who limited things to their appearance within human experience. Because of the temporality of the past, human experience should be conformed to the things, and we are untimely until we do so, as if we seek to escape the full dimension of human time. The aesthetics of present temporality is insufficient for truthfulness.

The temporality of the future lays an objective normativeness on human experience. Both interpretations (that might be true or false) and the selective directions of human life are guided by interests. As the pragmatists pointed out, truth is always qualified by the limited respects in which that which claims to be true selectively represents its objects. As they also pointed out in their more careful statements, the basic issue about human interests and purposes is not how to fulfill them, but whether they are the best ones. The normativeness in future temporality is not reducible to human purposes, but measures them. Human timeliness is thus in a double consideration of purpose: from present temporality comes the human constitution as being essentially interested or purposed, and in relation to future temporality these interests and purposes are normed as justified or not. Because the future exhibits structures crossing possibilities for everything, the norms for human purposes respect private human interests only incidentally. Human purposes are judged by norms for the good of all.

The temporalities of past, present, and future together constitute human temporality as respectful of the values achieved in process and of the obligations devolving upon the decisions of life. Process philosophy and pragmatism (less so existentialism) have distinguished themselves in this age of scientific and phenomenological positivism by their stress on the value-laden quality of life. Even when their expressions have emphasized the contours of present temporality, they have understood that value is characteristic of nature, not just the human sphere. To recognize the three-fold character of temporalities, past, present, and future, is to be in a position to characterize the values of things as normative for human life.

Having stressed the objective natural locus of reality and value, in contrast to an anthropocentric locus, it is safe now to close with some observations about the temporal development of human life.

Human character is an incremental affairs, achieved by the development of specific structures through the course of interaction with self and environment, particularly other selves. The account of the three modes of temporality contains guidelines for interpreting cumulative structured character. At the very least, an ethics of virtues grounded in biology and psychology is required to understand the human time of character development.

Human identity with reference to present time is a function of the norms that relate the essential features of past and future temporality in the present, constituting an enduring being identical through moral changes.

More than continuity of body, a person is identified as the one who did or became that and who therefore will be obligated to do or become this in the future. Such a conception of identity through time is not upset by change but in fact depends upon it.

Twentieth century philosophies have rightly seen that present temporality displays the only time in which people are free to do something about their circumstances. Without creative freedom, people would not be responsible: responsibility would be traced back to the indefinitely far past through the lines of coordinate connection. Without creative freedom, the norms of the future would never become anyone's personal responsibility. The temporality of the present is indeed the existential center of all human temporality.

Although the present moment of becoming might be isolated in its timeliness, its present and future constituents (the only objective constituents it has) are interrelated and social. The structuring of the past and interpretation of the future are both learned from socially developed structures. The time of human persons is thereby a social time, not of individuals alone but of individuals constituted in part by their interactions with social artifacts such as signs. As a consequence, the time-sense of human life is social, not individual *per se*.

If the account given above is on the right road, a human being in time has not one temporality but three. As a result, being in time is not only temporal, but an eternal togetherness of three temporalities. Neglecting the eternal dimension, one either falls into confusion about the temporal dimensions or acknowledges one to take the exclusion or reduction of the others. The age of science emphasized the temporality of the past, and translated the other temporalities into past terms insofar as it recognized them (for example, deterministic interpretations of choice). The jaded post-scientific age of our own time emphasizes present temporality where the translation of truth and moral value into aesthetics seems proof against de-existentialized past temporality. Not since the Christian middle ages in the West has a concern for the normative future dominated the sense for truth; the positivism implicit in modernity excludes normativeness, which leaves the future as bare subjunctive logical forms, not a matter of temporality at all. A balanced view of human time requires all three modes of temporality. This is a complex way to live—balancing incommensurables as it were. But the search for simplicity is merely an aspect of present aestheticism from which reverence for truth and commitment to real norms must rescue us.

The discussion of human temporality has added a dimension to the theory that truth is the carryover of value, properly qualified, from the object into the interpretation. Truth is faithfulness to the actualiy of the past and to that which the past can signify, including the future as structured by the past. But in addition, human temporality involves a commitment to the normativeness of the future, and to the value that any past thing's realization of its own future achieved. The normativeness of the future thus measures the propriety of the qualifications involved when truth is carried over: there is a commitment to value in intentionality as such. Subsequent chapters will develop this important conclusion.

It should be remarked here in closing, however, that the account of enduring individuals is grossly incomplete. Enduring individuals move, either with local motion or with shifting Galilean frames of reference. The characteristics of growth and loss mentioned above also require an account of motion. Motion in turn can be explained only in reference to an extensional field with spatial as well as temporal characteristics. If the theory of extensionality introduced in previous chapters is correct, asserting that the extensional field is not an independent container but is actually created by the harmonies extended in it, then an account of extensionality depends on an account of causation.

11

Space and Motion

I. SPACE AND EXTENSIONALITY

Motion is a largely neglected topic in recent philosophic discussions of causal agency. One source of the neglect is our century's preoccupation with time rather than space; space is essential to motion.[1] Another source of the neglect is the fact that process philosophy, the most original and powerful philosophy of nature in our time, treats motion plainly as a minor and derivative phenomenon.[2] Yet another source is the assumption by other philosophies of nature that science can tell us most of what we need to know about space, once philosophers have properly tied time to causation.[3] I will argue here that motion is a fundamental philosophic problem and that a philosophy of space needs to be developed on a par with the philosophic treatment of time.

Earlier it was argued that a harmony makes itself up out of the previously finished harmonies, and that it does so by creating for itself an extensional structure on the one hand harmonizing the extensional structures of all its antecedent conditions and on the other hand constituting its own position relative to those others in the extensional field. The field is not an independent matrix but is part of the cumulative character of the entities. In reference to time as commonly conceived this is not a difficult notion, because a new harmony's position is simply a succeeding time, arranging itself as following on the proper dates of its antecedent conditions, as being contemporary with other harmonies with the same or similar antecedent conditions, and as being before all the harmonies in which its own finished state can be a condition. This is Whitehead's theory.

But what is an account of a harmony's own place, given that it can take place in the same place as previous harmonies? Moreover, what is the account of the internal multiplicity of a harmony? It cannot be a temporal multiplicity of earlier and later with respect to a moment of present temporality, and yet present moments contain internal multiplicities. Further, it is unhelpful to say that space is the togetherness of contemporaries since contemporaneity is among the things needing definition.

A general account of extensionality is needed that includes space as well as time. In many respects, this account is merely a generalization of the account of temporality developed in the previous two chapters. Yet the deficiency so far has been any account of the otherness that extensionality is supposed to display. How can there be separate places in space? And how can these be related so that there is a singular space? Referring to the metaphysical notions of earlier chapters, these questions will be answered by understanding otherness in terms of separate essential features in diverse harmonies, and by understanding spatial relations in terms of conditional features. That, in fact, is how the three modes of temporality were described. But now these notions must be made specific to space. Space cannot be described except in reference to time, and of course the description of time earlier made implicit reference to the spatial character of things.

The first task here is to give a somewhat formal account of extensionality that allows for a description of space. The second task, in the next section, is to account for the dynamic integrity of space (like the eternal integrity of time) by showing how there can be motion through space. For the formal account of extensionality, four elements can be derived from the primary cosmology.

1. The first element in an account of extensionality is the logical structure of the future. The pattern of normative possibilities consists in layers of vague coherent structures partially specifying vaguer structures and standing ready to be specified further by less vague structures. Let us say that a given layer *G* of vague possibilities has both extensive and intensive magnitude. Its extensive magnitude consists in the array of contraries it presents as precisely coherent. For instance, suppose *G* consists of *a/non-a, b/non-b, c/non-c,* where the multiplicity measured by this layer has to do with *a, b,* and *c*. That the layer is vague means that any decisions about any members of its set of components would be all coherent with one another. Thus the following decisive outcomes are all coherent:

a, b, c
a, b, non-c
a, non-b, non-c
non-a, non-b, non-c

non-a, non-b, c
non-a, b, c
non-a, b, non-c
a, non-b, c

This is horizontal coherence. It amounts to saying that different things can happen together, different in their independence as embodied in the viable contraries; in five miniutes, you can stand up while I sit down, or vice versa.

Intensive magnitude refers to the vertical column, as it were, of relative specifications of a vague character. Suppose the decision in the first member above is for *a*, which is itself vague with respect to a lower level, *m/non-m, n/non-n, o/non-o;* any decisions among this latter set would be compatible with any others in the *m, n, o* set. Suppose finally the decision in the first of that set is *non-m,* which is itself vague with respect to *x/non-x, y/non-y, z/non-z,* etc. The pattern of increasing specification goes on to the point where the last bit of vagueness is eliminated by an actual decision that results in an haecceity. Notice that as specification increases, more things are made determinately compatible and coherent. The extensive magnitude of any layer of vagueness is its array of decision-points yet to be specified; that is, however this layer of vagueness gets specified, it will require the extensionality of having the horizontal array together. The extensive magnitude of a fully actualized state of affairs is the haecceity of the final decisions, bearing within them also the layers of vague common natures. The intensive magnitude consists in the value of the vertical column of decisions, for instance *a, non-m, y.*

If this were the full account of the future's contribution to extensionality, there could be but one spacey actualization and then a stop. Indeed, there could not even be one, for the determinateness required (from the past) to establish even the most vague precision within the future would be absent. The previous paragraph considered the future's structure from the standpoint of its essential, logical, timeliness alone. It needs also to be considered with respect to its temporality, in terms of which it relates concretely to fixed actualities and to the dynamism of present decisions.

Let the hierarchy of decisions be known by the date to be achieved for itself by the "present" decision moment which resolves the last indeterminacy and concludes with haecceity, T_1. That haecceity adds to the previously actualized things, with the result that there is a new multiplicity whose possibilities of harmony form yet another hierarchy of layers of vagueness, the date of whose haecceity, however it turns out, will be T_2. The structure of the hierarchy of T_2 is similar in some respcts to that of T_1, and different in others. Insofar as it is similar, such that the decision at each level of vagueness will have to be made again (even if they are made the same way), the relation between T_1 and T_2 is temporal, and the exact shape of that temporal relation, the spread of time within it, is determined by which decisions have to be remade and what else needs to be done in order to make those decisions a second time.

Insofar as the second structure is different from the first, it is because the decisions of the first are inherited into the second, providing definite structures of togetherness in the second where there was vagueness in the first. The conditions that T_2 inherits from T_1, plus the earlier past, includes some determinations that were vague in the hierarchy for T_1; T_1's hierarchy was conditioned only by the earlier past. This is to say that the second hierarchy has a layer of organization determined by previous actualization to be definite rather than vague; this layer constitutes an actual extensionality to which the second actualization must conform. It would be a mistake to view the second hierarchy as simply a more determinate version of the first. There are more differences in the second than derive from the mere inheritance of decisions. For the logical structure of possibilities opens to a whole new set of possibilities, given the fact it must integrate the actuality of T_1 with the previous multiplicity. Vagueness in fact may increase, as we hope it does when we act so as to increase rather than diminish our options. Further, there may be some leeway regarding which past actualizations end up with effective locations in a decision-making moment. If determinism were true, T_2 would have to inherit all of T_1's decisions; but the process of actualization may involve some decision-making freedom, and not all of the predecessors' decisions must be constitutive of the successor. The range of freedom, however, depends precisely on the alternatives for harmonization presented by the future.

2. Reference to the logical structure of the future alone is not sufficient to account for extensionality, however, because reference also must be made to the actual decisions that constitute the diversity in the horizontal array. The second element, then, in an account of extensionality, is the individual decisiveness of present moments. More precisely, extensiveness requires the separateness of the essential features of the diverse decisions specifying the contraries in the horizontal array. The essential features are those that organize the conditional features in ways unique to the decisive harmony.

In spatial extensiveness, the otherness of the essential decisions of different specifications of contraries is such that none of the conditional features organized derives directly from the other decision. Spatially different decisions thus are wholly independent of any direct conditioning of one another; nevertheless, they specify different elements in an array that is coherent.

In pure temporal extensiveness, by contrast, there is an asymmetrical relation between the different decisions or present moments with essential features. The later moments are those in which the earlier ones enter as conditions; the earlier moments are thus multiply located, with their own proper date and with the dates of the subsequent decisions that include them. Discursive continuity requires multiple location. Even in temporal extensiveness, where the later includes the earlier, there is a separateness of the essential features of both. The essential features of the earlier decisions do not bring the subjectivity of the process of integration into the later ones. Rather, that subjectivity marks the proper date of the earlier decision, and is objectified in its subsequent multiple locations. The integrity of the past over the present rests in the perishing of the subjectivity that makes the date of a moment's happening "proper."

3. So far it has been acknowledged that the future has an extensive structure in that it presents arrays of vague coherent contraries, and that these are separately actualized by separate decision points of change. This is sufficient to account for the otherness in extensionality, and also for the connectedness or unity of the extensional field. But it does not account for the individuality of space and time to which Kant so conclusively called attention (*Critique of Pure Reason*, B37–73). Kant's own account of the individuality of space and time need not be accepted in his terms. Indeed, insofar as space and time are supposed to be forms of the transcendental character of outer and inner sense respectively, as he argued, it is difficult to see how they can be individual at all. The obvious alternative is to account for the individuality of space and time by calling them (space-time) an individual. Thus Paul Weiss (1958; ch. 3) treats the extensive continuum as itself an individual thing within which extended things exist. The difficulty with views like Weiss's, however, is that nothing can be "in" an extensive field that is not extensional to begin with. If things are extensional enough to be in a field, they do not need the field to be in extensional relations with one another and with their insides.

The solution to the problem of the individuality of the extensional field comes from noting three things. The first is the unity of the past as actual. However independent the happening of decisions of extensionality separate changes might be, they issue in a unified actual past. The pattern of the unity itself derives from the coherence in the future possibilities that get actualized in the present decisions. The *actual* unity consists in the real achievement of a determinate singular past. The orders or structures achieved have varying degrees of tightness. Nevertheless, they are all included within the individual and singular achievement of the past. As actualized, the extensional field is singular. As being actualized, it is diversely emergent in separate decision points. As a possibility, the field is an array of connected possibilities that can be actualized by separate decisions.

A second and related point to note about the individuality of space-time is the logical structure of the future that requires either-or decisions about what can be actualized. The future cannot be actualized except as reduced at each decision point to one of the contradicting options.

The third point to note is the present's sheer feel of individual immediacy. The activity of decision making holds together both the future requiring decision and the singular past actualities to which the decisions must conform. Decision making is the effecting of changes that transform the to-be-decided future into a singular past. The individuality of the extensional field is thus both a norm defining the end of the decision and the ground to which the decision must conform. The decision process has the immediate feel or intuition of the singularity of its connection of its goal and ground. This must be much of what Kant had in mind when he remarked that we can conceive of space and time as empty of objects, but not of two spaces or two times. The way I would parse that is to say that a present decider only relates to space-time by virtue of mediating the singular past and the singularity-requiring future. To think that there is some other space-time than the one providing the locus of the decider is to suppose that the future does not encompass all possibilities in common, or that the past can have elements that are different from one another but also wholly irrelevant to one another; neither assumption is tenable. Present consciousness therefore experiences space as irreducibly spacey, and time as irreducibly timey, despite the fact that contemporary decisions are separate and can be experienced as separate. Augustine was right that we have a prereflective understanding of the uniqueness of space and time that always seems to be lost when we try to reconstruct them out of the non-spatial and non-temporal elements. Kant was right too that the immediate intuition of the individual characters of space and time cannot be learned *a posteriori*, but it is present in the very being of an extensional thinker.

4. A fourth point needs to be made about extensionality; namely, that while it embodies both the difference and connection of things, it also expresses their ontological harmony. That is, the being of extended things requires that the separateness of their essential features, whereby their difference is possible, rest within the ontological context of mutual relevance. This is a generalization of the argument made in chapter 9 about the being of time. Whereas that argument claimed that the modes of temporality have diverse essential features that require an ontological ground of mutual relevance, over and above the conditional features connecting them, the

present argument claims the same about any things extensively related, either spatially or temporally. Therefore the extensive position of any thing is not only extensionally related to other extensive things, but to the whole of the extensional field. "Wholeness" is impossible to define completely in terms of the extensive connections, for it involves a togetherness of essential features that make extensiveness possible. Wholeness has to do rather with that sense in which there is a togetherness transcending both unity and difference without reducing one to the other. Extensionality is itself possible by virtue of the non-extensional ontological creative act.

The influence of the primary cosmology on the account of extensionality is now apparent. The first element of the account, namely the logical structure of the future, is the temporal embodiment of limit or pattern as such; pattern becomes ingredient in actuality by virtue of the realization of the future. The second element of the account is the diversity of the actualizing decisions. By themselves they are the unlimited, separate, powerful sources of change. Only by virtue of their limitations by future possibilities are they coordinated, and since the possibilities are vague, they can be only partially mutually determined. The result of the first two elements is actual mixture, the singular extensional field of an achieved past. The wholeness of the extensional field, not reducible to either its separate elements or its connections, is the cause of mixture, its ontological grounding. The result is a world of things that is spatially diverse and temporally ongoing.

II. MOTION

The model developed in the previous section may now be made more complex in order to exhibit motion and interaction. Motion requires a distinction between an actuality and the field across which it moves from one position to another. Having argued that the extensional field is itself created by the actualities that occupy it, the distinction is not obvious in the categories developed here. It is not obvious because our sensibilities are predisposed to think too much in terms of present temporality alone. Within present temporality, a thing is simply in the place it makes for itself relative to other things. Process philosophy accepts this emphasis on the present and consequently says that although patterns move in social ways across spaces, temporally thick actualities do not so move. In contrast to process philosophy, it is important to account for the movement of temporally thick actualities.

Indeed, the temporal thickness of actualities is the clue to movement. A moving actuality takes in among its conditions at least part of the history of all the places it moves across, and as it occupies a place it harmonizes itself so as to exclude what was in that place before and what else might be in it at present. Among the limits of movement are those of a thing's capacity to push its way in, as it were, or to fall into a place. Because the histories of all the places through which a movement takes place are themselves related as having been compossible, there is a (perhaps shifting) pattern that structures space as a field for movement. Our common sense space is Euclidian; under certain conditions, the spatial patterns are non-Euclidian. Quantum phenomena reveal patterns of spatial occupation that run contrary to common sense but that are not at all unexhibitable as histories of places that various things have occupied and constituted.

The spatio-temporal field for movement therefore consists of the cumulative patterned histories of the places that present themselves as conditions for the sequence of changes in actual movement. The shifting pattern of possibilities for movement thus consists of a sequence of hierarchies of possibilities that successively makes it possible for the actuality to occupy the next place. To the degree that the future of the extensional field is determinate, that determinateness comes from the fact that past actualities have developed places and given them histories. To the degree that it is indeterminate, those histories are open to decision in the various change-points. Where those change-points are parts of a moving actuality, the open possibilities allow for coordinated movement.

The integrity of the extensional field over against actualities moving within it consists in the fixed givenness of the histories of places as coordinated by possibilities marking out what is determinate or indeterminate at any date. In no sense is the extensional field ever empty. Within the mode of the temporal present alone, the field exists as a bunch of actualized conditions needing to be harmonized, according to what is possible, into a position for the emerging thing. The dynamism of the present thus reflects the fact the business of that moment is to create itself as positioned. The conditions for attaining to position, however, are conformation to the integrity of the field.

The integrity of the actuality moving through the field depends on its kind of structure. A mountain quakes, or slowly moves with its plate over to the next continent, by virtue of the relatively common possibilities relevant to each of its coordinated parts. To be a temporally thick thing, a moving actuality must exhibit the discursive structure of the matrix. That is, it must not only possess present, past, and future states, but it must have, or have had, several present states so that its movement involves several connected changes of spatio-temporal position. Further, since most actualities have spatial extension involving many contemporary spatial parts, an actuality may involve the coordination of many movements at once. A social situation in flux is an obvious example. A running animal is another. Unlike the situation, the animal is a discursive individual, the character of which will be examined in the next section.

Temporally thick actualities are harmonies of harmonies of harmonies. A discursive pattern takes an extent of time to develop; but some such patterns, once developed, become part of the continuously inherited character of the actuality and enter into arrangements with other things so as to give rise to higher level harmonies. So, for instance, the experience for a human being of conceiving, gestating, and giving birth takes nearly a year; but afterward there is not only the new baby but also an important new dimension to the character of the mother.

Interaction is the moving of two or more actualities such that each harmonizes its movements in accordance with at least some part of the overall pattern of movements of the others. In this event, the common nature of the extensional field, both in its spatial and temporal dimensions, is extraordinarily important. Yet it not as if the field were empty and the things danced around it according to their own patterns. Rather, the field is constituted in all its parts by the interacting actualities and the background actualities. Therefore, each of the moving actualities takes account of (includes as components) the whole actual being of the other things, *vis-à-vis* the possibilities of occupying positions relative to the positions the others can occupy. Position is not an empty place, but a place that has been constituted by part of the moving actuality. Interactive movements require possibilities of positions shaped by the long-term movements of the interacting things.

Emphasis on the filledness of the extensional field makes it important also to bear in mind that vague elements are actualized as common natures in the actualization of their specifics. So, for instance, in government the specific personal relations between a set of persons may not be as important as the vague fact that some persons are in the judiciary, others in the executive branch, and that their interactions constitute a complex power struggle between the two branches. In the old story of the person who looked at all the colleges of the university and then asked where the university itself is, the response is supposed to be that the questioner made a category mistake: the university is nothing more than the set of colleges. But that response misses the point of the story. King's College would be a different actual place if the chapel were built thirty feet closer to the Cam, but it would not cease to be a component of Cambridge for all that: the College's role as a university constituent is vague with respect to many aspects of being just itself, and the questioner was right to ask for the vague characteristics of the colleges that went to make up the university, vague characteristics obscured by the particulars. Similarly with vague characteristics in interactions.

Hegel may have overstated the point; but he nevertheless was right that often the important elements in interactions are not the specifics that give individuality but the rational elements that might have been specified any number of ways.

This section has argued that space-time has the character of an actually filled, historically determined field insofar as its past. That past is what provides the determinate potentialities in which things emerge and that give determinateness to the future. We may now rehearse the overall structure of the dynamics of actualization in the space-time field.

III. DYNAMICS OF THE SPACE-TIME FIELD

The actuality of space is the growing structure of what has to be inherited in a horizontal array of levels of vagueness; it is internally related to all the structures that are forced on consequents by necessity. The actuality of time is the complex structure of temporality in which present temporality makes decisions within a hierarchy of layers of vagueness that is related to past and future hierarchies by certain similarities and differences. The present provides the creativity of decision making. The future provides each moment with a hierarchy of decision-points, and a relation to future hierarchies. The temporality of the past is to provide the singular structure to which hierarchies for future dates must be logically compatible.

The date by which a hierarchy is identified is the spatio-temporal position at which its decisions are immediately actualized; its internal content consists in the options and decisions at various levels of vagueness left open by previous finished actualities. In one sense, the sense celebrated by process philosophy, the present moment of deciding a hierarchy's vaguenesses is atomic, distinguished on the one hand from the past that is finished and that enters only as potentials to be integrated, and on the other hand from the future that is not to be brought to haecceity in this moment but in the next. In another sense, the temporalities of the three modes are locked together. At any given date, the structure of the future is fixed in part by what is past, and it is being changed by the decisions being made: as T_1 is being brought to haecceity, shifts occur all down the line of $T_{2,3,4}$, . . . n. These shifting future structures determine the various forms of multiple effective locations that past actualities have as potentials. The past things, of course, have their own proper date but also their subsequent multiple effective locations. Where they maintain themselves in space, not allowing subsequent future patterns for decision to be vague about them, they have temporal thickness, the everlasting hills, the enduring oak tree. Temporal thickness consists precisely in continuously occupying space so that subsequent moments have no choice about it. Where subsequent moments do indeed have a choice, and choose to reiterate a past thing, as when we reaffirm a tradition, there is not much true continuity of identity, but an ongoing reconstruction of identity; with respect to a tradition, the only true continuity would be in what Gadamer calls prejudice. Mountains and oak trees have much true continuity of identity, but they too change and grow with time. Living beings have not only continuity of identity but also the kinds of identity that are discursive, where the identity does not exist except as developing through time.

Although a decision-making harmony faces a hierarchy of possibilities as relevant to its own decision points, the conditional logical structure of the possibilities is determined by all the multiplicities requiring order. Hence most of a given harmony's future is shared in common with all other emerging harmonies. And since the shape of the future is not just the one hierarchy being brought to haecceity in a given harmonization, but the depth of the future as an infinitely projective and constantly shifting set of determinable hierarchies, enduring things interact so as to determine a common future. Although change within a present is atomic, causation involving a sequence of presents is united by a massive inherited spatial structure as well as a future with common elements binding any possible effects one things can have on another. Having said all this, we can call causation a discursive matrix, conveying spatially extensional determinations through many loci of decisive harmonization that are related horizontally in arrays of possibility as well as sequentially in patterns of causal order. What the structures of the inherited extensionality are, and the structures of the future, is a major question that we have not yet analyzed; it might be that the discontinuities are more striking than the continuities.

It should be admitted at this point that our account of space and time in terms of a multiplicity of hierarchies of layers of vagueness seems more complicated than it should. Would it not be simpler to represent the relation between present and future in a single "horizontal" hierarchy of vagueness, with the distant future very vague, being made more specific as its date gets closer? So, the vague possibility of a sea battle tomorrow gets more specific as the day wears on and the admirals respond decisively to various factors forcing them into a decision to fight or not. There is a truth to this representation insofar as we think ahead about a future date, wondering what is determinate and what is vague, and contemplating how to get form here to a desired complete determination. Nevertheless, this representation fails to capture two essential points, the spatiality of things, and the ongoing presence of actual vagueness as common natures. These should be recalled in turn.

It is necessary to represent time with a hierarchy of levels of vagueness for each proper date in order to maintain an inheritance of spread-outness through time. This can only be represented by indicating that positions that are vague and open to decision in earlier dates are determined and fixed for the hierarchies of later dates. Thus a moment of decision is not a dimensionless point creating for itself an inner extensionality. Rather, a moment of decision is internally extended by its inherited potentials that are common to other harmonies and by its possibilities that also are common to other harmonies so as to constitute a field. Its possibilities are given extensional spread by the actual decisions in the past that fix their vagueness within determinate limits. The temporality of present decision-making places the emerging harmony in a discursive matrix with the actualities of the past, with other emerging harmonies, and with the common future variously punctuated by the decisions.

Another advantage of representing time with a hierarchy of levels of vagueness for each proper date is that it displays the continuity of vagueness throughout the three temporal modes of actuality. It is not the case that when a level of vagueness has been resolved by relevant decisions, that the level itself does not receive actualization. Checkers does not cease to have the common nature of being a dog just because he is a Cocker Spaniel; being a dog is vague with respect to breed, and Checkers has that common nature as well as his specific breed nature. To give a temporal example, I am now at my desk in the study, and have vague possibilities regarding where I can be in two seconds; it is not determinate that I will still be at the desk, but it is quite determinate that I can't be outside the study; if I am still in my desk chair two seconds from now, it remains true of the reality two seconds from now that I am then bound to be in the study by being at my desk just two seconds earlier. To give another example, if a thing has a habit to behave a certain way, a habit that depends vaguely on being keyed off by special conditions, that habit is just as real when the conditions are absent and the thing is not exhibiting the habitual behavior, as when the habit is activated by the conditions.

Generally put, a hierarchy of levels of vagueness is actualized as a whole, with the higher levels remaining as common natures even though specialized or determined by lower levels. This is why we have general traits and possess universal characteristics, even though our actual natures are haecceities. Without an acknowledgment of this, interpretation of nature could never know actual things, only vague possibilities.

So far this chapter has presented a formal theory of extensionality, explicated particularly with reference to space. It has then developed a theory of the extensional field, both spatial and temporal, and shown how motion through that field is possible. Motion, of course, is crucial for a naturalistic theory of interpretation, for interpretation is itself a kind of motion through time if not also space. Finally, the theory of motion has been reintegrated with the previous theory of actualization. The next topic is that of causality. Of course, causality has been presupposed throughout in references to the conditional features connecting things. Causality itself has now to be thematized as a specification of the metaphysical theory, using the notions of extensionality and actualization developed so far.

IV. EXTENSIONALITY AND THE "METAPHYSICS OF PRESENCE"

Before causality is discussed, however, a general philosophic reflection is called for. The entire argument of this chapter has taken place within a naturalistic context that would be anathema to the bulk of philosophers who regard the Western tradition as a "metaphysics of presence." This is as true for those who want to reject such a metaphysics as it is for those who buy into it. Therefore it is important to put the metaphysics of presence in its place.

Although there are many focal points for the move to a naturalistic position in developing a theory of interpretation, the most decisive has to do with overcoming the implicit intuitionism of the view that consciousness provides either a model of reality or a direct access to it. The arguments here have made no reference to consciousness. David Weissman has shown decisively, in *Intuition and Ideality* (1987), that this intuitionism lies much deeper in the Western tradition than might be expected, given the innovativeness claimed by the so-called "phenomenological movement" initiated by Husserl. Heidegger made the same point in his critique of the "metaphysics of presence."[4] Yet as Weissman explicitly admits, and as Heidegger should have known, the metaphysics of presence, the "onto-theo-logos" philosophy, is only one story among the many in the Western tradition, and has even smaller currency when considered in the context of the great world traditions of metaphysical thinking.

The crux of the temptation to a metaphysics of presence has to do with extensionality, or rather with an inadequate theory of extensionality that reduces the temporally and spatially distant to their intentional meaning in the here and now. Derrida, in his critique of the metaphysics of presence (1973; p. 9), writes:

> The factor of *presence*, the ultimate court of appeal for the whole of this discourse ["metaphysics" and the phenomenology that only repeats the "original intention" of metaphysics], is itself modified, without being lost,

> each time there is a question of the presence (in the two related senses, of the proximity of what is set forth as an object of an intuition, and the proximity of the temporal present which gives the clear and present intuition of the object in its form) of any object whatever to consciousness, in the clear evidence of a fulfilled intuition.

The trace of an ontologising of presence is to be found in any philosophy for which the notion of horizon is fundamentally important. Horizon-language defines the extensional field by reference to a here and now relative to which things are proximate or remote. In philosophies of this sort, real difference is problematic. For, it should be possible to articulate an orientation to the extensional field by reference to any there and then, chosen indifferently, and that there and then would then function as its own proper position, as its own here and now. But how then can we understand two proper positions, two different here and now positions? Not by means of any definite horizontally defined extensional field, and extensive difference and then gets reduced to something merely ideal. An entirely different approach to extensionality is called for, one that integrates extentionality into the very identity of difference and connection. The phenomenon of here and now with its horizons is a trait of present temporality (and presence of spatiality) alone and requires integration into a larger theory recognizing the diverse temporal modes and the real nature of other things that are in other spatial places.

As remarked earlier, the twentieth century has come to a full appreciation of the temporality of the present, the time of change. There has indeed been an overreaction to the nineteenth century's ambivalent glorification of the Open Future and obeisance to the Determined Past. The overreaction consists in treating temporality as exclusively defined by the present, with the resulting reduction of past and future temporality to their conditional effects within the present. The past then loses its authority and the future its normativeness. In recognizing this overreaction, however, let us not lose sight of the crucial focus on the unique temporality of the present.

The aspect of causation focused in the present is change. Change is the actualization of something different from the situation before the change. Past actualities are indeed finished actualizations, but with respect to a present moment they are potentials for effectiveness in the changing situation. Contrary to the assumptions of the Aristotelian tradition, the twentieth century has seen that the power of actualization comes not from the already achieved actualities but from the present itself. The past is transformed from actual fact to potential effectiveness as it conditions the present, and existence or concrescence is the essential power of present temporality to harmonize the potentials, determining just how they will condition the whole. The result of present change is a new actuality that joins the others by means of its extensional connections. The process philosophers beginning with Whitehead have been the most cogent speakers to this point, and after decades of resisting Whitehead's technical vocabulary, many philosophers are now accepting his terms as common coin.

Although the past items provide the potential conditions—as it were the raw material for change—the future provides the structural possibilities for harmonization. The patterns for the outcome of change are value-laden, and since present creativity picks out to actualize what is in itself only a possibility, the creative work of the present is a kind of self-constitution of actuality with a value. The existentialists, particularly Sartre, have been most sensitive to this in their emphasis on freedom and self-definition.

Consciousness is peculiarly associated with change because of its intentional structure. An important aspect of intentionality is a sense of partial indeterminateness aiming at determinateness, oriented to possibilities as keys to determinateness, and feeling the weight of potentials each of which conveys its own force and value. Consciousness apprehends its array of components—initial potentials, patterns of integration at various levels, specific decision points—as the immediacy of the specious present in which things are changing.[5]

The critique of the "metaphysics of presence," so labelled by Heidegger and developed at length by Derrida, is a powerful force in the contemporary philosophical situation, yet ultimately a cynical one. On the one hand, the critique generalizes about the entire Western tradition from Plato through Husserl, claiming that all the conceptions of being have in common a commitment to being as presence. Further, this tradition is alleged to be logocentric, which means among other things that foundational principles are selected out in terms of which other things are to be measured, with the result that what does not bear an interesting relation to the principle is neglected; the use of the principle creates a hierarchical, either/or, good/bad mindset. On the other hand, this very critique selects a principle—the metaphysics of presence and logocentrism—to understand the entire tradition, and thus has to distort or neglect thinkers for whom those principles are irrelevant or are exceptions. Rather than admit the self-referential inconsistency of the critique, some deconstructionists congratulate the critique for deconstructing itself. But the conclusion they draw is not that a new look should be taken at the Western tradition, only that the tradition as well as the critique have now been transcended. If a genuinely new look is taken, however, a much richer field will be found.

Plato, for instance, does indeed have many elements in his theory of forms that could support a metaphysics of presence when isolated from the rest of his view, as was done by many "Platonists." Nevertheless, it should always be rememberd that the theory of forms was developed through a dialectical relation with the world of becoming and change. Only through the shifting plurality of the world's processes is it possible to articulate forms that measure its definiteness. As to priority, the forms are prior only with regard to identity and definiteness; the things participating in the form are prior with regard to motion, power, and interest. Further, for Plato the forms are definite only insofar as they have some plurality to measure. The form of the Good itself, isolated from the world that it creates, is not a determinate object in itself, and cannot be defined in terms of presence at all.[6] As to the definition of being, Plato's own definition was not presence but power:

> My suggestion would be, that anything which possesses any sort of power to affect another, or to be affected by another, has real existence; I hold that the definition of being is simply power (*Sophist*, p. 247; Jowett translation).

Whitehead in the twentieth century adopted much of Plato's characterization of being as power.[7]

To say that being is power is an insufficient generalization even of Plato's view. What he meant, and this is clear even in the brief quotation just cited, is that the being of a thing depends on its being conditioned by and conditioning other things. Sometimes this involves temporal conditioning, but not necessarily always. It would be better to say that being is having identity, where identity means harmonizing essential and conditional features and thus being ontologically related to other things. The important part of Plato's definition is that things exist by virtue of being constitutively related to things other than themselves. Precisely the opposite of a metaphysics of presence! Absence is constitutive of being just as much as presence, the way a harmony requires conditional as well as essential features. But the dialectic of presence and the absence is then not the crucial issue. The crucial issue rather is self-definition relative to otherness. This is the focal issue for the ontology developed above in chapters 5 and 6.

The genius of process philosophy is to have provided an exact account of creativity within a present moment. Past conditions are taken up as initial data, transformed, and rearranged so as to constitute an internally coherent new, actual, individual state of affairs. Part Three of Whitehead's *Process and Reality* is as important as Aristotle's *Metaphysics* or Newton's *Principia* for justifying a conception of a part of nature that is excluded or mystified by other theories. Before Whitehead, change involving novelty was thought either impossible, because of determinist presuppositions, or irrational because of romantic ones.[8] Whether his exact account is finally true is something he himself would have doubted. But that an account like his can be given indicates that the phenomenon of present temporality can be acknowledged without reduction. In addition, Whitehead's account gives a splendid rendition of the relation between physical and mental phenomenon *insofar as these are positioned in present temporality*. The physical consists in finished actuality, both among the initial potentials and the resultant outcome, whereas mentality is the creative process of making a difference. Of course, this makes the *content* of the physical an empirical matter, depending on what can be actualized. And the content of the mental defined in this way has little to do with human mentality that would involve interpretation passing through all modes of temporality. But Whitehead's account decisively rejects the Cartesian supposition that the difference between mind and body is a difference between substances: for Whitehead, everything which is, has been, or will be present has both physical and mental aspects, and from these can be built up phenomena of any complexity, extending the infinite range of Cartesian body and Cartesian minds.[9]

Change by itself is not as yet causation in a sense useful for an understanding of natural, personal, and social processes. Causation can involve a relation between temporally distinct things, such that a thing that happened long ago can affect a current situtIon, and such that a growing process exhibits continuous causality. The Aristotelian tradition in modern form recognized the temporal thickness of causation but ascribed to the whole of it the temporal structure of the past, that of progressive actualization with the actualizing moment being only a date. Among the difficulties with that account is that the antecedent has become fixed before it can do any causing. Therefore some Aristotelians say that causation takes place in a moment of simultaneous existence of antecedent cause and subsequent effect, which is but to rediscover present change.[10] Whitehead's own genius recognized the problem, and he acknowledged that concrescing occasions once finished are available as data in subsequent occasions. He went on in some passages to suggest that the transition from one occasion's finish to the next occasion in which it occurs as a datum is just as basic a sense of causation as concrescence itself. But his account did not deal with the identity of a continuous causal process or with the growth through time of an individual, except to note that there can be reiteration of an identical pattern throughout the occasions of an extended process and the conformation of emerging occasions to the actual past.[11] For causation beyond change, we must look beyond the existentialists and process philosophers to the pragmatists and their theory of growth.

12

Causation

I. CAUSATION, ENDURANCE, AND GROWTH

The discussion has now reached a point where it is possible to give a general characterization of causation. Causation is the structured three-fold temporal transformation of a discursive matrix. A discursive matrix is the whole of an extensionally connected field of actualities as entering into emerging actualities that integrate them according to the array of possibilities conjoined in various levels of vagueness. Causation is the transformation of this whole matrix, data by date. Although changes take place at various decision points, in specific emerging harmonies, those changes by themselves are not causation. Causation is the transformation of the entire matrix in which the various points of change are specific punctuation.

The transformation of the matrix is three-fold in reference to the modes of temporality. The temporality of the present applies to individual emerging harmonies, each inheriting the actual past as potential conditions, and each integrating these according to a future that coordinates its activity with what else is going on. The activity of a present moment is to bring a hierarchy of partially vague possibilities to haecceity. The present moments are causally related directly to the past and future in the ways described. They are not directly related to "contemporary presents" because they do not causally condition one another; nevertheless they are indirectly related by being parts of the same discursive matrix. The temporality of the future is a constantly shifting structure of hierarchies of levels of vagueness, responding to the changing state of actuality. The temporality of the past is the cumulative achievement of actuality, remaining fixed increment by increment, coordinated by its extensional structures, and shifting in its influence on successor states by virtue of its multiple effective location. Causation is a transformation of the matrix because any causal action shifts all three temporal modes, by virtue of the relation of each to the present in which change takes place.

Causation is a *structured* transformation in ways that have yet to be explored. For instance, causation takes place within the inner development of an enduring entity, in the interactions between entities, in the constitution of backgrounds for other causal happenings, in systems and systematic events, and in the formation and careers of special kinds of enduring being with a capacity to signify things, communicate, and build higher orders of organization in social life and civilization.

Before we turn to some of these structures, it is important to point out that the causal structures determine what we identify as things. Within present temporality alone, an emerging harmony can be seen as an entity itself, bounded by its initial conditions and by its final satisfaction of the individuality of haecceity; by itself, this is change, not causal identity. Within the threefold temporality of the discursive matrix, things take their definition or identity from the kinds of structures they have. Temporally thick actualities, from persons to situations, from gods to puffs of existence in far off space, all have structures distinguishing them from each other and from their environments; most take part in ecosystems of larger harmonies. And many can be discontinuous from one another, indeterminate with respect to the important elements in the other's being. Each actuality or group of actualities is internally extensional in temporal and spatial dimensions. The temporal dimensions are given by the order of what can condition what: the conditions are prior to the conditioned. The spatial dimensions are those by which horizontal arrays of elements in a level of vagueness are together, a combination of the demands of actual potentials and logical possibilities; the spatial dimensions are inherited through the actualization of positions determining subsequent states of affairs. One can conceptually abstract the particular things from their positions—the mountains from their space—but only if other things have come to give character to the space, or to represent the mountains' character. There is no such thing as wholly empty space. Geometries are logical possibilities whose determinateness arises from the particular past shorne of its special characteristics.

It is impossible, except by abstraction, to speak of the structure of actualities in contrast to their "content" (or whatever structure structures). Actualities are haecceities, thorough mixtures of limit and the unlimited. Nevertheless, because the vague levels of possibility are actualized along with their specifications, those vague common natures are structures that can be compared with the structures of others. Since the possibilities are often common to other things, there are overarching structures of which different harmonies actualize related parts. "Causal laws" are such kinds of overarching structures. It is ironic that so many thinkers who emphasize law in causality fail to hold to a Scotistic Realism of the sort developed here, and adopt instead a nominalism for which structures are external to the things structured. Nominalisms cannot make sense of why laws work, however, except by appealing to a human projection that creates the appearance of law-likeness, or by admitting that divine miracle pops the particulars into abstract positions in each case.

The next stage in the argument is to examine various structures or patterns of causation that in turn define different kinds of things. This section shall review and bring to greater complexity the discussion of endurance begun in chapter 10, and then take up the notion of growth, as promised at the end of chapter 11. The second section shall discuss inertial forces, regularities, and systems, all as patterns of causation. Section III shall bring the discussion round again to discursive individuals, those kinds of beings that might engage in interpretation.

Let us begin by reconsidering endurance. Suppose that the discursive matrix is structured so as to distinguish between an actuality and its environment. Like the distinction between a mountain and its environing floor in the continental crust, runoff lands, atmosphere, and climate, the distinction is not clear-cut; but suppose that, wherever we semi-arbitrarily locate the distinction, we can say what it is.

One factor in endurance is that the environment tolerating the actuality remains stable. The simplest model of environmental tolerance is that all the elements in the environment also endure, although of course the only necessity is that, whatever the changes in the environment, the net effect or function *vis a vis* the actuality remains tolerant of it. (Endurance of elements in the environment is modeled like endurance of the actuality under discussion.

A second factor in endurance is that the major extensional structures of the earlier dates be inherited and remain important in the later dates of the actuality. In the case of the mountain, the rock formations giving the overall shape, defining and occupying the mountain's shape, must continue, and they do so by virtue of the fact that the possibilities for later stages are not vague with respect to those extensional properties: there are no possibilities for the mountain to shift like a dancer. The reason the possibilities are determinate and not vague in these respects is because the prior actuality of the mountain allows no other way of being reharmonized.

A third factor in endurance is that the essential features of the mountain continue to organize the conditional features with much the same pattern. Mountains appear to have very little spontaneity, and so the range of opportunities for change, for essential features creating novel structures, is very small. The factors for endurance are mainly three: environmental tolerance, massive inheritance of conditional features shaping the basic extensionality, and limited novelty in essential features.

Despite their endurance, mountains do change, and it is instructive to model some of the ways. Rain and wind erode them. In this case, the extensional elements in the mountain surface share possibilities with the rain and wind that require erosion. The discursive matrix simply has no possibility of combining rock surface with the erosive elements without erosion. This illustrates the fact that the mountain does not have a possibility exclusively its own at any date, but a possibility common with weather; instead of marking off a mountain-environment boundary, we might mark off an ecosystem of mountain-wind-water that would have rather stable possibilities, to the diminishment of the mountain. Mountains also reside in crust plates that may sink, bringing lake or sea-water up to erode the rock from the base, and a similar analysis would be appropriate here. The more striking phenomenon is that mountains in their time do dance, when the subterranean pressures break through their caps, pouring foreign lava from the depths through the mountain's own veins, shaking its chunks like flour in a sifter. The analysis of this movement is that, with the change in the deep-earth environment, certain but not all change-points in the mountain, those long the fault lines, suddenly are faced with new possibilities of radical change. The upsurging lava, hot and pressured, introduced new potentials that the old repetitive possibilities for those fault lines did not have, and new possibilities suddenly become relevant; moreover, the old kind of possibility is determinately excluded by the actual lava.

This modeling of endurance reveals that endurance is a relative thing, measured by endurance that last longer and differences that occur more quickly. Moreover, it reveals that, although all the factors in the mountain and its environment are real and objective, the way they are divided up depends on the conceptual divisions we employ. The point is that the endurance of the mountain is caused by the solidity, the massive unavoidable extensionality of the actualized mountain. And the mountain's changes, its eventual transformation into a plain, are caused by equally unavoidable forces of extensionality altering the possibilities of the mountain-elements. The identity of an enduring actuality is thus a rough affair. By convention's sake, we can continue to call it a mountain when it has become a hill; the Ozarks are still called mountains even though they have become intervals between ravines. The identity involved here is nothing more than continuity with debatable margins. It is not the kind of identity a growing thing has.

A growing thing has a discursive pattern. That is, any of its parts, temporally or spatially distinguished, is itself organized in part because of some role it plays in the unfolding of a temporally extended pattern. The discursive pattern contributes elements to the essential features of each of the change points so that the cumulative causal transformations exhibit the unfolding of the pattern. Organic growing things are obvious illustrations, with DNA in proper relation to the environment calling for differentiation and maturations of parts and processes. But organic things are not the only instances. A situation might grow as a discursive pattern takes hold, determines more and more elements, and finally regulates much of the change that takes place within the situation. For instance, after a geological catastrophe, many new organisms and landface structures begin to interact with the pattern of a particular ecosystem. At the beginning, each seed, spore, microbe and animal reacted according to the possibilities of itself in its immediate environment. Some died, some changed, some flourished. As the immediate environments took shape, larger organizations became possible and actualized, reinforcing, changing, perhaps eliminating some of the smaller environments. Without new input, the system would reach equilibrium, and a pattern larger than any mere endurance of the elementary factors would contribute essential features to all the system's components.

Discursive individuals such as human beings constitute a class of enduring beings. They endure and change bodily, and they exhibit discursive patterns both in biology and in their personal careers. In addition, they have essential features in any moment of their lives deriving from past and future moments that give them a moral character. Before discussing them, however, it is important to discuss two kinds of causation that relate to, but are not paradigmatic examples of, growth; namely, inertial forces and regularities. These relate as well to systems.

Causation requires not merely a connection between one actuality and another actuality that it conditions. It requires an entire discursive matrix of all actualities in past temporality functioning as potentials in various harmonizations in present moments, and demarking the various levels of determination and vagueness in the shifting future common to all structural identities.

II. INERTIAL FORCES, REGULARITIES, AND SYSTEMS

One of the odious features of the metaphysical foundations of modern science, according to Whitehead, was its atomism requiring causal forces to be external to the things expressing them. On the social scale, this metaphysical mistake models human society as a group of atomic individuals united only by external convention or by externally imposed force. A proper metaphysics, Whitehead argued, would treat causation as immanent to the causes and effects. Immanent causation is that which arises from the characters of the actualities involved.

The weakness of Whitehead's own view is that although it accounts for regularity and irregularity, it does not provide focus on "tendency," on what Peirce called "Thirdness," connectivity and the drive toward more connectivity. Hence Whitehead's view, especially in its social applications, put too much stress on spontaneous choice to settle irregularities, and too little on the free management of tendencies which respect the various weights of the past. Further, although Whitehead quite rightly stressed the aesthetic power of patterns to lure process within a present moment of concrescence toward richer and more intense harmonies, he did not forcefully enough stress the normative status of distant possibilities that command the tendencies to produce values across a broad field of possibilities common to many things. Hence it is difficult on Whitehead's view to distinguish between an individual occasion's momentary aesthetic lure projected into the future, and objective ethical demands.

On the other hand, the difficulty with Peirce's view of Thirdness is its cumbersomeness at handling individuals. The purpose of this section is to employ the categories developed in this and previous chapters to describe immanent patterns of causation. The descriptions build upon process philosophy and pragmatism while minimizing their limits.

Inertial Forces. An ideal inertial force is an historic route of harmonies following some geometric structure of the extensional field with such intensive magnitude that the antecedent harmonies are important enough in each successor to (1) make the successor conform to the antecedents' geometric structure, and (2) condition further successor harmonies to do so likewise. The common sense geometry of inertia employs the straight lines of Newtonian mechanics; physics since quantum mechanics has made this issue more complex. For an inertial force truly to be ideal or pure, all the harmonies in the route would have to be alike except in temporal position; that is, force lingering at a point. If the point moves through time across a three-dimensional (or n-dimensional) field, the movement is ideal if no conditions alter the occupancy of the successive places except those of the antecedents. This would require that the separate histories of the various places to be occupied in the trajectory are trivial with respect to the moving inertial force. In a non-ideal inertial force, differences in the harmonies modify the route, both in force and in geometric structure. A run-away car in a crowd of people is a great inertial force, nevertheless one slowed down and deflected by the people struck. A hard-struck cue ball divides its inertia into many directions as it breaks the formation of billiard balls, finally slowing to a stop; but the directions and the slowing are to be accounted for by the shape of the balls, the angle of strike, and the friction of the table.

Where actualities tend to be homogeneous so that ideal inertial conditions are approximated, it is helpful to analyze causation in terms of vetors of forces. These conditions may obtain in matters of microscopic and macroscopic scale. For inertial patterns to be important, the vague traits in the harmonies along the historic route that make them similar must be more important than the differences between the harmonies. That is, the harmonies must tend to behave like their predecessors relative to the geometry of the extensional field.

Regularities. Despite the disadvantages of its externality, the atomism of modern science has led people to look at how things behave irrespective of prejudice about their "natural" motion. Kant, in fact, was led to formulate causality as the regular occurrance of one type of phenomenon following on another type of phenomenon: if *a*, then *b*. There need be no connection, in Kant's view, between the immanent natures of *a* and *b* other than the order and regularity of their occurrance.

On an immanent view of causation, regularity occurs when vague possibilities characterizing the cause-type occurrance are determinately connected with vague possibilities characterizing the effect-type. The characterizing possibilities are vague, depicting the cause and effect as types, and therefore can be instantiated in a number of individually idiosyncratic circumstances. This allows for regularity. That the regularity exists stems from the fact the actual past conditions the future to determine the connection between the vague types. What regularities there are depends on the empirically determined actuality of the past.

A regularity expresses what Peirce called a Third, a Relationship. As he pointed out, it is not enough to understand what Thirds are operative; we need to understand why there are the Thirds we observe (1935; pars. 287–317, 452–491, especially 490). Only chaos needs no explanation. The crucial cosmological questions have to do with why there are the regularities we find, and why regularities tend to develop.

To say with the determinists that every event in every respect expresses a regularity is to make an empirical claim for which there seems little evidence. Further, if events are determined by regularities, that affects only the types they exhibit, not their haecceities. On two counts, then, determinism seems implausible: things do not seem as regular as they should if determinism were true, and regularities apply only to the types in things, not to their individual natures. Kant would answer back that the only way we can tell whether some phenomenon is real, or just a figment of imagination, is by relating it to regularities that can be publicly checked. The response to Kant is twofold. First, he was right that we need to create some distance between our assertions and phenomena in order to see whether the former are true. But, second, there are other kinds of distance than that between regular order and mere order of occurrance in mind; in fact, there is the distance embodied in causality itself, the difference between a thing's proper location and its multiple effective locations, some of which are in our experience.

Systems. A system is a causal pattern in which roles are defined for actualities that interconnect. The interconnection between roles is such that (1) the playing of any role is sustained by the playing of some others and in turn sustains some others, (2) the alteration of any role requires an alteration in one or more other roles, (3) conditions 1 and 2 link individual roles in such a way that, either directly or indirectly, all the roles in the system are linked to form a causal unit; that is, the consequences of playing any role or altering any role are felt throughout all the roles.

Further, a system rests within a variety of background conditions. These include the conditions that supply the various actualities to play the roles and the conditions tolerating the roles played. Both kinds of conditions might be other systems, such that their support of the system under discussion is a role within their own pattern, or the result of several roles or of the playing of the pattern as a whole. Systems may intersect without forming one super-system if condition (3) does not hold.

The intersection of systems can be of several sorts. The intersection is *overlapping* if an activity that is a role in one system is also a role in another. The intersection is *conjunctive* if the activity of playing a role in one system is essentially connected (in the strict sense of essential) with another activity playing a role in another system. Giving birth is an example of overlap, playing roles both in the nuclear family system and in the larger system of population genetics. Performing labor in an economic system conjoins with food consumption in a food-chain system because one must eat to work. There are many degrees of partial overalp and partial conjunction. Systems can intersect at more than one point. In the case of overlap and conjunction, the points of intersection can exhibit regularities. But there is no systematic reason to find regularities between the two systems at points other than intersection. For instance, a diverse group of laborers at the same manufacturing plant all have to eat, but one group may be in a food chain for Hispanic food, another for Chinese, another for German; the ethnic cultural differences are the important variables determining the kind of food chain. An intersection is *accidental* if playing a role in one system affects a role in another system without itself being a role in that system, or if playing a role in one system conditionally but not essentially plays a role in another. An example of the former case would be wandering predators who destroy an ecology upon which they happen; Aristotle's lottery salesman who happens to make a sale at a dinner party is an example of the latter.

The actualities that can play roles in systems can be of many sorts. Individuals obviously do, as do aggregates of many kinds. Situations also play roles, as for instance a transition from one political regime to another plays a role in a political system. From tightly knit discursive individuals to diffuse situations, actualities have some kind of harmony of their own. That harmony includes the roles they play in various systems, and much else besides. It also includes the harmonizaton of the various roles together. And it includes the special haecceities that go beyond any roles in their definiteness. Therefore no actuality is reducible to any one systematic role, or to all its systematic roles together. Further, although an actuality can play a role in a developing discursive, though unique and unsystematic, pattern, it cannot be reduced to that role either. That is, an actuality is not reducible to its place in various histories any more than to its place in various sytems. On the other hand, the roles it plays in both systems and histories may be far more important to it and to the multiple things in which it is effectively located than the specifics of its haecceity; this at least was Hegel's view, dismissing the non-rational as mere accident.

We may suppose that the environment for an actuality, that which contributes its potential conditions when the actuality itself is emerging, is largely a great mass of systems. The systems may have many points of intersection so that by and large they hang together even if they lack the organic quality of a super-system. But because they have points lacking intersection, they are at various points indeterminate with respect to one another. The consequence of this is that the various sytems have partially independent careers, and the environment is not entirely stable. Further, environments can contain regularities whose occurance is accidental and not systematic. And they can contain inertial forces that wreak havoc with the systems in their path; for instance, a comet passing too close that sucks the atmosphere off the earth.

The contrast in primary cosmology between limit and the indefinite, between relative order and relative chaos, between the form-giving male god and the indiscriminate-birthing female goddess, is nowhere more evident in metaphysics than here. We image our environment as an arena of systems in which we take our being, act our parts, and aim to authenticate our lives by meaningful closure. The stability of this arena is precarious at best. The ancients knew that the mountains shake and that there are too many untimely births. The actual lives we lead betray the fact that the systems from which we had hoped to benefit never came together, or that they are falling apart, or that accidental happenings are suddenly more important that our stabilities, or that changes we desperately desire are blocked by rigid systems that seem immovable. The mixtures of our lives are between order and chaos, and in those moments when the shades of illusion are rolled away, we alternately struggle to cope and to relax into the maelstrom of causes. Finding the Tao, the true cause of mixture, is not attaching to a super-order, as some have thought, but is finding a center to orient the haecceities of life to that maelstrom.

III. DISCURSIVE INDIVIDUALS

Discursive individuals are temporally thick actualities such that any temporally present date is essentially determined in part by past and future states of the individaul. That is, any temporally present date receives essential features from the individual's past and future as well as from the spontaneity of the moment. The unity of a discursive individual is tighter than that of an actuality determined by a discursive pattern. Any unified developmental causal process is determined in part by a discursive pattern, but is not necessarily one and only one unfolding individual. A discursive individual has temporally distinct actual parts by virtue of their mutual determination by essential features.

A discursive individual at one moment is potentially conditioned by the whole past, but only the individual's own past essentially conditions; that is, among the conditions, some of those from the individual's own past function as essential features. A discursive individual at one moment has possibilities shared with a wide range of other actualities, but only those possibilities, or those sectors of possibility, that essentially condition the present are possibilities for the individual's own future. All possibilities present normative content, but only those relating that content to the individual's own future as normatively culpable constitute the person's future.

The notion of a discursive individual is a difficult one because it attempts to avoid both the process philosophy view that atomizes individuals in time too much and the substance philosophy that treats individuals as if they were merely past structures for which "present" means only unfolding. The heart of the concept of discursive individuals is the use of the category of essential features: a discursive individual is one whose past, present, and future are temporally diverse but essentially together. An essential feature, it will be remembered, contributes to the subjective ordering of conditional features, one that determines how the potential conditions are valued in the individual. An examination of some of the essential components of individuality in human life will illustrate the point.

Paul Weiss, in his fine book *Privacy* (1983), develops the thesis that every individual has a private power epitomized in various structures. For Weiss, the private power is temporally continuous, and he does not deal systematically with the important differences in the modes of temporality. Nevertheless, privacy in his sense can be interpreted as the subjective power of (1) the essential ordering of conditions in present temporality, (2) the results of essential order in past temporality, and (3) the normative demands of essential features in the future of the individual. A brief discussion of certain of his epitomies of privacy can illustrate the nature of discursive individuality; my discussion is not a faithful paraphrase of Weiss's own discussion, but an adaptation.

His first epitome is sensitivity, which means that the individual relates to the world through a body. At any moment, it is essential to the ordering of the welter of conditions that the individual's body be the medium of continuities between that moment and the actual world. It is the medium to the individual's own actual past, and to the rest of the world. Although a person's body grows, at each temporal point the past of that body is an essential medium, and the future of the body is essential to continuity of sensitivity. Relative to any dated present, the past and future of the body are essential to sensitivity. What is relevant about the body in this instance is its capacity to be a medium of sensitivity. The second epitome is sensibility, the structuring of the individual so as to be responsible to the values in things and appreciative of them. Sensibility requires the development of ongoing personal structures making room for the important values in the environment. Not exhausted in any temporal present, these structures are continuing and developmental. To have reached a stage in the development of sensibility is to be obliged to maintain and enhance the sensibility in the future, if possible.

Weiss also discusses need and desire as epitomies, but orientation is the next epitome that neatly illustrates discursive individuality. Orientation is the organization of life, present moment by present moment, to make desirable adjustments to the important and enduring aspects of the physical and social environment, especially background aspects. This entails developing habits of behavior and anticipation, well-engrained in one's physical and social nature. Although orientation is expressed at a moment, it is a temporally thick set of habits, and is never completely expressed at a moment. It requires past experiences to function essentially as habit forming, and it requires future behavior to be connected to current anticipations.

Several of Weiss's epitomies require action to take place with reference to internalized representations of a temporally spread-out self. Sociality, for instance, involves recognition of and relation to a social role; mind involves taking oneself to be normatively (though not necessarily actually) bound by norms of good thinking that any mind ought to be bound to, relating oneself to "any person." Resolution involves responding in terms of a representation of a long, complicated action, normed by values definitive of one's will as such. Acting as a person requires an image of how the parts of one's life make up a personal career. Autonomy requires not only a sense of resolution but of responsibility for the values implicit in one's action. And so on. In each case, a temporally thick structure serves as a set of essential features ordering the conditions of the moment. Fully to be a self is to act with a sense of responsibility for how that action fits in with one's ongoing identity in social, historical, cultural and personal circumstances. Not all the future-oriented sources of essential features are "moral" in the ordinary sense of being publicly objective obligations; but they are normative in the sense that they define the worth of the individual, epitome by epitome. A discursive individual is a harmony of many layers of discursive structures such as these epitomies, all embodied at every moment of present temporality, but none exhausted or even completely expressed in any one moment. A complete analysis of all the essential epitomies would indicate what is essential to human life, what collection of discursive traits make up essential humanity.

Of course, these epitomies are all vague. Sensitive to what? What sensibilities? Orientation to what? In what social, historical, or cultural contexts does one exercize resolution, mind, autonomy, live out a career, develop a self?

A discursive individual plays roles in many systems that extend beyond the individual, both physical and social. The epitomies are essential ways in which the individual harmonizes its various roles. There are also many conditional forms of integration. There are unsystematic regularities and nonsystematic discursive patterns—histories—in which discursive individuals play roles; and inertial forces use individuals blindly (that is, unsystematically). The harmonization of a discursive individual is thus a complex matter, subject to uncertainties and shocks. Substance philosophies give a false sense of security and continuity, although there are systematic forces such as the biological structure of the body that look securely coherent. Disintegration, or the failure to achieve continuing harmony in a new situation, is a constant threat. We may not be in a war of all against all, as Hobbes thought, but we are indeed in a fast-moving maelstrom. The range of possibilities, determined as it is in its complexity by the rush of actualities, simply might not have room for certain continuing discursive individuals. On the other hand, precisely by virtue of playing roles in causal patterns of all sorts, individuals can affect the flow of events to create some of the potentialities for their own life.

IV. CAUSATION, NATURE, AND INTERPRETATION

The purpose of Divisions II and III of this book is to rethink basic metaphysical assumptions that form our common sense. The justification of this purpose, relative to the topics of interpretation, truth, and reality, is that controversies surrounding those topics are limited by shared, inadequate common sense assumptions about the topic's basic context. Metaphysics is the philosophic discipline for a critical reworking of those assumptions. Only with an alternative metaphysical view will it be possible to approach the topic freshly.

A reformation of the metaphysics of common sense cannot be accomplished by importing a wholly new system. It can come, rather, only by judiciously tapping our own deeply embedded cultural resources, reorganizing them, making slight and perhaps polemically phrased shifts, and reconstructing a new system. Accordingly, these metaphysical chapters have reached into the philosophical, religious, and imaginative dimensions of both Western and Asian cultures, laying new stresses, pushing unusual connections, and tying the ideas together with a reconstructed technical vocabulary.

Chapter 5 analyzed the basic notion of identity, noting that an adequate theory must show how determinateness makes each identity different from every other, and yet the same as some others in some respects. A technical theory was then offered based on the categories of essential and conditional features, and harmony. In chapter 6, the assumptions about the nature of identity were contrasted with those about the being or reality of identity, and a theory of ontological creativity was presented representing determinate things as fundamentally diverse but also together in an ontological context of mutual relevance. Since ontological creativity, which makes the difference between being and non-being, has no determinate characters apart from the determinate things it creates, it can be approached through the basic categories of a primary cosmology that shows how there can be determinate things with harmonies of essential and conditional features. A categoreal scheme was adopted from Plato according to which the primary cosmology includes limit (form), the unlimited (chaos, plenitude), mixture (the concrete world), and the cause of mixture (the balance of harmony of mixtures). Religious resonances with each of these "creator defining" categories were pointed out. We now see that in the theory of extensionality, limit is associated with the logical form of future temporality, the unlimited with the diverse creative acts of present change, mixture with the actuality achieved in change, and the cause of mixture with the ontological harmony of these.

Chapter 7 picked up an implication of the theory of reality; namely, that by virtue of having form, any determinate thing has value. After situating the study of value in the current intellectual context, an analysis was given of harmony as an organization of essential and conditional features with complexity and simplicity; degrees of value, commensurability and incommensurability of value, and the uniqueness of values depend upon complexity and simplicity in formal configurations. Form itself was analyzed in terms of normatively measuring multiplicity, and this in turn gives rise to levels of vagueness, depending on the nature of the multiplicity. Complete specification of vagueness gives rise to a "this," a Scotistic haecceity, a concrete mixture. Nevertheless, a form maintains many levels, the higher ones being relatively vague with respect to the lower ones. Hence, the actualization of a form includes not only its haecceity but also its vague structures; therefore there is abstractness and generality even in haecceities. Form by itself is subjunctive: it would measure multiplicity if there were multiplicity to measure. Simplicity was then further analyzed in terms of the aesthetic categories of triviality, vagueness, narrowness, and width. The analysis then turned to explicate the notion of being a component of a harmony, as when it is said that conditional and essential features are components.

Through an analysis in chapter 8 of four senses of being a component—as claiming, as patterned, as achieved, and as harmonizing—a theory was presented for how harmonies are concretely embedded in the world, containing the past and referring to the future just by having form. In this discussion, the theory of identity as harmony was cosmologically contrasted with Aristotelian substance theory and Whiteheadian process philosophy, differences focused around the notion of extensionality. The chapter concluded with an introductory discussion of knowledge of value.

As the inherence of values in harmonies is one approach to the extensionality of the world, so is time. Chapter 9 proposed a theory of time that sharply distinguishes present, past, and future as modes of temporality. The modes of temporality are analyzed into their essential timely features, and their conditional features connecting them with one another. Various theories were criticized that reduce time to the paradigmatic elements of one temporal mode to the exclusion of others. The discussion was deepened by recurring to the ontological question of being of time, fleshing out the notion of ontological creativity and the context of mutual relevance.

The topics of identity, form, and value were then made more concrete in chapter 10 with a theory of endurance, perishing, and change through time, with some brief reflections on human-consciousness parallel to the reflections on the knowledge of value in the earlier chapter.

Chapter 11 attempted to specify the metaphysics by extending the previous notions to a theory of extensionality, focusing on space. Causation is distinguished from change, the causal role of present temporality, by virtue of ranging across an extensional field inclusive of the past and future as well. Whereas process philosophy can downplay the importance of space by virtue of limiting attention to present concrescences, each of which is isolated from contemporaries, the extensional field inclusive of the past and future depends on spatial as well as temporal togetherness. A theory of spatial extension was then offered in terms of the categories of past historicity and of shifting futurity. In particular, the future was analyzed as a shifting hierarchy of layers of vague compossibilities, specifying down to haecceity but maintaining the generality of the vague levels. Spatiality derives from compossibilities as determined by diverse actual decisions. Actual space is the singular achievement of all finished decisions. With a theory of space defined by actualized positions, it is then possible to model motion of actualities across positions or through space; a theory of motion and interaction is given.

Finally, this chapter calls attention to the patterns of causation defining the integrity of actualities moving through time and space. Specifically, patterns of endurance, growth, inertial forces, regularities, systems, and discursive individuals are analyzed. At this point, the basic categories of a full-blown metaphysics of nature have been introduced, ready to be employed for a theory of interpretation as an element in nature.

In particular, it will be argued that interpretation is a complex of essential features of human life. Interpreting is part of what makes people discursive individuals with unified changing careers through time. Interpretation is an epitome of humanity. Further, interpretation is not only an individual activity, but a social one, partly defining human sociality and ensuring that individuals' subjectivity is at once at least partly public. Finally, the ground has been laid for the thesis that interpretation distances the interpretive outcome from reality at the same time that it establishes causal connections so that reality can measure claims to truth.

DIVISION FOUR

Truth and Interpretation: A Measure Recovered

Preliminary Remarks

The purpose of the four chapters of this Division is to provide a speculative analysis of the basic concepts necessary for a theory of truth as measured by reality. Division I argued that the contemporary concern with interpretation is a manifestation of a deeper concern with the relation between human experience of the world and the reality of the world itself. Several current attempts to address this issue were discussed, and the hypothesis was formulated that truth is the properly qualified carryover of value from the objects of interpretation into the experience of interpreting. For this reconstruction of the issue of interpretation to be plausible, the metaphysical suppositions of our common sense themselves need to be reconstructed. Division II then attempted the rudiments of such a metaphysical reconstruction. The four chapters of that Division dealt with reconstructed conceptions of reality, through identity, being, value, and harmony, and with many related notions. Division III then specified those metaphysical notions into a cosmological interpretation of time, of enduring things, of space and causation, and of motion. The culmination of that discussion was a framework for understanding human life as discursive individuality in an environment of causal factors, a discursive individuality constituted across time by certain epitomies of what is essential to humanity.

The outcome of the speculative hypothesis is that thinking itself can be articulated as a complex but essential epitome of human life, and this in four dimensions of thinking. Imagination, the first dimension, has already been analyzed. *Reconstruction of Thinking*, in its second Part, argued that imagination is the original stratum of thinking by virtue of the fact that it consists in synthesizing natural conditions into the specific forms of experience. The norms determining the multiplicity of preexperiential conditions to have the basic experiential forms were analyzed as elements of beauty. Imagination *per se* is what it is by virture of conforming to aesthetic considerations.

Experience is not merely imaginative, however; it is also interpretive or assertive about the world, and its interpretations shape all its performative activities. The norms governing the interpretive or assertive relation between experience and the world are those having to do with truth, the topic of the current book. There are theoretical and responsibility-pursuing dimensions of thinking as well, to be discussed in later volumes. The unfolding, cultivation and exercise of these dimensions of thinking is a manifold epitome of human social and personal life. The specific topic of Division IV of *Recovery of the Measure* is the components of truth.

Distinguishing among the components of truth between concepts or meanings on the one hand and judgments or assertions on the other, it is customary to say that only the latter can be true or false. Concepts or meanings are used to make assertions but do not by themselves assert, it is ordinarily thought, and therefore cannot be true or false. This interpretation of concepts treats of them insofar as they are used in networks with other concepts, in assertions employing a network of concepts. The meanings of concepts can be explicated according to the networks in which they are employed. Late Wittgensteinians as well as semioticists explain conceptual meaning this way, and chapter 13 will analyze certain aspects of network meaning, especially those having to do with value.[1]

Concepts also have content, as the empirical tradition has argued, insofar as they are rules for integrating their various components. A valid concept is one whose components are real, and this is a crucial kind of truth, a carryover of the value of the components into the conceptualizing of them together. Even a valid concept can be inauthentically thought, however, when the particular social and personal experiences required for its components are missing and their roles are played by network meaning tokens alone. Chapter 14 analyzes this point, building on the discussion of components of harmony in chapter 8.

The discussion of concepts with both network and content meaning prescinds from their embeddedness in intentionality which must next be discussed. The forms of intentionality are manifest in imagination. A crucial function of intentionality, however, is to alienate the interpreter or interpreting community from the immediacy of imagination so as to deal critically with a world. Intentionality introduces the dyadic relation between interpretation and its objects that is necessary for truth to be a problem. This may not suppose that thought refers to something external; the externality might be contained within the orbit of interpretation. But the dyad is presupposed even in the formation of valid concepts, for those concepts are assumed to be ways of taking or interpreting the world. Chapter 15 analyzes interpretation as intentionality.

Chapter 16 must then weave these components of truth into a coherent natural structure of interpretation, indicating the assertive and performative elements.

13

Network Meaning

I. ON LANGUAGE FOR INTERPRETATION THEORY

The philosophic study of meaning and related problems has so cluttered the landscape with variant terms that it is necessary at the beginning to sort them out and stipulate some initial definitions. Of course, philosophy can come to defensible definitions only at the end of an inquiry, as Kant remarked, and so the introductory definitions here should be taken as preliminary (though not as preliminary as those given in Chapter 3, Section I). Nevertheless, even preliminary definitions carry an agenda, and the agenda of the present work is the development of a naturalistic theory of interpretation in contradistinction to several alternatives.

One strategy for terminology, employed by Peirce and Whitehead, is to invent neologisms for all new ideas and, even more important, for all minutely modified ideas. Peirce's invention of "pragmaticism," as a word too ugly for William James to adopt and abuse as he had "pragmatism," is a well-known story. The reasoning behind Peirce's position (1932; par. 223) is charming.

> The ideal terminology will differ somewhat for different sciences. The case of philosophy is very peculiar in that it has postive need of popular words in popular senses—not as its own language (as it has too usually used those words), but as objects of its own study. It thus has a peculiar need for a language distinct and detached from common speech, such as a language as Aristotle, the scholastics, and Kant endeavored to supply, while Hegel endeavored to destroy it. It is good economy for philosophy to provide itself with a vocabulary so outlandish that loose thinkers shall not be tempted to borrow its words. Kant's adjectives "objective" and "subjective" proved not to

> be barbarous enough, by half, long to retain their usefulness in philosophy, even if there had been no other objection to them. The first rule of good taste in writing is to use words whose meanings will not be misunderstood; and if a reader does not know the meaning of the words, it is infinitely better that he should know he does not know it.

Further on (par. 226) Peirce established rules for teminology, the sixth of which is this:

> For philosophical conceptions which vary by a hair's breadth from those for which suitable terms exist, to invent terms with a due regard for the usages of philosophical terminology and those of the English language but yet with a distinctly technical appearance.

The difficulty with the way of neologisms is that it is immediately disconnected from relevant neighboring projects. What reason has the reader to take them seriously, if the work of understanding the new meanings is considerable? Both Peirce and Whitehead have suffered from the appearance of irrelevance and idiosyncrasy. In the long run, disciples and devotees can bring a master's terminology into the general forum of philosophic language, and this has begun to happen with Whitehead's terminology. No one yet, however, has, for instance, brought Peirce's (1936, par. 302) crucial distinction between tychasticism, anancasticism, and agapasticism into the mainstream of the discussion. Still, there is a certain justification for neologisms when one's project is so new that it has no serious neighbors. Both Peirce and Whitehead were reinventing philosophy of nature after Kant and his positivistic followers had dismissed it in favor of natural science and epistemological philosophy of science. Unless one is willing to adopt prescientific language, or the romantic language of Goethe or Hegel, philosophy of nature does have to invent its own terms, and the chapters above have borrowed many of Whitehead's neologisms and defined new ones.

The case with a theory of interpretation, however, is different. There are many neighboring theories on the ground, and the explicit purpose here is to suggest a reorientation of those approaches. Therefore, the best strategy regarding terminology is to employ the terms that are current in the discussion and to criticize and modify their meanings. As Peirce would warn, this invites misunderstanding if the reader expects an uncritical use of a term in the technical sense defined by an alternative approach; readers should be warned that terms here are introduced as meaning less than they do in certain other systems, and are developed to acquire somewhat different meanings. To counterbalance the danger of misunderstanding, it is important to seek out the benefits of critical dialogue. The terms here are employed in ways that are intended to translate the insights and distinctions of alternate approaches into the strategic orientation of a naturalistic theory of interpretation.

The terms used in the analysis of interpretation below, and that already have been used informally, can be characterized by comparison with John R. Searle's language in *Speech Acts.*[1] But first an important dissimilarity should be noted. Searle's theory, like Habermas's and that of most hermeneutic philosophers, is based on communication; that is, on the nature of getting thoughts from one mind to another. This supposes a separation of minds that should not be given such philosophic importance. Stanley Cavell's brilliant but tortured *The Claim of Reason* illustrates the grief to which this supposition is heir; to suppose that interpreting minds (or *Daseins*, or Speakers, or Text-writers) begin essentially separate is a legacy of Descartes. Sometimes minds are separate, but other times they think together. Gestures, word utterances, and other forms of communication between people might be slower than trains of firing neurons in an individual's brain, but they probably are more efficient connectors for interpretative purposes. A theory of interpretation should deal with the interpretive process that might go on within a single individual, or be shared among many.

Searle's topic is a theory of language, and it analyzes speech acts. My topic is a theory of interpretation, with interpretive acts; language is but one mode in which interpretation takes place, or perhaps is but a part of interpretive acts that include much more.

As to comparative parallels, the first is that I shall use the more general "interpretation" and "interpretive acts" as the inclusive term, where Searle uses "language" and "speech acts."

Second, I shall use "signification" and its cognates "sign," "signify," and so on, where Searle uses "perlocution," with an important qualification. Searle defines perlocution as the consequence or effect on the hearer of saying something; being persuaded, taking warning, being committed, for instance. To write one's name on a contract or to say "I do" at the right place in a marriage ceremony is not merely to express a thought, but also to make the contract or the marriage. Searle distinguishes perlocutionary acts from illocutionary ones by saying that the former are the consequences of the latter. If, however, one adds to Searle the qualification that understanding an illocutionary act which has no other consequences than transmitting a message is itself a perlocutionary consequence, then every successful illocutionary act is also perlocutionary. And a perlocutionary act can be construed to contain illocutionary acts with their propositional, referential, predicative and other elements. This qualification parallels signification, which is the complete act involving object, sign, and interpretant in which the sign is successfully interpreted as standing for the object in some respect.

In one sense, concepts are only signs. They are not true or false except insofar as they are involved in significations or judgments, and then it is to the signification that the category of truth might apply. As signs, concepts refer to one another and are interrelated significantly in systems or codes. The topic of this chapter is network meaning in this sense.

In another sense, however, concepts are indeed true or false insofar as they mediate content that is real in the concept being thought as it is thought. In this sense the connotation of the term is that a concept grasps things together as its content. The content meaning of concepts is closely related to their network meaning as signs, and all concepts have both. Concepts regarded according to their content meaning are good or bad not only according to how efficiently they serve the uses of the networks in which they are embedded, but also according to how well they mediate their content to those who think with them. That is, concepts are true to the extent they carry over (the value of) their content into the experience of conceiving with them.

Because there are several words that have been used commonly as substitutes for one another—concept, meaning, sign, and representation, it is appropriate to lay down some stipulative conventions for the following discussion. "Sign" has been used throughout as defined by its mediating function between an object and interpretant, according to the theory of interpretation put forward by Peirce and others. One of the major theses of this book (and of Peirce's writings, for example, 1932, p. 302; or 1958a, 220–245) is that all of nature exhibits the process of interpretation, and hence everything (every harmony) is a sign, a point properly recognized by Derrida (1976, pp. 50–52).

Some signs are involved in human experience and are distinguished from the other signs by virtue of their connection with intentionality; these will be called "representations." Representations are not only verbal, but include any kind of gesture, perceptive structure, or instrumentally organized action that signifies in an intentional way.

A concept is a constructed intentional rule for representing, and it can be embodied in any appropriate representation; most concepts are best understood through verbal descriptions and metaphoric presentations. Most words or phrases are representations of concepts, and frequently it is not misleading to discuss words as if they were the concepts themselves.

A schema is a rule for uniting any sign as a harmony of components. A form is what is common to a schema and a concept representing it (Neville: 1981, ch. 6).

Any sign has meaning insofar as it is capable of referring and is capable of being interpreted. For most purposes in this book, however, the crucial meaning is intentional meaning, the meaning of representations or concepts.

That concepts have both network meaning and content meaning stems from the fact that they are rules for organizing manifolds, as Kant said. The second section of this chapter shall explore this point and develop the idea of networks. The third section shall dispute the point important to French semiotics and structuralism—that the networks constitute codes. It will be maintained that, instead, networks grow and diminish, and that the interesting question is how the network grows from a relatively uncoded form to a determinately coded form. The discussion thus returns to the topic of levels of vagueness and the importance of vagueness for generality. The fourth section provides a general theory of networks as displaying the structure of formal value discussed in chapter 7; namely, vagueness, triviality, narrowness and width.

II. RULES, NETWORKS, AND REFERENCE

In the *Critique of Pure Reason*, Kant wrote:

> All knowledge demands a concept, though that concept may, indeed, be quite imperfect or obscure. But a concept is always, as regards its form, something universal which serves as a rule. The concept of body, for instance, as the unity of the manifold which is thought through it, serves as a rule in our knowledge of outer appearances. But it can be a rule for intuitions only in so far as it represents in any given appearances the necessary reproduction of their manifold, and thereby the synthetic unity in our consciousness of them. The concept of body, in the perception of something outside us, necessitates the representation of extension, and therewith representations of impenetrability, shape, etc. (1956: 135;A 106)

His extraordinarily fruitful remark mixes at least two senses in which concepts are rules. First, in knowing outer appearances, a concept is a rule unifying a manifold that is thought through it. In this sense, the rule relates the concept's own manifold to other things in the process of objective knowing. Here the rule is a knot in a network, and Kant's remark points to network meaning. Second, in unifying its own manifold, the concept as rule calls up representations of that manifold, as we must think extension, impenetrability, shape, etc., when we think about an external thing as having a body. This second sense is content meaning, the topic of chapter 14.

Although he created the conceptual scheme for getting beyond it, Kant in this passage still assumed, perhaps only rhetorically, what seems now to be a naive relation between concepts in us and outer things to which concepts can be referred. When used a certain way in judgments, concepts can be referred to objects; put more circumspectly, concepts are among the tools allowing us to refer to objects. Whatever reference consists in, it is part of the network nature of a concept as rule to be able to refer; I shall argue that reference involves an interaction guided by network meaning that connects a referring representation with an object that is a sign but not necessarily a representation. In Kant's example, the concept of body is a rule not only in unifying extension, impenetrability, shape, etc., but also in applying these, organized by the concept, to the outer object.

Further, as a rule for referring, the concept provides organizational principles for how its own manifold can be referred. That is, by referring to the object as a body, the concept can be used in a judgment to refer to the object as extended, impenetrable, having some shape, etc. Its manifold contents are themselves concepts or rules, the logic of which, as referrable to the object, is given by the concept as rule. All of this is to say that a concept as rule is a sign that refers to its object when implicated a certain way in a signification, and by virtue of that reference allows the object to be interpreted with further signs that are its own manifold. As rule, the concept prescribes the organization of the interpretations to be drawn from its reference. This is precisely Peirce's insight, inspired by Kant, when he defined interpretation in terms of object, sign, and interpretant. The sign says the interpretant sign can be referred to the object in a certain respect, and the rule-character of that first sign defines the respect in which the interpretant can be applied.

What does this have to say about objects? The objects themselves are implicated in the concept's network by virtue of being objects, and therefore they themselves are rules of some sort tying themselves as objects into the network. By virtue of recognizing the network relation of reference, we can reject as naive the view that conceptual networks in some mysterious way transcend themselves and refer in some non-network fashion to external objects. Interpretation is a triadic relation implicating object, sign, and interpretant in one network, and this network is a structure of a complex of natural interactions. Whatever kind of rule-form an object has, it ties into the interpretive network by virtue of which it is referred to. Moreover, any concept or referring term can itself be an object referred to by its manifold content insofar as that content can be referred to it as its content, *ad in-*

finitum. There can be interpretations of interpretations of interpretations. So the simplest hypothesis is that objects too have the form of rules unifying manifolds that can both be referred to other objects and themselves referred to by other signs.

The standard philosophic difficulty with this position is that it collapses into subjective idealism; namely, the doctrine that we think only our own concepts and refer only to our concepts. A contemporary defense of this idealism is the deconstructionist claim that all thought is the interpretation of a text, with nothing non-textual to which the text refers. This is a difficulty when it collapses into implausible solipsism.[2]

The way around that difficulty, first explained by Peirce, is to recognize that knowing is an activity within certain parts of the network that connects to other parts of the network that may not be knowings. That is to say, all nature has the form of a network of signs, and it is precisely because of the natural interpretive connections, causal if you will, between one part of the network and another that the first can be known by the second. Representations can refer to signs that are not themselves representations, as well as to those that are.

The theory of nature and causality elaborated above is a way to make sense of this. The causal conditioning of one thing by another makes the conditioned thing a sign of the condition. The overall harmonic structure of the conditioned thing is the rule for the network allowing one to get from the conditioning thing to the further things that the conditioned thing conditions, and to the other things harmonized with the condition in the conditioned thing. As we shall see in Section III, the general form of network meaning is the aesthetic form of harmony, involving triviality, vagueness, narrowness, and width.

Some of the mysteries of reference, at least with regard to the simple model of referring to past things, disappear with this naturalistic or causal account. The objects referred to have their own proper position in the extensional field, possibly far distant from the knower. They are present in the knower, as conditions, possibly through a dense chain of mediations—conditions of conditions of conditions. This model does not yet explain the intentionality of referring, that is, the judgment character of the activity of taking one harmony as a sign referring to another (see chatper 15); but it explicates the several senses of the presence and absence of the object in the knowing reference to it.

How does a network give rise to reference? It is never as simple as a theorist would hope. Charles Peirce, for instance, thought he had accomplished a great deal by devising a theory of signs based on the possible trichotomous combinations of three kinds of signs: icons, indices, and symbols (for example, 1932, pp. 134–173). Indeed this was a great accomplishment, and subsequent reconsiderations of his division of signs have given rise to only minor improvements. But there is more to the network of meaning than the formal relations among signs; there are levels of syntax and semantics.

The concepts of both syntax and semantics are analogies developed from the study of language, and in most twentieth century treatments have been expressed as characterizing properties of formal languages. Syntax, however, can be defined more broadly, in accordance with the naturalistic theory of interpretation, as the vague formal possibilities of conditioning within a discursive matrix as determined by the mostly invariant actual structures of a cosmic era; semantics is the less vague formal possibilities that develop historically within an era and attain to sufficient generality as to characterize a domain. Reflecting recursively on the *language* by which we describe possibilities, syntax is the formal structure of language as such, and semantics is the structure required to express the specific meanings in any particular language. The domain of a language is the culture within which it is used, and the borders of such a domain are ambiguous.

A naturalistic theory needs to stress the primacy of the syntactical and semantic meaningfulness of the world, to which our languages give resonance and communicability. As Wittgenstein and others have shown, meaningful human activity includes the use of language, among many other forms of behavior, to interact interpretively with the world and to communicate about this with others. Not only are speech acts more various than descriptions, the repertoire of interpretive behaviors includes habitual actions that are meaningful interpretations and that themselves are signs for further interpretation. In a practical sense, of course, we do not deal with the world wholly beyond our reach (assuming that includes our conceptual reach). But insofar as we do deal with the world, or parts of it, we shape our responses as best as possible to acknowledge and be responsive to the harmonic structures, to the meaningful interpretive conditionings, of the environment. Language is but one way of registering the world's meaningfulness in the way we make up our own discursive natures. The networks of our various meanings are partly continuous with the networks of conditions and harmonies in the world; the discontinuities mark our errors.

Language is a special kind of interpretive behavior because of its involvement in communication. Communication is not merely the expression to one another of what people internally mean. It is rather one of the chief modes of conditioning whereby people attain to the human epitomies. If one says that communication is artificial because it involves conventions, then Aristotle would have been right to say that people are not naturally human but artificially so, since so many human potentialities are posterior to communication. Verbal language is by no means the most basic structure of communication. Dewey (1981, ch. 5) was insightful in defining a sign as anything that is taken by one person as playing a role in the experience of another. Cuddling, fighting, gestures to represent these and other overt signs, are all basic communicative signs. Dance and especially music are important modes of communication for their human-making powers, and require pervasive and intense networks of nuance. But verbal language is probably the most flexible medium of communication developed so far, capable of great distance in reference, of a wide range of controllable intensities, of self-reference, irony, and humor. In particular, verbal language is an adroit tool for the explicit and intentional creation, development, and care of human relations and institutions. Communication at all levels is part of the conditioning necessary for most of the qualities we associate with humanity.

As mentioned before, however, it is a mistake to build a theory of meaning on a theory of communication, because that makes it seem as if people were separate enjoyers of private meanings that then have to be communicated. Rather, the theory of meaning should be built on a theory of networks, causal networks including non-cultural nature as well as other people and human artifacts such as symbols and language. Communication between people can be understood as a variant of network interpretation rather like the continuous thinking of a single individual.

The network meaning of a concept carries thinking along regulated paths. Of course, one of the crucial variables determining the direction of thinking is the structure of intentionality in the thinker or thinkers, the purposes, motives, and activities at hand. The network meaning of concepts, however, bounds the possibilities for directions of interpretation. Given sufficient motive, a train of thought can go on indefinitely. When people learn the network of their society's communication system, its rituals, gestures, langauges, etc., they can spin on and around the network forever. This unlimited connectability of elements of a network has a good side and a bad side, both of which stem from the fact that the network meaning can be relatively empty of content meaning. On the good side, a network extended into a new domain provides at least analogical purchase on the novelty. We can move along the network, testing whether the imported meanings can be used here, and how they have to be modified. The rituals for social gatherings stand us in good stead when we encounter new groups, for instance, although the missionary who says grace for the cannibals' meal makes a great mistake regarding which part of his network to pursue (he ought to pursue the network regarding falling into a den of lions, the proper interpretant of which is running like hell). On the bad side, the potential content-emptiness of network meaning may be deceptive. We may think we properly understand something just because we can talk about it glibly. The crucial difference between an experienced and an inexperienced person makes the point.

From the perspective of the metaphysics developed earlier, the possibility for network meaning rests on the fact that actuality contains within itself the levels of vague determination as well as the specifications of these vague levels down to haecceity. Therefore, when a potential condition is taken in by a harmony, it can play certain roles and not others; that fact is a general feature. Of its possible roles, it must be cast in a definite, individual positions: that fact gives it a concrete universal character to which reference is also possible. Both the roles it actualizes in the harmonies, and its possible roles not actualized, constitute aspects of the ways the harmony interprets the original condition, and they themselves are open to further interpretation by subsequent harmonies. Network meaning includes both irrevocably general elements referrable to all harmonies, and less general, finally concrete, elements that are referrable only to historical harmonies as historical. The character of intentionality, the judgment that refers, depends on the mix of these two arrangements of generality.

In order to explore network meaning further, it is necessary to examine the organization of meanings in codes. A code is one specialization of a network.

III. THE DEVELOPMENT OF CODES

Galileo prophesied we would come to understand nature only when we had grasped its alphabet, namely mathematics. His point was a major inspiration to the development of mathematical science. Its metaphysical implication was that the formal structure of things, that which is mirrored or revealed by mathematics, is the interesting part to know. On that assumption, the uninteresting parts drop from attention and some kind of formal idealism becomes the supposition of common sense.

Descartes was a better philosopher and apologist for the new physics. He knew that, besides form, there are existential elements to reality, real spaciness to extension, and real mentality to thinking minds. For all the perverse consequences of his separation of body and mind as separate substances, at least he preserved the tradition's insight, from Plato and Aristotle through Aquinas and Scotus, that existence is more than a plane of formal possibility. In order to preserve the completeness and closure of mathematical science, therefore, Descartes hit upon the idea that all realities are purely positive creations of a God who is outside the sphere of knowable realities. For Descartes (1934, pp. 248–251), God creates even the formal conditions for the possibility of things, and the norms by which they are judged. God's creating is like the divine or natural light we share with God. Since there is nothing in reality God does not create and simultaneously know, our own knowing, finite though it is in comparison with God's because of the hastiness of our will and the limit of our attention, in principle can penetrate completely through all objects of knowledge. There is nothing in the world, no mysterious matter, that is not transparent to the natural light. Although reality is not reduced in practice to mathematics for Descartes, it does consist in "simples," by which he meant units penetrable by the natural light, the paradigms of which are mathematics and the existential logic of the *cogito*. Descartes' "intimate union" of existence and mathematical form in intuition was not maintained by his successors, although Spinoza, Leibniz, Pascal, and even Kant struggled with it.

Descartes' twentieth century successors applied his fundamental position, now viewed as an hypothesis, to language and culture, its success complete in transforming common sense about nature even as its plausibility utterly vanished from contemporary physics. Saussure (1959) proposed that language was to be studied as codes of signs. Levi-Strauss (1967) extended the theory of codes to myth and culture and his structuralism achieved the status of a full-blown method in the minds of many. That is, it became a hypothetical metaphysics, though always defended according to its usefulness in investigation. Indeed the idea of codes was fruitful in both linguistics and more comprehensive cultural studies. But it is a lie to experience. It has the metaphysical effect of imposing a deceptive order on things. Although codes might look good from a distance, close examination of a text reveals not the homologies of structure, but Derrida's *differance* (Derrida, 1976). Deconstruction gains its energy from the revelations of the cheats of structuralism. The Saussurean-inspired study of linguistics has yet to recover from its deconstruction.

Stated metaphysically, the structuralist position is that reality is made of building blocks whose important relations are exhausted in the systematic connections expressed in codes. By knowing the codes, one knows how things fit together. Descartes' existential intuition gives plausibility to the conception of the building blocks; Galileo's views on the mathematical alphabet of nature, now applied to culture, define the goal of knowing: to be able to speak the sentences and paragraphs of reality. But if we look closely, the structuralist position is plausible only by its power to force its frame of reference on the inquirer. The texts of nature, literature, and culture are much more than codes, and the codes applicable only vaguely.

How are we to understand this metaphysically? The first point is to recall the distinction between the vague characters of things and haecceity. It might be that structuralism applies only vaguely to the fields it studies, and that it does indeed apply in some cases at that level. With this understanding, it is to be expected that any given speech act, the set of family relations for a given family, will be much more particular and various than the structural analysis would say. Further, the haecceity might even be contrary to the structural role it is supposed to play vaguely. For instance, the mother's brother might be expected to be the family authority, when in fact the authority is exercised in a particular case by the boy next door who adventitiously assumed an authoritative role. The distinction between vagueness and haecceity explains some but not all of the discrepancies in structuralism.

A more profound metaphysical observation about structuralism is that it errs in thinking that reality is composed of structurally related building blocks, of alphabet elements or Cartesian simples. Reality is rather a maelstrom of discursive processes, illustrating the principle of context-dependence. In light of that principle, any structures discerned, especially any simple elements that can function as place markers in mathematical relations, must be selective abstractions from the maelstrom, more or less well-founded. The maelstrom context is not a totality or whole, appeal to which would contextualize abstractions determinately. Rather, the context is the interaction of a host of discursive processes, unified by whatever vague possibilities they share and motivated by whatever actual processes have been set in motion.

Any temporally discursive process involves levels of vague structure that are decisively specified down to haecceity as actualization takes place. As a particular level of vagueness becomes actualized, an actual history accrues around it so that it becomes a stable structure, as for instance when family patterns settle down. Within that structure, as its specifications, other decisions may become structured, so that the structure is a complex hierarchy. On the other hand, it might be that whereas the higher levels of vague structure become stabilized by actuality, the lower levels down to haecceity are not so stable, and are the result of more or less idiosyncratic decisions. A society might be vaguely structured, for instance, to have both men and women in constant care of affairs, with a communal knowledge of what must be taken care of, but without a stable, repeated, and socially normative definition of gender-specific work or authority roles. The growth of that society might see some of those roles developed and stabilized. Peirce

(1935; pp. 190–215) was the first to see the importance of this phenomenon of the growth of structure, and called it Agapism, growing Thirdness. By reference to agape he meant to indicate that the value achieved by a local and temporary structure might enhance the larger environment if it were stabilized and extended in scope. So, the fortuitous family relations worked out in one family might become the model of family roles for the larger society, with proper reinforcements to ensure that it continues to be actualized, and with permissible variations so that it might be adapted to various circumstances. This growth in generality and stability is a kind of evolution.

Just as vaguely structured actual conditions can come to be supplemented by more specific structures, so those specific structures can become destabilized, returning to a more chaotic process of specifying the vague structures. Any number of causal events could break up specific structures. A cosmic cataclysm could break up even very vague structures, although some higher-level vague structures would have to remain intact if there is anything at all left of the world. Peirce, with his progressivist enthusiasm, was not as sensitive to such devolution as he might have been.

The image our metaphysics suggests for nature and culture is this. There are slowly evolving, very vague structures of discursive processes within which more specific structures evolve to stability and then sometimes devolve. As the various discursive processes interact, different stable structures of specifications become possible, and then perhaps impossible. These structures of course build on one another and interact in both systematic and unsystematic ways. The growth of personality structure in a person for instance might be systematically determined to devolve with senesence. One hopes that the difficult growth of a society-wide, maybe eventually world-wide, institution of law and justice will continue without devolution, or at least not until society no longer needs justice.

Within the cosmic era of human life, capacities to organize experience so as to represent the world are among the structures actualized in human genes, social habits and culture, and subject to change as these actual historical conditions change. These capacities include the development of representations with network meaning, especially language. For reasons cited throughout the above, it is important to emphasize first the fact that the capacity to represent is a part of nature, a specification of signification, like the development of a cultural or biological structure.

Of course, the major adaptive variable for the stabilization of a network of signs is its effectiveness in representing what is real, according to the various practical and aesthetic uses of representation. A network should allow the representation of the vague as vague, the specific as specific, the evolving as evolving, and the devolving as devolving, as well as other forces, regularities, idiosyncracies and haecceities. A *theory* of signs, a semiotic, therefore, must include as a major principle the explanation of the evolution and devolution of codes. More particularly, it needs to give an account of how our representations can develop from relatively vague structures to more specific codified structures, and of the reverse devolutionary process. Study of language merely as code, bracketing out the genetic factors, is sheer deceptive abstraction, perhaps harmless enough if one does not need to look too closely. Neither French structuralism nor Carnapian syntactic-semantic theory is about real language in its concreteness (neither *langue* nor *parle*). As Peirce said, it is regularity, law, that needs an account, not chaos. Evolutionary/devolutionary explanation is what accounts for structures.

But then what are the semiotic structures to be accounted for? Are they not codes? Is there not a fruitful and legitimate semiotic science of at least the formal structure of codes? Of course. The next section will describe just such a structure for meaning networks as such. Semiotic structures are not intentional objects, however (except insofar as the study objectifies them). They are rather the structure of intentional acts. Carnap's study of the logic of formal languages and the linguistic study of language structures deal with language as itself an intentional object. Language is actually a complex of structures evolved within the maelstrom that embodies intentionality (among other things). Instead of the Cartesian account of language as built up from structurally related simples—the relations of course are more simples—the study of representations should focus on their emergence from the maelstrom, and their context there.

IV. FORMAL STRUCTURE OF NETWORK MEANING

According to chapter 7, the nature of form is the achievement of value through triviality, vagueness, narrowness, and width. In *Reconstruction of Thinking*, I defended the theory that those properties constitute beauty, the norm of imaginative form. The purpose of the current section is to discuss their involvement in representing form. A representation is a harmony with vagueness, triviality, narrowness, and width. In brief, the hypothesis is this: Vagueness and triviality constitute the background in which representations can be asserted meaningfully. Narrowness and width are properties of the interpretive functions of representations themselves, roughly corresponding to referring and predicative functions. Representations cannot be part of an intentional process without the background elements; network meaning includes both focal and background elements. These properties shall be discussed with reference to research projects for understanding network meaning.

Triviality. Triviality is the character of harmony corresponding to what Kant (1956, "A Deduction") called "synthesis of apprehension of the manifold." With regard to the network meaning of a representation, this means that the representation is constituted as it is by supposing an array of conditions to obtain. This array includes (at least): (1) the physical conditions for representing, such as a world, life-systems, brains that think, behaviors that include representing; (2) the cultural conditions for life that involve representing, such as social life, communication, and the specific orientations of culture determining the main respects in which interpretations are made; (3) the sign system of which the representation is a part, such as the language, the gesture system, the musical system, and so forth; (4) the purposes according to which the representation might be involved in interpretation, the motives or interests that the use of the representation might serve; (5) the specific connections to unique context and use that accrue in a given historical instance of the employment of the representation.

This manifold of "trivia" is trivial in the sense that the representation supposes them without actually requiring any interpretive move to make them explicit. That is, the use of the representation does not require that these conditions themselves be represented, only that they obtain. Nevertheless, the fact that they must obtain means that further interpretation could indeed follow out the network of the representation and get to them, indicating the roles each condition plays. Triviality might be a misleading term here, if it is taken to suggest that the conditions for a representation are not important. They are indeed important as the conditions without which the representation could have no network meaning. They are trivial only in the sense that the representation does not have to represent them and they do not have to represent it; they are supposed conditions.

The research program of exploring the manifold synthesized in the bare unity of a representation might be a fruitful orientation for cultural anthropology. The neglect of the trivial conditions of representation leads to the false belief that representations can be treated merely according to their network connections in a code. Most of the supposed trivial conditions, however, are related to the representation in ways other than code relations.

Vagueness. Vagueness corresponds to Kant's "synthesis of reproduction," and in this context consists in the openness of the representation to further interpretation according to the specification of further signs. Although a representation determinately legitimates certain interpretations, it is vague with respect to an indefinitely large set of other interpretations; those other interpretations can be made only by means of an intervening specification. For instance, the representation "dog" determinately legitimates the interpretation that anything to which it is applied in the ordinary sense is a mammal; but it is vague with respect to whether there is anything to which it can be applied that is a pet of my daughters. Vagueness thus contrasts with the determinate sign functions of a representation by virtue of needing an intervening set of specifying signs.

The domain over which a representation is vague consists, first of all, in all the items that are in the representation's trivial comprehension. Further specifying signs can trace out the connections with any of the supposed conditions. Explicitly hermeneutical inquiry, asking what the representation means, frequently proceeds by tracing out these connections with supposed conditions.

Second, the domain over which a representation is vague includes just about any item in the system of representations of which it is a member, or in any other system to which a translation can be made, because the intervening specifying representations can make whatever transformations are necessary. For instance, to imagine how "loud" can interpret "black," we can suppose that black is the color of a blaring loudspeaker. The respects in which a representation is vague are mostly unimportant, and therefore are simply among the trivial conditions that could be traced out if ever there were a reason to. Sometimes, however, the purpose of thought is precisely to specify an otherwise vague representation because its vague potential with respect to something is the issue at hand. "Where are my glasses?" is an existentially potent expression of the vagueness of my knowledge of my glasses with respect to place.

The research project exploring representational vagueness is hermeneutics in its various sorts. Nineteenth century hermeneutics was concerned principally with the vagueness of translations: how to make the culture and language system of biblical times determinate with respect to modern times. More recent hermeneutics has generalized the project to a concern with communication. Supposing that another person or group has a determinate expression that is vague with respect to our own understanding, how can we grasp that expression? The more usual way of putting that is to say that our own understanding is vague with respect to the determinate meanings of the other. But this is to give an unnecessarily subjective interpretation of the hermeneutical circle: the task is for the other's meaning to unfold or specify itself to us, not the other way around. A third and even more general sense of hermeneutics is simply the process of inquiry. Any putting of a question has the form of treating the current representation of the subject matter as vague with respect to what one would like to know about it. Of course the subject matter itself might be vague—"what will five years bring?"; but to know that is to have an answer of sorts to the question.

Narrowness. Narrowness corresponds to Kant's "synthesis of recognition in a concept." With regard to representations, it consists in that element in the representation that effects the contrast between the object and the interpretant. The representation is a rule unifying its contents in such a way as to mediate between the object to which it is referred and those other representations with respect to which it is determinate. A representation's narrowness is its unity that legitimates the ascription of its interpretant to the object. As the earlier discussion indicated, narrowness is a contrast in which at least two elements of a harmony are juxtaposed. The several elements are themselves complex harmonies, and in the contrast their integrity is respected. The more intense the contrast, the greater the diversity in the integrity of the things contrasted.

The narrowness of a representation involves two dimensions of contrast. Simply as a harmony, a representation is a contrast of its contents, as in Kant's example "body" is a unity of "extension," "shape," "impenetrability," and so on. In this dimension, the narrowness of the representation "body" consists in the ordered juxtaposition of its content representations. Each of those in turn is a highly complex and well-defined representation, so that "body" is an intensely focused notion. This "content narrowness" is not the whole of the representation's narrowness, however, nor is it the interesting dimension for network meaning. The second dimension, or network, is the contrast between the referring function of the representation relating to potential objects and the interpreting function relating to the other representations that the representation legitimates being ascribed to the objects. A representation's network narrowness consists in the contrast it effects between object and interpretant. It is to say that whatever is a body is extended, has shape, resists penetration, etc. Network narrowness is not merely the dyadic juxtaposition of object and interpretant, but the triadic juxtaposition according to which an object juxtaposed to extension is also juxtaposed (according to the representation as rule) to shape, impenetrability, and so forth.

The research project exploring the network narrowness of a representation, of course, is that of definition. Narrowness is the definiteness of a representation as a representation. Dictionary definition is only one form of definition, and holds only for verbal representations. Behavioral definition is a broader notion. The process of definition is related to the width of a representation.

Width. The width of a representation is the form it has by virtue of its syntactic, semantic, and pragmatic functions. Inseparable from narrowness, width consists of those network elements governing the applicability of the representation as defined within an interpretive process. Whereas the narrowness of a representation is achieved by the contrast of its content with its potential references, its width is the context in which that narrowness is applicable to potential references and interpretable in terms of its content. Without narrowness, the representation would be a mere marker in a network that could not actually be employed in interpretation. Without width, the representation would be isolated from the rest of the network; with width, the interpretive process has formal lead-ins to and inferences from the representation. The width of a representation consists in the systematic roles it plays that give it extension.

Syntax, semantics, and pragmatics are research projects that usually apply to verbal representations. Their extension into gesture, say, or vision remains at a primitive stage. Further, even the organization of research regarding verbal representations is overdetermined in light of the fact that a larger theory of participation in the cultural enterprises of representation is necessary to give them context. Even the category of "verbal representations" or "language" blends off into gestures, into habits of representatively organizing visual and other kinds of sense perception, and even into movement guided by representations of ourselves as moving. Any behavior taking its orientation from a representation of ourselves as continuous beings through time, or from a representation of a group with which we identify, is representative behavior, and therefore structured with network meaning. To speak English, for instance, is not only to exercise competence in that language, which may be explained in terms of verbal representations, but is also to represent ourselves as speakers of English; the latter representation is not a verbal representation, although some of the signs by which we represent ourselves as English speakers are acts of speaking English. People who represent themselves as French speakers comport themselves toward their language differently from the comportment of those who represent themselves as English speakers, as American-English speaking tourists to Paris and London invariably experience.

Network Meaning. Although it might seem as if network meaning has but one dimension—the flow from object to sign to interpretant, a flow whose intelligibility comes from the rule character of the sign as representation—there are in fact four dimensions of network meaning: triviality, vagueness, narrowness, and width. It follows from this that an understanding of the use of a representation in an interpretive process must alert to the shifts in all four dimensions.

The background dimensions, triviality and vagueness, share content with other representations and constitute the common fabric required for the interpretive process. Of course, the harmony required for that background is an extraordinary achievement. Who could imagine that the vague processes of nature articulated by physicists and chemists could harmonize and harmonize and harmonize so as to provide actual structures that specify possibilities for an interpretive field? The organization of nature required for representation is not surprising when one asks what it is worth: the exquisite subtlety of harmonies involved in representation makes even beautiful sunsets seem like shadow-play.

14

Content Meaning

I. PRAGMATISM AND THE LINGUISTIC TURN

The "linguistic turn," characteristic of so much twentieth century philosophy (Rorty, 1967, pp. 1-39), is a turn away from experience and the empiricist philosophies associated with experience. To model mind on language is to stress the network meanings of representations, their connections, and the successful transition in thinking from one representation to another, from one representer to another. The advantage of the language model is that it makes logic immediately applicable to thinking, articulating mind in terms of the nature and legitimacy of its transitions. Machines whose workings have a form like that of mental logic then can be understood as analogies to mind. In its informal, ordinary language varieties, philosophy of the linguistic turn can be highly revelatory of experience as linguistic nuance reflects experiential nuance. To some extent, at least, what we experience is to be understood and grasped in terms of what we say about it. Nevertheless the saying is different from the experiencing.

There have been many motives for the linguistic turn. First and foremost, there was exciting work ready to be done with the linguistic forms of logic and language. Second, the linguistic turn offered hope for certainty and scientific grounding for philosophy, through intuition in logical matters and empirical science in the actual uses of language. Third, although twentieth century philosophy defined itself in a rejection of the great systems of idealism, it could carry on much of the idealist project by shifting the subject from the network meanings of the world to those of language, formal or otherwise. Fourth, emphasis on network meanings provides a philosophic escape from appeals to uncontrollable introspection that had so plagued empiricism.

Nevertheless, there is an important truth in the empiricist tradition; namely, that the interesting content of mind comes as the content of experience. Relative to this insight, network meaning seems only the processing of the content of experience. Hobbes hypothesized that a person is a collection of perceptions, each of which is like an inertial force compromised with the others against which it rubs in the person. Whitehead gave a sophisticated version of this hypothesis in his doctrine of prehensions. The truth in the empiricist conception needs to be separated from its objectionable components.

The root problem of empiricism (and much else in the Western tradition, according to David Weissman, 1987) is that in its classical form it employed a vision or intuitionist model of knowledge. That is, the way to possess an experiential content is to look at it. The content is supposed to have appeared before the mind's eye as a perception of an external thing or of an inner mental state. Insofar as classical empiricism shared the Cartesian Fallacy, it attempted to analyze experiential contents into what it hoped are simples, and employed them as a foundation on which to build certain knowledge. Hume was a brilliant example of empirical Cartesianism, adding a spicier skepticism than Descartes would have enjoyed. Where Descartes practiced methodical doubt to purge error from thought, Hume (1988, Bk. 1) aggressively wielded his *a priori* classification system—either impressions or logic—like a sword: any claim not exhaustively analyzable into the elements of that classification is to be cast upon the fire (Hume: 1955, p. 173). Even supposing that there is merit to Hume's classification system, the observations required to classify candidate mental contents cannot be controlled. Hume himself was sensitive to this. Force and vivacity are not clear criteria to distinguish impressions from mere copies in marginal cases. And logical analytical truths too seem to fade off into conventions in marginal cases.

Charles Peirce (1934, pp. 135–189) made the decisive critique of classical empiricism, and all other intuitionist philosophies of simple starting points, when he asked whether the judgment that mental content is an intuition (impression or empirically pure given) is itself an intuition, or some other kind of judgment. If it is an intuition, there is an infinite regress of question-begging claims. If it is not an intuition, and yet if it is supposed to yield new knowledge, knowledge of a matter-of-fact rather than a logical implication, then it itself requires further interpretation that someday ought to come down to impressions or logic, *ad infinitum*. The conclusion of Peirce's argument is that if we have empiricist impressions or intuitive mental contents, we couldn't tell whether a given instance were such a case. As a result, no inference, about certainty or anything else, could be derived from a claim that a given judgment is based on an empirical given. There is no pragmatic meaning whatsoever to the claim that a given perception or other judgment is empirical or intuitive.

Peirce must receive credit also for developing an empirical alternative to the empiricism he criticized; namely, an alternative conception of the meaning of "possession" of empirical contents. Although his view was far more brilliantly developed by James, Dewey, and Whitehead, he better than his followers saw the root of the mistake: the intuitionist model. Empirical content is not something we possess by looking at it. Rather, it is possessed, he suggested, by influencing or shaping our activity. Whether the mental content is an abstract meaning or a brute part of the world immediately encountered, its reality is possessed by experience in precisely the ways in which it makes a difference to activity. Not to have the content is to act in ways shaped only by other things.

The pragmatist conception of experience is empirical in ways that subtly reject common assumptions about intentionality and logic. With regard to intentionality, since Brentano, Frege, and Husserl, it has been commonly assumed that the content of thought, or of experience, is the intentional object. A thought "of" something is like a look "at" it. Without denying that intentionality is oriented toward an "object," a pragmatist can describe the object in terms of the purpose, focus, intent of intelligent activity, not in terms of its content. The contents rather are the experiences integrated into the activity that make it possible and give it its shape.

One kind (or a family of kinds) of intentional purpose is to represent the content of experience. In this we select out the experiential content for conscious objectification. Contrary to any intuitionist view, however, this conscious objectification is surely a matter of *representing* the experiential content, with the qualifying abstractions attendant on the signs used to represent, the respect in which the representation is made, and the purposes of representation. Becoming conscious of perceptual experience, for instance, means identifying it in terms of the kinds of lines, shapes, and volumes we are trained to employ, employing the colors and textures we recognize, and so forth. Patrick Heelan has shown (1983) that even the "pure experience" bias of the phenomenological tradition should acknowledge that perception is conditioned by learned categories of interpretation. Perception thus is not merely uninterpreted sense experience, but a complex act grasping content by means of representations. There is every reason to believe that the actual experiential content is far, far richer than conscious objectifications of it, as evidenced by the fact that unusual experiences can give us new interpretants that suddenly show us more of what was there all along, or surprise us out of customary perceptual representations to a new vision. So much of our experiential content is on the fringes of consciousness, or beyond the fringes except in decisive moments. To discover what that content is and represent it, we may attempt to bring it to consciousness; but we can also approach it inferentially from the ways we act. Consciousness is not as important a category as many intuitionist philosophies have required. Pragmatists from Jesus onward have argued that we understand our experience best by means of the fruit it bears in our actions.

With regard to logic, both Peirce (1932, 1933) and Dewey (1916, 1938) wrote extensively about the topic, and the conception of network meaning is my version of their concern. A crucial distinction needs to be drawn, however, between the ways by which intelligent activity is shaped by network or logical meanings, and the ways content meaning shapes it. The former has to do with the rules according to which signs can interpret one another, and mind thus move from one thing to another. The latter has to do with the inner texture of intelligent activity. That activity is the outcome of many historic routes of influence, embodied both in the person and the things with which the person interacts, including the solid places through which the activity moves. All those causal conclusions are the pieces, as it were, to be organized intentionally in intelligent activity, integrated and redesigned so as to play roles in the discursive unity of the activity itself. Those are the experiential contents, or the stuff ready to be made into experiential content by imaginative synthesis.

An argument could be made that pragmatism collapses the distinction between logic and content. It translates logic into the habits of thought, the network connections, that lead to warrantable assertions. As to content, by denying the intuitionist objective view of experiential content, it translates content into the contours of the habits are themselves the content of experience if their causal provenance is taken into account. There is, nevertheless, an important distinction between logic and content. Whereas logic deals with the legitimacy, with the routes of carryover of value, from one sign to the next, all from the triadic standpoint of the interpretant, the content is the actual reality of the process of interpretation itself, the material reality as well as what is signified in subsequent interpretation. Whereas network meaning is always mediated, content meaning is always immediate though mediable.

The pragmatists' corrected conception of experience properly emphasizes interaction. The content of experience is not "present" to consciousness, but manifested in the shape of activity. By interacting with things, we conform ourselves to their conditions, and we shape them in terms of our own intents and accidents. More important, by interacting with other people while interacting with things, we shape the representations that are so important among the contents of experience. The interactions are not posterior to set purposes, but reveal the things about which purposes are worth having. Both purposes and interpretive signs are continuously reshaped in experiential interactions (Smith, John E.,: 1978; 1983, pp. 3–37 and 115–160).

In certain respects, our experience is the product of causal influences that impinge on us, both from our own past development and from the systematic and unsystematic causal lines of the environing world. If these impingements were to be objectified with nondistorting representations in consciousness, we might in fact find something like the visual and auditory sensations of the empiricists, and the fillings-in of inner sense. But these causal influences are never received with total passivity. At the very least, they must be made compatible with one another and arranged so as to fit in with the overall make-up of the experiencer. More likely, they must be bent to conform to roles in the experiencer's own ongoing, purposefully directed, life. Further, since human life is social, the signs of language and other media are used to modify these influences in any particular instance so that they can be experienced in common. To say that the content of experience comes through interaction calls attention to the fact that the content is taken up and reshaped in experience.

Like all causation, the interactions involved in providing the content of experience involve the carryover of value. Truth-seeking experience aims to carry over value in interpretive ways, so that the sign is interpreted as having the value of its object in a certain respect, and so forth. Perhaps there is a truth-seeking dimension to all experiential interactions. There are other kinds of value carryover, however, such as in pleasure and pain, happy or sad experiences, and the like. A proper analysis of the content of experience can show how it embodies itself as an intensional field of value.

As contours of activity, experiential content has a discursive form. It is in fact a rule-governed harmony of other contents. The previous chapter quoted Kant to the effect that concepts are rules for integrating other representations and what he called intuitions. The content meaning of any representation is the experiential result of having appropriately encountered the representations united by the conceptual rule. The network meaning might allow for those contents to be separated out and interpreted on their own. But so often, especially in matters of affection and religion, the content-experiences cannot be separated out for interpretation without destroying the whole content meaning.

II. THE STRUCTURE OF CONTENT MEANING

The content meaning of a sign (representations are signs involved in the exercise of intentionality) is the set of other signs united in the sign's universal rule structure. Each of those signs has content, and so on down. In this respect, a sign is a harmony of the sort analyzed earlier, with components. A sign differs from other harmonies in having a semiotic rule structure as its overall pattern. Yet any harmony can be made into a sign by interpreting its overall pattern as a semiotic structure whereby its components are signs of the external things conditioning and being conditioned by it. Here is the payoff for joining a naturalistic metaphysics and cosmology to the theory of interpretation. The theory of natural harmony articulates a pattern of connections, universal to all things to which reference can be made. This pattern is equivalent to the nature of a sign in the theory of interpretation; the relation between the essential and conditional features of a harmony is identical to the relation between a sign as rule and the other signs constituting its network connections. Although not all natural harmonies are actually involved in intentional interpretations—they may have no bearing on any mind whatsoever—their structure is such that they can function as signs whenever they are actually involved in interpretation. This is a wholly nonidealistic way of saying, with Peirce and Derrida, that everything is a sign or text. Of course, the sign-character of a natural thing may be far more complex, indeed infinitely so, than any finite set of semiotic-based interpretations can render.

As a harmony, the logical space of a sign is its extensional field relative to other signs. Any sign is infinitely deep or dense in its contents, although perhaps only trivially or vaguely so. Just as a natural harmony can be reconstructed as a sign, a sign can be reconstructed as a natural harmony. The logical space of a sign—the domain of signs it interprets and that can interpret it—is identical to the extensional field of the sign as a natural thing. The set of semiotic representations on hand to interpret the sign might be inadequate to the exploration of its logical space. Indeed, it would have to be, since the logical space is infinitely complex and the network-meaning of a semiotic system is finite. This is only to say that our signs are more than we know. Our language and other representations are "mysteries" in this quite intelligible sense.

As mentioned above, a sign is a character in an activity. It mediates another sign to an object so as to constitute an interpretation. The temporal structure of interpretive activity is crucial to understand in noting the role of content-meaning. A distinction needs to be drawn between "base interpretation" and "intentional interpretation." The temporal structure of base interpretation is that of the activity of interpretation, moving through its own immediate content time; this is the primary concern of the present chapter. The temporal structure of "intentional interpretation" has to do with the temporal locus of the intentional logical object, which might be in past, present, or future, and with the loci of logical consequences and evidences, which also might be in any temporal mode. Pragmatism often confused the presentation of its theory by failing to distinguish base from intential interpretation.

The base object of an interpretation is in the mode of the past. It has a character that enters as a condition into a present interpretive moment. The change in the present moment is to give the object the significatory role of being the object of the interpreting sign. The interpreting sign has a network meaning expressed in the process of the present change that identifies and actualizes the object role and the sign role. Part of the network meaning of the sign is the potential implication of future signs functioning as interpretants to spell out how and in what respect it is a sign of the object; the interpretants are in the base future temporal mode. The implication of future interpretability is essential, in the technical sense, to the network meaning of the sign in the present; without that implication, the sign cannot stand for the object, and the object cannot enter the interpretive process as object. Which future signs will actually interpret the sign is conditional to the sign's being a sign, although they may be logically essentially to the sign's network meaning.

Just as a sign is an interpretive activity, so its contents are sub-activities within the same process. The network meanings of a sign can be signs in earlier or later processes, but the signs in the content meaning are coincident with the actualization of the sign itself. The network points beyond the actualization or thinking of the sign itself to its references and interpretations, to the other signs involved in it vaguely, trivially, broadly, and narrowly. In this sense, the network meaning is the real lawfulness of the world. By contrast, content meaning is the presence of those component signs in the activity of the signing itself, sub-activities occurring within the activity of interpreting, broadly construed.

Because signs are harmonies, and harmonies include their components in the extensive and intensive ways discussed earlier, signs must have both network and content meaning. It is not necessary, however, that a sign's network and content meanings be identical. To speak for a moment of representations (a kind of sign), the content meaning can be magnified and the network meaning minimized, as in strong emotions and gushy feelings; the reverse may be true in the thinking of abstract ideas.

The organization of the subactivities of the content meaning of a sign is a function of its rule structure in combination with the rule structures of the subactivities organizing subsubactivities, and so on. The rule structure of content meaning need not be the same as that of network meaning. The rule structure of content meaning must observe the requirements for exercising the activity in the particularities of the action. These include the physical and biological organism doing the interpreting, and not only that but the exact states of the organism, its environment and context, as well as any historically specific purposes, cultural and semiotic elements at play. Content meaning always requires a contextualizing of the rule structures, and content meaning rule structures lend themselves to this: there is no content meaning without an appropriate organism, in an appropriate environment, with appropriate forms of particular participation. The network meaning of a sign, by contrast, can (though need not) prescind from the particularities of the physical nature of the process and its historical content.

Functionalism in the contemporary sense debated by philosophers such as Jerry Fodor (1981) contributes much to an account of network meaning. Part of that account is the universality of the function; the sign-function is what it is regardless of whether it is performed by a meat brain or a silicone chip computer. Since the content meaning of a sign is relative to the material embodiment of its activity, the content of the sign occurring in a meat brain is radically different from that in a computer. Functionalism defines itself as distinterested in content meaning. If the metaphysical position I have defended has merit, then the computer must have some content meaning just as the human brain does. The reason is that there is an inherited physical reality to the silicone chips, and to the structure of algorithms in the program. This reality, giving content to the present harmony of the computer at any moment, need not have any relation to the network meaning of its sign-activity except to be the condition for its process. The structure of the program's algorithms is physically present in any interpretive activity as the marks on the magnetic field of the disk; but its logical structure containing the network meaning is, by definition of the "first this and then that" nature of algorithms, not present in a whole way. Whatever content meaning computers of the sort we know might have, it is semiotically specific to the network meanings of its interpretive activity.

Human thinking stands out in sharp relief from computer activity. Because of its content meaning, human thinking must take place in biological human beings, with human culture, human systems of representation, and guided by intrinsic human purposes. (As we invent more human-like computers, grown biologically and acculturated like our children, computers may approximate human thinking; but it seems a shame not to appreciate ordinary sex and the development of human children as having achieved this goal already. Computers are needed to accomplish network interpretations different from those human beings can do; there is little need to nudge them toward human content meaning except in cases where they might be used prophylactically for elements in a diseased or injured human being.) Human thinking is identified not only by its running through network meanings that can be simulated by computer activity, but also by the experientially dense immediate content of its interpretations. Human beings not only think about things, they think with things, and on many levels interpenetrating and activated at once. Unlike machines that can act with network meaning alone and have unrelated content meaning to their parts, human beings have at least a partial identity in their thinking between the network meanings and content meanings. The having of the content must be in part the way by which the network is followed out. Thinking with this particular content is a way of thinking along that network. Where these become disconnected, or divergent, we think self-deceptively, with a consciousness divided between conscious and unconscious, non-mutually reinforcing, elements.

III. HUMAN REPRESENTATIONS

The shift to a focus on human thinking requires that the discussion shift from signs in general to representations or mental signs. The argument of this book so far has been that nature is all of a piece in that its elements have the general character of signs and its processes have the structure of interpretations. The problem addressed by this argument is to show how human thinkers, and intelligent human cultures, can imaginatively interpret the real world without reducing the world to a construct of the imagination. Having laid out a conception of nature as material and significatory, it is now appropriate to show how human thinking is a special kind of interpretation, one that can know the rest.

A representation is a special sign used in human thinking. Unlike other signs, it must have four kinds of defining characteristics. These are the four kinds of qualification modifying the carryover of value as articulated in the theory of truth presented earlier in chapter 3 and explained in 4.

First, it must be embodiable in the human organism. Visual representations, for instance, the colors we discriminate, the lines and textures we pick out and imagine with, are those related to the human physical anatomy. Flies and bats most likely represent the world very differently because of their different sensing organs.

Second, a representation must have cultural form. Most likely, the vast majority of our representations are learned through social interactions, and surely the very form of our representations is modified by the fact that the process of representation itself is culturally influenced if not learned wholly. We have representations of the sort and for the kinds of things our culture represents. In individual cases where the imagination breaks cultural forms or invents new ones, there is still the negative relation to cultural representation. As noted often above, the greatest influence of culture is the identification of what is valuable to represent.

Third, a representation must be related to other representations in a semiotic system. This is part of culture but, by virtue of network meanings, has a life partially of its own. Representations are not static; they grow in generality or specificity, and hence are in changing relations within the semiotic system.

Fourth, representations are relative to human purposes, sometimes developed to serve those purposes and surely modified by the requirements of purposive behavior at the same time that they modify the purposes.

Not all of the signs in human interpretation are representations. Many are the natural objects in the world with nothing of intentionality about them. But all human experience includes some representations. At the experiential minimum is the interpretation of some nonrepresentative object by means of an imaginative representation, the interpretant itself, or interpreting activity, being a complex of nonrepresentative and representative signs. Most human experience has vastly complex objects that combine representational and nonrepresentational signs, and equally complex signs and interpretants.

Our epitomizing activities of sensitivity, sensibility, and orientation always frame interpretive terms in which the world is interpreted in conjunction with the interpretation of our body's interpretation of the world. We experience with what Whitehead (1978, Pt. 4, Ch. 4 especially) called the "withness of the body." Merleau-Ponty (1968) and others have made much of the bodily orientation of human experience, rejecting the narrow claim that we experience only our body without the rest of the world. Some religious adepts claim to be able to think without any ambiance of bodily, nonrepresentative signs; this is not a widespread practice. The content of any interpretation must have bodily signs present at least in a trivial position; most interpretations use these signs for vague orientation. And in any interpretation attending to something in the physical or social environment, nonrepresentative signs function to give breadth if not narrow focus.

By virtue of the fact that representative signs fit into semiotic systems, they are explicitly distanced from the nonrepresentative signs in their objects by the form of the semiotic system. In language, signs fit into propositions, and the propositions can be referred to their subject matter as complex interpretive signs. There may be analogues to propositions in all semiotic systems. The special structure of the system means that a specific process of selection takes place in the process of the carryover of value from the object to the semiotic representation. Although we may not often be conscious of it, there is an alienation intrinsic to human representative interpretation; namely, that we think what things are *in terms of our representing systems.* Since the things about which we think usually are already caught up in our thinking with imaginative terms, there would rarely be a representation of a non-representative sign. But even where the object itself has imaginative form, to think about it is to represent the object-with-imaginative-form in the terms of a semiotic system. To put the point more strongly, even when we think about something wholly contained within a semiotic system (for instance the definition of "bachelor") using other terms within that same system (the English language), the activity of interpreting is using the English language on two levels: as object, and as selective representing language. All signs are selective embodiments of their objects, with finite network meaning. Representations are selective in the terms of the biological, cultural, semiotic, and purposive systems within which they are made.

A representation thus has rule structures for both its network and content meanings that express the semiotic systems of which it is a part or to which it is related. The rule structures for network meanings may also express the biological, cultural, and purposive contexts of interpretation, and the rule structures for content meaning must do so. Insofar as the content meanings of a representation include other representations, or complexes of representations and other signs, those component representations have both network and content meanings. And so on down. The worth of a representation—not its applicability in a judgment to a subject, but its intrinsic worth as a representation—depends on the quality of both the network and content meanings of its contents. A content representation deficient in network meaning is unclear, brute, not well-formed or thought out. Deficient in content meaning, a network representation is formally efficient but empty, and therefore deceptive.

IV. VALUE AND DEFICIENCY IN CONTENT MEANING

To think a representation in the process of employing it within an interpretation is also and simultaneously to think its contents. The contents are layered and interrelated within the harmony of the representation so as to give intelligent solidity, nuance, and depth to the thinking. Regardless of whether further interpretation of the network meaning of the representation draws out the significant content, it is present in the thinking. The being of the thinker as thinker consists in the solidity, nuance, and depth of the representations thought. Insofar as thinking is possessing the world (as qualified by one's biology, culture, semiotic systems and purposes), the quality of that intelligent engagement of the world rests with the quality of the contents of the representations. Since the contents of a representation have contents that have contents *ad infinitum*, a representation has infinite depths. Most of the contents are possessed trivially and vaguely, and so for most purposes it does not matter whether they can be brought to attention through the pursuit of network meaning. Nevertheless, because of its infinite depths, no representation can be analyzed exhaustively. It has no simple elements, and its analysis must always be pragmatically selective regarding the analytical context.

Because every component of a representation is itself a harmony containing infinite depth, and every harmony is an achievement of value, each representation is a summary achievement of value. Put overly simply, each representation is a selective accumulation of the values in its potential objects, selective according to the qualifications of interpretation. A deficient representation fails by excluding or distorting the value of its potential objects.

The truth of a representation is thus equivocal, depending on whether its network or content meaning is intended. As to network meaning, a representation has no meaning by itself but only in the context of being asserted or assumed to hold of an object in some illocutionary interpretive act. Then, it is better to ask whether the interpretation is true or false. As to content meaning, a representation is true to the extent that it cumulatively integrates the value involved in being a ready sign to interpret its potential objects.

The following are examples of representations that are untrue or deficient with regard to their content meaning. (1) We lack (in Spring, 1989) a concept of physical force, being unable to integrate the several forces physical cosmologists have identified. (2) No youth has an adequate notion of senescence because the feeling of senescence is self-reflexive on growing old oneself. (3) An uncultured person's view of art is inadequate because art is appreciated with cumulative comparative judgment. (4) A person deprived of essential kinds of love in childhood cannot feel mature love in its fulness. (5) The fool says in his heart there is no God because an idolatrous notion of God blocks apprehension of divine fulness. Each of these examples can be analyzed to draw out important aspects of content meaning.

1. The problem with the integration of the various forces recognized by the present state of physical cosmology is that no theoretical concept has been invented that relates all the forces or shows them to be different manifestations of a more basic force. Perhaps this is because one or several of the forces are currently misconceived, or because there are more forces than have been recognized. But perhaps it simply is because no integrating representation has yet formally been imagined. The difficulties are mostly with

network meaning. The network meanings of the various forces do not cohere with one another (although they are consistent). Nor is there an overall network meaning expressing them all. The content meaning of the vague notion of force is deficient because the network meanings of the several contents cannot be integrated. The network meaning of the vague notion is appropriate to the present state of knowledge precisely because it shows where the incoherence lies; that is, when interpreted, the vague notion of force can be specialized several ways that do not cohere with one another. The resolution to the problem of content meaning for that vague notion rests not (necessarily) with altering the notions of the several kinds of force, but in providing a content rule-structure that harmonizes them. That content rule-structure may very well reinterpret them without altering their present assertions. The vague notion of force is not false when asserted of our world's cosmology; it just is not specifically applicable: the specific applications are those other meanings of force.

2. A young person cannot have an adequate notion of senescence because part of that notion would have to be how it feels to be growing old oneself. The young person can know just that logical point, and therefore have as part of his or her representation a sub-representation of growing old oneself. But all that sub-representation could contain would be the network meaning of growing old oneself, not the content meaning. The content meaning would have to reflect the young person's own experience. This is not like having a network idea of Europe from reading but lacking the content meaning that would come from traveling there; it is rather the logical point of self-reflexivity. The content meaning can come only as the person grows old himself or herself.

3. Art is historical and contextual. Any work of art has its relation to some tradition and society as part of its meaning. Recent art has also become self-consciously cultural. An uncultured but sensitive person can look at several works of art and perhaps derive some notion of art as artifactual, requiring excellence of design and craftsmanship, and as exhibiting aesthetic excelence. Yet a notion of art formed from those elements is inadequate to the historical, contextual, and self-referentially cultural elements. Further, in interpreting a particular work of art, an uncultured person would miss and thereby misinterpret those elements in the work having historical, contextual, and cultural significance. The difficulty with the uncultured person's notion of art is thus at least twofold. On the one hand, the historical, contextual, and cultural elements are simply missing as contents. On the other hand, although the content-response to the formal immediate elements might be rich, the network meaning of those formal elements relative to the contextual ones is distorted. To be sure, everyone is inadequately cultured

to appreciate the full meaning of art, just as everyone is somewhat insensitive to the immediate formal elements.

4. A person deprived in infancy of oral gratification, say, assuming that something like Freud's theory of oral, anal, and genital stages is correct, will not have the full meaning of oral expression upon reaching maturity. Kissing, for instance, can be learned through its network meanings, and the lover might become adept. But without the background, the essential component to oral pleasure, the lover's heart cannot be in the kiss. Because so many of our intelligently directed activities, such as love-making, are built up of layer upon layer of subactivities, each of which is essential to the whole, substitute components can be learned and faked, components that perform the network function but that lack the real content. Love-making requiring a kiss may be full and rich in all other ways, but not with regard to the kiss itself. Most psychological problems take the form of missing or distorted essential prior experiences. We learn to cope with tokens that perform the network function of the missing deficient element, but that takes its toll. Many psychotherapeutic techniques attempt to provide the missed experience indirectly, through transference, for instance, or to reconstruct a distorted experience.

5. Anselm's fool who said in his heart there is no God did so because, logically, he substituted a determinate and hence idolatrous conception (the golden mountain) for God in the ontological argument. Anselm's formula, that than which nothing greater can be conceived, says nothing determinate about God but only about what is not God. The logical mistake be as it may, the reference to "his heart" suggests a motive for the idolatry, and religions classically say that the motive is something like selfishness, personal attachment, or personal pride. The result of any of these self-oriented activities is that their representations within overall interpretive life block out or distort the communication among the content meanings of the rest of life. The problem is not that they interrupt the systematizing of our network meanings—that may not be a wise task anyway. The problem rather is that they inhibit the feeling of one content meaning through another. Samadhi, enlightenment, the bliss of divine vision, all have to do with taking each and any element of the world as a harmony giving access to any and all other elements without obstruction. The self-nature of any one, individual though it may be, does not stand out as important so as to cast other things into triviality and vagueness. The other things are not registered as mere conditional features in some one thing, or in onself, but as full entities with conditional and essential features on their own. In the divine vision, all things are seen in their multiplicity and relations. Just as each thing then is grasped as itself-and-not-these-others, it is grasped as itself rather than nothing. The

concept of God, though involving many discordant cultural and conceptual elements—the network meaning is highly controversial—has as its content meaning a mystical vision of the ubiquity of the divine ground in all things. Thus no thing is God without idolatry, and God is not a thing, perfect as Guanilon thought or otherwise. The sagacious say in their hearts, even if lacking a representation with much network meaning, that a true recognition of anything, or of all limited things together, is a recognition of the ontological ground manifesting its creativity in and through them. The remedy for a fool's vision is a spiritual path that leads along the tao wherein one constitutes one's own position as a center for all other harmonies that is closer to no one rather than another—the circle whose center is everywhere and whose circumference is nowhere.

In all these cases, it is the structure of the notion or representation that is in question, not whether it is asserted correctly. Judgment concerns the appropriate assertion of a representation (usually itself propositional) of its object. Good judgment depends on the representations themselves being adequate to the subject matter. From the standpoint of science in the short run, or of logic or professional philosophy, the truth issue is saying of what is that it is, and of what is not that it is not. This issue of truth, however, depends on the interpreter having adequate signs to assert in the first place. For civilization, the truth issue is whether we have the representations worth ascribing to the subject matter at all. Civilizations advance or decline as the major representations develop in accord with the achieved value in their objects. Because most important civilized objects, for example, birth, growth, death, love, work, play, and art, are themselves partially functions of the representations current to appreciate them, there is an intimate connection between the career of civilizations and the accessibility of representations adequate to frame them. It is at least a necessary condition, if not even more important, to have true representations than it is to assert them truly. The achieved value of a civilization comes more from the adequacy of the content of its current representations than from the fitness of their employment in assertive interpretations. Because of this, the influence of logic on twentieth century philosophy has been baleful indeed.

A significant part of the "two cultures" conflict between science and the liberal arts in Western culture is that the former is ostensibly concerned with network meaning and the latter with content meaning. Whereas the work of science seems to be to make true rather than false assertions, the work of the liberal arts is to have true representations available to assert. In fact, these orientations are not as different as they are commonly understood. Our very first example of a concept with deficient content meaning was from the realm of science. Science needs imagination as much as art does. The liberal arts also cannot rest with well-formed representations sloppily deployed. Nevertheless, science thinks of itself as protected by skepticism about inappropriate assertions, a Cartesian concern. The liberal arts think of themseleves as creative; that is, as giving content meaning.

The discussions in this chapter and the previous one of network and content meaning have been somewhat estranged from the process of thinking itself. The reason for this has been that they have prescinded from any concern with intentionality. The activity of meaning anything with network or content meaning is intentional activity. The next topic then is intentionality.

15

Intentionality

Whatever intentionality is, it marks the difference between the play of signs in thinking and their play in functional, algorithmic inference. Artificial intelligence may deploy representations in interpretive patterns according to programmed alogorithmic instructions, but in this it is not yet intentional. Intentionality is an essential component of human thinking in its interpretive aspect. Specifically, intentionality is the trait of human experience that contextualizes interpretation.

Medieval Western philosophy employed the notion of intention to indicate the "object" of intellect. "Being" was said to be the first object of intellect, particular beings the second object, representations the third object, and so on. "Intention" meant the content of an intellectual act. Intentional "inexistence" was the phrase used to indicate fictions, mistakes, or objects of thought that lack the existence their nature seems to require. After Descartes, who characterized mind as a substance of its own whose acts might have objects that are other substances, intentionality came to mean having an object of consciousness. Brentano, Frege, Meinong, and Husserl particularly provided theories of intentionality as a mental act that is "about" something (Chisholm, 1960); intentionality came to mean the "aboutness" of consciousness irrespective of whether the object is real in itself or only a mental construct. Husserlian phenomenology then could conceive itself as neutral with respect to the reality of intentional objects and limit itself to analysis of noetic acts and noetic objects, assuming thereby that it can analyze everything since nothing can fail to be at least an intentional object (Husserl, 1962).

The subjectivism of much contemporay understanding of intentionality, and its following of an intuitionist model, has already been criticized. The argument turns now to the development of an alternative theory of intentionality coherent with the naturalistic approach to interpretation. However the naturalistic view of intentionality comes out, it must be able to account for the direction of thinking activity, for unreal objects of thought, and for phenomena of consciousness. It needn't take consciousness, nevertheless, as the paradigm of intentionality; consciousness may be a special case of intentionality, blending off into other kinds.

I. EXPERIENCE AS PROCESS

Intentionality is a dimension of experience, and experience has temporal thickness. A characterization of intentionality thus must have temporality relative to the present, past, and future. This seems paradoxical, however, because intentionality has been taken rightly to be the feeling of subjective immediacy in the present. Nothing in the past intends anything any longer; its subjective immediacy is over. The future cannot intend anything yet, however much it is a possibility for being intended, because it has no actualizing agents. So intentionality is peculiarly a dimension of present experiencing. Admitting this, we must still admit that intentionality has essential connections with past and future because of the temporal thickness of experience. Not to recognize the essential connections with past and future is to fall into what Heidegger called "the metaphysics of presence": the assumption that what we mean (intend) must be something available in a present moment, something that directly or indirectly presents itself.

In order to indicate its peculiar relation to the present and still acknowledge essential relations to the other modes of temporality, intentionality can be characterized initially in terms of the causality of the present. Whitehead's (1978, Pt. 3) characterization of present causality or concrescence has not been surpassed in twentieth century thought, once its limits are recognized and controlled for. He pointed out that the present is a temporal mode of coming-to-be. The conclusion of the previous moments leaves finished facts arranged in actualized structures. The reality of the present is to integrate these diverse facts into a new being. Whitehead called the grasp or prehension of facts "feelings." That language is far too anthropomorphic for his cosmological purposes, and lends itself to a panpsychic interpretation. Chapter 8 in this study has reinterpreted Whitehead's discussion in terms of harmonizing "components;" this ties in with the theory of extensionality developed in chapter 10 through 12. For purposes of analyzing intentionality in human experience, however, the language of feeling is just fine. The "bodily" sense of feeling so central to Whitehead (and also Dewey) is an important linchpin in the theory of intentionality here that denies special importance to consciousness.

The process of integration in moments of human experience can be looked at in two directions.[1] One can look back toward the past, and from this perspective the process is the integration of feelings of past things. The norms for process in this perspective have to do with respecting and incorporating as much of the values of those past things into the integration as possible. Because of this, intentional experience is a cumulative inheritance of appreciation, of value-laden interpreting, though of course the values inherited might not themselves be broken out with representations. Nor is the actual process of integration identical with the content of intentionality: one might be thinking about an airplane about to land, and that thinking integrates one's sense of the environment, previous experience with airplanes, and like things, without those being objects of intention.

One can also look to the future; that is, to how the outcome of the present concrescence will determine possibilities. This is the direction of intentionality. Human thinking does not focus on the close of the present moment but on the onward flow of events into the imagined future. Nevertheless, although the objects intended may be far future, the reality of intentionality is to resolve the present plurality now with an eye to continuities with the future. Therefore the norms for intentionality have to do with finding the right patterns according to which the feelings can be integrated into a singular and definite event fitting in to the causal tissues related to the intended future. The immediate interest of intentionality is in satisfying the requirements of definiteness in the moment.

The content aim, and the proximate outcome of an intentional act is a judgment or action. Judgment and action have much the same form, differing only in the degree to which the latter is expressed through large scale observable behavior. With regard to judgment, tied to human thinking, I have argued (1981, Pt. 1) that there are four broad areas; namely imagination, interpretation, theorizing, and the pursuit of responsibility. The last blends off into overt action. The norms for judgment are beauty (for imaginative form), truth (for interpretation), unity (for theory as contemplated), and goodness (for responsibility).

Intentionality is intimately associated with the spontaneity of the present, with its creativity. Were there no spontaneity, the past things would achieve location in the present without modification, or would fail of present location at all; the causal structure in this case would simply be that of the extention of previously actualized things according to the vectors of forces they established. Were there no spontaneity, the future would merely be the outcome of the past, deterministically organized, and with no need to refer to human thought. Intentionality employs the spontaneity of the present moment to relate past givens with future possibilities, and these relations may involve integration of the givens in possible ways that differ from their natural propensities. The special norms for spontaneity are novelty of patterns for data, a sense of presence in immediate process, and the relevance of pattern to the plurality to be integrated.

Actualization is that part of process whereby the diversity of potential past conditions is brought to harmony according to patterns that yield a wholly definite individual actual outcome. The activity in actualization, therefore, is the creation of relevance of pattern to data, of limit to the relatively unlimited. To continue the language of primary cosmology, actualization is the making of the individual mixture out of limit and the unlimited. The nature of present spontaneity and creativity is thus relevance-making. The essential features of spontaneity may be sheer poppings-into-existence-out-of-nothing. But its conditional features are of at least three sorts. (1) Its products have to be somewhat novel with regard to given data. This is what seems so important to the freedom of mind, and is the point at which some people contrast the great spontaneity in human intentionality with the minimal spontaneity (glitches) in computers. (2) Its spontaneous patterns must be relevant to the past data so that they enter as conditions to a possible outcome of the present process. In this respect, the spontaneity connects the future possibilities with the forces of the past. (3) The spontaneous process of integration itself has an immediacy to it; its content is the mediation of possibility and achieved actuality, but its own being is the immediate coming into existence of the new integrated individual.

The feel of present immediacy is the urge or lunge toward the definite satisfaction of unresolved indeterminacies of integration, an aim at actual concreteness. This immediacy is articulated by the logically successive decision points in the moment as level upon level of vague structures are resolved, down to haecceity. The directional character of immediacy is thus from the vague toward the specific. With the attainment of haecceity, complete specificity, that moment is no longer present nor immediate. It is a mistake to think that the direction of intentionality is toward the future; intentional objects can be anywhere in our representations of the temporal field. The directionality of intentionality is toward actualization, toward bringing the vague to specificity. This is felt in its immediacy, but not necessarily in the context of its objects. Its intended objects themselves might have any temporal (or non-temporal) location. Intentional interpretation in this regard differs from base interpretation, which is always oriented to the future continuity of interpretation.

What has been said here about spontaneity and intentionality in fact applies to just about any present moment in process, not only to moments of human thinking. Human thinking involves not only signs but representations, a special class of signs. We ought therefore to restrict discussions of intentionality to those processes involving representations as patterns for integration (and usually also as given data and intended future states of affairs, as in thinking something through). There is not a clear line between unthinking and thinking moments, however, since there is no clear line between signs and representations. A representation is involved in a semiotic system, and, as argued above, it is a developmental character of signs that some of them can become involved in such systems. Signs lie on a continuum from the brute natural to the sophisticated intellectual, experientially available by yogic investigations and biofeedback at one end to conscious reflection at the other, ranging from noninvolvement in a semiotic system to complete involvement. Signs shift in their network meanings, and can come into involvement, and leave it. Therefore signs can sometimes be representations, sometimes not.

The genius of Whitehead's position is that he defined all of the process governed by concrescence within the moment as mental, and all finished moments as physical. Although this abuses the notion of the mental since it applies to every present occasion within the existence of anything, it allows the complications of spontaneity to be built up so as to express whatever a Cartesian might like to say about the extent and subtlety of mental, subjective life. In a strict sense, only in the present moment is a thing the subject of its own actualizations. At the same time, Whitehead could say that any occasion viewed as past is physical, and whatever a Cartesian might want to say about physical nature could be found there. No occasion is ever mental only, or physical only. The mental contents and physical contents are both matters for empirical investigation, and the cosmology of present actualizations that yield past actualities, within the limits set by future possibilities made relevant to past potential conditions, neatly integrates mind and body. I intend to preserve the structure of Whitehead's account while extending the notion of modes of temporality and limiting mental langauge to human and similar realities.

Combining the aspects of novelty, presence, and relevance in intentionality, its essential character is to contextualize. That is, intentionality necessarily has as its foundation an imaginatively constructed experiential field within which it orients and relates the important matters it must integrate. Nothing has meaning for intentionality except insofar as it is oriented within an experiential field that is its context. The directional activity of intentionality, making specific the otherwise vague, is the contextualizing of its components.

John Dewey and Alfred North Whitehead, though differing in historical roots and particular philosophical interests, shared many points in the reconstitution of the conception of experience in American philosophy. This is nowhere more evident than in their approach to intentionality.

Dewey hardly used the category because it was not helpful to his emphasis on the ongoing, interactive character of experience. To experience something, for Dewey (1981, ch. 8 and Appendix), was to go through it, like experiencing a thunderstorm, or a wedding, or Freshman Year. Intentionality of course was present, sometimes passively when we "suffer" and "have," sometimes actively when we "act" and "do." But no present moment could stand out as definitive of experience for Dewey except insofar as it is the locus of consummatory qualities (Dewey: 1984, ch. 10; 1934, ch. 3). In such a consummatory moment, there is an intentional "quality" of experience, uniting its elements and expressing more or less well the ontological quality of contingent being that Dewey discussed in *A Common Faith* (1934a; 1984a, pp. 243-262, "Qualitative Thought"). The difficulty with Dewey's account of quality as the immedaite unity of the moment is that it seems to lose precisely the direction element so characteristic of his emphasis on the ongoing, interactive nature of experience.

Whitehead far more than Dewey remained within the epistemological orientation of modern philosophy, and hence thought that the character of experience has to be wholly manifest in a moment defining subjectivity. Even the *revised* subjectivist principle allows for the treatment of the experiencer as wholly a subject with only incidental reference to past and future objective states. But he turned that epistemological position on its head in his criticism of Hume's doctrine of the immediacy of impressions and ideas (1929, Pt. II, ch.7). He argued that we do not experience subjective qualities except by great abstraction from concrete experience. Rather, we experience those qualities as part of vectors of forces coming to the present from organized and solid trains of causation (1929, pp. 86-87 and 133-135; Pt. II, ch. 4; Pt. IV, ch. 4). Through those vectors of forces, things far distant in space and time become present to experience. By being taken up with intentional form, those vectors of forces give temporal thickness to experience that occurs in the moment.

These two accounts, Dewey's and Whitehead's, need to be combined so that we can understand how intentionality acts, moment by moment, with an experiential field of which we can be conscious, through a temporally thick process of interaction. I shall begin by expanding the notion of vector force in the direction of Deweyan interactionsim, and then turn to the qualities of presentational immediacy.

II. THE VECTOR CHARACTER OF EXPERIENCE

The root of the idea of vector forces is the conception of historically defined places discussed above. In chapters 8 and 11, I argued that space consists of particular places that have been defined through time by thc serial inheritance of the things that have occurred there. Movement across a spatial plane is thus to be conceived according to the capacity of the moving thing to play a temporally appropriate role in all the places it successively occupies. Therefore, the state of a thing at any one moment is densely determined by (1) its inheritance of the multiplicity of its own past elements, (2) the requirements set upon it to accommodate to and embody the history of its place in the spatio-temporal environment, its extensiveness, (3) the adjustment of both of those to its own movements, intentional and otherwise, and (4) its accommodation to the things with which it interacts physically, metabolically, and socially, according to their own characters as defined by the past, their places, and their vectors. The vector of forces is thus at least fourfold: (1) the discursive vectors of one's own past, and future as determined by the past; (2) the extensive vectors of one's environmental position; (3) the motile vectors of one's processes of integrating these first two in movement, and (4) the interactional vectors that include the vectoral composition of the things with which one interacts. All of these vectoral forces impinge on any present moment of an individual and require integration according to the relevant possibilities. Intentionality is the form of the process by which an intelligent, representation-employing person provides a context and acts within the context to bring them to harmony.

It would be a great mistake, however, a disastrous capitulation to the modern epistemological tradition, to suppose that the problem is how to bring external things into the subjective experience of the present moment. This was the problem as Hume and Kant saw it. The problem rather is to expand the nature of the present moment of experience so as to include direct experience of objects that are not here and now. Although perhaps some objects of experience are immediate qualities of a here and now intentional act, the great texture of experience, its very orientation to direction and temporal location, comes from experiencing an array of spatially diverse things, often things that are temporally thick. Even prescinding from memory and anticipation, most of the things we experience as "present" in a present moment are experienced as discursive, essentially showing something of their past and future. So whereas an intentional act of experiencing at a moment might be defined in present temporality (actually, that too is an abstraction since an interpretive process takes time), the objects of experience, even of consciousness, are both temporally and spatially extensive.

The fourfold vectors of forces, exhibiting as they do the multiple location of things, serve to bring things into the experiencing individual's present moment of intentional life. Although of course each temporal present in each vector involves modifications of what conditions it and what it passes on as conditions for its future, the actualities of past things are real potentials for being conditions in a temporal present.

Nevertheless, the mere brute presence of past things is not experience, whatever other kinds of causal influence it might exhibit. Experience, except in extreme cases, is not of past or distant things as they immediately impinge on the here and now, but of them as then or there. Experience requires the alienation of present conditioning so as to attain the distant condition.

Therefore, what characterizes intentional experience is not passivity with regard to external causes, as the intuitionist or classical empiricist perception model might suggest, but rather the use of representations to mediate the direct presence of the distant object. Causal influence by a distant thing is not experienced except insofar as it is joined with a representation that objectifies the vectoral connection, identifying an object. The representation, among other things, objectifies the vector of forces so as to pick out the features that define its referent. Our representations of color-sensations, for instance, pick out surfaces as the objectified elements in the causal vector; and insofar as we also employ "surface" representations organizing the colors, we identify bodies with volume as the relevant objects, and so forth. Experience, as opposed to other kinds of caused and causing reality, involves a synthesis of vectors of forces, at least fourfold in kind, with representations. The representations articulate the vectors into objects to which they refer, according to the character of the representations.

The synthesis of causal vector and representations has at least two possible modes or levels. Most basic is imaginative synthesis. As I argued in *Reconstruction of Thinking*, imagination is the synthesis of causal conditions into images so as to form an experiential world. The form of an imagined experiential world includes a background, with vagueness and triviality, and a focal foreground with narrowness and width. These characteristics of vagueness, triviality, narrowness and width constitute the goodness of experiential form, or beauty. Imagination by itself is non-assertive. It prescinds from whether the objects involved are really constitutive of vectors of forces, and also from whether the imagery is appropriate to and well grounded in the real world.

The second mode or level of synthesis of vector and representation, however, is interpretation. Interpretation is inevitably assertive, or assumptive, about the reality of the object as identified by the representation in the vector of forces. The assertive interpretation of course is made by yet another representation. The interpretive representation asserts the first sign to represent the object in a certain respect, thereby affirming the first representation's identificaton of the object amidst the vector of forces.

In this discussion it must be remembered that in any imaginative synthesis or interpretation there is not just one object, but an indefinitely rich field of objects organized according to vagueness, triviality, narrowness, and width. Similarly, there is not one vector of forces but an indefinitely rich array of at least four kinds—discursive, environmental, motile, and interactive. And there is not one representation but a whole network of representations, some employed actively, each of which has indefinitely rich content.

Without acknowledging the causal power of the vector of forces, we might think that experience consists only in representations of representations. This was the fault of classical empiricism, perhaps of the entire modern European tradition. Under this faulty supposition, it is possible to conceive the intentional mind as an inner show, unrelated to external reality except by third-position correlations infinitely difficult to attain. Interpretation under this supposition is mere interpretation of mental representations with other mental representations, and the problem of truth seems to be to leap outside the mental sphere to compare representations with a measuring external reality. That leap plops into the abyss.

By acknowledging the causal power of the fourfold vector of forces, we are committed to a naturalistic theory of interpretation. Real actualities, distant in extension from the experiencer, can enter through multiple location into the experience, and can be identified by representations signifying some or all of the causal vectors. The representations might be mistaken, but this is possible only because there is a truth about which to be mistaken. The truth, of course, is the carryover of the actualized value of the actuality as mediated by the vector of forces into the experience, qualified by biological, cultural, semiotic, and purposive factors. The representations employed are elements in semiotic systems, and are qualified by biology, used according to cultural themes, and for various purposes. Because objects are experiences only as conjoined in imagination or interpretation with such representations, they are always mediated by our biology, culture, semiotic systems, and purposes. There is never the unmediated presence of a natural object in experience. Actualities are experienced only in those aspects that our representations can pick out, and they are hidden in those aspects that our representations obscure. Nevertheless, albeit mediated by representations, actualities are directly present as objects. As John E. Smith (1961, pp. 179–183) has long argued, experience is direct but mediated.

The other side of that point is that representations occur in experience always or nearly always joined imaginatively and interpretively with the direct presence of objects in the array of vectors of forces. Any representation that can be actualized necessarily must be harmonized with the assorted causal forces. But more than that, representations have their form and present relevance because they interpret, or at least imaginatively form, the conditions of one's past, one's environment, one's motions, and one's interactions. Even in the most abstract reverie, there is some feeling of the world through the thoughts. Although it would be foolish to attempt to classify the vectoral presences in the nuances of thought, in light of the extraordinary diversity in their array so far beyond the capacities of our representations to assemble, nevertheless it is instructive to recognize some broad categories. These categories sketch the naturalistic version of the phenomenological tradition's transcendental theory of the "lived body" (as in Merleau-Ponty, 1968). The descriptive or phenomenological account of experience underlying the naturalistic theory in fact is that of William James, in his famous *Principles of Psychology* (1890). Perhaps because he wrote before the reductionist modernist philosophies of the twentieth century, but probably just because he was an intelligent despiser of program philosophies, James' account has the advantage of cleanliness. It does not presuppose a mind-body dualism, and hence does not have to overcome it. It does not presuppose a transcendental standpoint, but rather a naturalistic one, and hence does not have to overcome any transcendental subjectivism, as Merleau-Ponty tried to do. Finally, James' account was written before the popularity of the notion of function, yet after the limit of the idea of mechanism had been exposed by the idealists, so that his theory is thoroughly contextualistic.

Whitehead (1929, pp. 258; and Pt. IV, ch. 4) pointed out that all experience is characterized by the "withness of the body." However distant actualities are, the vectors of forces by which they become directly present move throughout bodies. Objects are touched with our flesh, heard with our ears, seen with our eyes, smelled and tasted with nose and palate. Of course they are not to be reduced to the forms their carryover takes in these organs; but they are not present as ready to be conjoined with representations except as exhibiting the history of the bodily portion of the vector of forces. Actually, these organs of sense carry the objects over into pressed nerves, vibrated eardrums, wave-like excitations of the optic nerve, etc. These in turn are not experienced except as conjoined with coordinating neural activities represented by palpable feelings, sounds, signs, and the rest. So an experience of an object involving simple perception is a highly mediated set of conjoinings of various stages in the vector of forces, articulated by various representations. Our sense of body, when that is directly objectified for interpretation, is not a clear demarcation point relative to the environment, but is thick and multi-layered. To touch someone's cheek is to have the person, the cheek, the pressure and warmth of one's fingertips, the feel of the texture of skin, the kinesthetic sense of one's arm, one's bodily orientation to the person, arousal, flush of embarrassment, and all the representations identifying each one of these and countless more elements of the vector of forces, as well as whatever high-level interpretation is put on the touch.

Further, our sense of a single bodily action is combined with the vast array of similar experiences of actions to give a sense of the wholeness of our body. Most of the time this sense of bodily self is not objectified at a conscious level in experience. But it is objectified as the medium through which our experience takes place. Were it not so represented, we would be unable to control for the special selections our bodies make. In practice, we are quite adept at distinguishing what external things are in their own sphere from the special forms required for their mediation through our nervous system. Babies learn that most things do not cease to exist when we stop sensing them. We know further that our sensations are automatically interpreted according to standard conditions, and control for deviations—we are not often fooled by dusk or the Doppler effect. Only by representing how our body is "with" the objects we experience is it possible to represent, as we easily and habitually do, how the objects are "without" our body. In some sense, of course, all experience is perspectival relative to the experiencer. The search for pure "primary qualities" is vain. But we are more or less adept at developing not only appropriate representation but also appropriate bodily feelings and actions so as to be able to prescind from at the least the more variable and idiosyncratic "secondary qualities."

Not only is experience qualified by the "withness of the body," it is also qualified by the "warmth" of its own representations, as William James (1892, chs. 11-12) put it. A representation, of course, is a cultural and semiotic thing, but it too has a history of actualization. Only by an act of abstraction, or of plain forgetting, can a representation be prescinded from its cultural history. More to the point, an individual gives histories to representations. As I learn an idea, for instance, it is conjoined, often with network and content meanings, to the situations in which it is learned. My uses of it also enhance the history. The idea comes to me in a given experience, therefore, warmed by its past. Insofar as its past is within my own experience, conjoined to the vectors of body, environment, and activities, it comes warmed as "my" idea.

In addition, the vectoral histories of both bodily mediations and representations are qualified by their roles in the essential epitomies of the person. They are involved diversely in sensitivity, sensibility, need, desire, orientation, sociality, mind, resolution, autonomy, and the pursuit of responsibility. Each of these and other like epitomies shape the histories of the various elements of life. Therefore, it should be noted that any experience has elements that could be analyzed according to the status of the components of essential humanity in the life of the individual.

The vector character of experience, conjoined with the representations identifying objects, is incredibly rich. Compared with the classical empiricists' experience of sense impressions and their ideational copies, or with the deconstructionists' experience of representational textuality existing as nothing but its own interpretation, the vector character reveals experience to be physical and extensive far beyond the immediacies of intentional activity in a temporal present.

Underlying this richness is the fact that the actualities experienced and the representations involved in mediating their direct presence are achieved values. Experiencing then is valuing. Its richness is a world of worthy things, albeit the worth can be negative as well as positive, depending on its position in the world. Every actuality is a harmony with triviality, vagueness, narrowness, and breadth, exhibiting complexity and simplicity. Every actuality conditioning another actuality is integrated into a wider harmony with those elements defining value. Finally, the experience of any one of these actualities, or vectors of sequentially conditioning actualities, integrates them into the experience with vagueness, triviality, narrowness, and width as characteristic of the imaginative field. The representation of this indicates why, as the pragmatists claimed so often, experience is shot through with values felt, values insistent, and values aimed at.

III. PRESENTATIONAL IMMEDIACY

The real character of a present moment of experience is the coming-to-be of an actual state of affairs. By the time it has determinate existence of its own, it is past. Yet the character of experience is such as to be in a world with things present; further, it is to be in a world with a past and future, observing and taking part in actions that take time. We experience things as having a history, and their contexts as having more inclusive histories. The present moment is thus an abstraction from a temporally thick character of experience, of enjoying, acting, and interacting with things in the context of the world. At each present moment, we are immediately present in the world, a world that is temporally thick. How is this possible?

The vector character of experience accounts for how distant parts of the world can be directly present in a here and now intentional act, and the representations with which they are joined in imagination and interpretation account for how they can be given experiential form and made objects of reference. This still does not account for the immediate character of experience, the way it seems in consciousness and in its subconscious spread appearing at the fringes of consciousness. Consciousness itself is a very difficult concept, one that has been abused by philosophies taking it to be a primitive given that can be described but not explained. Nevertheless, intentionality is organized around awareness, its field and its objects, what Whitehead called presentational immediacy. This must now be analyzed.

Let us, at least heuristically, take consciousness as the most complete form of presentational immediacy. It consists in at least three aspects: self-presence, a field character, and a contextual character.

In an interactive process of experience there are many interpretive acts, some forming active processes, all operating within the world of imaginative construction. Through the four-fold vectors of forces there are many dimensions of direct involvement of actualities other than the experiencer. Consciousness arises when the integration of these things includes not only an interpretation of an object, say, but also an interpretation of the act of interpreting the object. That is, the sense of the "presence" of things comes in part because the acts of interpreting them that are existentially present in temporal reality themselves become objects of interpretation. Consciousness thus involves a complex object. One part of the object is the representation of the interpretation of, say, the distant thing; this representation includes the actual interpretation of the distant thing as a proper content meaning, but it integrates the interpretation into a wider field of other interpretations of objects—the interpretation of the tree is integrated with the other things interpreted as landscape. The other part of the object of consciousness is the representation that the first part is going on as part of the intentional process. As Whitehead (1929, p. 245) said, consciousness involves an element of negativity: not a direct gaze at an object, but an interpretation of the gaze at the object as an act of the subject doing the interpreting, with the implicit recognition that the object might be otherwise than is interpreted in the gaze. By abstraction, one can suppress the sense of self involved in being conscious; in this extreme case, one is filled with the object—semiotically represented by itself. This might be pure awareness, but it is surely not self-consciousness, and perhaps not even consciousness; religious adepts call it a kind of self-less bliss. By alternate abstraction, one can suppress the vector element in the object and be filled only with representation. Of course it is really impossible to divest all representations of their conjunctions with vector forces—there is always a sense of body, of the hardness of one's seat if nothing more. But we can think we are bracketing out all senses of existential force when we focus on a particular representatoin in exclusive terms of its roles within our experience. Both abstractions, that losing the experiencer and that losing the actual world, are extreme, rare, and hardly to the point in much experience. The ordinary course of experience, particularly that in which interactions with others takes a dominant part, is to have consciousness flickering, spreading, or contracting over a larger field of orienting awareness (James, 1890). Consciousness does this by virtue of the fact that intentional activity includes within itself representations of its own activities conjoined to the activities themselves. Consciousness thus is always partly self-consciousness, and by intensifying the self-reflexive character, can deepen into profound self-consciousness. The immediacy of consciousness is the harmonized contrast between the representations of the intentional acts and the representations of how those acts are involved in one's own experience.

In addition, consciousness has a field character. That is, in order to represent our intentional acts as part of our own experience, we must be able to conjoin them to representations of the extensional fields they exhibit relative to ourselves. These include some representations of space and time, embedding any intentional act in an imagined world with some articulation of the three temporal modalities. The conscious representation of motion and interaction requires some schema for mapping a future with possibilities. Further, our sense of the field is articulated by continuities of motions and interactoins, of systems and changing situations. We may try to think an empty space-time, for instance, but it can not be done without thinking some points and movements within it. In particular situations of consciousness, the field needs to encompass only the elements involved in the intentional act (including relevant background). But since the representations involved are tied semiotically to other elements, they include broader and broader systematic representations. Behind all of the vagaries of the representations of the intentional field are those very broad categories of expectation about what a thing is, its natural powers, what causation is, time, space, and what can be expected. Metaphysics examines the broadest assumptions about what can be within an intentional field.

Although consciousness can expand or contract its focus, that focus always entails a field; the representations making intentional acts present to themselves connect them to the representations of the field. That representations of the extensional field are employed in consciousness does not mean that those representations are true. But they can not be far off if consciousness has pragmatic value. That is, the representations of the field must carry over some of the value of the extensional field itself.

The directional part of intentionality consists in employing the representation of the field to provide a context in which two intentional elements can be related. One element is the first intentional act, say a perception or an interpretive reaction to a vector of forces. The other is the representation of how that first act fits into experience. In a present moment, these two are vaguely related. Or put better, the vagueness of the initial relation between them must be brough to specificity if the moment is to come to definite individuality. The directional character of intentionality is the process of decision within a moment of present temporality determining how an intentional act can be fitted singularly into singular experience. Because of the field character of intentionality, the future outcomes of alternate possible determinations are factors in the decision project. To this extent, the directionality of intentionality is anticipatory. But the anticipation is a function of the field character of intentionality, representing the world into which the intentional act must fit as having a future. The field is a context, and the work of intentionality is determining how the content of experience, as determined in specific intentional acts, will fit into that context. When intentionality is problematic, as in inquiry, the issue is what potential condition or content of experience can be elicited to answer the needs of the context.

With respect to its contextualizing function, intentionality puts a great premium on the truthfulness of the intentional representations of the extensional field. For the contextualizing of an experiential element to work, it must actualize real possibilities; hence the future must be accurately represented. The future, of course, is articulated by already actualized structures and the alternatives these allow for potential actualization. The intentional field then must accurately represent the actualized past in its extensional interconnections. Further, for any given experiencing agent, there are other agencies, both individual and otherwise, acting contemporaneously. Therefore there must be an accurate representation of the range of activities and probabilities of contemporary actions. In all, the representation of the spatio-temporal field of activities needs to be accurate enough to allow the intentional context to represent the real extensional context, for the intentional contextualizing is the creating of a determinate state of affairs for the real context. The intentional representation of the context functions only within the present moment of coming to exist, and in subsequent present moments. The outcome of an intentional act is an actual state of affairs in which the particulars of the action are contextualized in the real extensionality of the actual world.

Doubtless pragmatic action warps the imagery of intentional contexts into reasonably accurate shape. Only philosophers make the contours of the content itself an object of attention. But in times of cultural crisis, people lose the required degree of accuracy in their representations for an intentional field. In doing this they lose the world, not the real world that continues to impinge on them with the fourfold vector of forces, but the experience of that world.

I cannot stress enough that the transformation of causal impingements into experience is the carryover into interpretive experience of the value of the objects experienced as qualified by biology, culture, semiotics, and purpose. Our intentional field is constituted by representations fit for our biology, for perceptual, tactile, olfactory, kinaesthetic and other bodily elements. The intentional field of course develops through time by the accumulation and buildup of intentional acts having bodily vector forces in them. So the field brings to the contextualizing even of new bodily feelings the history of the body's formation of the field. The intentional field also is deeply shaped by culture, by the hermeneutic elements embedded in the cultural themes that select certain respects for interpretation and not others. Even the perception of space is "carpentered" by cultural forms, as Patrick Heelan (1983) says: only a culture of Euclidian geometry, with straightedges and T-squares, sees things in Euclidian space. Of course, our semiotic systems affect the representations of the intentional field; the capacity of artists and priests to change that field consists only in their control over the shape of our representations in systems. Purposes too, especially those that are habitual and that underly a full texture of activities, affect the representation of the intentional field. The truth of the intentional field thus is not a repetition of form of the extensional field and its contents, but a carryover of the values there as qualified by the special selectivities of intentionality as such: biological, cultural, semiotic, and purposive.

Because culture, semiotic systems, and purposes are not had at all except as socially shared, and because our biological nature is shared through nature, and its manifestations through culture, the intentional field is a shared artifact. Pathological or poetic madness is required for an individual to contextualize in an idiosyncratic intentional field. Only persons with deep experience, those who take up the commonly shared representations and press them to individual and perhaps novel uses, can have significant variants on the culture's general intentional field.

Consciousness is a kind of self-reflexive awareness of experiencing. At sub-conscious levels there are also representations, derived from biology, culture, semiotics, and purposes, that integrate elements of intentional life.

At unconscious levels, there are other representations, often at odds with the first kinds, that integrate intentional activity in ways Freud (1920) characterized as "primary process." Probably this is too crude a classification; there may be many levels, many functions of culture, many overlapping, partly coordinate, partly irrelevant, and partly conflicting semiotic systems and purposes. The representations forming the overall intentional field in which our actions are contextualized, and the subcomponents of that field, are not necessarily coherent. Where the incoherence prevents successful contextualizing, its price is high. The incoherence cannot be so great, however, as to prevent the achievement of definite singularity and haecceity in the present moments of intentional life. Likely there is a bio-cultural-semiotic-purposive deep structure, vaguely unified in itself but specified in diverse partially related ways underlying our historically developing intentional field. Likely also, this intentional deep structure is rather true in a qualified way of the content-filled extensional structure of reality. Peirce (1935, parts. 476–477) suggested that only an hypothesis like this could account for the otherwise mysterious fact that we are ever right any of the time in our guesses about how to act.

Whatever the genetic or cultural origin of such a deep structure, it seems sure that consciousness arises as we learn to live with our culture, symbols, and purposes. Only when we have the requisite representations can we conjoin them to the vectors of forces and to one another so as to have conscious experience. This is not to say that apart from consciousness there is no experience or nothing but mechanical reaction. On the contrary, there can be experience wherever representations are used in interpretation, resting on the base of imaginative synthesis. Most of our activity is nonconscious appreciations and behavior, often of a very complex, if habitual, sort. Consciousness requires the very special kind of representation that makes our intentional acts themselves their own objects, not losing the direct presence of the vectors of forces. It is therefore a fleeting thing, coming and going, expanding and contracting. Often it is extremely desirable, since it vastly widens the range of deliberation, and allows us not only to enjoy but to enjoy the fact that we enjoy. On the other hand, when the object of experience is painful, we often seek the surcease of consciousness. There is a neurological operation for patients with excruciating cancer that breaks the neurological function necessary for consciousness of pain. If asked whether their pain remains after the operation, the patients say yes; the intentional acts of the pain remain. If asked whether the pain still hurts, they say no; the peculiar self-reflexivity of consciousness, combining the pain and its hurtful role in their experience, is no longer possible for them.

IV. THE TEMPORALITY OF INTENTIONAL LIFE

Our discussion of intentonality has brought to the fore two loci of relevant temporality that now must be integrated. One is the temporality of experiencing, in which the existence of intentionality is especially associated with present temporality. The other is the temporality of presentational immediacy, of the intentional field itself. The mediating link between these two is the fourfold array of vector forces.

On the one hand, as Dewey says, experience is an interactive affair, with any one experience stretching over many changes in the date of the now. On the other hand, experience has an immediacy to it, presentational immediacy, so that any given now entertains an experiential field providing the context for present action. How are these related?

The first point to recognize is that the temporality of the present contains within it both past and future. With respect to the past, any present moment of experience has the previously developed field of presentational immediacy carried over into it. The carryover has both structure and power as a vector of forces. As to structure, the field is not a mere datum handed down as a potential condition. It is structured by the essential epitomies, for instance, so that there is continuity of both form and content, of sensitivity, sensibility, pursuits of needs and desires, orientation, sociality, rationality, autonomy, responsibility, and self. All of these qualities articulate the intentional field. There is carryover also from the environment: the factors that shaped earlier fields of presentational immediacy continue to shape the emerging one, and the environmental factors that have changed urge changes in the new moment's field. Because the experiencer is a full natural being, likely to be in motion relative to something, there is an ongoing trajectory of integration of the person's developing essential epitomies and the histories of the places through which motion passes. Indeed, there are interactions that require and contribute to continuity of intentional field. The simple interaction of a conversion itself requires that the intentional field of both participants continue to sustain, share, and mutually accommodate to the culture and language of their speech, both of which provide baseline representations for the field of presentational immediacy. The fourfold vector of forces virtually assures the continuity of basic structures from one moment to the next in an experiencer's life, and from one experiencer to another in a situation with any important social communication. Because the physical embodiedness of ongoing life is transformed imaginatively to a relatively stable structure for presentational immediacy, there can be a relatively stable context for continuing action throughout the many changes of an interactive causal process. This is the heart of the naturalistic theory of interpretation, however uncongenial it might be to classical empiricism or phenomenological conceptions of consciousness arising from a bracketing procedure.

The fourfold array of vectors of forces assures not only relative stability of structures in continuity, but also continuity of immediacy. The directional character of immediacy is not essentially future-oriented, but rather oriented to attaining definiteness in the moment. As argued in Division III of this study each moment faces a complex possibility that in part is determinate and in part vague; the business of the moment is to determine the vague part in appropriate ways. Because of the stability of the structures provided in continuity by the fourfold array of vectors of forces, each moment has something of the same job to do, determining, as its predecessors had to do, the options left open by the inherited structures.

Some decisions, of course, are actions; that is, they determine once and forever some vague possibility. Later moments can not make the same decision, or an alternative one, because the deciding moment's decision alters the possibility structure for the future. A discursive action, or interaction, is a series of decisive changes that add up according to the unfolding of the discursive pattern. Even in an unfolding continuous action, however, the context within which the action continues to make sense and have direction must remain relatively stable. This happens insofar as (1) the respective essential epitomies achieve continuous intentional attention for reenactment, (2) the environment maintains a roughly stable structure of potentialities that must continuously be determined, (3) the orienting motions of things, including the experiencers, maintain roughly stable patterns requiring accommodation, and (4) enough interactions, for example, metabolism or conversation in a known language, require constant adjustment.

Thus there is a continuity of immediacy consisting in each moment of experience having to determine much of the same vagueness that its predecessors determined and its successors likely will have to determine. Since the task of each moment is inherited into the next that must repeat it, there is no atomicity of immediacy in the transition from the finish of one moment of actualization to the next. There is indeed an atomicity in that each present moment's determination of vagueness comes to an end in haecceity, thereby actualizing itself; at that point, the moment is past and actual, having achieved the value of integrating its various components in the singular way done. But there is no discernable bump in the immediacy of flowing experience, even consciousness, because the direction of intentionality is not to the future but to the concrescent achievement of definiteness, which is much the same moment to moment. In fact, were there no decisive change altering future possibilities, no action affecting the future, consciousness would be almost an unaltered and unself-conscious immediate identity through time. Only discernable change enables discernable bumps in consciousness; Secondness, as Peirce (1931, pars. 322–336) would say, is required to break the simple immediacy of consciousness.

My remarks in this section so far have focused mainly on continuity and discontinuity of intentionality from the side of the experiencer. The experiencer is also aware that the field of presentational immediacy contains continuity and discontinuity. At any given moment, an experiencer takes the intentional context to have a temporal depth in which things have histories, in which there are environments for any focal point, in which movements take place with structure through historical places, and in which interactions happen, some of which are regular and ongoing, while others are unique and only partly predictable in outcome. Because of the continuities in intentional field cited earlier, this vast, swarming, but orienting field of presentational immediacy is the context in which the experiencer in the next moment contextualizes activity, and in the next and the next. It is impossible for an experiencer to entertain the project of even a simple action such as walking over to the tree without maintaining the contours of the intentional field and following out the trajectoris of various elements in it, including the walker's own movements. In order to organize oneself to walk, that walking has to have a context, and the context must remain consistently throughout the activity, or at least consistent enough that the activity can take place. While walking one counts on one's path from the porch across the road to the tree in the lot to remain relatively fixed in space. One counts on the dog not to interrupt the walk with an attack of affection or viciousness, and one plots the movement of cars on the road so as to pass over when it is safe. Only a few of these elements would be in consciousness, but all would be elements of the intentional field in which the walk is contextualized. Consciousness might in fact be focused on something quite alien, say a metaphysical problem; but the walk with its intentional field is itself a context for the metaphysical thinking.

The continuities of the intentional field, and of experiencing things in the intentional field, are as diverse as the structures of representations and represented actualities involved. I should stress, however, that there are some essential continuities—those of the experiencer. Within experience many internal and external factors are present in force and in representation, but the internal ones constitute the continuing identity of the individual over time and throughout the collection of the individual's enjoyments and actions. The continuity, as argued earlier, consists in essential features connecting the various parts of the individual's life, mainly along the structures of the essential epitomies. By the interactions between the individual's essential epitomies and the historically unique features of environment, the person has a unique identity that itself is represented and functions as an organizing representation in the intentional field.

Perhaps more than any other representational feature, an individual's representation of his or her own personal identity at all levels of specificity organizes the intentional field. This existential fact has dangers that clearly need to be recognized, since it is the formula for selfishness and narcissism. It can only be partially compensated by the universal shared structures of culture and the semiotic systems. The ontological truth of the matter, of course, is that the existential field is filled with many unique actualities, of which oneself is but one. The norms for good behavior come not from the fact that it is possible, or even necessary, to see the field from one's own unique standpoint, but from the fact that one's unique standpoint puts one in the position to do certain things and not others. What things one ought to do depends on the values involved, not on how they serve any private interest of one's own history.

The intentional field is not to be conceived as an imaginative projection of representations organized as an image of the world. This was the conception I drew out in the first chapter as the seeming consequence of the importance of imagination and the imperial triumph of hermeneutics. The conception is inadequate, however, because it ignores the very many ways by which our representations are formed and exist in experience as the outcomes and interpreteres of the vectors of forces by which we are caused and causing creatures. Sustaining the representational order of the intentional field requires feeling its vector appropriateness for our existential context. Of course there can be crazy imagined worlds, distorted intentional fields. But these are crazy precisely because they differ from the representations that better organize and interpret the causal impingements on our being. Wildly false representations cannot be sustained except at the price of mental or social illness. Poetically creative representations, to the contrary, gain reinforcement because they reveal and provide intentional orientation to otherwise unnoticed elements in our natural-cultural world. Although we have yet to consider the truth of representations in detail, it is clear that our imagined intentional field is not merely an artifact, but is rather the means by which we operate naturally, as causal agents, in the real world. It is both an instrument of life and a product of the interactions. In ways not too difficult to imagine, the intentional field has pragmatic value, and is corrected according to its pragmatic uses.

The discussion has now recovered Dewey's point: experience is interactional. More precisely, the very ability of experiencers to sustain an intentional field through the passage of time, encompassing both continuities in the flow of experience and continuities in the flow of the things experienced, comes from the function of the intentional field in interactions. The interactions, containing within them the various essential, environmental, and motile vectors of forces, provide the complex causal ground, the correcting medium, and the value of the intentional field. The field serves to contextualize our actions, the actions of others, and everything else for which intentionality seeks to determine a place. Intentionality is the activity of determining for its objects a specific place in context. This happens at every experiential moment, but is never complete or satisfied in a moment. Any intentional activity requires at least the movement of making a change through time, even if only a change of idea. The continuities required for making a change, even if only a change in consciousness, are those manifesting themselves in interaction. Interaction is the engagement with real things with the result of representing them and responding to them. Both representation and response take place in the context of an intentional field, itself the result of steady interaction.

16

Interpretation

The project outlined in Division I called for the development of a naturalistic theory of interpretation. The components of that theory now are largely in place. Affirming the triadic character of the network meaning of signs, a theory has been put forward that analyzes a sign as a complex rule for relating interpretant to object relative to triviality and vagueness in background, narrowness and width in foreground; the representations involved in intelligent interpretation are species of signs. The content meaning of signs has been analyzed as the comprising, within the experience of thinking, of all the components integrated by the sign's rules. Another way of putting this is that the value achieved in the sign's content is the integration according to the sign's rules of the values achieved in the components, and in the components of components, on down. By virtue of its content meaning, a sign, or representation, can be true as the carryover or embodiment of the value of its integrated objects. The discussion of signs and representations has been extended further through a theory of intentionality. That theory accounted for the intentional character of experience as the directional contextualizing of signs in ways that combine both the phenomenological "object of attention" sense of intentionality, and the Deweyan sense of intentionality as a function of real interaction of the interpreter with things in the world. The purpose of the present chapter is to collect these components into a statement of an integrated theory of interpretation as a natural function. The goal is to demonstrate that such a theory supposes and explains the reality of the world as interpretations' measure.

There are four main topics to the discussion. First, interpretation must be related to purposive activity; intentionality was clearly distinguished from purpose in the previous chapter. Second, interpretation as an activity, or a family of activities, must be discussed with reference to other aspects of life and nature so as to be contextualized; according to the analysis of context above, interpretation itself is meaningful only within a larger context. Third, a theoretical restatement of interpretive truth as the carryover of value must be developed, integrating the naturalistic positions taken. Finally, the question of the reality of the world as measure must be addressed.

I. PURPOSE

The central theme for the American pragmatists in their reconstruction of the ideas of interpretation and truth was the relativity of interpretation to purpose. This was especially true for William James, though both Peirce and Dewey, as well as Mead, Morris, and Quine, accepted the point. They pointed out, in ways richly funded by their various systematic positions, that the context for interpretation is the interpreter's purposive activity. Roughly put, they argued that an interpretation is true or false relative to the needs of representation in purposive activity. In this way, at a stroke, they rejected the static correspondence assumptions of the empiricist, rationalist, and transcendental schools of European philosophy.

Against the empiricists, they objected that the question is not whether there is some object or quality corresponding to an idea impressed on mind. Rather, an object is represented in mind by a form that is appropriate for how the object bears on the purposive activity of the interpreter. With the empiricists, however, the pragmatists affirmed that there must be some causal relation between the object and the representation.

Against the rationalists they objected that the question is not whether an idea is adequate to its object, but rather whether it is adequate to the object as its representation in the purposive activity that might deal with the object. With the rationalists, however, they affirmed that ideas, and interpretive assertions, must be adequate to objects, not that objects may be pared down to suit human purposes.

Against the transcendental philosophers, the pragmatists objected that there can be no transcendental conditions of knowability to which objects and interpretants, respectively, should conform in order to relate to one another. Rather, the conditions for knowing must be invented and perhaps periodically amended in order to be faithful to the hard edges of reality. Nor should we conceive the matters of cognitive interpretation to be in another dimension from that of purpose; rather, for the pragmatists our purposes should be amended to conform with what is most appropriate in the world to value in purposive behavior. With the transcendental thinkers, however, the pragmatists urged that interpretations be regarded as vulnerable to criticism, and that criticism arise from discernable practical considerations.

The logical heart of the pragmatic reference to purpose is the following. Suppose that, in interpretation, a sign stands for an object in a certain respect as taken by an interpretant. Other signs could stand for the object in other respects, as other interpretants would mark. Purpose is that which selects the respect for interpretation. It is logically necessary that such a differential selection be made: otherwise interpretation would stand baffled like Buridan's ass at the array of all the possible respects in which the object might be interpreted.

The requirement for defining the respect of interpretation, or for giving direction to interpretation, is that purposive activity requires some particular respect of interpretation for the intentional function of relating the elements of the purpose to a context. The interpretation-in-a-particular-respect, in other words, is important for some element of the function of placing the purposively relevant objects in a context within which the purpose can achieve definiteness. It might be, for instance, that achievement of the purpose requires a particular object to be identified and described. On the other hand it might be that the purpose requires walking around the object such that interpretation has to figure out the characteristics that might make the object an obstacle. Descriptive interpretation is likely to be conscious or marginally conscious, whereas interpretations of the contours of the place relative to moving through it are likely to be largely unconscious.

Purposive activity is by no means a simple matter to understand, although no one doubts its importance for interpretation. It is a mistake to believe that all human behavior is purposive. Because of the importance of the biological sphere for the qualification of the carryover of value in interpretation, it is necessary to set purpose in its limited context as a kind of human activity. William James, of course, limited purposive behavior to those elements of life that involve representations, which is exactly right. He also (1890) gave what is still the most comprehensive account of the nonpurposive elements of experience. Nevertheless, his emphasis on purpose in the context of meaning or interpretation needs to be understood as circumscribed by what is not purposive. Several points can be made to lay out this context and to show how the pragmatists might have over-emphasized purpose.

1. Many activities of the human body are organized as subsystems of the organic whole, and these activities have their regular operations or play that are not purposive. Empirical science is bringing many of these subsystems to light and there is no adequate simple catalogue of their kinds of activities. Among the rough classes would be activities of fairly straightforward self-maintenance, activities of systems organized as feedback loops performing

a variety of functions in the larger organism, activities of subsystems performing specific homeostatic functions for the larger organism and for the larger environment, and activities such as sex, dance, music, and talk that, whatever other useful functions they serve, are intrinsically valuable and are engaged in often for no reason other than simply engaging in them.

2. For want of a better term in advance of a more detailed discussion, these subsystems of human activity that are not themselves purposive can be called elements of the "biopsychic dance." The reference to dance picks up a paradigm case of non-purposive activity that clearly lies within the realm of conscious experience. It emphasizes the "circularity" of these subsystem functionings, and also their physiological base. Dance is an intently energetic activity, and yet a passive one in the sense that the experience is indulged as its own reward. It often makes little difference whether one says we dance because of inner or social compulsion, or because it is enjoyed for its own sake. Dance, like many of the subsystems that lie within or on the margins of experiential awareness, allows of being engaged in special circumstances as purposive activity: "Do you want to have fun? Let's dance." But ordinarily we dance just because we feel like it. "Dance" also is an apt metaphor for the play of bodily processes, for the interchanges of hormones and neurotransmitters, for the activities of the metabolic processes, for the mobilization of immune defenses. It can serve as well to connote the deep psychic processes, the stuff of dreams and shamanic trances.

3. The adjective "biopsychic" wallpapers over a deep crack in our professional languages for human activities. But it is the languages with their disjunction and incommensuration that are at fault. Biology tends to describe things from the outside, applying a linguistic style modeled on physical and chemical mechanism. "Psychic" languages tend to describe activities from the inside, in terms of the ways they connect with person's own intentional (though not necessarily purposive) behavior. The phenomena of the biopsychic dance should not be misunderstood by being identified with the incommensurable abstractions with which we commonly identify them. Some subsystem activities, for instance, the chemical and electrical functions that regulate the heart rate, or the output of adrenalin, are not often part of experiential awareness, even when their products, the heartbeat and energy surges, are clearly noticed. But who is to say that yogic techniques, or biofeedback, cannot bring these activities across the margin of experiential awareness by putting them into an imaginative context with background and foreground? Other activities, such as ritual dance itself, are socially learned and thus to be understood in terms of the intentions and semiotic systems of "psychic" life. Yet they also are biological phenomena, more akin to pigeon mating behavior than to the rituals of the Christian Eucharist

(though the cannibalistic dance of the Eucharist ought not be understood too domestically). Many of the most interesting of these non-purposive systematic activities lie across the margin that distinguishes the phenomena that are psychic because they have the form of the imaginative world, and those that are biological because they lack that form. The deep structures of personality, the feelings or impulses that can be named and brought to consciousness by Jungian archetypal analysis, the bizarre psychophysical motions of trance that are named in shamanic practice, the elementary interactive behavior such as sex, grooming, or nursing: all these are inadequately analyzed by either biological or psychic terms.

4. Yet the play of these non-purposive routines are most of the stuff of which life is made. They are adaptive and the results of adaptation; they motivate evolutionary changes, and are evolutionary outcomes. Much of the depth of life consists in the running of these routines, in their interactions, changes, frustrations, developments, and deformations. Whether or not they are taken up in imaginative form, fitted into a world so that they can be experienced with imaginative form, the subsystems are felt as the solid mass of substances in biological life, the physical and psychic body moving through the world and providing a sense of locus and temporal lineament. Any purposively shaped experience takes these subsystems as fundamental elements of its background.

Purposive behavior differs from the subsystem of the biopsychic dance.

First, it takes its form from the elements of imagination, organizing focal elements against the background of a world. To be sure, many components of purposive behavior are wholly lacking in imaginative form. A purposive pointing of the finger requires setting in motion a subsystem of chemical neurotransmitters, excitable neurons, and muscle contractions and relaxations, none of which has the imaginative form of world except as known from the outside; the pointer is unaware of it all except perhaps the muscular effort. However many nonimaginative elements are involved in a purposive action, the overall contour of the action has a world-experiencing imaginative form. Further, although there are occasions in which the non-experiential subsystems might be set running by means of a variety of non-purposive causes, in the instance of a purposive action, the contours of the purpose, the roles the systems play in the purposive action itself, are necessary conditions for their operation (Pols: 1975; 1982). Reference to the purpose is necessary to understand the organization and actual functioning of the elements otherwise limited to the biopsychic dance. This is by no means to suggest that the activation of the subsystems is not "mechanical" at some level, limited to what can be understood in terms of nonpurposive behavior. Rather, the activation of the subsystems here in this particular purposive action, in this configuration, is simply insufficiently explained on that "mechanical" level. The configuration of running subsystems is expressed only on a higher level of organizaton, and is to be understood on that higher level in terms of purposive configuration. To reduce the understanding of the subsystems to the level of the biopsychic dance alone would be like explaining a complex business office in terms of typing and filing without reference to the economic organization of accounting and commercial correspondence.

Second, purposive activity requires a representation of the goal, a representation so formed that it ties in to the activities that are engaged in to accomplish it. The representation of the goal might not be realistic nor need it be conscious. Freud's and the other psychodynamic sciences have exposed many kinds of unconscious purposive behavior, often though not necessarily at cross-purposes with conscious intentions. Conscious and unconscious goals share the common features of representing some outcome of the organization of activities within one's world; their form as representation connects with activities imagined as part of the world.

Complex or sophisticated goals can be problematic. That is, we can have goals and not know how to achieve them. The complexity here consists in representations having semiotic forms that seem not to connect with activities that are part of our world. Deliberation is required to find connecting activities and, as we sadly learn, many goals are unreachable. Nevertheless, in order to be goals at all, these complex representations must involve connection with at least representations of activities that might achieve them, even if the represented activities are unavailable to us. Getting rich can be a pauper's goal, unrealizable in fact, because the pauper imagines how other people get rich; world peace can be a goal because we can imagine people beating their swords into plowshares. Nevertheless, these complex goals whose means we can only imagine would not be real goals unless somehow the imagined means were connected with some real activities that can be organized by the purposive person. The pauper can talk an excited line about the luck that will come tomorrow because that anticipation has a magical symbolic relation to the imagined ways the truly rich get that way; when the pauper gives up the illusions, the goal of wealth is abandoned as well. The peace advocate may admittedly not know how to motivate the superpowers to beat their swords into plowshares, but can continue to act on the conviction that convincing a few people in the neighborhood, a realistic hope, might contribute to the larger suasive power.

Third, a goal is not only represented in terms of activities that might accomplish it; it also is represented as connected with a representation of the agent as contributing to bringing it about. A given agent might be the sole contributor to purposive activity, or play a role in conjunction with others. To have the activity as purposive, however, the agent must connect the representation of the goal with a representation of self as contributing agent. The connection of the two representations requires a subtle representation of time. On the one hand, the temporal dating and spread of the purposive activities and their contribution to achieving the goal needs to be represented. On the other hand, the temporal significance of the contributing activity in the overall life of the agent or agents must be represented. That is, the activities must be felt as issuing from the resources built up out of the agent's past, as determining certain of the agent's overall activities at the time in which they are undertaken, and as determining the value of the agent's future as having been a contributing cause to the pursuit of the goal. Purposive activity can be successful or frustrated, adroit or highly costly, moral or immoral: whatever, the value of engaging in it accrues to the value of the identity of the agent according to the real contributions of agency. This identity for the agent is what is represented either clearly or vaguely, accurately or inaccurately, authentically or distorted by fantasy, as connected with the representation of the goal itself. Without this, the goal is not the agent's goal, and hence not a goal itself.

Fourth, purposive activity not only involves these representations, but also the existential act of adopting them. That is, in present action, the bringing of vague possibilities to the haecceity of actuality includes, among other things, the adoption of the goal and the related real or symbolized activities, and the adopting of the relevant identity. There may be little or no free choice in what one purposes, but where there is purposive activity, there is a making up of the individual to be a temporally determined agent, acting to contribute to the realization of the goal. Another way of putting this point is that purposive activity has the special value of organizing the individual so as to achieve the various values in the goal, in its pursuit, and in the resultant moral identity. The individual is the outcome of the composite value achieved by putting together the potential values that enter the existential process of actualization. To organize the potentials for experience so as to result in purposive activity is to achieve both the values of purposive activity as such and those of pursuing the purpose at hand.

The analysis of purpose thus has at least four dimensions: (1) the analysis of its imaginative form, (2) the analysis of the representation of the goal and its connection with activities to accomplish it, (3) the analysis of the representation of the purposer as agent, and (4) the analysis of the actual individuating of the purposer as having and acting on the goal. These correspond roughly with the four areas of qualification of the carryover of value in interpretation: biological participation, cultural participation, semiotic participation, and the participation that consists in being purposive.

The relevance of the analysis of purpose to interpretation is that purposive activity is required to select the respect in which a thing might be interpreted by the signs at hand. Rarely would the relevant purpose be to interpret the thing itself; that we often purpose to interpret is an academic's fantasy. Rather, we need interpretations of things in order to act purposefully. Interpretations are required in each dimension of purposive activity. (2) They are required to imagine a world in which the actual routines of the biopsychic dance can be organized according to the contours of purposive activity. (2) They are required to represent the goals and its connectons with actions. (3) They are required to represent the agent's identity as relevant to the activity. And (4) they are required to sort the potentials for integrative individuation into the forms of purposive action.

Our purposive actions thus are always within a highly interpreted context. In a given context, the interpretations that are inherited from the past are themselves functions of previous purposive behavior. Part of the activity of making up purposive behavior therefore is the adjustment of inherited interpretations to the purpose at hand, and conversely the forming of the purpose at hand through the adjustment of interpretations.

II. CONTEXT

The context within which interpretation is to be understood to take place is larger than purposive behavior or the biopsychic dance. It is in fact the entire context in which the human emerges and exercises itself, as marked out in part by the essential human epitomies discussed earlier. This is not to say that animals other than human beings are totally devoid of interpretive behavior; indeed perhaps most mammals interpret in rudimentary or not so rudimentary ways. It is rather to say that the context for understanding human interpretation includes all the dimensions required for the emergence and exercise of interpretation on the full human level. There are four principal dimensions to contextuality that can be understood on the basis of the philosophy of nature, meaning, and contextuality developed so far: the natural, the imaginative, the intentional, and the responsive.

1. Natural contextuality. Quite apart from imagination, for a thing to be in a context is for it to integrate the four kinds of vectors of forces, as described in chapter 15. That is, a thing has to be a harmony integrating the discursive vectors of forces of its own past and future as described in chapters 9 and 10, the extensional forces of things in its environment as described in chapters 8 and 11, including the historical determination of its space-time field (as described in my *Cosmology of Freedom*, 1974, and *The Puritan Smile*, 1987), the motile forces of its movements as described in chapters 11 and 12, and the complex of interactive forces involved in taking account of and affecting other things as described in chapter 12.

The vectors of forces are the basic classes of components integrated in a natural harmony, as described in chapter 8. They are the root conditional features that must be harmonized by essential features to constitute a harmony in nature, as articulated in chapter 5 and 6. Each element in those vectors of forces is itself a harmony of some sort or other, as outlined in chapters 10 and 12, and has a value. As chapter 7 argued, that value in each thing is itself the result of its integration of the values of its own fourfold vector of forces with its essential characters.

Thus, irrespective of whether the natural harmony has anything like imaginatively formed human experience, it has a generic interpretive form. A harmony integrates all its vectors of forces as conditional features so as to be itself in the context of them all. Any one conditional features functions as a sign for others in the vectors of forces, and the way by which the harmony integrates that conditional feature is the way by which it interprets the sign as signifying the others. Though a generic sign need not have a semiotic network meaning, with the conventional structure of a code, it does have an internal pattern or rule that gives it a network relation to other things, a relation that can then be represented in human interpretation. The sign as a conditional feature of a harmony also has content meaning in the sense that its own components are contained, according to its structure, in the larger containing harmony. Because the very identity of a natural harmony has the form of a contextualized interpretation, it is possible for human representational interpretations to spell out that natural identity. Here is the affinity between nature and human knowing.

All natural harmonies, human or not, have a natural context in the sense discussed here. This is part of the essential causal constitution of a thing. The imaginative, intentional, and responsive dimensions of context are built on the natural context as specifications and additional levels of interpretive harmony. There are no grounds whatsoever for assuming that experiential contextuality is an inner subjective construction projected toward an outer world. There can be no real question of whether the representative levels of contextual interpretation have a world. Rather, the question is whether those representative interpretations interpret the world correctly. The imaginative, intentional, and responsive dimensions of contextuality might involve error and misinterpretation, but not disconnection from reality. They are always, even when wrong or utterly irrelevant, interpretations arising from within the real natural context in which the interpreter takes identity, and the experiential elements of context can only be modifications of the natural context of the world.

2. Imaginative contextuality. The imaginative dimension of an interpreter's context is an extra level of synthesis integrated with the natural dimension. It transforms at least some of the fourfold vector of forces from mere causal components into an integrated whole having the form of experience. In *Reconstruction of Thinking*, Part II, I analyzed the form of experience into the construction of a world with background and foreground. The elements making up form are those that integrate things so as to embody or schematize the norm of beauty, and thus triviality and vagueness are associated with background, narrowness and width with foreground.

Imagination synthesizes the vectors of forces by means of images. Any image allows of being used as a representation; that is, an interpretive process can take it to be a representation of something in the material in the vectors of forces. To treat an image as a representation, however, is the work of interpretation, not of imagination by itself. Imagination is simply the feeling of the vectors of forces as organized by images making up a particular worldliness. Some imaginative forms might be biologically determined, others by culture or particular semiotic systems. Imagination is an integration of conditional features according to images. It is not the contemplation of an image in abstraction from grasping reality as a world-form; such a contemplative vision is a highly complex semiotic act.

Having an imaginative grasp of the vectors of forces is a precondition for representative interpretation. As such, it is neither true nor false. A given imaginative synthesis might very well integrate the fourfold vectors of forces so as to carry over the values of things into its structure, as qualified by biological, cultural, semiotic, and purposive conditions. But that it does so requires that some of its elements be taken as signs of objects, and imagination by itself does not do that. An imaginative synthesis might, alternately, distort and pervert the values an interpretatiion would suggest it carries over; again, however, the representational function is not found in imagination but in an interpretive dimension added to imagination. Norms for imaginative construction are solely aesthetic. Nevertheless, there can be no representational interpretation except insofar as imagination both presents the vectors of forces formed as a world and provides image-elements that can take on the role of representing.

Imagination is always perspectival. The vectors of forces can be integrated in countless ways by virtue of elevating and suppressing different elements. An imaginative construction must have the aesthetic coherence of some one way of integration. Imagination as such is but one of many ways of natural integration, one that depends on the imagery given by the biological, cultural, semiotic, and purposive elements of human life; those elements impose perspectival conditions on imaginative integration. There are several biological structures for potential imaginers, several cultures, several semiotic systems, and a vast array of purposes. That imagination is perspectival does not mean that it lacks value of its own. At least, any imaginative integration has the value of some beauty. Even a fragmented imagination, such as our Western one, has coherence at some levels, incoherence and discord at others, and minimally it has at least a modicum of beauty. Nor does the perspectival character of imagination mean that interpretations constructed from a given imagery are false: they are limited in perspective, but perhaps true as qualified by the biological, cultural, semiotic, and purposive limiting conditions.

3. Intentional contextuality. The intentional dimension of a context for interpretation is added to, or forms a further complex level of, the natural and imaginative dimensions. Intentional contextuality is the integration of the fourfold vectors of forces as already integrated with semiotically formed representations. The intentional character of the context means that the context is already filled with interpretations, that among the important elements of the context are representations functioning to form and simplify the vectors of forces. This acknowledges the point that no experiential context provides uninterpreted givens, while insisting that the interpreted elements are still given in the vectors of forces.

Intentional contextuality means that the interpreter's discursive nature functions contextually as already interpreted by representations of the interpreter's identity. The various human essential epitomies discused above were shown to involve representations and also to express representations making up the person's identity through time. To the extent these epitomies are imaginatively registered in the intentional context, they come already interpreted with representations that take meaning in part from the network connections of the person's and culture's codes. The extensional vectors of forces, similiarly, are synthesized by representations articulating the extensional coordinates of the interpreter's semiotic systems. Scales of space and time differ from one culture to another, and often are functions of social organization and technology. It is culturally interesting to note that whereas Westerners think in terms of North, East, South, and West, the Chinese think of East, South, West, North, and Here. The forces of motion and interaction are similarly formed by representations, in the intentional dimension of contextuality.

The upshot of the intentional dimension is that the world apprehended as the context for interpretation presents a depth of interpretation. The environment, for instance, is not framed with representations in its proximate positions and with un-representational signs in more distant time and space, as if behind a screen of subjective projection. Rather, the representational interpretations appear up and down the vector of forces at the points where pragmatic reasons have installed appropriate representations. We now appreciate the characters of micro-particles (not to say "elementary" particle) by means of physical theories unavailable a century ago. We have not yet come to appreciate even simple contextual elements such as vision or locomotion in semiotic terms that represent brain processes. Mostly, the context for interpretation is formed by representations that pick out or form the "objects" of the everyday world.

The semiotic codes providing representations for intentional contextuality are many, various, and not necessarily coherent, consistent, or commensurable; the sole unifying criterion is that they all be compatible with the imagery constituting the experiential world. The various codes may be in dynamic processes of change, altering the definitions of their representation, increasing or decreasing their determination. An inexperienced automobile driver, for instance, will have a driving context with much vaguer representations of the meaning of traffic conditions than an experienced driver. The codes by which Western medieval people read the virtue of the persons in their context were much more determinate than those of the nineteenth century Europeans who tended to be determinate only about efficiency, rationality, and aggressiveness. The context for forest-dwellers represents many more distinctions of green than the context of a desert dweller; not that there are not as many shades of green in the natural context of the desert, but that they are not pragmatically important enough there to call forth discriminating representations.

Insofar as the context for intentionality is appropriate for consciousness, there are representations articulating the context to have a field character and to distinguish the field and its contents from the self of the interpreter, as discussed in chapter 15. That is, representations articulate the vectors of forces so that distant things are presented through the medium of intervening things to the self, qualified by the intervening things along the way, and recognized to be both within the proximate things and that which is without those things. An intentional context thus presents the world as ready to be alienated as well as embraced by the interpreter. This brings the discussion to the fourth dimension of contextuality.

4. Responsive contextuality. The responsive dimension of contextuality integrates the other dimensions with representations presenting the world as ready for the interpreter's response. This involves, in addition to the representations mentioned in the previous point, those that define certain relations between the interpreter and the world articulating relevant boundaries, openings for response, and the causal powers by which a response might be made, as discussed earlier in Section I. There are two main sides to reponsive contextuality; the representation of the interpreter as capable of response, and the representation of the context as ready for or demanding of response.

In order to be interpretively responsive to something in context, an interpreter must have some ways of representing responsiveness and using those representations to organize a readiness to respond (and then the response). The discussion of epitomies of the essentially human in chapter 10 spelled out much of what might be involved. The range of elements necessary for human responsiveness is far wider than that, however, and doubtless variable relative to the different kinds of contexts of response. A response itself can be of many kinds. Some responses are merely interpretive or intellectual. Others are performative in different ways with the interpretive elements functioning in passing. The study of the structures of self-representation necessary for responsiveness is a fruitful field for psychology and sociology.

The grasp of the context as ready for or demanding of response is more interesting than the contextual grasp of oneself as ready to respond. On the one hand, it involves seeing the context as organized in such a way that a response can fit in and be effective; this was discussed above at some length in connection with purpose. On the other hand, the context must include representations that reveal it as fit for a response. The context must be represented as a potential source of food to allay hunger, of safety from danger, of companionship, of aesthetic delight, of moral demand, of spiritual fulfillment. This is to say, the responsive dimension of contextuality represents the contexts as containing things of value to which it is also an appropriate value to respond. Put the other way around, responsive contextuality represents the response as a fit, appropriate, or good way of responding to the good and ills of the context. Whereas all the dimensions of contextuality present the context as articulated by the assorted values of its context, the responsive dimension represents those value as determining the worth of a potential response, determining in fact that there should be a response with some value.

It was mentioned in chapter 2 that pragmatism, at least in its Peircean and Deweyan forms, says that, although purpose guides interpretation, the most important interpretation is the determination of what purposes are worth having. Now I shall generalize this point. The very context for making an interpretation is formed already so as to be ready for responses (purposive or not so purposive). Readiness does not mean just an opportunity for the interpreter to cause something. It means rather an opportunity for responding in a value-laden way, an opportunity formed by the values at stake in the relation between the context and the potential responses within it. The fact-value distinction makes no sense at all in light of the consideration that all interpretation takes place within an "appropriate" context. Part of the value of a potential responder is to respond in ways that respect the values of the fourfold vectors of forces. Interpretation itself is just one kind of response, though perhaps a dynamic part of all other kinds of responses. An interpretation might be mistaken, or inappropriate as dictated by some high-level code; but it cannot have a context at all unless it is appropriate to take place, in some form. The context for interpretation presupposes that interpretation is called for.

The discussion has now returned to the relation of the values in the context to the values achieved in a response. Focusing on interpretive responses, or interpretive aspects of other kinds of responses, the relation between those two loci of worth is the condition for truth. Truth is the carryover of value from an object in the context to the interpretation of it in the interpreter. This elementary claim of chapter 3 can be fleshed out with the categories developed through the philosophy of nature.

III. TRUTH

The hypothesis that truth is the properly qualified carryover of value from object to interpretation can be elaborated under three main heads: logical truth, generic truth, and the truth of texts.

1. Logical Truth. Logical truth is the truth of representations that have network and content meaning within some semiotic system. Rightly timed gestures, winks, and ritualized behaviors are examples of such representation; but for purposes of analysis here, I shall focus on propositions as themselves represented by linguistic expressions. My thesis is that a representation is true if and only if its form is such as to convey the properly qualified value of its object into the interpretation of the representation as representing its object. There are several issues that must be addressed to clarify this thesis.

That the value of an object can be carried over into the interpretation of it was asserted, in chapter 3, but not grounded in a theory of causation that explains carryover. Divisions II and III have provided that theory. Chapter 5 began by elaborating a theory of identity as consisting in essential and conditional features, thus showing how things are determinate in themselves and in connection with other things. Chapter 6 showed how identities embody the primary cosmology, with form, components, actuality, and goodness. Chapter 7 analyzed goodness in detail, relating it to both form and actuality. Then Chapter 8 discussed how identities are harmonies in an extensional field and how one harmony can be a component of another, contributing its value through the qualifications of multiple location. Chapter 9 introduced a theory of time that allows for the specification of "conditioning" as dynamic causation. Chapter 10 explored the discursive or temporal nature of harmonies and, along with chapter 11, showed how the conditioning of things by each other takes the form of motion and interaction, all transforming value. Chapter 12 then brought together a comprehensive theory of causation according to which value is carried from one thing to another. The way by which a temporal thing integrates the vectors of forces coming to it is iconic of the way by which an interpretation takes a sign as standing for an object.

Most theories of truth presuppose a philosophical nominalism of simple location, according to which the actuality of a thing is only in its place and cannot be carried over into something else; by the same token, value cannot be conceived to be carried over on a nominalist theory.[1] The metaphysical and cosmological theory summarized just now is a clear alternative to that. Chapter 3 and, more thoroughly, chapter 4, indicated how the carryover of objects into the interpretation of them involves the qualifications of their transformation into biological, cultural, semiotic, and purposive forms. These qualifications indicate how a thing, in being interpreted, becomes qualified by the context of the interpreter.

The contextuality of *objects* is equally important to stress, in opposition to the usual presupposed nominalism. Contemporary nominalists (Quine, 1961) might very well admit that an object can be referred to only from within the interpreter's context of a language or a culture, or even a biology or set of purposes. Within this nominalist assumption, there is debate as to whether one can still refer to the objects as really independent of the context of the interpreter's reference to them, or whether they are to be reduced to the logical place of reference itself, a form of subjective idealism derivative from nominalism (both positions are maintained, I believe, in Putnam, 1978). Contrary to the nominalist assumptions about objects, I have argued that objects themselves exists only in contexts, as spelled out in the previous section. Contextuality is required by the fact that identity involves conditional as well as essential features. This point can not be related more specifically to truth in interpretation.

For an interpreter to take a representation as standing for an object, it is necessary to pick out the object. The work of "referring" is identifying an object in its own context. An object is something that is, or is part of, a harmony integrating itself in its own proper place among all the vectors of forces that are its conditional features. Reference involves coordinating the object's real context with the interpreter's biological, cultural, semiotic, and purposive contexts. Reference by itself is possible when there are aspects of the interpreter's context that identify the object in contrast to other possible objects. The interpreter's context thus must itself involve enough true interpretations of the real context of the object in order to make that reference. "The third man from the left in the lineup" is referential if that man is in a context adequately interpreted by the notions of the lineup, of being distinguished from other men by the number of positions left to right, and so forth. If the interpreter is trying to identify a murderer but there is in fact no lineup, only the dream of one, then the phrase is not referential. Under ordinary circumstances, the evolutionary development of the imagination of the interpreter, and the always already (Tracy, 1987) prior interpretations of the world, provide ready congruence of the interpreter's referring signs with the world of objects to which reference might be made. Exceptions would be when a person is taken into a radically new situation, and does not know how to pick out what is important, or when a new phenomenon is noticed for which current codes cannot conceive a cause.

Within interpretation, an object is referred to only as being within its context, where the interpretive apparatus of the interpreter takes the world as already interpreted enough to allow of reference. This is to say, we do not interpret objects *per se*, only objects-in-context.

As discussed in chapter 15, to intend an object is to take it to be both within the interpretation and without the interpretation. It is within the interpretation as being in the logical place of the object. But it is over against the interpreter (or against the interpreter's current interpretation in cases of self-reference) by virtue of being apprehended in a real context relating the object to the interpretation causally. The causality expressed in the appropriate vector of forces both connects the object to the interpretation and externalizes it from the synthetic act of interpretant. This point is necessary to account for the reality of objects over against the interpretation of them. Only an account of the logic of interpretation that includes a causal relation between object and interpretation can protect the realism of reference. We of course make mistakes about references, as in hallucinations, dreams, and the like. But the mistake precisely is to assume that the customary causal connections and exteriorizations are there when in fact other causal factors are in play. Experienced hallucinators, and most of us when dreaming, do understand the different causal nexuses causing the hallucination or dream, and accept the hallucination and dream as such, without being deluded. The customary validity of reference requires that our context of interpretation have the causal connections of things adequately identified with representations of their important causal properties, how to judge distances, tell colors in various lights, discern when someone is poking fun at us. (The semiotically ordered system of a teasing conversation is just as much a causal system as one exhibiting the propagation of light.)

An interpretation not only refers a representation to its object but also takes the object to be what the representation means. That is, an interpretation says that the object falls into networks of connection that, in part at least, are described by the network meanings of the representation, as indicated in chapter 13. Part of the network meaning of a representation is reference itself, and the obverse of this is the object's network relation to the representation that allows the representation to refer to it. The content meaning of the representation says that the object, with the proper reverse biological, cultural, semiotic, and purposive qualifications, is a harmony of components that can carry over to the representation as its contents, organized by the representation's rule nature. The object, of course, has many more components and patterns than any finite representation can mean—an infinite number of components and patterns in fact. But those that a particular component picks out might indeed truly be part of the object, and important.

A true interpretation carries over the achieved value in the object into the interpretation by means of both the network and content meanings of the representation. A representation true in its network meaning allows the interpretation to entertain the object, properly qualified and so on, in its contextual connections. A representation true in its content meaning allows the interpretation to entertain the object, properly qualified and so forth, as the achievement of the value of harmonizing those of its components contained within the content meaning. Network meaning allows for an appreciation of the value achieved in a thing's connections. Content meaning allows for an appreciation of the value achieved in a thing's actualization, or possible actualization. A representation's network and content meanings largely overlap because the rule articulating the network meaning is also what organizes the contents. An interpretation can grasp a thing's network meaning, and predicate it truly, without having much or any of the content meaning (if the network meaning is sufficient by itself to provide reference to the object). To have content meaning the interpreter has to have attained the properly qualified actuality of the content in question. This might be done through a direct perceptual or other experiential encounter with the object. But in most of our experience, the empirical contents of our meanings come from other areas of experience and are reorganized in our integrating representations. Memory of the heavy yellow solidity of my father's gold watch provides a content for my understanding of what my wife means in talking about her father's gold cuff links, as organized by the concept of gold. The network meaning of "gold" connects the watch and the cuff links in my experience, and the direct content of experiencing the former gives content meaning to my reflections about the latter. My emotional experience of "an artifact of my father's" gives poignant content to my reflections on my wife's feeling for the "artifact of her father's."

Meanings, of course, are common natures, both in objects and in representations of objects. Any actualized harmony is more than its common nature: it is an haecceity. Sometimes a thing is experienced in its haecceity. Part of that experience is the discernment of common natures, which are just as real as the thing's haecceity. But another part of the experience is of the thing's haecceity itself, as mediated through the haecceity of intervening vectors of force. It is an interesteing question whether some haecceity, some thisness, is required in all indexical reference.

There is no value, of course, apart from a harmony with components organized in patterns. Thus, to say that truth is the carryover of value is also to say that it is the carryover of the harmony. But the qualifications in the carryover can greatly change both the components and the patterns. The physical reality of a mountain is stony and the reality of a mother's love is personal, cultural and psychological, yet both can be represented in minds whose components are meat organs.

Functionalists (Fodor, 1981) can say that the components of thinking do not matter so long as the patterns of the functions are carried over. Yet the patterns of thinking are biological, cultural, semiotic, and purposive, while the patterns in mountains are none of these, and the patterns in the actuality of mother love are very different from those in thinking about mother love. The qualifications in causal carryover can alter both components and patterns. The carryover carries truth when the value of the object, and the harmony of its complexity and simplicity, is carried over. In this case, the interpreter possesses the object, subject to the qualifications, as an achievement to be integrated into the interpreter's own reality. Since most interpretation is not limited to an individual person, interpretation in its truth is the enrichment of a society of interpreters.

Truth is the condition of making the interpreter true to the objects in the respects interpreted. Being true to an object in network and content ways is just one part of the interpreter's life, and that truth has to be reconciled with the other components of the interpreter's discursive life, and with the life of the interpreting community. This reconciliation depends on, and is facilitated by, the biological, cultural, semiotic, and purposive qualifications of the carryover. Any achievement of truth in an interpretation itself has a proper place in the discursive life of interpretation, and in its subsequent multiple locations can become an untruth, or part of an untruth. Truth is the possession of the value of the object by means of the representation's connection with the object in interpretation. The network value of the object's connections mediated by network meaning, and the content value of the object's achievements in the content meaning, both allow of distortion when subsequent interpretation keeps the representations but distorts the value.

In all this talk about value, it is easy to slip into the assumption that it is some mystical or "simple non-natural property," in G. E. Moore's phrase (1903). With this assumption, it would seem that the carryover of value can only refer to feeling, so that truth is reduced to mere swarmy good feeling. On the contrary, it must be remembered that an account has been given of what it is that makes something valuable, an account employing the categories of simplicity and complexity, and of triviality, vagueness, narrowness, and width. Thus, to grasp the value of something is to grasp just what it is, how its components are harmonized in an organizaton respecting simplicity, complexity, and the rest. Of course, this might not be an adequate analysis of what makes something valuable. But a better analysis would show even better what the properties are that make a thing what it is. Whereas the preliminary hypothesis about value in chapter 3 had to assume that things' nature is constituted by what makes the things valuable, chapters 5 through 12 have defended that assumption with great detail. To be sure, there are many more questions that could have been asked at every step of the way in, in light of the diversity of topics covered, even after the lengthy treatment of detail, we must admit that the axiological philosophy of nature is only provisional, looking for correction. But now, nearing the end, we can reaffirm with Aristotle (*Metaphysics*, 1011b 26) that truth is saying of a thing what it is and not saying of it what it is not, and mean by that, that interpretation contains what and how a thing is valuable by referring to it with the appropriate meaningful representations.

2. Generic Truth. The account of truth as a logical matter has focused on truths expressed in representations affirmed interpretively of objects. Underlying the whole of the discussion, however, has been the thesis, mentioned several times, that true interpretation is the value to be achieved by human beings in their cognitive dimension. The metaphysical underpinning for this is that our world provides ready opportunities for interpretation, for carrying over its assorted and structured values into specific human lives and societies. Part of human reality, as depicted in the essential epitomies, is to be responsible to the world's values by representing them in the human context, in biological, cultural, semiotic, and purposive form. Therefore it is important to say that, in the cognitive dimension, human beings not only ought to know the truth, but in knowing the truth, be true. Further, since all of human life is affected by interpretations, if not directly interpreting, all of life may be said to be true or false. No life can be wholly false. But most lives fail to be sufficiently responsive to the valuable things around them. They lack orientation to what is important. They suffer from insufficiently worthy purposes. To show how and why we have so much knowledge of objects but so little feel for their worth, and how that worth ought to determine the moral and aesthetic shape of our lives, is a proper task of critique of culture. To say our lives are false to the reality of the world is not to say merely that we have the facts wrong. Often we have the facts right, but abstracted from the concrete realities in which their value is apparent. To say our lives are false is to say we are profoundly morally wrong.

3. The Truth of Texts. The theory of interpretation I have developed arises from the American tradition for which the paradigm case is the interpretation of nature. I have argued (1974, Pt. III) that culture, even human mentality, is part of nature. The dominant European tradition of hermeneutics takes as its paradigm the interpretation of texts.[2] Can that be represented as an important proper subset of the interpretation of nature? Can the theory of interpretation developed here say anything useful about the interpretation of texts? A literary theory is a topic that extends beyond the intent of this book. But an indication of the direction of a naturalistic literary theory can be given.

A text is an artifact whose message is of interest to literary theory. An interpretation of the text involves identifying the various elements in the message in their connections and achievements; as a harmony in a context, of course the hermeneutical circle must be observed. The work of interpretation involves developing a language that is sensitive to the connections and achievements in the messages.

Part of a text's message might be that it aims to give a true account. But what does "true account" mean? That depends on what kind of value the message aims to embody. A representation of an historical event is one kind of truth; drawing a moral from the historical account is another. Mythic accounts seemed for a long while to be of historical form, or pseudo-history; now they are understood to be "about" world-formation in some sense (for example, Eliade, 1959) or other (as in Berger, 1969). Epics, novels, poems, memoirs, diagrams, scientific papers, all have various specific kinds of carryover of various specific kinds of value. One function of literary theory is to distinguish and spell these out for each text. The question of what truth a text contains on its own terms is different from the question of whether its representations are true in our context.

The interpretation of a text is to interpret for us how it interprets its subject matter in its world. Where it is not obvious, such interpretation means creating a connection between the subject and world of the text and our own interpretive context. This is another dimension of the hermeneutic circle. Of course, every interpretation, of an interpretation of an interpretation of an interpretation, is a carryover from a previous interpretation. Each carryover is qualified by cultural and other differences. Thus Derrida (1976) and others (Taylor, 1984) are right to insist on the constant play and equivocation of terms (Lentricchia, 1980). They are right too to object to a logocentrism that insists on a univocal meaning of discourse throughout Western history. Each text is its own unique integration of the vectors of (mainly cultural) forces in its world, and interpretation needs to be sensitive to constant variance and play of inexplicit differences.

Yet is is a mistake to think of the Western tradition as logocentric. The Western tradition contains a great many approaches to texts, and a richly textured array of texts. To insist on reading the Western tradition through the Heideggerian categories of lococentrism (or even worse, of onto-theo-logocentrism) is blatant logocentrism. Not even Hegel, who was as logophilic as one can be, was that reductionistic in hermeneutical logocentrism.

There is a profound sense in which Derrida is right to call everything a text, on the analogue of a writing. That sense is the one recalling that the imaginative, intentional, and responsive dimensions of context are formed by representations that are already given in any act of interpretation, all this in addition to the fact that objects of interpretation are referred to in terms of already interpreted vectors of forces. This is similar to Peirce's point that everything that can be integrated is also a sign. I have argued here at length that natural identity and connection have the form of signification of interpretation.

Applied to literature, however, Derrida's dicta about grammatology are highly misleading. Often a text's meaning is best understood by relating to the geography and climate in which it was written, to the scientific understanding of the day, to the history and interests of the author and readers. In these connections much can be said about the text's truth and worth, and although the saying of these things is another text, our own, our text might be quite true about the interpreted text in context. There is no reason to suppose literary interpretation need fall into relativism any more than is required by the mere fact of fallibility in interpretation. There surely is no reason to suppose that, because any interpretation of a text is different from the text itself, the interpreter is free to say the text means anything at all. If an interpreter intends to be true to the text interpreted, then the text in its context must be taken to be the measure of the interpretation. Like any interpretation, our interpretation of a literary text is qualified by our biology, culture, semiotic systems, and purposes. Given those qualifications, we may still be true to the text, taking it as our measure.

IV. THE WORLD AS MEASURE

I have come now to the end of a long argument that began as the endeavor to justify our naive sense that the world is the norm or measure for our interpretations, despite the seeming consequence of interpretation-theory that the world is just to be reduced to interpretations. The consequence of that reduction is a disastrous relativism. The thrust of my argument has been to articulate a philosophy of nature in which interpretation is understood as a causal part. True interpretation is thus a certain kind of causation, one that carries over the value of the interpreted object into the interpretation of it. I have argued that, seen in context, this is what we mean when we say something is true.

My argument has not been to prove anything from agreed upon premises, but rather to articulate a categorial expression for a reformed common sense that can indeed take the world as measure. The hope is that when people think about the theory presented here from enough angles, and correct its deficiencies, they will come to see that the world is the measure of our interpretations, and get on with improving, enriching, and extending interpretive life.

We must ask again, however, why it is so hard in our day to see that the world is the measure. Once we admit that any culture or line of intepretation is perspectival or contextual, why are we tempted to take the next step to subjective relativism? And to the cynicism and nihilism to which that leads? Of course there are a great many important answers to that question. I will mention two, both of which are philosophical mistakes arising out of cultural developments.

The first is what chapter 2 identified as a Cartesian thesis that the world consists of simples, and that knowledge involves isolating the simples and then reconstructing their connections. The fault in the Cartesian thesis is its failure to recognize the ontologically constitutive importance of context. The present chapter has linked the idea of simples to metaphysical and epistemological nominalism, which has roots even earlier than Descartes. That objects are constituted in part by context is such an obvious part of experience that only a philosophical theory could have blinded us to the fact. I have argued since the second chapter for another philosophical theory that explicates our experience of contextuality. Many people believe that modern science requires a nominalistic theory. I do not see, however, where anything in the theory I have presented as an alternative needs to give the lie to science. What might indeed be required of science is that it give a contextualistic redefinition of the meaning of "controlled experiment." Science, as it is often practiced, and more often publicly advertised, reinforces the idea that reality is but our interpretation. What an ironic twist on the positivist origins of modern science!

The second is that, with the failure of a simple correspondence theory of truth to make its case, recent philosophers and others have argued for the confusion of the meaning of truth with criteria for truth. Hilary Putnam (1983, p. 272), for instance, writes

> What happens when metaphysical realism becomes dubious? Philosophers who reject metaphysical realism (Kant, Peirce, and in the present period, Dummett, Goodman, and myself, to name just a few 'specimens') typically argue for a conception of truth as (idealized) justification or rational acceptability.

Putnam had to present an argument to include Kant in that list, but it is clear that Peirce made the confusion when he defined truth as that opinion ultimately fated to be believed by the community of investigators in the infinite long run. Peirce's underlying argument was that the community would be corrected in its false opinions by appying his method of determining error, and toward the end of his life he came to give up that belief, and hence the definition of truth (Wells, 1965). Kuhn (1969) and Toulmin (1972) have contributed, perhaps unwittingly, to the confusion of the meaning of truth with criteria for truth by their magisterial accounts of why scientific communities exchange one theory for another; it seems easy to believe that the truth of a theory consists merely in the case to be made for it at a time. Richard Rorty (1979) has popularized the view that we do not even have truth, only beliefs for which a persuasive case can be made. And the advocates of philosophy as rhetoric have argued that reference to truth is just a misleading holdover of the nasty onto-theo-logocentric sins of the West.

But the conclusion simply does not follow from (1) the fact that we can judge claims for truth only by seeing what cases can be made for them that (2) truth is nothing more than a claim with a good case. Truth is rather the peculiar correspondence involved in the carryover of value from the object to the interpretation. Any interpretation has a hypothetical character; this is true even of perceptions, which makes them fallible in principle. Further, since the identification of objects for reference requires accepting a preinterpreted context, the fallibility in interpretations extends in all directions, not just to its immediate assertions. Therefore, *whether* some interpretation is true, or how far it is true, or how misleading further interpretations of it might be, is always a crucial question. Criteria for truth are needed.

Some philosophers in the past have tried to provide criteria that are not acceptable today; for instance, appeals to intuition, to revelation, to deductive certainty. Sensitivity to the multifariousness of the interpretive context, particluarly in philosophy, makes it wise to accept a very open approach to criteria: accept as true only those claims for which a good case can be made, and then be suspicious of the case (Toulmin, 1958). I have argued (1982, ch. 1) that this open-ended appeal to "best case" is required for a claim to be properly public and vulnerable. In all this, however, that for which one examines the case is whether an interpretation is true in the sense of saying of what is that it is and of what is not that it is not.

The heart of making a case for an interpretation is finding some avenue, or map of avenues, for checking the various causal connections between the object and the interpretation. This means not only the overt physical and social causal connections, but also those involved in the biological, cultural, semiotic, and purposive qualifications of the object in the interpretation. The more each of these connection points can be interpreted, the more a case can be made for or against the interpretation in question. Most of the time this simply means that we must reflect thoroughly on our lives and civilization in order to have good habits of judgment about interpretations. But some of the time it means reflectively undermining our interpretive habits. All of this is to allow the reality to be the measure of our interpretations, when we never get at reality except through interpretations.

Recovery of the Measure is merely the title of a heuristic task. Reality has always been the measure of our interpretations, even when we have deceived ourselves into believing the contrary. Like it or not, the actual world with its real normative possibilities is the standard against which our interpretations measure up well or badly. To be sure, there is no single "right" interpretation. Each interpretation represents its object in some respect, and that respect is conditioned by biological, cultural, semiotic, and purposive elements. In principle there are an infinite number of respects in which a thing can be interpreted, though in practice these are thrown into a finite number of classes or family groups by the unities of human nature, culture, semiotic systems, and culturally cultivated purposes. Relative to each respect of interpretation, there is a truth to be had and errors to be avoided; that is, worthy things to be appreciated and distortions of value to be avoided. Alternate respects of interpretation are neither true nor false relative to the first, just different, sometimes commensurable and sometimes not. The contextual relativity of cultures or even of personal points of view come from the fact that thematically different respects of interpretations are employed. Sometimes commensurating interpretive standpoints or respects can be found, and sometimes not; a commensurating standpoint would be able to show how all cultures or persons have possibilities for true interpretation according to their kind. That cultural or personal claims are different and incommensurable does not suggest that some one or other is not true in its own way. Far less does it suggest that no interpretations are true of the real world. Rather, all interpretive perspectives set themselves the task of attaining to the truth of the world according to the respect defining their nature, culture, signs, and purposes.

The contextual relativity of cultural and personal perspectives is by no means a moral relativity. The representationally defined structures that make up the intentional world of an interpretive project provide meaningfulness relative to the project. Yet the things of the world have real values, and it is an open question whether the carpentered representations of an interpretive project do much justice to those values. The subordination of women to men, for instance, is thought an evil in cultures deeply shaped by egalitarian principles, but a great good in cultures shaped by sternly patriarchal traditions; the subordination is wrong in any culture, however, whether or not the culture approves, because women and men are equally intelligent, conscious, and socially interrelated in all cultures. To make that judgment is not to stand outside every relative culture; it is only to occupy some culture that can see the natural characters of women and men that are universal irrespective of differences among cultures. Just as the real values in the world make demands on the purposes individuals ought to have, they make demands on the imaginative representations that go into defining cultures.

Although reality is the measure of interpretive human life, so much of our own culture seems to have lost its nerve about the fact. I have not tried to explain the motives for that loss of nerve (though see Cahoone, 1987). But I have tried to explain why it is a mistake that need not be made. A proper response to the recognition that the real world is the measure of interpretation is to embrace the multitude of tasks of testing our interpretations, extending them and making them more critical, responsive, and rich. Rather than accept Kant's Copernican Revolution, identifying reality only as it conforms to our conditions, the philosophic task for our civilization is to cultivate the critical disciplines of piety before the real, thereby recovering something of our measure.

Notes

INTRODUCTION

1. The phrase "lose the world" is an allusion to Richard Rorty's influential essay, "The World Well Lost," reprinted in 1982, pp. 3–18 (from *The Journal of Philosophy*, 69(1972), pp. 649–665). Although he diametrically opposes my point that it is not at all well that the world is lost, we agree in the main that the dominant proponents of interpretation-theory are the ones who lose it and get along without it. The historical issue is complicated in the case of the pragmatists. Whereas Rorty rightly calls attention to their theories of experience, and of the contextualizing of interpretation, he truncates his account of them, particularly of Peirce and Dewey, by neglecting both their philosophies of nature and their metaphysics. Thus he fails to see their proximity to Whitehead, and fails also to take the opportunities they afford to develop a different conception of world or reality that is compatible with the conclusions of interpretive philosophy. These issues shall be explored in subsequent chapters.

2. The most comprehensive interpreter of American philosophy, sensitive alike to the conceptions of community, experience, value, nature, and metaphysics, is John E. Smith. See, for instance, his *Purpose and Thought* (1978) and *The Spirit of American Philosophy* (1983). For a highly epistemological approach to pragmatism, see Margolis, 1986.

3. I have traced out and defended Peirce's critique of Kant's argument at the end of the *Critique of Pure Reason* against the "method of hypothesis" as a means for metaphysics, in 1981, pp. 150–52.

DIVISION I THE WORLD AS MEASURE

PRELIMINARY REMARKS

1. Still the clearest exposition of the strategies of the correspondence, coherence, and pragmatic theories is that laid out by Brand Blanshard (1939). Blanshard himself holds to the coherence theory. The best recent critical review of the ideas is by Carl

Vaught (1987). The moral Vaught draws from the review is that any account of truth must capture the insight of "otherness" at the base of correspondence, and "openness" at the bases of coherence and pragmatic conceptions. His own account develops notions of metaphor and analogy to preserve both otherness and openness. See also Hesse, 1988.

CHAPTER 1 THE PROBLEM OF TRUTH

1. I have argued (1986) that both Hegel and Whitehead make illegitimate appeals to the notion of totality in their systems, but that systematic philosophy is still possible without claims for totality.

2. "Being in a world" is a phrase reminiscent of Heidegger's characterizaton of *Dasein*, "being in the world." Heidegger (1962) was surely right that people experience themselves as in a world, and that they experience the world as a context for themselves. He intended his phrase to mark a transcendental condition for human life; that is, "being in the world" is the condition under which natural processes can be conceived. As it is used in the present context, however, "being in the world" indicates a special set of causal processes within a larger range of nature. Although human beings cannot experience or think of nature except under the conditions of the form of experience, this fact does not entail that those experiential conditions themselves are the only conditions of nature. The experiential priority of the forms of experience can be rendered within a naturalistic theory without recourse to a transcendental turn such as Heidegger's. Further, where Heidegger assumes "the" world for *Dasein*, the very fact that all interpretation takes place within the prior conditions of imaginative forms of experience renders the uniqueness, indeed the reality, of "world" problematic. Does a person have one world or many, or even any "real" worlds?

3. I have explored this view of judgment at length (Neville: 1981, Pt. II). Imagination is not necessarily limited to human beings. Perhaps the basic structure of imagination should be taken to be definitive of "experiencing beings." The point of the discussion in the text is to acknowledge the limit or autonmy of human imagination. David Hall agrees with this distinction of imagination from interpretation, or what he calls "referencing" and "ordering," but draws quite different conclusions from mind; he holds that the concern for truth is a special case of moral concern (I think morality is a special case of truth-concerns) and that moral concerns are a bad thing. The reason they are bad, in his view, is that they involve imposing an order based on human interest over the intrinsic diversity of the world. See Hall, 1987.

4. I analyze and criticize Peirce's view of sign, object, interpretant, and "respect" in "Intuition," 1967. This essay contains the germ of the theory developed in this book, but without sufficient awareness of the problem of reality on an interpretation model.

5. For a contemporary defense of the Aristotelian position, see Walhout, 1978.

6. See Moore (1903), especially p. 10, where he wrote

> It may be true that all things which are good are *also* something else, just as it is true that all things which are yellow produce a certain kind of vibration in the light. And it is a fact, that Ethics aims at discovering what are those other

> properties belonging to all things which are good. But far too many philosophers have thought that when they named those other properties they were actually defining good; that these properties, in fact, were simply not 'other,' but absolutely and entirely the same with goodness. This view I propose to call the 'naturalistic fallacy' and of it I shall now endeavor to dispose.

7. For a subtle development of this thesis see M. M. Bakhtin (1981), who argues that the very form of the novel, especially for instance in Rabelais, involves a subversion of the "finished narrative" perspective characteristic of the epic. The deconstructionists, of course, take pride in their techniques of subversion (Culler, 1982; Lentricchia, 1980).

CHAPTER 2 PHILOSOPHICAL STRATEGIES

1. When a tradition has fallen into confusion, it is too easy to criticize its founders; poor Descartes is taking his lumps in the literature these days. He should be given proper credit for rescuing the struggling impulses of modern science from the confusion of the late medieval and Renaissance periods. Indeed, the philosophy textbooks of a generation ago did just that and perhaps we now are only riding out the opposing swing of the pendulum.

2. Rene Descartes (1956, p. 12). In this work, in the *Meditations*, and in many other writings, Descartes discussed the nature of "simplicity" as the smallest part that is wholly perspicuous to "the light of nature." John Locke attacked what he took to be Descartes' notion of simple ideas; but he substituted his own version of simplicity, the idea of sense data or simple perceptions. Thus both the rationalist and the empiricist traditions were concerned to find basic units of reality, and to conceive of things as complexes built up out of these units.

3. Often this substitution is unconscious, as in Descartes' case. With Kant, the substitution was conscious and given an honorific title: a Copernican Revolution; Kant's philosophy affirms both Descartes' theory of analysis and reconstruction, and the principle of context-dependence; its strategy is to give the analytical construct a transcendental status, defining criteria of reality.

4. Describing his theory, Fodor writes, "The theory of mind it looks a lot like is Descartes', blending, as it does, elements of mentalism and nativism. But much of Descartes' ontological and epistemological baggage has gone overboard, and what is left has recognizable affinities with the Empiricist tradition too" (1981, p. 1).

5. For a basic statement of functionalism, see Fodor (1983); see also Rozin (1976). For sympathetic philosophical evaluations of these views, see George Wolf (1984) and Jay Schulkin (1987). For an interesting discussion of whether functionalism can do without reference to mental staes, see Fodor's Introduction (1981).

6. See Gallistel (1980) for an extended explanation and defense of the hierarchical model of intelligent behavior.

7. In *Schools for Tomorros*, republished in Dewey: 1979, pp. 309-313; see also his criticisms in 1980, p. 160.

8. For a definitive exposition of this point, see John E. Smith, 1978.

9. See Rosenthal, 1986, especially chapter 8. Rosenthal discusses (p. 188) the following statement by John Dewey: "Man is under just as much obligation to develop his most advanced standards and ideals as to use conscientiously those which he already possesses" (Dewey: 1982, p. 180).

CHAPTER 3 TRUTH: AN AXIOLOGICAL HYPOTHESIS

1. The theory of imagination I elaborated in 1981 Pt. II, argued that form is a function of value rather than the other way around.

2. The claim that knowledge is not intuitive is by no means innocent, and it will be defended throughout this book. See the brilliant attack on intuition in David Weissman, 1987. He too makes the case that philosophy is hypothetical, as illustrated in this book and defended at length in Neville, 1981.

3. The array of imagination, interpretation, theorizing, and responsibility is the ground plan for my axiological theory, and is explained in 1981, ch. 1.

4. The point about the corruption of value language is well made by Allan Bloom, 1987. His chapter on "The German Connection" traces the degeneration of moral language through Nietzsche, Heidegger, Weber, and Freud. His anti-German racism, of course, is not to be respected.

5. Actually, the modern Western tradition has associated itself with a thesis that in fact constitutes a reason to truncate the interpretive process from its object. Most modern philosophy has assumed a metaphysics of causation positing that objects do not themselves enter the consequent things that respond to and interpret them, but instead are self-contained and might be only represented or mirrored later. This modern conception perhaps is an adequate metaphysics of causation for a scientific procedure noting only the regularity with which causal features appear, not the existential means by which they do so. But it is not an adequate conception for explaining the natural processes of interpretation by which knowledge arises. Whitehead (1925) has sufficiently criticized the modern conception of causation that supposes what he called "simple location." In line with Whitehead's point, the development of a doctrine of "multiple effective location" is key to the theory of causation presented later in chapters 11 and 12. Hermeneutical philosophies, which do not pay much attention to revising the modern conception of causation, continue to run grave risks of losing the real full object with its constitutive value. For they view objects not as involved in a natural process of interpretation, but only in terms of their objectification as intentional objects defined by the outcome of interpretation.

CHAPTER 5 IDENTITY

1. This is the point so well brought out in Justus Buchler's principle of ontological parity (1966). Anything that has identity, which he characterized as being a natural complex (a point consistent with the theory below), is real just insofar as it has identity.

2. For my own acount of the difference between metaphysics, ontology, and cosmology, see Neville: 1974, pp. 26–28.

3. "Ontological parity" is Justice Buchler's term by means of which he characterized all "natural complexes" as being equally real. He criticized Whitehead for sometimes giving ontological priority to actual occasions, speaking of them as the "true beings." But Whitehead's point is that some realities are inclusive of other realities, whereas the others cannot exist without the inclusive ones. This is to point out the important difference in kind between realities, a point Buchler would have to accept. See Buchler, 1966 and 1983.

CHAPTER 6 BEING AND PRIMARY COSMOLOGY

1. Another and more profound manifestation of the death of God is loss of confidence in an extra-worldly protector, with the consequence that we had better meet other things within the world on their own terms; in Altizer's theology (1977), the way to do this is through a self-emptying like Jesus'.

2. Paul Weiss is the contemporary thinker who probably has thought most thoroughly about the nature of what I have called primary cosmology. In *Modes of Being* (1958), whose categories I listed above, he treated the categories precisely as modes of being, tracing their intricate interactions. The interactions illustrate the distinction between essential and conditional features, each mode having its essential features and each being conditioned by the other three. But what is the being of which they are modes? On reflection, Weiss abandoned the being-mode distinction and reconceived the modes as Finalities, those things which are ultimately appealed to in order to account for appearances. That is, appearances, or our concrete world, is a product of the interaction of the Finalities. By the time of *Beyond All Appearances* (1974), Weiss had elaborated the theory of Finalities in some detail, and added being as a finality to actuality, ideality, existence, and God.

3. For a more detailed analysis of the implications of this paragraph for normative description, see Neville: 1987, chs. 4, 6, and 7.

4. For more discussion of this irony, see Hall, 1982; and Neville: 1987, chs. 1, 10, and 11.

CHAPTER 7 VALUE

1. See Bernstein, 1971, 1976, and 1983. I have disputed Bernstein's way of reading Aristotle, and his surprising neglect of Plato on the topic of action, in Neville: 1981, pp. 58–60.

2. Robert Bellah and his associates (1985) detail in intereseting ways the contemporary American approach to personal values.

3. For an analysis of the historical problem and an overview of the "axiology of thinking," see Neville: 1981, ch. 1; for a discussion of the role of metaphysics and cosmology, see chapter 2 in that work. The most effective popular attack on the dualistic assumptions of modernity is Richard Rorty, 1979. See also Bernstein, 1971, 1976, 1983. Perhaps the most persuasive analysis of the fact-value distinction and problems of "objectivity" is Lawrence E. Cahoone, 1987.

4. An earlier and alternative expression of this theory was presented in Neville: 1974, ch. 3, and yet in a different form in 1981, chs. 3–4. A practical explication of the theory is found in 1987, chs. 4, 6, and 7.

5. See the various discussions of the Good in Books 5, 6, and 7 of the *Republic*, and of normative measure in the *Statesman*.

6. See *Republic* Bk. VI, 506e–509b. For instance, at 509b Plato wrote (I quote first the Greek because many people dismiss my conclusion as a bad translation):

> Kai tois gignoskomenois toinun me monon to gignoskesthai phanai hup' ekainou autois proseinai, ouk ousias ontos tou agathou, all' eti epekeina tas ousias presbeiai kai dunamei huperboles.
>
> In like manner, then, you are to say that the objects of knowledge not only receive from the presence of the good their being known, but their very existence and essence is derived to them from it, though the good itself is not essence but still transcends essence in dignity and surpassing power (Shorey translation).

7. See my detailed analysis of Plato's text in 1974, ch. 3. See the *Statesman* 283c–287b. Plato wrote, for instance

> In our present discussion too there is an additional postulate on which we must insist, and it is this. 'Excess and deficiency are measurable not only in relative terms but also in respect of attainment of a norm or due measure.' For if we cannot first gain assent to this postulate, we are bound to fail if we advance the claim that a man possesses statecraft, or indeed that a man possesses any other of the special forms of knowledge that function in human society. . . . When one day we come to give a full exposition of true accuracy in dialectic method, we shall find the need of this postulate concerning the due measure which we have just enunciated. However, the statement in the form that we have made it and with the demonstratoin – adequate for present purposes – which we have given of it, is a very great help to us, or so it seems to me. For it shows that two propositions stand or fall together. The first is that the arts exist; the second is that excess and deficiency are measurable not only relatively but in terms of the realization of a norm or due measure (284b–d; Skemp translation).

CHAPTER 8 HARMONY: A THEORY OF COMPONENTS

1. I have discussed this difficulty in Weiss's theory in several places: 1968, ch. 2; 1970; and 1972. Weiss has restated his position in 1974 and 1977.

CHAPTER 9 MODALITIES OF TIME

1. Time is not a new question, of course. Perhaps the most telling characteristic of any culture in any period is its assumptions about time and history. In the Western philosophical tradition we still orient ourselves by the options posed by Heracleitus and Parmenides; the views of Plato and Aristotle, Plotinus and Augustine, Locke and Descartes need to be assessed as our contemporaries. Kant and Hegel determined the major options for our own thinking. Yet the twentieth century has made

time most problematic because its common sense has been shattered in theory and in practice. In theory, relativity and quantum mechanics have upset our assumptions about the continuity and regularity of time. In practice, our wars, oppressions, and economic exploitations have brought assumptions of cumulative temporal progress to ruin. Three of the four most influential philosophic books of the first half of this century were centered on the theme of time: John Dewey's *Experience and Nature* (1st ed., 1925; 1981), Martin Heidegger's *Being and Time* (1st ed., 1927, 1962), and Alfred North Whitehead's *Process and Reality* (1st ed., 1929, 1978). Only Ludwig Wittgenstein's *Tractatus Logico-Philosophicus* (1922), of the founding books of our century's philosophy, escapes a serious concern with time, not because the author was unaware of either the new physics then brewing or of the Great War, but because their very harsh proximity knocked him into a mystical retreat from the scale of things measured in time; see Russell Nieli, 1987.

2. See for instance Dewey, 1981; Heidegger, 1962; and Whitehead, 1978.

3. See, for instance, his poem "Mr. Burnshaw and the Statue," in 1972, pp. 119 and 125.

4. This paragraph expresses ideas analyzed in great detail by Whitehead as genetic division in 1978, Pt. III. For an explanation and practical expansion of them, see Brumbaugh, 1982.

5. From the first and fifth chapters of the *Tao Teh Ching*, as translated by Wing tsit Chan, 1963, pp. 139 and 141.

6. Hartshorne, following Whitehead, sharply distinguishes ontological creativity from God. But on his scheme they work together to create in much the way the text here depicts. That is, creativity always makes a spontaneous new one out of the previous many; God lures each spontaneous process of concrescence. Therefore, God plus creativity account for everything new in any entity, and they also account for what is old in that entity by having cooperated to create it in its own dated present. See for instance Hartshorne, 1962; and Neville, 1980.

CHAPTER 10 TEMPORAL THINGS: ENDURANCE, PERISHING, AND CHANGE

1. Only in the biological works did Aristotle pay much attention to the internal relation of individual final causes to one another. For instance, the shark, he said, rolls over on its back to attack in order to blunt the efficiency of its powers, because otherwise it would eat up all the fish in the sea.

CHAPTER 11 SPACE AND MOTION

1. By now the classic discussion of these problems is Adolf Gruenbaum, 1963. The first part of that work discusses the "metric" of space and time, showing how in the twentieth century they have come to be measured together as space-time. Part II analyzes their topology, and our era's preoccupation is displayed in that four of the five chapters of that part are about time, and only one about space. Philosophy of science, of course, is not the only philosophic discipline concerned with space and time. Heidegger's *Being and Time* is one of the most influential books of the century, almost wholly neglecting space or relegating it to prepositional status ("withness,"

"beforeness," "at handedness," relative to temporally defined things). Much twentieth century philosophy has been motivated in its thoughts about nature by a rejection of the "spatialization" of nature, as Bergson complained, with a consequent emphasis on its dynamic, temporal elements. This expressed itself in Peirce's theory of interpretation, in James' emphasis on passage in pure experience, and in Dewey's identification of things by their origins and consequences. Although emphasizing process, as is so well known, Whitehead joined space to time in his metrical conception of space-time, yet with an irony. The dimensional analysis of space-time in Part IV of *Process and Reality* is so abstract as to apply indifferently to space or time, or to any other dimensions; as a result, the concrete analysis of space-time is almost wholly exhausted by the theory of prehension and succession in other parts of the book. The best attempt to flesh out Whitehead's theory of space is in Jorge Luis Nobo, 1986; the success of this attempt depends on altering the standard interpretation of the theory of prehension, however, and thus the controversy reverts to questions of succession. It is instructive that in a recent quite brilliant collection of essays by and about the work of Bohm and Prigogine on motion, edited by David R. Griffin (1986) of the Center for Process Studies, the title gives "ultimacy" to time alone: *Physics and the Ultimate Significance of Time: Bohm, Prigogine, and Process Philosophy*. Dorothy Emmet, 1985, attempting to unite both the insights of the early Whitehead and the discussions of nature in twentieth century analytic philosophy, argues persuasively that causation should be conceived as organic interaction of elements within events rather than as exchanges between events; yet the "within events" side is not developed into a theory of space, or even space-time, except in an early Whiteheadian sense.

2. On Whitehead's theory, motion is possible only for a society of occasions, not for an occasion itself. Only actual occasions, for him, are *res verae*. Philosophers since Paul Weiss in *Reality* (1938) have argued that the kinds of unity possible for Whiteheadian societies are insufficient to account for unified agency in motion. The most original attempt to save Whitehead's view is F. B. Wallach's expansion of the idea of an actual occasion to conceive large occasions containing smaller ones (1980).

3. Indeed, the problem is more difficult even than this. Kant's critique of metaphysics had the effect, for those who believe it, of relegating *all* discussion of nature to the natural sciences, and limiting philosophy to epistemological discussion of the sciences. This effectively eliminates philosophy of nature itself, transforming it to the epistemological business of philosophy of science. Of course, Kant need not be believed.

4. See, for instance, his detailed analyses in *Being and Time* (1962, ch. 4, pp. 334f); or see the essays in *The End of Philosophy* (1973).

5. My *Reconstruction of Thinking* (1981, ch. 4, especially pp. 187–190) provides a detailed analysis of the "natural act" of thinking in terms of feeling (the past), judging (intentionality with a future orientation), and spontaneity (present concrescence); general norms for each of these aspects are discussed. Consciousness, as opposed to thinking, which has many non-conscious elements, is not as important or central a phenomenon, surely not philosophically constitutive, as many twentieth century thinkers of the phenomenological and existentialist traditions have believed.

6. See Plato's discussion in the *Republic*, Book VI, especially around 509, where he wrote the passage quoted in Chapter 7, note 6, above.

7. See his various discussions of John Locke, of the ontological principle, and the principle of relativity in *Process and Reality* (1978); for instance, in Part II, chapter 1, sections vi and vii.

8. Many philosophers before Whitehead of course had acknowledged creativity within the present moment, but none had given an elaborate theoretical account. Peirce was one of the most inventive in this regard in his doctrine of chance and growing Thirdness; but his view was still romantic in its appeal to vitalist sensibilities.

9. A detailed critical analysis of Whitehead's treatment of change, including its capacities for explaining experiential phenomena, was given in my 1981, chs. 3-8. While acknowledging the categoreal distinctions between what Whitehead called the physical and mental, it is important to reserve mental language for only those few instances of what he described as univeral mentality, and what his disciples have proclaimed as panpsychism, that have the form of experience in something like a human sense. *Reconstruction of Thinking* gives a careful analysis of the distinction between universal prehension and experience, in which the latter is only the prehension formed by the special syntheses of imagination. All experience has the form of imagination. In Whitehead's language, this is close to saying that experience is to be identified with presentational immediacy, except that experiential syntheses also include the felt depth of vectors of historical forces and the normativeness of transcendent possibilities.

10. See, for instance, Norris Clarke, 1961.

11. One of Whitehead's best statements is the following (1978, pp. 214-215):

> To sum up: There are two species of process, macroscopic process and microscopic process. The macroscopic process is the translation from attained actuality to actuality in attainment; while the microscopic process is the conversion of conditions which are merely real into determinate actuality. The former process effects the transition from the 'actual' to the 'merely real'; and the latter process effects the growth from the real to the actual. The former process is efficient; the latter process is teleological. The future is merely real, without being actual; whereas the past is a nexus of actualities. The actualities are constituted by their real genetic phases. The present is the immediacy of teleological processes whereby reality becomes actual. The former process provides the conditions which really govern attainment; whereas the latter process provides the ends actually attained. The notion of 'organism' is combined with that of 'process' in a twofold manner. The community of actual things is an organism; but it is not a static organism. It is an incompletion in process of producton. Thus the expansion of the universe in respect to actual things is the first meaning of 'process'; and the universe in any stage of its expansion is the first meaning of 'organism.' In this sense, an organism is a nexus.

A very interesting recent study of this issue in Whitehead is Nobo, 1986.

DIVISION IV TRUTH AND INTERPRETATION

PRELIMINARY REMARKS

1. I used the term "network meaning" in a coordinated distinction from "content meaning" in *The Tao and the Daimon* (1982, pp. 225–229), and the discussions later in chapters 13 and 14 elaborate the relevant notions. Mary Hesse (1988) has independently used the phrase "network meaning," however, in an excellent article that argues that all language is metaphorical. I agree thoroughly with her position, though I believe that the defense of the claim that all language is metaphorical will have to acknowledge content meaning as distinct from but related to network meaning. Network meaning refers to meaning in codes. Content meaning refers to the way the coded elements organize much experience that is not itself significant for its coded form. On the ubiquity of metaphorical language, see Vaught, 1987.

CHAPTER 13 NETWORK MEANING

1. Most of his terms to which I refer are explained in Searle (1969, ch. 2).

2. See the discussion of this trend in deconstruction in Caputo, 1987.

CHAPTER 15 INTENTIONALITY

1. My adaptation and amendment of Whitehead's theory is thoroughly discussed in Neville: 1981, Ch. 4.

CHAPTER 16 INTERPRETATION

1. Nominalism is a difficult and controversial position to define, and really ought not be characterized outside the system of some particular nominalistic philosopher, as nominalists would insist. For present shorthand purposes, I take nominalism to be the claim that only individuals or particular substances have actual reality; further, their reality is simply located. Nominalism thus stands opposed to "realism" where "realism" means the theory that universals or generals have reality in the actual world as well as in mind. With the Scotistic theory of "common natures" advocated earlier, I follow Peirce in being a realist in this sense (see John F. Boler's *Charles Peirce and Scholastic Realism*, 1963). "Realism" is also a term that has come to mean the theory that things have reality independent of mind, and this is the meaning of the term in most modern discussion. Realism in this sense of mind-independence contrasts with one meaning of idealism, which is that the objects of mental intention are only mental constructs, and not "really" independent. Nominalists can be realists in this sense of mind independence (as in Kripke, 1977) and other nominalists (such as Putnam, 1978) can be idealists, believing that what the mind intends are particulars though not independent of mind; epistemological idealism is a nasty word in contemporary philosophy (though it was not in the previous generation, as for instance in the work of Brand Blanshard, 1939) and so most such idealists talk about the "con-

vergence of theories." Idealism also has another meaning, associated with Plato, according to which it signifies those theories that say that actual things are to be understood as embodying value, and thus can be judged with regard to whether they embody as much as they should or the right kind; moral idealism contrasts with materialism, which asserts that there are just facts. The axiological theory I have put forward here is a moral idealism. Moral materialism of the sort that contrasts with moral idealism can be different from cosmological materialism. Cosmological materialism is the view that both actualities and possibilities, including norms and ideal forms, are to be understood as elements of temporal process; it contrasts with cosmological idealism which says that the realm of universals or eternal objects is metaphysically independent of the realm of temporal process. Whitehead is a cosmological idealist with his theory of eternal objects; by virtue of explaining eternal objects as the essential features of the future, I am a cosmological materialist. To summarize the application of these confusing labels to the theory defended here, it is a metaphysical realism with regard to universals, and thus not nominalism, an epistemological realism with regard to the mind-independence of things, and hence not epistemological idealism, a moral idealism with regard to norms, hence not moral materialism, and a cosmological materialism with regard to universals, hence not a cosmological idealism.

2. In his wonderful essay, "Existence and Hermeneutics," Paul Ricoeur wrote:

> It is useful to recall that the hermeneutic problem was first raised within the limits of *exegesis*, that is, within the framework of a discipline which proposes to understand a text—to understand it beginnnig with its intention, on the basis of what it attempts to say. If exegesis raised a hermeneutic problem, that is, a problem of interpretaton, it is because every reading of a text always takes place within a community, a tradition, or a living current of thought, all of which display presuppositions and exigencies—regardless of how closely a reading may be tied to the *quid*, to "that in view of which" the text was written. (1974, p. 3, translated by Kathleen McLaughlin)

In addition to that essay, for a history of hermeneutics from a European point of view, see Bleicher, 1980. Derrida is one of the few representatives of the European tradition to see much of value in the American tradition begun by Peirce; but he does not appreciate the extent of the difference caused by the difference in paradigmatic interpretive object—nature vs. text.

Bibliography

Altizer, Thomas J. J.

1977 *The Self-Embodiment of God.* New York: Harper & Row.

1985 *History as Apocalypse.* Albany: State University of New York Press.

Bakhtin, M. M.

1981 *The Dialogic Imagination: Four Essays*, edited by Michael Holquist and translated by Caryl Emerson and Michael Holquist. Austin, Texas: University of Texas Press.

Bataille, George

1986 *Erotism: Death and Sensuality*. Translated by Mary Dalwood. San Francisco: City Lights Books. Original French edition, 1957.

Bellah, Robert, *et alia*

1985 *Habits of the Heart.* Berkeley: University of California Press.

Berger, Peter L.

1969 *The Sacred Canopy: Elements of a Sociological Theory of Religion.* Garden City: Doubleday Anchor.

Bernstein, Richard J.

1965 Editor, *Perspectives on Peirce.* New Haven: Yale University Press.

1971 *Praxis and Action*. Philadelphia: University of Pennsylvania Press.

1976 *The Restructuring of Social and Political Theory*. New York: Harcourt Brace Jovanovich.

1983 *Beyond Objectivism and Relativism: Science, Hermeneutics, and Praxis*. Philadelphia: University of Pennsylvania Press.

Blanshard, Brand

1939 *The Nature of Thought*, in two volumes. London: George Allen and Unwin.

Bleicher, Josef

1980 *Contemporary Hermeneutics: Hermeneutics as Method, Philosophy and Critique*. London: Routledge & Kegan Paul.

Bloom, Allan

1987 *The Closing of the American Mind*. New York: Simon and Schuster.

Boler, John F.

1963 *Charles Peirce and Scholastic Realism: A Study of Peirce's Relation to John Duns Scotus*. Seattle: University of Washington Press.

Bordo, Susan

1987 *The Flight to Objectivity*. Albany: State University of New York Press.

Brumbaugh, Robert S.

1982 *Whitehead, Process Philosophy, and Education*. Albany: State University of New York Press.

1984 *Unreality and Time*. Albany: State University of New York Press.

Buchler, Justus

1966 *Metaphysics of Natural Complexes*. New York: Columbia University Press.

1983 "A Strain of Arbitrariness in Whitehead's System," in Ford and Kline.

Cahoone, Lawrence E.

1988 *The Dilemma of Modernity: Philosophy, Culture, and Anti-Culture*. Albany: State University of New York Press.

Capaldi, Nicholas

1987 "Copernican Metaphysics," in Neville, 1987a.

Caputo, John

1987 *Radical Hermeneutics*. Bloomington: Indiana University Press.

Cavell, Stanley

1979 *The Claim of Reason: Wittgenstein, Skepticism, Morality, and Tragedy*. New York: Oxford University Press.

Chan, Wing-tsit

1963 *A Source Book in Chinese Philosophy*. Princeton: Princeton University Press.

Chisholm, Roderick M., editor

1960 *Realism and the Background of Phenomenology*. New York: Free Press.

Clarke, Norris, S.J.

1961 "Causality and Time," in *Experience, Existence, and the Good: Essays in Honor of Paul Weiss*, edited by Irwin C. Lieb. Carbondale: Southern Illinois University Press, pp. 141–157.

Cobb, John B., Jr.

1980 "Three Responses to Neville's *Creativity and God*," with Charles Hartshorns and Lewis S. Ford, in *Process Studies*, 10/3–4 (Fall-Winter).

Cobb, John B., Jr. and Franklin Gamwell, editors

1984 *Existence and Actuality*. Chicago: University of Chicago Press.

Colapietro, Vincent M.

1988 "Human Agency: The Habits of Our Being," in *The Southern Journal of Philosophy*, 26/2, pp. 153–168.

Culler, Jonathan

1982 *On Deconstruction: Theory and Criticism after Structuralism*. Ithaca, N.Y.: Cornell University Press.

1986 *Ferdinande de Saussure*, revised edition. Ithaca, N.Y.: Cornell University Press.

Davidson, Donald

1974 "On the Very Idea of a Conceptual Scheme," in the *Proceedings of the American Philosophical Association*, XLVII (November), pp. 5–20.

Derrida, Jacques

1973 *Speech and Phenomena, and Other Essays on Husserl's Theory of Signs*, translated with an introduction by David B. Allison. Evanston: Northwestern University Press.

1976 *Of Grammatology*, translated by Gayatri Chakravorty Spivak. Baltimore: The Johns Hopkins University Press.

1979 "The Supplement of Copula: Philosophy *before* Linguistics," in Harari, 1979, 82–120.

Descartes, Rene

1934 *Philosophical Works of Descartes, Volume II*, translated by Elizabeth S. Haldane and G.R.T. Ross. Dover reprint, 1955.

1956 *Discourse on Method*, second edition; translated by Laurence J. Lafleur. New York: The Liberal Arts Press.

Dewey, John

1916 *Essays in Experimental Logic*. Chicago: University of Chicago Press.

1934 *Art As Experience*. New York: Putnam's Sons.

1934a *A Common Faith*. New Haven, Conn.: Yale University Press.

1938 *Logic: The Theory of Inquiry*. New York: Henry Holt.

1939 *Theory of Valuation*. Chicago: University of Chicago Press.

1978 *The Middle Works, 1899–1924, Volume 6: 1910–1911*, edited by Jo Ann Boydston. Carbondale: Southern Illinois University Press.

1979 *Essays on Education and Politics: The Middle Works of John Dewey, 1899–1924, Volume 8: 1915*, edited by Jo Ann Boydston. Carbondale: Southern Illinois University Press.

1980 *Democracy and Education: The Middle Works of John Dewey, 1899–1924, Volume 9: 1916*, edited by Jo Ann Boydston. Carbondale: Southern Illinois University Press.

1981 *Experience and Nature*, in *The Later Works, Volume I*, edited by Jo Ann Boydston. Originally published in 1925.

1982 *Reconstruction in Philosophy*, in *The Middle Works, Volume XII*, edited by Jo Ann Boydston.

1984 *The Quest for Certainty*, in *The Later Works, Volume IV*, edited by Jo Ann Boydston. Originally published in 1929.

19894a *Essays et alia*, in *The Later Works, Volume V*, edited by Jo Ann Boydston. Material published in 1929–30.

Edwards, Jonathan

1959 *Religious Affections*, edited by John E. Smith. Volume II of *The Works of Jonathan Edwards*, Perry Miller and John E. Smith, general editors. New Haven: Yale University Press.

Eliade, Mircea

1961 *The Sacred and the Profane*. New York: Harper Torchbook.

Emmet, Dorothy

1985 *The Effectiveness of Causes*. Albany: State University of New York Press.

Findlay, J. N.

1970 *Axiological Ethics*. London: Macmillan.

Fodor, Jerry A.

1981 *Representations: Philosophical Essays on the Foundations of Cognitive Science*. Cambridge, Mass. MIT Press.

1983 *The Modularity of Mind*. Cambridge, Mass.: MIT Press.

Ford, Lewis S.

1980 "Three Responses to Neville's *Creativity and God*," with John B. Cobb, Jr. and Charles Hartshorne, in *Process Studies*, 10/3–4 (Fall–Winter).

Ford, Lewis S. and George L. Kline, editors

1983 *Explorations in Whitehead's Philosophy*. New York: Fordham University Press.

Freud, Sigmund

1920 *Beyond the Pleasure Principle*. Volume 18 is the *Standard Edition of the Complete Works of Sigmund Freud*, edited by J. Strachey. London: Hogarth Press, 1886–1939.

Gadamer, Hans-Georg

1975 *Truth and Method*, edited by Garrett Barden and John Cumming. New York: The Seabury Press. Original publication, 1960.

1976 *Philosophical Hermeneutics*, translated and edited by David E. Linge. Berkeley: University of California Pres.

1986 *The Idea of the Good in Platonic-Aristotelian Philosophy*. Translated by P. Chrisopher Smith. New Haven: Yale University Press.

Gallistel, C. R.

1980 *The Organization of Action: A New Synthesis*. Hillsdale, N.J.: Lawrence Erlbaum Associates, Publishers.

Goodman, Nelson

1978 *Ways of Worldmaking*. Indianapolis: Hackett.

Griffin, David R., editor

1986 *Physics and the Ultimate Significance of Time: Bohm, Prigogine, and Process Philosophy*. Albany: State University of New York Press.

Gruenbaum, Adolf

1963 *Philosophical Problems of Space and Time*. New York: Knopf.

Hall, David L.

1982 *Eros and Irony*. Albany, State University of New York Press.

1987 "Logos, Mythos, Chaos: Metaphysics as the Quest for Diversity," in Neville, 1987a.

Harari, Josue V.

1979 *Textual Strategies: Perspectives in Post-Structuralist Criticism*. Ithaca, N.Y.: Cornell University Press.

1979a "Critical Factions/Critical Fictions," in Harari, 1979, pp. 17–72.

Hartshorne, Charles

1962 *The Logic of Perfection and Other Essays*. LaSalle, Ill.: Open Court Publishing Company.

1980 "Three Responses to Neville's *Creativity and God*," with John B. Cobb, Jr., and Lewis S. Ford, in *Process Studies*, 10/3–4 (Fall–Winter).

Heelan, Patrick A.

1983 *Space-Perceptions and the Philosophy of Science*. Berkeley: University of California Press.

Heidegger, Martin

1949 "On the Essence of Truth," translated by R. F. C. Hull and Alan Crick, in *Existence and Being*, edited with an introduction by Werner Brock. Chicago: Henry Regnery.

1962 *Being and Time*, translated by John Macquarrie and Edward Robinson. London: SCM Press. Original German edition, 1927.

1968 *What is Called Thinking?*, translated by J. Glenn Gray. New York: Harper and Row. Original German edition, 1954.

1971 *Poetry, Language, Thought*, translated by Albert Hofstadter. New York: Harper and Row.

1973 *The End of Philosophy*, translated by Joan Stambaugh. New York: Harper & Row.

Hesse, Mary

1988 "The Cognitive Claims of Metaphor," in *The Journal of Speculative Philosophy*, 2/1, 1–16.

Hobbes, Thomas

1959 *Leviathan*. Introduction by A. D. Lindsay. New York: Dutton. Original edition, 1561.

Hume, David

1888 *A Treatise of Human Nature*, edited by L. A. Selby-Bigge. Oxford: Clarendon Press. Original edition, 1739.

1955 *An Inquiry Concerning Human Understanding*, edited by Charles W. Hendel. New York: Liberal Arts Press. Original edition, 1748.

Husserl, Edmund

1962 *Ideas: General Introduction to Pure Phenomenology*, translated by W. R. Boyce Gibson. New York: Collier Books. Original edition, 1913.

James, William

1890 *Principles of Psychology*. Two volumes. New York: Henry Holt.

1892 *Psychology*. New York: Henry Holt.

Kant, Immanuel

1956 *Critique of Pure Reason*, translated by Norman Kemp Smith. London: MacMillan.

1956a *Critique of Practical Reason*, translated by Lewis White Beck. New York: Liberal Arts Press.

Kripke, Saul A.

1977 "Identity and Necessity," in Stephen P. Schwartz, editor, *Naming, Necessity, and Natural Kinds*. Ithaca: Cornell University Press.

1980 *Naming and Necessity*. Cambridge: Harvard University Press.

Kuhn, Thomas S.

1962 *The Structure of Scientific Revolutions*. Chicago: University of Chicago Press.

Lasch, Christopher

1979 *The Culture of Narcissism*. New York: Warner Books.

Lentricchia, Frank

1980 *After the New Criticism*. Chicago: University of Chicago Press.

Levi-Strauss

1967 *Structural Anthropology*, translated by Claire Jacobson and Brooke Grunfest Schoepf. New York: Anchor Books.

Locke, John

1947 *Two Treatises of Government*, edited by Thomas I. Cook, New York: Hafner. Original, anonymous, incorrect edition, 1690.

Lucas, George R., Jr.

1979 *Two Views of Freedom in Process Thought: A Study of Hegel and Whitehead*. Chico, CA: Scholars Press.

1983 *The Genesis of Modern Process Thought: A Historical Outline with Bibliography*. Metuchen, N.J.: Scarecrow.

1986 *Hegel and Whitehead: Contemporary Perspectives on Systematic Philosophy*, editor. Albany: State University of New York Press.

Margolis, Joseph

1986 *Pragmatism Without Foundations: Reconciling Realism and Relativism*. Oxford: Basil Blackwell.

Merleau-Ponty, Maurice

1968 *The Visible and the Invisible*. Evanston, Ill.: Northwestern University Press.

Millikan, Ruth Garrett

1984 *Language, Thought, and Other Biological Categories: New Foundations for Realism*. Cambridge, Mass.: The MIT Press.

Moore, G. E.

1903 *Principia Ethica*. Cambridge: Cambridge University Press.

Neville, Robert C.

1967 "Intuition," in *International Philosophical Quarterly* 7(December), pp. 556–590.

1968 *God the Creator: On the Transcendence and Presence of God*. Chicago: University of Chicago Press.

1970 "Paul Weiss's *Philosophy in Process*," in *Review of Metaphysics*, 24(December), pp. 276–301.

1972 "Knowledge and Being," *Review of Metaphysics*, 25(June), pp. 40–46.

1974 *The Cosmology of Freeedom*. New Haven: Yale University Press.

1978 *Soldier, Sage, Saint*. New York: Fordham University Press.

1980 *Creativity and God*. New York: The Seabury Press.

1981 *Reconstruction of Thinking*. Albany: State University of New York Press.

1982 *The Tao and the Daimon*. Albany: State University of New York Press.

1986 "Hegel and Whitehead on Totality: The Failure of a Conception of System," in Lucas, 1986, pp. 86–108.

1987 *The Puritan Smile*. Albany: State University of New York Press.

1987a *New Essays in Metphysics*, editor. Albany: State University of New York Press.

Nieli, Russell

1987 *Wittgenstein: From Mysticism to Ordinary Language*. Albany: State University of New York Press.

Nietzsche, Friedrich

1956 *The Genealogy of Morals* and *The Birth of Tragedy*, translated by Francis Golffing. Garden City, N.Y.: Doubleday Anchor. Original German of the *Genealogy*, 1887.

Nobo, Jorge Luis

1986 *Whitehead's Metaphysics of Extension and Solidarity*. Albany: State University of New York Pres.

Peirce, Charles Sanders

1931 *Collected Papers of Charles Sanders Peirce. Volume I, Principles of Philosophy*, edited by Charles Hartshorne and Paul Weiss. Cambridge, Mass.: Harvard University Press.

1932 *Collected Papers of Charles Sanders Peirce. Volume II, Elements of Logic*, edited by Charles Hartshorne and Paul Weiss. Cambridge, Mass.: Harvard University Press.

1933 *Collected Papers of Charles Sanders Peirce. Volume III, Exact Logic*, edited by Charles Hartshorne and Paul Weiss. Cambridge, Mass.: Harvard University Press.

1934 *Collected Papers of Charles Sanders Peirce. Volume V, Pragmatism and Pragmaticism*, edited by Charles Hartshorne and Paul Weiss. Cambridge, Mass.: Harvard Univerity Press.

1935 *Collected Papers of Charles Sanders Peirce. Volume IV, Scientific Metaphysics*, edited by Charles Hartshorne and Paul Weiss. Cambridge, Mass.: Harvard University Press.

1958 *Collected Papers of Charles Sanders Peirce. Volume VII, Science and Philosophy*, edited by Arthur W. Burks. Cambridge, Mass.: Harvard University Press.

1958a *Collected Papers of Charles Sanders Peirce. Volume VIII, Reviews, Correspondance, and Bibliography*, edited by Arthur W. Burks. Cambridge, Mass.: Harvard University Press.

Pepper, Stephen

1942 *World Hypotheses: A Study in Evidence*. Berkeley: University of California Press.

Pols, Edward

1975 *Meditation on a Prisoner: Toward Understanding Action and Mind*. Carbondale: Southern Illinois University Press.

1982 *The Acts of Our Being*. Amherst: The University of Massachusetts Press.

Post, John F.

1987 *The Faces of Existence: An Essay in Nonreductive Metaphysics*. Cornell University Press.

Potter, Vincent, S.J.

1967 *Charles S. Peirce on Norms and Ideals*. Amherst: University of Massachusetts Press.

Putnam, Hilary

1977 *Meaning and the Moral Sciences*. London: Routledge & Kegan Paul.

1983 *Realism and Reason: Philosophical Papers, Volume 3*. Cambridge: Cambridge University Press.

Quine, Willard Van Orman

1961 *From a Logical Point of View*, second revised edition. New York: Harper.

Rawls, John

1971 *A Theory of Justice*. Cambridge, Mass.: Harvard University Press.

Ricoeur, Paul

1969 *The Symbolism of Evil*. Translated by Emerson Buchanan. Boston: Beacon. Original edition, Harper & Row, 1967.

1974 *The Conflict of Interpretations: Essays in Hermeneutics*. Edited by Don Ihde, various translators. Evanston: Northwestern University Press.

Rorty, Richard

1967 *The Linguistic Turn*. Chicago: University of Chicago Press.

1979 *Philosophy and the Mirror of Nature*. Princeton: Princeton University Press.

1982 *Consequences of Pragmatism*. Minneapolis: University of Minnesota Press.

Rosenthal, Sandra B.

1986 *Speculative Pragmatism*. Amherst: University of Massachusetts Press.

Royce, Josiah

1899 *The World and the Individual, Volume One*. New York: Macmillan.

1901 *The World and the Individual, Volume Two*. New York: Macmillan. Dover reprint, with an introducton by John E. Smith, 1959.

1908 *Philosophy of Loyalty*. New York: Macmillan.

1968 *The Problem of Christianity*, with a new introduction by John E. Smith. Chicago: University of Chicago Press.

Rozin, Paul

1976 "The Evolution of Intelligence and Access to the Cognitive Unconscious," in Sprague and Epstein, 1976.

Sallis, John

1987 *Spacings of Reason and Imagination in Texts of Kant, Fichte, Hegel*. Chicago: University of Chicago Press.

de Saussure, F.

1959 A Course in General Linguistics, translated by Wade Baskin. New York: McGraw-Hill.

Schulkin, Jay

1987 "Possibilities and Constraints," in Neville, 1987a.

Searle, John R.

1969 *Speech Acts*. Cambridge: Cambridge University Press.

Smith, John E.

1961 *Reason and God: Encounters of Philosophy with Religion*. New Haven: Yale University Press.

1978 *Purpose and Thought: The Meaning of Pragmatism*. New Haven: Yale University Press.

1983 *The Spirit of American Philosophy*, revised edition. Albany: State University of New York Press.

Sprague, J. M., and A. N. Epstein, editors

1976 *Progress in Psychobiology and Physiological Psychology*. New York: Academic Press.

Stevens, Wallace

1972 *The Palm at the End of the Mind*, edited by Holly Stevens. New York: Vintage.

Taylor, Mark C.

1984 *Erring: A Postmodern A/theology*. Chicago: University of Chicago Press.

Toulmin, Stephen Edelston

1958 *The Uses of Argument*. Cambridge: Cambridge University Press.

1972 *Human Understanding: The Collective Use and Evolution of Concepts*. Princeton: Princeton University Press.

Tracy, David

1987 *Plurality and Ambiguity*. San Francisco: Harper & Row.

Vaught, Carl G.

1987 "Metaphor, Analogy, and the Nature of Truth," in Neville, 1987a.

Walhout, Donald

1978 *The Good and the Realm of Values*. Notre Dame, Ind.: Notre Dame University Press.

Wallach, F. B.

1980 *The Epochal Nature of Process in Whitehead's Metaphysics*. Albany: State University of New York Press.

Weiss, Paul

1938 *Reality*. Princeton: Princeton University Press.

1958 *Modes of Being*. Carbondale: Southern Illinois University Press.

1974 *Beyond All Appearances*. Carbondale: Southern Illinois University Press.

1977 First Considerations. Carbondale: Southern Illinois University Press.

1983 *Privacy*. Carbondale: Southern Illinois University Press.

Weissman, David

1987 *Intuition and Ideality*. Albany: State University of New York Press.

Wells, Rulon

1965 "Charles S. Peirce as an American," in Bernstein, 1965.

White, Hayden

1978 *Tropics of Discourse: Essays in Cultural Criticism*. Baltimore: The Johns Hopkins University Press.

Whitehead, Alfred North

1925 *Science and the Modern World*. New York: Macmillan.

1933 *Adventure of Ideas*. New York: Macmillan.

1978 *Process and Reality: An Essay in Cosmology*, corrected edition by David Ray Griffin and Donald W. Sherburne. New York: The Free Press. Original edition, 1929.

Wittgenstein, Ludwig

1922 *Tractatus Logico-philosophicus*. London: Routledge and Kegan Paul.

Wolf, George

1984 "The Place of the Brain in an Ocean of Feelings," in Cobb and Gamwell, 1984.

Wyschogrod, Edith

1985 *Spirit in Ashes: Hegel, Heidegger, and Man-Made Mass Death*. New Haven: Yale University Press.

Index